Linguistic Penalties and the Job Interview

Studies in Communication in Organisations and Professions
Series Editors: Christopher N. Candlin† and Srikant Sarangi, Aalborg University,
Denmark

This series aims to build bridges between communication and discourse studies and
a broad range of professional, organizational, and workplace sites by foregrounding
authoritative analyses of real-life practice – in collaborative, informed and explanatory ways. The series provides an interdisciplinary and interprofessional forum for
dialogue between academic researchers and professional/workplace communities
and organisations. Examples of appropriate fields of inquiry include: social and community welfare, medicine and healthcare, counselling and therapy, education, law,
media, management and business, policy and government and development studies.
Coherence among books in the series is achieved through their common concern
with cross-over concepts such as power, diversity, identity, agency, decision-making,
expertise, risk, appraisal and evaluation.

Published:
Dialogue in Focus Groups: Exploring Socially Shared Knowledge
Ivana Marková, Per Linell, Michele Grossen, Anne Salazar Orvig

Discourse and Responsibility in Professional Settings
Edited by Jan-Ola Östman and Anna Solin

Understanding and Interaction in Clinical and Educational Settings
Barry Saferstein

Writing the Economy: Activity, Genre and Technology in the World of Banking
Graham Smart

Forthcoming:
Communicative Contingencies in Handling Emergency Medical Calls
Srikant Sarangi

Interpreter Mediated Healthcare Consultations
Edited by Srikant Sarangi

Morality in Practice: Exploring Childhood, Parenting and Schooling in Everyday Life
Edited by Jakob Cromdal and Michael Tholander

Team Talk: Decision-making across the Boundaries in Health and Social Care
Edited by Srikant Sarangi and Per Linell

Linguistic Penalties and the Job Interview

Celia Roberts

SHEFFIELD UK   BRISTOL CT

Published by Equinox Publishing Ltd.

UK: Office 415, The Workstation, 15 Paternoster Row, Sheffield, South Yorkshire
      S1 2BX
USA: ISD, 70 Enterprise Drive, Bristol, CT 06010

www.equinoxpub.com

First published 2021

British Library Cataloguing-in-Publication Data

A catalogue record for this book is available from the British Library.

ISBN-13   978 1 84553 768 5   (hardback)
          978 1 84553 769 2   (paperback)
          978 1 80050 000 6   (ePDF)
          978 1 80050 039 6   (ePub)

Library of Congress Cataloging-in-Publication Data

Names: Roberts, Celia (Professor of Applied Linguistics), author.
Title: Linguistic penalties and the job interview / Celia Roberts.
Description: Bristol : Equinox Publishing Ltd, 2021. | Series: Studies in
   communication in organisations and professions | Includes
   bibliographical references and index. | Summary: "Linguistic Penalties
   and the Job Interview looks at the role of language and interaction in
   constructing the job interview and how this role produces disadvantage
   in the linguistically diverse communities of the western world. It
   relates the specific activity of the job interview to the wider field of
   institutional discourse and discusses relevant social theories in the
   light of the data"-- Provided by publisher.
Identifiers: LCCN 2020050127 (print) | LCCN 2020050128 (ebook) | ISBN
   9781845537685 (hardback) | ISBN 9781845537692 (paperback) | ISBN
   9781800500006 (PDF) | ISBN 9781800500396 (ePub)
Subjects: LCSH: Employment interviewing. | Interpersonal communication. |
   Language and languages--Variation.
Classification: LCC HF5549.5.I6 R58 2021 (print) | LCC HF5549.5.I6
   (ebook) | DDC 658.3/1124014--dc23
LC record available at https://lccn.loc.gov/2020050127
LC ebook record available at https://lccn.loc.gov/2020050128

Typeset by S.J.I. Services, New Delhi, India

Contents

List of Figures

Acknowledgements

I would like to thank Sarah Campbell and Yvonne Robinson, research associates on the DWP-funded projects on which this book is based. Lauren Small, Annia Hussan and Prita Chopra also gave research assistance. My colleagues at King's College London – Ben Rampton, Roxy Harris and Constant Leung – provided constant support and insights. I received practical advice on interview training from Joanna Channel, Jennifer Bright, Ann Janssen and John Twitchin. I would also like to thank Anthony Johnson and Liz Such at the DWP, as well as Glenda Pattenden for her design and editing support, and Dave Doyle for his excellent copy editing. Finally, many thanks to the following for reading chapters of the book and providing such trenchant comments: Sarah Atkins, Mike Baynham, Renata Coray, Melanie Cooke, Alexandre Duchène, Mi-Cha Flubacher, Kamila Hawthorne, Kobe de Keere and Srikant Sarangi.

Transcription Conventions

The examples are transcribed using, in most cases, minimal notation drawing on conversational analysis (CA) (Psathas, 1995; Stokoe, 2012). Where the analysis includes features of microanalysis, the notation draws on interactional sociolinguistic (IS) systems (Gumperz, 1982a and b).

Transcription Notation

[	Overlap, e.g.
]	A: … out [of curiosity
	B: ooh I don't know]
=	Latching, i.e. where the next speaker's turn follows on without any pause
	A: monday to friday=
	B: =god
hhh	Laughter
(.)	Untimed brief pauses
(1)	Timed pauses in approximate seconds
((fine yeah))	Unclear talk or possible hearings, indicated by stretch of talk in parentheses
((^ ^))	Unrecognisable talk
(xxx)	Proper name omitted
(h)	Audible inhalation/exhalation
(writing)	Non-verbal sound or movement; description of conversational scene, e.g. (bell sounds)
:	Sound stretch, e.g. e:rm
-	Cut-off previous word/sound; false start or unfinished utterance, e.g. I thou- well I thought
<u>Yes</u>	Emphasis, with perceived stress indicated by volume and pitch change

(lo)	Low tone
(ac)	Accelerated speech
{ }	Period over which phenomena occur, e.g. interviewer writing while candidate talks

1 Introduction

The front cover of this book shows an installation by two Scandinavian artists, Michael Elmgreen and Ingar Dragset, ironically called *Social Mobility (Staircase)* (2005). It consists of a set of stairs leading to a door with the word 'Administration' on it. The irony lies in the fact that all the lower steps are missing and lie broken on the floor, thus effectively preventing those aspiring to climb up the social and institutional ladder from even getting to its first step. The administrator's door is shut so, although there may be some way of circumventing the broken steps, there is still the problem of how to pass through the door. At this point in most institutional encounters there is a real or symbolic doorkeeper or gatekeeper whose task is to evaluate those on the threshold and, possibly, allow them through the gate.

Social mobility depends upon understanding and managing those institutional rules and practices which take you up the steps and open the door or gate. Those unfamiliar with them are penalised; the penalty imposed for infringing the social rules of the gatekeeping interview is to be shut out. Since you are what you talk in the interview, this becomes a 'linguistic penalty.' This is the combination of all the disadvantages experienced most acutely by linguistic minorities – but also by other disadvantaged groups – when talking their way into accessing scarce resources, particularly in the labour market. And since the job selection interview is one of the most explicit and ubiquitous gatekeeping processes in bureaucratised societies such as the UK, which is the setting for this book, the linguistic penalty helps to produce social and linguistic inequality.

We have all been through job interviews and most of us have experienced the frustration and failure that can go with them. I remember, when I was twenty-four years old, having to field the question, 'And are you courting?' Luckily, I had not enough wits about me to reply with a smart or rebarbative answer, which might have cost me the job. But if you are reading this book, you are probably rather adept at the interview game, take it for granted, and have been successful at it, managing the hidden power which excludes those who are not.

I will argue that these processes of exclusion are both unfair and unnecessary. In the first part of this chapter, I introduce the overall argument of the book: how migrants are particularly subject to the indirect discriminatory processes of the job interview, the tensions built into the design of the interview in highly diverse societies, and the linguistic demands of constructing a particular self. These exclusionary acts all lead to the task of challenging the taken-for-granted institutional discourses around employment inequalities. The second part of the chapter looks at the theoretical landscape which provides the critical take on these everyday encounters. This book also aims to describe the secret life of language in these moments of intense gaze on it, and comment on what an extraordinary place we find ourselves in when opportunities depend so much on such a narrow and particular way of talking and interacting. This book therefore treats the job interview as an extended case study of a much wider phenomenon: the language gaze in public life.

1.1   Migration and Indirect Discrimination

All disadvantaged groups – and this includes most migrants as well as many local Black and minority ethnic (BAME) groups, local white people from low-income backgrounds, and many groups of women – are more subject to the bureaucratic gatekeeping procedures that give access to scarce resources than those who are in a more secure socioeconomic position. These disadvantaged groups are all subject to the dominant Western discourses, based on classical Greek philosophy, which still show the traces of a fundamental duality between rational man and, in Plato's terms, 'women, slaves and barbarians' all categorised as 'other.' The selection interview contributes to the production of social inequality for these counted as 'other' and their voices can be heard in the narrative of this book, along with the many successful candidates who experience much less intensively the weight of the selection process.

However, the experience of exclusion remains far more common amongst migrants. Geographical mobility, despite the fluctuations in migration policy, is still more attainable than social mobility. Arriving, settling and bringing up children in a new country bring no guarantees of movement up the socioeconomic steps and through the gate. For this reason, the focus here is on migrants and mobile citizens from BAME groups, and how the bureaucratic entanglements they face become entrapments. Lured into what seems like a friendly conversation, the migrant candidate is caught up in the complexity of the interview and finally penalised for not being adequately social.[1]

The job interview may not seem as high-stakes as, for example, the asylum interview. Indeed, its ubiquity makes it seem almost banal. But it remains the final hurdle for all but the lowest-paid contract jobs (and for those who are self-employed) and is routinely used as an example of the archetypal formal situation. Additionally, the gap between BAME groups and majority group applicants in access to jobs is regularly used in the media to illustrate inequality.

The linguistic penalty that migrants face is the product of current ideologies in which nearly everyone is increasingly subject to being constantly classified and measured, and either punished or rewarded. This regime of assessment is the institutional response to a market-based society in which the workplace produces a battery of measurements to select out the losers. As the critical journalist George Monbiot (2016) argues in his book *How Did We Get into This Mess?*, it is the wider neoliberal context which has produced such an environment. 'This mess,' he says, is the result of the neoliberal reliance upon universal quantification and comparison:

> Workers, job seekers and public services of every kind are subject to a pettifogging, stifling regime of assessment and monitoring, designed to identify the winners and punish the losers. (Monbiot, *The Guardian*, 15 April 2016)

The proliferation of psychometric tests and assessment centres – and the early sorting and surveillance work now done by employers, such as checking applicants' Facebook pages and using algorithms to exclude the majority – are just some of these assessment processes. The continuous rumble of the audit culture affects all of us. But at the end of the line – despite new, largely digital techniques – it is often the face-to-face encounter which is the final measure. It is in these encounters that talk is on trial, where the confluence of all the impressive resources we possess is used in the ultimate metric of success or failure.

It is for this reason that the fieldwork discussed in this book is based on video recordings of interviews for low-paid work and for junior management posts in a range of service and industrial jobs, where there are large numbers of BAME candidates: delivering mail, packing coat hangers, receptionist and supermarket work, for example. Despite the routine level of many of these jobs, the interviews often lasted up to an hour and ranged over many topics. Our ethnographic fieldwork also traced through some of the practices and processes – from interview design, through post-interview 'wash-up' sessions and candidate and interviewer reflections – in order to understand how well-intentioned procedures lead to indirect discrimination.

Of course, in one sense job interviews are designed to discriminate. In terms of psychometric testing and the general discourses of occupational psychology, discrimination refers to the capacity to distinguish between pass and fail, good and less-good candidates. Beyond this world, and in the context of equal opportunities and institutional fairness, discrimination has a very different set of meanings. In this context, no human resource manager or occupational psychologist would talk of designing to discriminate. Yet research on the outcomes from interviews suggests that, despite institutional regimes that require equality of opportunity, selection interviews discriminate in the second sense of this word. So discrimination *as* selection can turn into discrimination *in* selection. People are sorted into those who will fit in and those who will not; into people like us and the others. It is the tension between the conflicting demands of universal quantification and equal opportunity requirements that produce interview designs with questions such as, 'What are the advantages of repetitive work?'

1.2   Tensions in the Design of the Job Interview: Standardisation and Diversity

The context for this study is the institutionalised workplace in a period of globalisation and marketisation; a time of tension, contradictions and paradoxes, many of which are masked by the institutional processes designed to manage them. While the globalised marketplace has produced uniformity in the shopping malls and products around the world – the so-called McDonaldisation effect – it also contributes to the migration of people from poorer to richer states, producing the pluralism or 'superdiversity' (Vertoveç, 2007) of major urban centres and, increasingly, of smaller towns and villages. Globalisation, with its market-driven ideology, requires 'a stifling regime' of standardised classification and assessment to manage diversity and sort out winners from losers in the name of equal opportunities.

Gatekeeping, and the tensions and paradoxes it poses, is central to one of the most profound social struggles in globalised societies: 'how to be uniform *and* tolerant of diversity' (Heller, 2007: 636). How can institutional and objective norms and standards be applied fairly to applicants whose origins are in societies differently structured from those where they are now experiencing the gatekeeping process? Organisations, both in the public and private sectors, are caught between the taken-for-granted norms and standards of institutional life and the requirements to be sensitive to and manage diversity. And this is increasingly a dilemma, since it is widely assumed that 'increasing globalisation requires more standardisation' (Timmermans and Epstein, 2010: 75).

Institutions built on a history of relationships, discourses and ways of speaking now face a labour market characterised by difference and perceived difference. They are expected to regulate their procedures so that they can be defended as objective and consistent but they are also required to acknowledge, be responsive to and even celebrate the fact of difference in their workforces. In the selection process, these differences are judged by the prevailing norms of conduct; the performance of some groups of applicants is routinely valued as less competent or inappropriate. These differences – which stand out through processes of classification and standardisation, and which in other contexts and places would be valued – become inequalities (Lamont, Beljean and St Clair, 2014). This also raises questions about how institutions defend themselves and how such defensiveness can add to the weight of the assessment experienced by those who are gatekept.

Equality legislation on indirect discrimination is not, on the whole, very helpful when looking at what can make the job interview unfair. It tends to look at overt practices such as dress codes, inflexible working hours or lack of provision for religious observance, where particular groups are disadvantaged by a practice that everyone is expected to comply with. And it suggests that indirect discrimination can be tackled with good intentions and by following equal opportunity procedures. But inequalities in interview outcomes are routinely more covert, relating to the design and implicit assumptions of the contemporary interview plus the social evaluation of perceived difference in institutional talk.

1.3 Linguistic Demands in Constructing the Entrepreneurial Self

Some of the cultural and social processes at the root of inequality have been traced by sociologists and greatly influenced sociolinguistic research, but there has not been much reciprocal influence in the recent sociological literature. Yet selection interviews are a key institutional site for analysing the production of social inequality for several interconnected reasons: the focus on assessing the entrepreneurial self, the communicative demands of the interview and the 'language' explanation.

Firstly, interviews reflect the cultural shift in which new forms of capitalism have led to what is called the enterprise culture, and so in turn to the enterprising or entrepreneurial self. There are two concepts wrapped up in this phrase: the idea that the individual is their own microbusiness with a market value which can be sold to the workplace, and that the capital or skills on sale are those of resourcefulness and the self-organisation and self-awareness that underpin them. This alignment of personhood and the workplace puts a special emphasis on the self and more precisely on the communicating, performing and expressive self. This underlying motif or trope of the enterprising, communicating self as a motivated, self-expressing employee is in sharp distinction to other historical and traditional notions of the relationship between work and the individual. Rather than selling professional, technical or craft skills – or even 'a pair of hands' – to the employer, an applicant has to sell the self through the so-called soft skills of communication, team working and leadership, together with their social and emotional fit with the job and the culture of the workplace.

The social and cultural self, and its capacity for self-presentation, becomes the centre of attention in assessment and selection since ways of behaving and being are what matter. The face-to-face interview is the activity where such assessment is most keenly carried out. Any group within society that does not take this for granted and is not able to access the necessary resources is disadvantaged. Also, the concentration on the enterprising self is itself disadvantaging for any groups not socialised into the business of accepting the value of the constantly reflective and reshaping self, simultaneously authentic and flexible.

Secondly, interviews are at the epicentre of another powerful contemporary phenomenon, related to neoliberalism, which values communication skills above all others in workplace selection and assessment – as well as in other spheres of our lives including the personal, as the sociolinguist Deborah Cameron discusses (Cameron, 2000). Although the interview is the default method for assessing candidates' oral communication, the fact that the whole event is made of talk and text is not attended to. While it evaluates a set of what Cameron calls codified communication skills – a general set of constituents such as active listening – paradoxically, it does not address the language and interpretive processes of both sides in constructing the interview. In the world of human resources (HR) and occupational psychology, language is only a transparent channel through which ideas and attitudes travel, and so need not be recognised or studied in its own right.

The interview is constituted of talk, but language is hardly ever mentioned in its design, structure or in the social interaction of the interview itself. So the powerful role of language in decision-making in the interview is masked, and all the more powerful because it is. In the decision-making after the interview, comments on candidates' competence or personal adequacy – such as, "I didn't really trust him" – are based on how trustworthy their talk was judged to be, but this is not acknowledged. The linguistic complexities of the job interview remain hidden and the work that language does remains largely unrecognised. The upshot is that candidates are blamed for the 'quiet sorting process' (Goffman, 1983) that fails them.

Thirdly – and somewhat paradoxically again, while language is largely ignored in interview design and most decision-making – when candidates are perceived as foreign or other, or assumed not to be expert in the interview language, then language can be invoked to rationalise specific decisions or as a clarion call around which doubts and negativity may coalesce. Language in these decision-making contexts is used as a criterion for failure or incompetence – much as it is used in the wider discourses in society where poor English, Spanish, German and so on (or 'not enough language') are routinely used to explain lack of success. So in these circumstances, the complexities of managing the job interview can be reduced to a narrow and poorly defined notion of linguistic competence to account for a candidate's failure. Non-linguistic issues that relate, for example, to a candidates' foreign work experience are reworked as linguistic ones, as doubts are raised about whether they are up for the job. Language is paradoxically both under-specified/recognised and, in some cases, over-specified/recognised. Language as no problem or language as *the* problem create a linguistic penalty in the labour market.

1.4 Challenging the Taken-for-Granted Discourses around Employment Inequalities

One of the main goals of this book is to provide insights and an analytic language which help to challenge widely accepted discourses in the workplace around the role of language and cultural processes: for example, that a lack of command of the majority language explains the gap in labour market success between local and overseas-born job seekers, or that inequality or 'cultural or unconscious bias' can be simply tackled by searching for objective measures which screen out the incompetent. These notions of good language skills, bias, objectivity and individual competence ignore the interplay of values and ideologies with which these ideas are so charged but which are rarely voiced in workplace assumptions and formal practices. This critical take puts the job interview as an activity – and its particular interactional constraints and ideologies – at its centre rather than language or 'culture,' while recognising the wider social, cultural, linguistic and economic regimes that produce the current job interview in late modernity and which feed into the interview at all points.

Here is a short example taken from a forty-minute job interview for a low-paid job in a delivery company, which illustrates this interplay of interactional strategies, values and ideologies. This section of the interview assesses candidates' competence in being resilient, reflexive and strategic in managing repetitive work:

Example 1: Ire – Nigerian Migrant, Borderline Successful

```
 1. I:   right what would you tell me is the advantage of a repetitive job (1)
 2. C:   advantage of a
 3. I:   repetitive job (1)
 4. C:   er I mean the advantage of a repetitive job is that er:m
 5.      it makes you (.) it it keeps you going (.)
 6.      er it doesn't make you bored (.) you don't feel bored
 7.      you keep on going and (.)
 8.      I mean I me- a (.)
 9.      and also it it puts a smile on your face
10.      you come in it puts a smile on your face
11.      you feel happy to come to the job
12.      the job will ((trust)) you
13. I:   you don't get to know it better
14. C:   sorry
15. I:   you don't get to know it better
16. C:   yeah we get to know the job better
17.      we I mean we learn new ideas
18.      lots of new ideas as well
19. I:   right what is the disadvantage of a repetitive job
20. C:   well (.) disadvantage er:m (.) er disadvantages (1)
21.      you may you may f- offend customers
22.      you may f- offend our customers
23.      in there that's a disadvantage of it
24. I:   you don't find it boring
25. C:   yeah it could also be boring (.)
26.      to be boring and you and you (.)
27.      yet by being bored you may offend the customers
28. I:   how how would you offend them by being bored
29. C:   by not putting a smile on your face
30. I:   right
```

This short extract exemplifies many of the themes discussed in this book:

1. **The counter-intuitive rituals of the job interview:** The question, 'What are the advantages of repetitive work?' in any other context

might seem absurd or ironic and its literate, analytic style rests uneasily with the communicative demands of most low-paid jobs. It illustrates some of the tensions in the design of the interview.

2. **The hidden assumptions which serve to construct inequality when there is no shared definition of the interview:** Here, the interviewer's question about repetitive work is responded to with some markers of upset, suggesting a struggle with how to respond. Then the candidate comes up with an idealised view of how workers should respond to such work: that all work should make you feel happy. But underlying this competence question at lines 1 and 13 is a set of conventionalised expectations that while repetitive jobs are boring, enterprising, self-managing candidates will recognise this and find ways of dealing with the boredom which will maintain their identity as motivated workers who do not have to be closely supervised. The special inferencing required of the job interview which eludes this candidate is a clear example of the linguistic penalty of the job interview.

3. **The interactional constraints and expectations of the interview and how its outcomes are jointly accomplished:** The design and location of the interviewer's questions are intended to assess the candidate's ability to reflect on experience and show how he has learnt from it. The opening section of this example gives some evidence of perturbation, such as hesitation and false starts. There is a one-second pause after the opening question, a partial repetition by the candidate, a further pause after the interviewer's completion of her utterance (line 3) and then several fillers and vocalised pauses. The interviewer's further questions indicate that he has not given an acceptable response and these questions both evaluate his performance in the moment – for example, 'you don't get to know it better' – and feed into the final decision that he is a borderline case.

4. **The permeability of the encounter:** Corporate discourses of competences, together with those of the 'entrepreneurial self,' leak into the process at all points as do the institutional norms of interaction and assessment.

In discussing these themes, I take a questioning stance which asks how we ended up with a form of institutional assessment that appears so self-evident to organisations, but is at best inappropriate and often dysfunctional, unfair and unnecessary.

This extract is a telling example of how some of the routine acts of institutional life feed into and are fed by wider processes of domination. And a close analysis of how institutions process and place people within categories of relative (dis)advantage is grounded in the interdisciplinary foundational work in early sociolinguistics, interactional sociology, linguistic anthropology and critical theory. This early, critical work was in turn informed by fundamental notions of ritual and classification processes in defining group sharedness and difference in the work of Durkheim, Weber and Douglas.[2]

The key concepts developed by Foucault, Goffman, Gumperz and Bourdieu have been widely interpreted, critiqued and reinterpreted over the last twenty to thirty years in overviews and edited collections (Duranti, 1997, 2001; Blommaert, 2005; Coupland and Jaworski, 2009; Arnaut et al., 2016) and remain central reference points for any studies on institutional inequalities, including this book. In the second part of this chapter I will therefore only sketch out some of these concepts as they relate to the job interview and some of the connections between their theoretical work, before providing a brief summary of the research on which this book is based. But first, I give an overview of the rest of the book.

1.5   Overview of the Rest of the Book

The idea of the self as a constantly performing and governable set of entities is discussed in chapter 2 and linked to some of the theoretical background given in chapter 1. The different, somewhat conflicting selves are accounted for by the way in which institutions 'think' and act. This chapter moves from the entrepreneurial self to performing the institutional self, setting the scene for why the interview is a punitive encounter.

Chapter 3 examines the role of linguistic penalties in the selection process. Earlier research on discrimination in employment and the sociolinguistic studies of the job interview are reviewed. This chapter then outlines the methodological approach from linguistic ethnography that is used in this book and which takes sociolinguistic analysis beyond the four walls of the interview room.

Chapter 4 discusses the design and underpinning discourses of the contemporary job interview and how these shape its detailed conduct. After a brief look at the history of the job interview in the UK, the design of current interviews in terms of competences and soft skills is outlined. Then the role of 'diversity' in the workplace in masking some of the contradictions of competence management is considered.

Chapters 5–10 analyse the interview process based on the data from two projects. Chapter 5 is the first of two chapters to focus on the candidate's contribution. Here the hybrid discourses of the interview are introduced as key elements in the linguistic technologies of the interview. Two of the three central discourses – the institutional and personal – are analysed.

In chapter 6 the third mode of discourse – professional discourse – is realised through candidate narratives which are a central mode of engagement and basis for judgment. This chapter examines the relationship between narrative and institutional order, the structure of narrative and stance taken up in it, the grounded experience of story and how reporting talk is managed through narrative.

In chapter 7 we look at the interactional conduct of interviews and how the environment of the interviews and their outcomes are interactionally produced. Each interview is relatively more conversational or institutional and this dynamic is an indicator and producer of success of failure.

Chapter 8 traces the processes by which final decisions are made. It shows how interview judgments are embedded in the social evaluation of all talk and interaction and discusses how these subjective processes are masked by institutionally required objective standards. The slippage from objectivity to a pure subjectivity is traced through changing interviewer criteria and the business of record keeping.

The linguistic penalty imposed specifically on migrant candidates is the focus of chapters 9 and 10. In the former, common sense ideologies around language are discussed as they serve to produce negative ethnic stereotypes and inequalities. The linguistic capital required of job interviews amplifies the differences between local and migrant candidates, putting unnecessary demands on the interpretive and cohesive resources of the latter. This subjects them to a double weight in the interview as it becomes more institutionalised.

Chapter 10 focuses on those aspects of the linguistic penalty which stem from different experiences of work and of selection processes and of presenting the institutional self, before coming to the UK. This somewhat different cultural capital is then compared with the discursive and communicative regimes of the interview.

Chapter 11 is about practical relevance and making a difference. It stems from trying to affect some kind of institutional change with my own research for quite a long time, and from my continuing frustration with the role of the job interview and other face-to-face assessments in producing inequality. After a brief discussion of the current debates about application and 'impact,' I explore the possibilities of combining independent and critical research with practical outcomes and partnerships with organisations. These ideas are then worked through two case studies: one based on the research analysed in this book and one from a medical setting.

The next sections in this latter, more theoretical part of the chapter examine briefly four key themes that inform the book, and critical sociolinguistics more generally: the power of discursive technologies, how interactional work amplifies differences, the production of linguistic inequality and how this is done through hidden processes.

1.6   Knowledge/Truth and Subjectifying Technologies

In 'The Order of Discourse' (1984), Michel Foucault argues that that in constructing, controlling and distributing power and knowledge, discourse is itself dangerously powerful. It needs to be regimented by institutions which are in turn held together by the regulating discourses they produce. Through discursive policing only certain types of empirical knowledge, systems of classification, codified knowledge and modes and registers of language are allowable and true at any one historical time. We live in a time, Foucault asserts, when truth is conflated with knowledge. The current focus on evidence-based practice – and, increasingly, the lure of big data – is part of this wider discourse. Accumulated evidence is not only useful knowledge but is taken as the truth of the matter, however ideologically motivated its accumulation was. Institutions can use this overarching truth/knowledge discourse to maintain and defend themselves and increase their power; all the more so, since this kind of 'truth' masks itself and the act of its production. We are unaware of 'the will to truth, that prodigious machinery designed to exclude' (1984: 114).

This machinery – this order of discourse, by being so abstract and hard to conceptualise or tie down – is able to conceal its own power. It becomes impossible for institutions to operate outside this discourse and those who attempt to do so are seen as mad or bad or merely sad. So for example, the current dominant discourse in workplace selection enshrines the job interview as the final act of judgment and competence as central to its design. Any interrogation of this discourse is almost bound to fail.

The selection interview, designed around the competence framework, is used 'to establish over individuals a certain visibility through which one differentiates and judges them' (Foucault, 1977: 184). This production of a certain kind of visible self is one of the most distinct processes of the Foucauldian notion of subjectification as realised through 'technologies of power,' which discipline and punish through centralising control and surveillance. Foucault identifies two key technologies: the examination as the technology of discipline, and the confession as the technology for subjecting the self to an authority who can judge and, in some cases, forgive (Fairclough, 1992a: 52–56). In both examination and confession, 'technology' implies a set of scientific mechanisms designed to exercise surveillance over and produce and control, in a systematic way, the less visible and less codified aspects of an individual's social life.

Job interviews are an obvious example of the technologies, games and ceremonies that the workplace constructs and through which a certain self is produced, socially evaluated and either rewarded or punished. This self is classified, judged and – in the case of most job interviews – penalised or punished. It is the punitive nature of examinations that requires them to be so highly ritualised and turned into ceremonies of objectification, from which the truth can be determined (Foucault, 1977: 184–185). The penalty imposed on the individual is mediated through the seemingly objective – because ritualised – processes of the interview design.

While Foucault also sees the confession as leading to forms of discipline and punishment, these two technologies come together in the selection interview in complex ways. It is not a simple matter of confessing the truth and being pardoned or punished, but of performing self-revelations within the orthodoxy of the workplace. In a confession, the individual is made visible as part of the ceremony of subjectification. While there is the potential for the confessional in all aspects of the selection process (in psychometric and attitudinal questionnaires widely used by employers, for example) it is closest to the interactional admission of weakness in such job interview questions as, 'What do you consider are your weaknesses?' or, 'Can you give me an example of how you dealt with a mistake you have made?' In answering, candidates have to admit failure before projecting a more positive self. Some confessing is seen as both appropriate and indeed necessary as a technology of power since it serves to establish authenticity in the candidate. Through the rituals of the institution, punishments and confessions are 'euphemised' (Bourdieu's term), made allowable, and so mitigate the 'symbolic violence' done to the interviewee. These rituals also require of those at the gate an understanding of how to do them, how to have 'a feel for the game.'[3]

1.7   Interactional Work and the Amplification of Interactional Differences

While the metaphors of technology and game suggest ways in which power is designed and functions discursively – and so how talk-based selection comes to be produced – they give no detail of how talk and interaction work to regulate and evaluate. To examine the interactional processes that constitute the job interview we turn to Erving Goffman, where the face-to-face domain is an analytically viable unit to be studied in its own right (1983) – and then to Gumperz and his central concern with the detailed ways in which people negotiate conversational involvement and so achieve their day-to-day communicative goals (1982a).

Goffman's notion of 'the interaction order' stems from his definition of a social situation as an 'environment of mutual monitoring possibilities' (Goffman, 1967: 63) between people that are co-present, where 'each one is accessible to the naked senses of all others' and where the banal rituals of everyday interaction serve to promote well-being and ease any discomfort. This constant vulnerability to others' gaze and talk has echoes of Foucauldian subjectivity, although Goffman's guiding interest and conceptual apparatus is in how we manage relations, identities and involvement in the heat of social interaction:

> It is not only that our appearance and manner provide evidence of our statuses and relationships. It is also that the line of our visual regard, the intensity of our involvement, and the shape of our initial actions, allow others to glean our immediate intent and purpose, and all this whether we are engaged in talk with them at the time. (Goffman 1983: 3)

Goffman – in summarising the interaction order, in a late overview of his work – shows a particular interest in selection processes or what he calls 'people-processing' encounters and how those involved are 'readable' (1983: 8). Implied in Goffman's people processing is his underlying interest in the management of reputation and the management of authenticity, and how the outcome of this management is continuously evaluated. In the impression management of the interview, where both sides have reputations to make and keep, it is possible to identify several of Goffman's key concepts: the interpretive work done through interactional frames, the value that each side gives the other through their facework, how this value is enacted in the ways in which both sides engage in and respond to the other – their interactional footwork – and the production formats which concern the sense of ownership and authenticity of utterances.

Frame, Face, Footing and Formats

His concept of frame describes this socially defined reality. In any given stage of an encounter, speakers and listeners establish or negotiate what is going on: we are in the frame of a preliminary chat about the weather before the interview proper begins, then an assessment of competence and so on. The frame constitutes what is happening and also works as a filtering process through which general principles of conduct apply. As such, the frame we are in at any moment is embedded in larger frames, reaching out from the wider institutional frame to the awareness and tracking of each other in a social situation and finally to the way in which we are framed by the physical world. Another order of framing is what Goffman calls 'fabrications,' which add another level to the multiple layers of social reality of which interactants must be aware (1974: 156–200).

Facework – 'the positive social value a person effectively claims' (Goffman, 1967: 5) – involves a tension between the positive and negative aspects of face. The requirement to claim some level of social connection with the other – positive face or solidarity – while maintaining one's own face and respecting the other's desire to maintain theirs, termed negative face or deference (Brown and Levinson, 1987), is acted out on both sides of the encounter. Facework feeds the indirectness which permeates the interview. Candidates must temper their positive facework with deprecating and crafted confession and interviewers use the ritual of the interview to mitigate its more punitive aspects – for example with 'thank you' and 'good' to move the candidate on from what is often an inadequate answer. Such indirectness causes its own interactional problems and often widens the gap between candidate-perceived success and interviewer negative evaluation.

Facework determines interactional footing. Drawing on the everyday notion of 'getting off on the wrong footing,' Goffman defines footing as a 'participant's alignment, or set, or stance, or posture, or projected self ... held across a strip of behaviour,' adding that a 'change of footing implies a change in the alignment we take up to ourselves and the others present as expressed in the way we manage the production and reception of an utterance' (1981: 128). The ways in which we relate to others in the moment, through small linguistic and bodily changes, establishes the footing we are on and so the impression we intend to convey (7.3). Changes in footing, Goffman argues, are not sudden switches from one stance to another. Instead he sees different footings, like frames, as embedded in each other, with one momentarily in the foreground while others rumble on behind: 'And within one alignment, another can be fully enclosed. In truth, in talk it seems routine that, while firmly standing on two feet, we jump up and down on another' (Goffman, 1981: 155).

This energetic metaphor captures the complications of embedded footings and frames, but rather hides the delicacy of the work involved. For example, candidates may have to manage institutionally how they can 'take ownership' of a mistake they made (showing a weakness and then defending themselves) and within this vulnerable moment also lighten the environment as one successful candidate, Gladston, frequently does.

One element of the stance or projected self, held for a time in interaction and particularly salient in analysing the job interview, depends on 'production formats.' These are concerned with the sense of ownership or responsibility or authenticity of utterances. Is the speaker merely an animator of someone else's words, the author of them or the principal who is responsible for the message that is intended to be conveyed – or indeed, a combination of these (Goffman, 1981: 146–152)? The extent to which interviewers are the authors or merely the animators of their utterances depends largely on the structural constraints of the interview: the extent to which it is a highly institutionalised and regulated interaction. Candidates, on the other hand, are expected to present themselves as author and principal, but not animators. If they are judged as only animating other people's words in a formulaic way, questions about their authenticity and trustworthiness are raised.

Inferencing and Contextualisation

Goffman orientates to the social world as an interactive accomplishment, but not to the micro details of conversational involvement: how, precisely, language and cultural processes enter into the achieving of communicative goals. This is the terrain that Gumperz has mapped out where 'grammar, culture and interactive conventions' are integrated and culture is constituted in speaking practices (Gumperz, 1982a: 4):

> A general theory of discourse strategies must therefore begin by specifying the linguistic and sociocultural knowledge that needs to be shared if conversational involvement is to be maintained, and then go on to deal with what it is about the nature of conversational inference that makes for cultural, sub-cultural and situational specificity of interpretation. (Gumperz, 1982a: 2–3)

As a sociolinguist whose work is grounded in the early linguistic anthropology of the ethnography of communication (Hymes, 1964; Gumperz and Hymes, 1964, 1972; Gumperz, 1999; Auer et al., 2014), Gumperz's concern with cultural framing and variety is used to examine the social and cognitive work participants must do to make sense of each other. This involves two key concepts: conversational inference and contextualisation. Gumperz developed the ethnomethodologist Harry Garfinkel's 'et cetera principle' (1967) – that as we talk and listen, we are continuously filling in all that is unsaid but necessary for sense-making – into a theory of conversational inference. We make sense of what we hear by continually looking for relevance, tying what is systematic in language to cultural conventions. We do this at the most micro level, connecting up small linguistic signs to 'scenarios' or hypotheses. These are always suggestive and tentative and this has implications for the analyst as well as the interactants (Gumperz, 1999: 465).

The inferencing work that speakers must do depends upon not just understanding the context, in the taken-for-granted sense of the word, but being involved in the 'contextualisation' work of talk (Cook-Gumperz and Gumperz, 1976). 'Contextualisation' acts in two ways: Firstly, it creates local opportunities for interpreting both the so-called literal dimension of talk and all its meta functions – what is outside and beyond the literal in language (e.g. the pragmatic, indexical and metaphorical functions of language). Secondly, it has a reflexive function in which talk invokes contexts which shape the interaction moment by moment, in the very act of being shaped by it. This shape-shifting quality of contextualisation accounts for the unstable nature of an institutional encounter, for example, when there is a sudden dip in its emotional temperature; also, and more often, it helps to explain how an either positive or negative environment becomes further entrenched as the interaction proceeds.

'Contextualisation cues' (Gumperz, 1992a, 1992b, 1996; 8.2) are the detailed sign systems through which contexts are created in combination with lexis and grammar. These small, barely perceptible signs are a collection of different phenomena: prosody, paralinguistic features, code or style switching and formulaic expressions, which nudge the inferential process in a certain direction and may have large interactional consequences if the conditions for shared interpretation are not present. For example, in an interview for an electrical installation training course, the question, 'Have you <u>done</u> jobs in your home?' (with the extra prominence on 'done') is expected to cue the inference, 'Have you actually done some relevant electrical work at home and what is the evidence of this?' (Gumperz, 1992b: 316).

There are several intriguing aspects of contextualisation cues. Firstly, they cannot be assigned stable meanings but function relationally. A pause or the prominence given to a particular word does not mean anything in itself, only in relation to what proceeds and follows in the interaction and, crucially, depends on the associations and conventions that speakers bring to what they hear (Gumperz, 1997: 8). The interpretation of these signs is always only suggestive and tentative. Secondly, these small signs connect to what Gumperz calls 'scenarios.' These may be any aspect of sociocultural knowledge – either quite mundane or reaching out to wider social and political events, conduct and ideologies. Thirdly, these cues are not subject to conscious control or awareness. They do tremendous work in establishing coherence, relevance and appropriacy, but this goes largely unnoticed. Yet their very multifunctionality makes them powerful but hidden triggers for judging the competence and adequacy of speakers. All three aspects play a crucial role in understanding how linguistic inequality is produced in institutional settings – and how difficult it is for either those who are assessed or their assessors to recognise that small interactional differences can have large consequences.

1.8   The Production of Linguistic Inequality

Linguistic inequality, now a widely accepted notion (Coupland, 2003a: 465–466; Piller, 2016a), stems from a post-war trend in sociolinguistics – in which Gumperz played a central role – concerned with social problems of equity and access in multilingual and other linguistic diverse settings. It is also influenced by critical theory, notably around discursive and linguistic power in the theories of Foucault and Bourdieu. Gumperz's goal of developing a general theory of understanding from an interactional perspective became directly linked to issues of diversity and equality in what he came to call interactional sociolinguistics (IS). The aim of IS, he argues, is to 'provide insights into the linguistic and cultural diversity characteristic of today's communicative environments and document its *impact on people's lives*' (Gumperz, 1999: 453, my italics).

IS methods trace how small-scale struggles over meaning feed into large-scale sociological effects. Macro issues to do with inequality, institutionalisation, urbanisation and discrimination – plus sociological notions of ethnicity, social identity, networks and gatekeeping – are linked to micro issues of discourse coherence, sequential organisation of conversations and pragmatic concepts of, for example, face and footing. So while Gumperz's work does not explicitly theorise power, there are connections to Foucault's central concerns: the capillary effects of power and how power works on the ground in mundane ways (Rampton, 2014).

Linguistic Markets and Linguistic Capital

The symbolic economy, like the financial one, has its own marketplace and capital. Like the acquisition of material wealth, the accrual of cultural capital (knowledge, skills and particular ways of behaving) locates individuals within a powerful position in the social structure. Within the symbolic economy, the linguistic market is particularly powerful since 'every linguistic exchange contains the potentiality of an act of power and all the more so when it involves agents who occupy asymmetric positions in the distribution of the relevant capital' (Bourdieu and Wacquant, 1992: 145). The linguistic market functions through the 'legitimate language' which Bourdieu defines as the official language of the state, 'a system of norms regulating linguistic practices' (Bourdieu, 1991: 45). Just as material capital has value, so do linguistic practices and this value depends upon the fact that the linguistic market must be a unified one. All talk is measured against the legitimate or official language, the language of the dominant group:

> In order for one mode of expression among others … to impose itself as the only legitimate one, the linguistic market has to be unified and the different dialects (of class, region or ethnic group) have to be measured practically against the legitimate language or usage. (1991: 45)

Bourdieu does not give an explicit definition of linguistic capital, but throughout his discussions of language and symbolic power he associates linguistic capital with legitimate language:

> The constitution of a linguistic market creates the conditions for an objective competition in and through which the legitimate competence can function as linguistic capital, producing a *profit of distinction* on the occasion of each social exchange. (1991: 55)

This competence is associated with standard and educated varieties of lexis, grammar and phonology and what Bourdieu calls 'euphemisation' (Bourdieu et al., 1994: 84). This is the increased censorship that the legitimate language requires of the speaker, depending on the sanctions in a particular field (1994: 137–162). In institutional settings, such euphemisation makes talk more indirect, more overtly polite and often more distant and abstract.

Linguistic capital is not simply a matter of linguistic competence, but also entails an understanding and mastery of the situations where this capital will have value. Displaying this capital marks out the speaker as part of, or potentially part of, the dominant group within the social structure and one who feels naturally comfortable in this position (1994: 11). This sense of ease – of knowingness – is frequently commented on. Thompson, in introducing Bourdieu's work, describes it as a 'feel for the game' (Bourdieu, 1991: 13). Elsewhere, Bourdieu argues that those without enough linguistic capital to talk comfortably in these situations not only perform less well, but are constrained by their awareness that they lack this legitimate competence – this linguistic 'sense of place' (1991: 82). With Wacquant he developed the metaphor of the fish out of water to describe the sense of being in or out of place. Knowing the value of one's own ways of speaking contributes to one's own sense of social worth, and vice versa. The fish with the linguistic capital, so to speak, does not 'feel the weight of the water' as opposed to those without such capital who feel its weight pressing down on them (Wacquant, 1989: 43).

Bourdieu's general theory of the unified linguistic market could be read as suggesting an absolute connection between the official/legitimate language and the bureaucratic workings of powerful institutions, and between the legitimate language and linguistic capital; in other words, that all institutional talk that determines our position in society uses the formal code, standard variety and euphemised register of the legitimate language.

But as later chapters explore, the institutional encounter of the selection interview is not carried out entirely in the official language or institutional discourse, as Bourdieu also calls it. While the job interview from an institutional perspective is formal, censored and discreet – fitting with Bourdieu's central thesis that the legitimate language prevails in all aspects of institutional life – the practices on the ground are only partly characterised by the formal legitimate language. The capital for actually succeeding is more discursively complex, variable and dynamic. There is more than one form of linguistic capital in these settings. These forms of linguistic capital include an understanding that being adequately institutional and social in formal activities means drawing on other, less institutional discourses within an overall institutional frame. Those with sufficient linguistic capital can both perform adequately, using the discourses that are appropriate, and play with these discourses – flouting the rules of the game and, in doing so, showing their familiarity with them.

1.9   Hidden Processes and Concealment

A thread running through sociolinguistics and social and cultural theory is that of concealment, masking and indirectness, as I have already alluded to. Interactional and institutional life cannot manage without these hidden processes, at whatever scale they may operate. Discourse and the symbolic marketplace classify and regulate what is thinkable and mask the powerful processes and groups which determine what is acceptable. Reasons for exclusion are seen as a matter of the incompetence or inadequacy of individuals or social groups, rather than a judgment based on the prevailing discourses and symbolic economy which serve and service the dominant class.

In the specific context of the selection interview, Goffman also sees institutional concealment at work; again, this aligns him at times to a more critical stance than he is usually associated with. His early work on the presentation of self (1959) discusses performance as deliberately staged to conceal (although later 'performance' was reworked as a way of being genuine). In the 'quiet sorting process' (1983) the focus is on the quietness, the implicit or invisible ways in which decisions are made and the objectifying language used to hide them. So while individuals may fabricate or conceal aspects of themselves, institutions are not even aware of their acts of concealment:

> Deciders ... can employ an open-ended list of rationalisations to conceal from the subject (*and even from themselves*) the mix of considerations that figure in their decision and, especially, the several weight given to these determinants. (Goffman, 1983: 8, my italics)

In the job interview much evidence is amassed, but the actual decision-making is based on a whole lot of considerations and weightings hidden from the candidate and rationalised by the institutional lists of criteria of suitability and acceptability – and other, often unspoken factors to do with the institution and its local level politics. Although Goffman wrote little about power and equality, he suggests here how many forms of talk are policed and interpreted within power relations and how these relations are masked in the very act of working within them.[4]

It is these quiet sorting processes that Gumperz traces systematically in his studies of intercultural gatekeeping encounters. As mentioned above, it is inferential processes functioning below the level of consciousness which, when not shared, can lead to rapid negative evaluations. It is the very taken-for-granted quality of the inferential process which allows gatekeepers to be so assertive in their judgments when, paradoxically, these are at least in part based on cues which are only suggestive. The slippage from local inferencing to a fixed subject is, therefore, a hidden process. And yet, in another paradox, the invisible nature of the people sorting process is made possible by its techniques of surveillance which make the objects of its gaze startlingly visible. In a recently-coined German term, *gläserner Bürger*, people become 'glass citizens.' The transparent, totally seen-through and amplified self shifts all attention from the technologies that produce it, seeming to subdue their powers while positioned to maintain them. And in this regard, Foucault and Gumperz share a view on how the truths about people are silently constructed through the institutional processes which judge them.

1.10 Research Sites and Data

The research on which this book is based was carried out in two linked projects between 2004 and 2008. Both led to detailed reports published by the Department for Work and Pensions (DWP).[5]

The first, *Talk on Trial*, looked at entry-level job interviews and was concerned about the gap in employment levels between BAME groups – particularly migrants – and their white counterparts, which stood at sixteen per cent in 2004, when the original research began. The second study, *Talking Like a Manager*, investigated selection and promotion interviews for line management and junior management positions and also afforded the opportunity to consider some of the wider organisational discourses and practices which, unwittingly, create a glass ceiling within organisations for BAME groups and migrants. Although this research was undertaken more than a decade ago, recent UK studies have shown that there is still an ethnic hierarchy in the workplace, in terms of employment and pay, and that migrant job seekers and staff are still particularly disadvantaged (2019).[6]

While policy research indicates that some of this disparity in opportunities can be accounted for by direct discrimination and lower human capital amongst BAME groups and migrants, a third factor in explaining the extra 'penalty' suffered by ethnic minorities (Heath and McMahon, 1997) is that of indirect discrimination. British legislation and policy research has for decades identified how apparently neutral workplace cultures and relations can work to exclude minority ethnic candidates (Noon, 2005; Sanglin-Grant, 2005; Pager and Shepherd, 2008; Lewis et al., 2015). But neither this research nor the psychological research on selection practices has analysed the detailed interactional processes which lead to unrecognised and indirect discrimination. This research presented an opportunity to extend, revisit and recontextualise research on job interviews and inequality which had begun in the UK in the mid-1970s with John Gumperz, Tom Jupp and colleagues and myself working in the Industrial Language Training service.[7]

Data for the two recent projects were collected from both public and private sector organisations in London, the Midlands and Scotland in eight different research sites: a large national delivery company, a supermarket, two further education colleges, a packing factory, a food factory, a hospital and an agency recruiting for low-level, white-collar work. The combined core data from both projects were seventy-six naturally occurring recordings of the selection interviews (seventy-four video recorded and two audio recorded) lasting between thirty minutes and one hour, plus a range of ethnographic data. There were brief pre- and post-interviews with candidates, recordings or field notes of decision-making processes (where applicable), video feedback sessions with the interviewers (where possible) and documentation related to the interviews including preparation for candidates, assessment sheets and notes filled in during the interviews, plus organisational materials on recruitment and selection practices.

These data are all highly sensitive for interviewers and organisations, as well as for candidates, and so not easy to access. So we collected data wherever we could get an entry and where informants consented. For the promotion interviews and interviews for junior management posts, the ethnographic focus broadened out to include some of the organisational systems, practices and communicative environments of the organisations. Sixty-two ethnographic interviews were carried out with a mix of senior and middle managers, HR personnel, work-based language teachers, union representatives and shop floor staff. While these provided ethnographic background, the core data to which we made ourselves accountable were the recorded interviews.

Studies of globalisation and language tend to be associated with new industries such as the new media, tourism and call centres (Heller, 2003; Coupland, 2010), and undoubtedly these are rich research sites for mining the changes in language use and language value – both generally and in connection with migration and multilingualism. However, the more traditional manufacturing and service industries, although relatively under-researched by sociolinguists and those working on interaction, are also strategic sites for understanding language and migration.[8]

Apart from the contract work outside the formal labour market, it is the low-paid jobs in these more traditional industries that are the ones available to those in the lower socioeconomic groups where BAME groups are most likely to be positioned. Similarly in the public sector, where minority groups are more likely to gain employment, much of the entry-level and low-paid work remains routine and only partially restructured by new media and technologies. In all cases, the institutional processes of recruitment and selection have been affected both by legally enforced equal opportunity requirements and by the day-to-day practices of working with and making judgments on a labour force which is increasingly diverse.

Many of the interviews recorded in our data were for jobs termed 'entry level,' which are low-paid and do not require specific educational qualifications. However, they represent a significant improvement on the type of employment endured by most recent migrants and the very lowest-paid workers, which are categorised as the lower-tier labour market. This 'lower-tier' labour market, in contrast to the higher tier, is also more insecure (Doeringe and Piore, 1971). Poor conditions, no job security, no union support and pitifully low pay – in short, a precarious existence (Del Percio, 2016) – is the lot of the many contract workers often employed in the least visible jobs as workplace or domestic cleaners, as care workers, in construction, agriculture or in sweatshops (Anderson et al., 2006) or in food processing, transport driving and catering (Wadsworth, 2017). 'Entry-level' jobs in the public sector and well-established companies in the private sector, by contrast, offer pay and conditions which are significantly better and so are part of the high-tier labour market – although this is clearly a relative tier. However, access to this high tier comes at a high price: the successful deployment of complex communicative resources in order to pass through the interview 'gate' and enter into the organisation. This working up of the institutional self is the subject of chapter 2.

1.11 Note on the Term 'Migrant' and Race/Ethnic Categorisations

It is difficult to find a term which does not come with stereotypical associations and which is sufficiently general to characterise the super-diversity of most countries today. I have opted for the term 'migrant' and use it here 'to refer to any mobile citizen who migrates or is mobile for various reasons such as work, leisure, asylum or some other reason' (Duchêne et al., 2013: 6–10). Chapter 3 discusses the problem of social categorisation in this charged field. In public discourses in the UK, 'migrant' is coming to have a more general connotation along the lines that it is used in this book. However, British 'migrants' who live overseas are still called 'expatriates.'

The same difficulties arise with terms related to race and ethnicity. In this book, the term BAME is used to refer to all Black and minority ethnic groups, including most migrants. This term has also been contested. As this book goes to print a UK Government report, *Race and Ethnic Disparities* (March 2021), specifically recommends that BAME should no longer be used. The term AAEM – African, Asian, ethnic minority – has also begun to be used, but is not yet recognised in many institutional discourses.

2 Performing the Institutional Self

Central to the idea of linguistic penalties is how the design and interactional dynamics of the job interview, with all its institutional constraints, lead to the final assessment of an individual candidate. So this chapter draws on the theoretical background in chapter 1 to look at the contemporary self and how it is shaped by the institutional order. We look at institutions from a more human and intersubjective stance, at how institutions think and act in the particular instance of the gatekeeping encounter, and then at how individuals perform the self, given these institutional constraints and practices.

The overarching dialectic between these different elements is addressed through two central tensions of the job interview: Firstly, between the market-driven, expressive self on the one hand and the classified, institutionalised self, on the other. Secondly, between authenticity and performance. These tensions are managed through the quiet processes of institutional discourse and through the performance of several selves disciplined as one.

2.1 Contemporary Ideas of the Self

A thread already introduced is the idea of the self as an object of scrutiny and evaluation. I will concentrate here only on those aspects which, while being part of widely circulating discourses of the self, are worked up for institutional purposes and traceable in the practices of the job interview. They arise from contemporary social and economic conditions of late modernity and from the neoliberal economy and globalisation, briefly introduced in chapter 1.

These discourses are of the self, driven by its own sense of self. It is discursively organised as the centre of awareness, feelings, judgment and action (as opposed to being a self which is attributable to other social structures such as the family or the community). This notion of an autonomous self is both an active and a calculating one (Rose, 1996) in which, in Foucauldian terms, the self governs itself as a moral regulator, responsible for its own success and sense of coherence.

These 'technologies of the self' (Foucault et al., 1988) are a set of models for rational self-reflection, but the contemporary self also works on itself through story, as Giddens suggests. In late modernity, as traditional certainties and structures are erased, Giddens argues that the self has to become a project, constantly aware of itself and working on itself to produce a coherent narrative:

> In the post-traditional order of modernity and against the backdrop of new forms of mediated experience, self-identity becomes a reflexively organised endeavour. The reflexive product of the self which consists in the sustaining of coherent, yet continuously revised biographical narrative takes place in the context of multiple choices as filtered through abstract systems. (Giddens, 1991: 5)

In the job interview, candidates are expected to display a coherent story of themselves, one that Giddens would describe as an ongoing narrative (1991:54). And this reflexive self – one who is self-aware, shaping and building the self from the experienced world – has now been imported into institutional and corporate discourses as, for example, in the competence models of selection processes.

Neoliberalism and the Entrepreneurial Self

The self as a project has to be responsive to the changed practices of capitalism in a neoliberal phase. The 'new spirit of capitalism' reinvented work as no longer alienating and machine-like but as an instrument of self-expression and self-actualisation (Boltanski and Chiapello, 2005).[9]

And an important element of this transformation was the capacity to be enterprising, as was briefly noted in chapter 1. Drawing on the notions of new capitalism and neoliberalism, discourse analysts talked of a 'new work order' (Gee et al., 1996) which embraced an 'enterprise culture' (Du Gay, 2000) and 'post-bureaucratic organisations' (Iedema, 2003). The new capitalism was a response to globalisation and to new technologies where there was demand and technical capacity to constantly change products/services and customise them in order to compete in the world market. This constant change led to a new work order where flexibility was required and new responsibilities were pushed down to workers so that they could react to change without waiting for top-down decisions:

> The fact is that with authority now being redistributed throughout the organ-
> isation, there is no *the* leader. Everyone must be a leader; everyone, that is
> to say, must answer questions about the business's purpose – and ask ques-
> tions, too. (Champy, 1995: 41 quoted in Gee, Hull and Lankshear, 1996)

With flattened hierarchies, ordinary workers were expected to manage themselves, to develop an 'entrepreneurial self' (Du Gay, 1996; Peters 2001,
Garrido-Sardà and Sabaté-Dalmau, 2019; Flubacher, 2020). As the name suggests, the entrepreneurial self was and is driven by the market. The seepage
of market forces and discourses into all aspects of public and private life
is the most significant marker of the neoliberal economy and, by extension,
to the commodification of the self (Harvey, 2005). Neoliberal concepts have
recently become the focus of some critical sociolinguistic studies (Allan and
McElhinny, 2017), but in this book I only want to illustrate how, in the job
interview, the market drives the performing self. It becomes a product which
manages itself not only in the workplace, but in any environment where it
could be for sale. The selection process is one of the most explicit encounters
for selling the self and candidates are expected to do this through a mix of
reflexivity, expressiveness and self-marketing.

Individuals actively construct and define themselves as, summatively,
made up of a 'bundle of skills' (Urcioli, 2008: 211) sellable in the marketplace (Kelly-Holmes and Mautner, 2010). In contrast to the notion of craft
or technical skills, the focus within the new economy is on the soft skills of
communication, team working and leadership and on the flexible, communicative self, aligned to the workplace culture and so transportable to new
environments and conditions – technologies of the self (Urcioli, 2008). These
skills form the competences now widely used in the competence-based interview. For example, Pippa, a successful white British candidate, reads into the
interviewer's question about repetitive work (in contrast to Ire, 1.4) that she is
being asked about self-management and responds at lines 6–7 with evidence
of this:

Example 2: Pippa – White British, Successful

1. I.1: you know delivery work (.) you know that there's quite a routine to it
2. C: mhm
3. I: ehm and that I imagine sorting (.) gets quite repetitive
4. C: mhm
5. I: ehm (.) is that any problem to you
6. C: no er I try to er make it more interesting by (.)
7.   to set a goal for myself to beat the goal
8. I.2: mhm
9. C: (.) you know (.) hhh

This evolving notion of the self is well illustrated in an analysis of professional advice literature from 1930 to the present (De Keere, 2014: 311–324). It traces the shift from self-control, in much of the advice in the early and mid-twentieth century, to self-expression: a self increasingly conceptualised as expressive, authentic and autonomous (Rose, 1998; Giddens, 1991; Taylor, 1989). This expressive, authentic self is realised in the performative work of the job interview and the kind of reflexivity expected of candidates. The coherence of the stories they tell will affect judgments of authenticity; their display of self-analysis must not only display competence, but also the fit between their inner feelings and desires and the job itself (De Keere, 2014). So the notion of authenticity defines much of the work of the interview for both sides (Allan, 2013: 67; Boltanski and Chiapello, 2005; 10.8) and is central to the candidates' performance, as is discussed below.

This new self – as well as being self-managing and part of self-managing teams – is also expected to be engaged in the organisation's vision. So although apparently being relatively empowered in their work, the enterprising self is required to align with the organisation's overall culture and its values and regimes. Individuals are expected to increase efficiency by responding to change in a relatively autonomous way, but always buy into the organisation's mission:

> A manager's statement of purpose and vision is important in this task of *signification.* It's the master script, if you will, in which we all play out our different roles. It's the corporate meaning in which we find our personal meaning. (Champy, 1995: 58 quoted in Gee, Hull and Lankshear, 1996)

The neoliberal self is not a freewheeling individual. Rather, from a Foucauldian perspective, the cultural change which has produced a self-governing self is engineered by the state and its institutions. As Rose argues, the individual self is a significant element in producing useful citizens through 'governmentality' (Rose 1998: 11). Power and technologies of power work through subjectivity. Institutions and the institutionalised workplace shape the entrepreneurial self. And the surveillance and bureaucratic regimes of recording and assessing to measure people's 'bundles of skills' are in apparent tension with the unregulated enterprise culture they espouse.

In the next sections of this chapter we consider this institutional order from the perspective of the active agents that make up institutions and produce inequalities. Firstly, the work of Douglas and Weber traces how institutions which are set up to maintain social order and benefit communities – built out of commonalities and notions of equality – come increasingly to develop boundaries through processes of standardisation, classification and categorisation which lead to exclusion and inequality. Secondly, the literature on institutional interaction is discussed to establish the institutional character of the job interview, and how classification and assessment arise through its joint production. Finally, we turn to the gatekeeping interview and how, despite its orderliness and apparent fairness, it comes to be 'rigged' in favour of those who attune to its hidden processes.

2.2   'How Institutions Think'

Some of the Foucauldian machinery of surveillance, control and subjectification has been touched on in the technologies of the exam and the confession. But institutions are made up of people and how they work in organisations; people tend to disappear in the material metaphors of 'machinery' and 'technology.' So the ritual and classificatory processes produced in social interaction out of continuous acts of meaning-making (also briefly discussed in the first chapter) need some further exploration. These processes of objectification and classification are the means whereby the institutional self is produced. We look at classification as a sense-making, value-laden habit and then as rational, objective conduct.

Douglas's Thinking Institutions

First, a more anthropological take is helpful to see how, in Mary Douglas's term, 'institutions think.' In her quirky book with this title, institutions are like living organisms busily creating and defending themselves: 'This is how … we build institutions, squeezing each other's ideas into a common shape' (Douglas, 1986: 91). Gradually, classifications and categories are built which squeeze and bind people together until this knowledge is presented not only as natural and reasonable but also as necessary to grow and defend institutions: 'Institutions survive by harnessing all information processes to the task of establishing themselves' (Douglas, 1986: 102).

Douglas sees categorisation as the root of inequality. Contrasted with a relatively open set of meanings that candidates bring to the interview gate is the system world of closed and abstract categories. Institutions' texts and modes of talking are increasingly distant from active doing and saying, becoming timeless and taken for granted in abstract formulations and jargon (Mumby and Clair, 1997; Sarangi and Slembrouck, 1997; Iedema, 2003; Maryns, 2006; Mehan, 1993: 241; Tranjaeker, 2015). The open set of meanings are 'squeezed,' in Douglas's term, into a closed set of criteria and categories which become the dominant and habitual meanings that only some candidates have access to, and which cannot be readily learnt in interview preparation courses. Power inheres in these increasingly abstract forms, as the examples of competence models in chapter 4 illustrate.

This stock of common cultural knowledge is partly codified in regulations, training manuals, mission statements and so on. But there is also the 'recipe knowledge' that is not necessarily written down, but which forms the routine practices of everyday institutional life:

> The primary knowledge about the institutional order is knowledge on the pre-theoretical level. It is the sum total of 'what everybody knows' about a social world, an assemblage of maxims and morals, proverbial nuggets of wisdom, values and beliefs, myths and so forth … every institution has a body of transmitted recipe knowledge, that is, *knowledge that supplies the institutionally appropriate rules of conduct.* (Berger and Luckmann 1967: 83, my italics)

Through the gradual sedimentation of repeated actions – such as job interviews – features of institutionality come to appear as given, unalterable and self-evident, and can be referred to indirectly or in a kind of shorthand by those in the know: those with a feel for the game. Many of the interviewers, when asked about candidates, could not understand why so many failed so badly since 'all they had to do was talk about themselves.' And Pippa for example, after stating her preferences as to where she would like to work, adds, 'but you've got to be open for these positions (.) flexible' – thus signalling to the interviewers her awareness of the institutional frame, the categories that they were working with, and so how to perform the institutional self. In this way, for those who are fluent in institutional modes of behaviour – who have a shared definition of the interview – the encounter becomes (relatively) predictable and this fluency progressively affirms the orderliness of the activity, as well as the acceptability of the candidate and their ability to play with the rules. While Douglas does not address power directly in this book, implied is an understanding that institutional thinking becomes exclusionary and does so quietly, in order that its power over others is not explicitly acknowledged.

The Weberian Legacy

While Douglas describes the processes whereby staff in institutions come to form a defensive group based on shared categories, beliefs and values, Weber looks at the origins of modern bureaucratic institutions from a rational and ethical perspective (Weber and Parsons, 1947). Du Gay, in *In Praise of Bureacracy* (2000), argues that Weber sees the modern bureaucrat as profoundly ethical in their rationalism and detachment from the personal. Rather than judging people on the basis of their status or ascription, each person can be judged as a case and thus bureaucracy can help to undermine corruption and nepotism by introducing consistency, efficiency and neutrality. Weber's arguments for rational, objective and standardised forms of work arose from his pluralist tendencies and concern for fairness in increasingly diverse societies. Rules, adherence to procedures and impersonality were a source of democratic equalisation for the good of the whole. Put like this, rational, rule-governed accounting practices seem both fair and reasonable, releasing institutions from the personal and producing categories and cases against which individuals can be objectively judged.

The Weberian legacy is enduring. Belief in rational and legitimate procedures underpins the efforts in private- as well as public sector workplaces to design and carry out thousands of gatekeeping interviews every year. The standardised rules and structures to which interviewers adhere are based on these Weberian principles, and have increased in superdiverse and globalised societies (Timmermans and Epstein, 2010). The critical sociolinguist needs to acknowledge the moral base of these principles, while at the same time drawing attention to how these very processes – designed to defend institutions against accusations of inequality – can contribute to its production. The equal opportunities interview, the asylum interview, the audit culture and risk assessment scripts attest to institutions' genius for ratchetting up their bureaucratic and technocratic procedures. And the greater the mismatch between these and the people processed by them, the less fair they are. So the tension between consistency and standardisation on the one hand, and diversity and plurality on the other, finds its perfect setting in institutional interaction.

2.3   How Institutions Interact

All job interviews are instances where typical features of institutional discourses and 'institutional interaction' (Drew and Heritage, 1992: 3, 21–24) are present; indeed they can be taken as a prototype of an institutional encounter in that they are goal-orientated, ritual encounters, jointly produced and marked by a range of interactional constraints. Levinson encapsulates these features in his definition of 'activity types.' He puts particular emphasis on the rational organisation of such activities and the constraints and inferences that shape formal or relatively formal interactions, such as

> teaching, a job interview, a jural interrogation ... I take the notion of an activity type to refer to a fuzzy category whose focal members are goal-defined, socially constituted, bounded, events with *constraints* on participants, setting, and so on, but above all on the kinds of allowable contributions. (Levinson, 1992: 69)[10]

The constraints on allowable contributions determine the institutional character of such encounters as highly ritualised legal settings (Atkinson and Drew, 1979), the total institutions of the justice system (Heydon, 2005; Rock, 2007) and selection interviews. Levinson, drawing on Gumperz's work on inferences, goes on to show how what counts as allowable depends upon a set of inferential schema which guide how what is said is read, and how these are tied to the activity in question. In other words, there are activity-specific rules of inference and these not only define what is an activity type, but also what institutional talk is like.

These constraints, which entail special inferences, are drawn from both background knowledge and from the structural properties of the activity. This is well illustrated in Levinson's telling example from courtroom testimony of a rape victim. Here, the sequencing of the questions builds up a set of inferences to make what appears a natural argument for the jury: that the victim's behaviour encouraged the defendant. The fact that the defence barrister has control over what topics are initiated and over the turn-taking system – and that the young woman is positioned by these structural constraints – means that she has no or little opportunity to challenge or rework the argument, and has her identity constructed as someone who is 'loose' or 'asking for it.'

In the job interview, these special inferences may be required of a particular question, as in the repetitive job question, or of a line of questioning or a phase of the interview; or indeed of the whole activity, since all aspects of the candidate's display and performance are subject to scrutiny and evaluation, determined by institutional priorities. The machinery of the institutional interview is oiled both by these special inferences and by the fit of candidate self and performance, discussed below. Like the barrister, the interviewer has an intuitive grasp of these inferences and, like the young victim, many candidates are positioned as incompetent by institutional constraints and their presumptions.

While rules, rituals and constraints imply some fixity in institutional activities, the idea of fuzziness and the potential for instability and uncertainty in the notion of inference also emphasises that such activities have elements of unpredictability. Flouting the rules, dealing with the tripwires and fabricating impressions when performing the institutional self suggest there are always aspects of improvisation as well as rule-governed behaviour, and the management of and tension between them is also a constant theme of this book.

2.4 Gatekeeping

So far, we have looked at some of the processes developed by institutions as they think and talk: how they establish themselves through taken-for-granted systems of knowledge and the interactional rituals which constrain – although not always – allowable inferences and contributions. We now focus on that most banal and yet high-stakes encounter: the gatekeeping interview.

The anthropologist Fred Erickson introduced 'gatekeeping' into studies of discourse and interaction – in an early paper on education counselling (Erickson, 1975) and later in Erickson and Shultz (1982) and subsequent discussions (Erickson, 2004: 72–85, 172–174; 2011: 395–406) – demonstrating the subjectivities of gatekeeping judgments and how, unwittingly, key elements of sharedness determine the outcome:

> Gatekeeping encounters are not a neutral and 'objective' meritocratic sorting process. On the contrary, our analysis suggests that the game is rigged, albeit not deliberately, in favour of those individuals whose communication style and social background are most similar to those of the interviewer with whom they talk. (Erickson and Shultz, 1982: 193)

In a later definition, there is some shift away from differences in communicative style to a more general social evaluation of the person at the gate:

> In social research, *gatekeeping* as a metaphor has been applied ... to situations of face-to-face interaction in which some issue of institutionally authorised social selection is involved – inclusion or exclusion at an institutional boundary that is based on an institutional officer's judgments of the worthiness of the person who is being considered for inclusion. (Erickson, 2011)

Recent studies have expanded the gatekeeping concept used by Erickson and by Gumperz and his associates in several ways (3.4). Getting through the gate – whether a real turnstile, imaginary portal, a rite of passage or a bureaucratic assessment – is all too familiar and has spawned many well-known metaphors as a form of symbolic boundary crossing (Angouri, Marra and Holmes, 2018). In these studies, the concept of gatekeeping does not necessarily involve some formal acceptance or explicit judgment of people (Tranjaeker, 2015: 82–88) and the 'gate' may relate to a more general acceptance of newcomers into working practices (Holmes, 2007); in other words, a more 'back stage' [*sic*] than front stage process. But the job interview is one of the starkest examples of a barrier which includes or, more often, excludes.

'Gatekeeping' suggests the fact of being let in or not, but the 'glass ceiling' above the heads of junior management – or the 'invisible gate' at the entrance to the interview room – is as much about the institution maintaining and defending itself through the taken-for-granted processes of classification and normalisation mentioned above, as it is about reaching out to its potential new members. Janus – the god of doors, gates and thresholds in Roman mythology – is usually represented as facing two ways, both outward and inward. And the selection interview is Janus-like in that interviewers look out to the candidate but also back to their own organisations and its institutional order (Auer and Kern, 2001; Mäkitalo and Säljö, 2002; Sarangi and Slembrouck, 1997; Sarangi and Roberts, 1999b).

The following example, taken from training material for interviewers from one of our research sites, is clearly defensive in the manner in which it instructs them to ask standardised questions: 'Deviation from these questions can mean that the candidate is treated differently from other candidates, which provides them with the opportunity to appeal against the decision and could provide grounds for indirect discrimination.' For the interviewers then, the original ethic of standardisation is transformed into a protective mechanism to save them and their management from potential loss of institutional face – and expensive legal costs – while maintaining a social environment. The implications for candidates are that they should comply with standardised procedures, while performing an authentic and expressive self. How then do both sides perform this complex activity and manage its paradoxes, and how do interviewers then manage to sort candidates into successes or failures?

2.5   The Gatekeeping Interview as a Joint Production

The idea of interaction as a joint production of social order underlies the whole project of ethnomethodology and conversation analysis (CA). The founding notions of turn taking, sequential organisation and mutual orientation to the people and task in hand presume a joint, co-constructed, intersubjective activity (Garfinkel, 1967; Sacks et al., 1974; Heritage and Clayman, 2010). In analysing the asymmetrical nature of institutional talk and interview encounters, the goals, controls and constraints described above determine the design of questions and responses, the allocation of turns and the differential distribution of participation rights (Drew and Heritage, 1992: 47–53; Llewellyn,

2010). This talk, summed up as the 'interview orthodoxy' (Button, 1992), has influenced similar sociolinguistic studies of gatekeeping encounters which are discussed in the next chapter.

All these studies show that the interview and its apparent 'truths' about candidates are absolutely the product of both interviewers and candidates, as Erickson and Shultz discuss in terms of the 'ecosystem' of which both sides are part (Erickson and Shultz, 1982: 181). There is no one-woman or one-man act in this drama. These studies also illuminate two contrasting effects of co-production: control and special help. The first arises when the interview is, ironically, designed to minimise any dynamic elements between interactants. This control is most evident when the interview is highly structured and/or conforms to the demands of equal opportunity legislation. In these cases, there is little or no opportunity for repair or negotiation sequences (Birkner, 2004; Button, 1992) by either side. In Birkner's study:

> Participants' roles and turn-taking systems never gave rise to repair or negotiation sequences throughout the forty-one hours of our corpus. (Birkner, 2004: 295)

So the very design of the interview intended to address issues of subjectivity, inequality and potential bias in its conduct produces a regime which prevents misunderstandings from being repaired and actively disadvantages candidates.

The second example of the hidden joint production of the interview and its outcomes is the phenomenon of special help given to subsequently successful candidates (Erickson and Shultz, 1982; Kirilova, 2013; Kerekes, 2003; Komter, 1991). Special help is given when interviewers guide the candidate into playing the interview game with positive responses, joint storytelling or cues that candidates are offered to help them adjust their position.

Both cases, in different ways, show the co-construction of candidate success or failure and, in the case of the latter, how candidates are routinely blamed for the interviewers' own less-than-helpful performance (Gumperz, Jupp and Roberts, 1979; Button, 1992; Roberts and Campbell, 2006; Kirilova, 2013). This is less a matter of individual interviewers' lack of competence than of being subject to some of the same communicative dilemmas as candidates, since both are controlled by the boundary making and standardisation of the institutionalised interview.

But the dominant institutional discourses of selection disregard such co-construction. Within a predominately positivistic and psychometric tradition, the performance of the candidate is treated quite separately from the interviewers' questions and their conduct is taken to be determined by institutional norms and requirements, and therefore part of the objectivity which goes with rationalisation, standardisation and (apparent) fairness (Bolander and Sandberg, 2013).

The idea of a joint production is incontrovertible and needs to be insisted upon at all points – but there is one caveat. In some of the CA literature, terms such as 'joint achievement' or 'interactional accomplishment' may suggest something positively engaging, cooperative and egalitarian, but this does not sit easily with the shaping of candidate failure in so many examples here. So here the notion of 'joint production' does not come with any positive associations of equality or mutuality.

Since the neoliberal regimes of the institutionalised workplace demand a close identification between the individual and the culture of the employing organisation, the seamless integration of workplace and personal identity and desires has to be artfully performed in the interview to produce a convincing synthetic self (Fairclough, 1992a; Wodak, 1996). To perform their entrepreneurial selves, candidates must manage the tension in their performance between being authentic, expressive and true to themselves but also flexible, adaptable and open to change. The presentation of self, even in the banal contexts of low-paid work, becomes a central marketing and economic force and the particular linguistic capital which renders candidates attractive – as well as competent – in the interview will earn them a (relatively) better job, since neoliberalism prioritises the local markets where individuals can impress (Coupland, 2010).

In the twenty-first century, the artful performance of the self is even more valuable than in the previous one, since it must be simultaneously entrepreneurial and institutionally tuned to the bureaucracy of the interview (Ritzer, 1999). Before arriving at the institutional gate, job seekers are expected to prepare this self or selves for their interview performance, as several recent critical studies have explored. The self-disciplining of job seekers to enable entry into the 'high-tier' labour market puts excessive weight on this linguistic capital (Del Percio, 2016; Del Percio and van Hoof, 2017; Flubacher et al., 2017) and its moral and cultural values tuned to the standards of the workplace (Lorente, 2012; Allan, 2016; Allan and McElhinny, 2017).

2.6 Performing and Performativity

The idea of performing in a job interview is now taken for granted. There are innumerable 'how to' texts, training courses and tips on 'selling yourself.' But a much more nuanced account of the self as a performing entity has been developed in anthropology, sociology, philosophy and linguistics, as well as performance studies in literature. The notion of 'performing the self' has drawn on the strictly formal accounts of speech act theory and on more pragmatically complex processes in the ethnography of communication and folklore studies.

Nested in the idea of 'performance' are two apparently contradictory concepts. Firstly, the ordinary, everyday act of talking is a performance (Duranti, 1997: 16). But secondly, performance is a special and heightened act of verbal artistry. This tension is present in the kind of advice meted out to those who face an interview: you are told to 'just be yourself' – that is, act the way you habitually do – but also to rehearse for the institutionally framed activity of display to an audience. In other words, 'You've got to sell yourself.'

Everyday Performance

The everydayness of performance is central to Goffman's work: 'What minimal model of the actor is needed if we are to wind him [*sic*] up, stick him amongst his fellows, and have an orderly traffic of behaviour emerge?' (Goffman, 1967: 3). This image of the clockwork performer, like many of Goffman's descriptions of social interactants, is a dramaturgical one. Metaphors of actors, the stage and performers are repeated throughout his work and are recast as he develops his central concerns with how we manage the small and everyday impression of ourselves to and with others.

In his early work he talks of what we might call two interactional selves. One he calls 'the harried fabricator of impressions involved in staging a performance' and the other 'a character,' a 'dramatic effect arising diffusely from a scene' (Goffman, 1959: 253–254). In job interviews, the former of these two is perhaps represented by the candidate mustering their personal resources to manage the immediate social trauma of the event; the latter anticipates the overall 'character' the candidate hopes and intends to convey to the interviewers – the calculating aspect of the self. In both cases, the notions of fabrication and drama suggest something unreal, or deliberately staged to conceal (1.7).

In a later work, *Frame Analysis*, the everyday performer is presented as a more nuanced creature whose performance arises from the 'maintenance work that needs to be done by both parties to maintain the semblance of reality.' The author then asks, 'Under what circumstances do we think things are real?' (Goffman, 1974). Here, there is a shift to a moral requirement to display ourselves in ways that others expect of us, so that a sense of shared reality is allied to a sense of authenticity. Again, authenticity becomes a key criterion in assessing candidates – not so much in terms of a general fit with the organisation but as part of how we are, as Goffman says, 'accessible to the naked senses of others.' Performance is reworked as a way of being genuine – as a display of the true self. In front stage work, such as performing in the job interview, this assumption of reality and authenticity depends crucially on being in shared frames and managing multiple frames – one nested in the other – as with footing. In the interview, candidates have to perform in a socially engaged way while monitoring the self, managing their conduct vis-à-vis the interviewer and being conscious of its institutional design. Working within these multiple frames depends absolutely on aligning to the special inferential processes of the institutional activity, discussed above.

Performance as Heightened Display

Performance also implies a heightened and artful expressiveness. Bauman's definition fits well with the staged performance required of the job interview. He defines it as a display of communicative competence which is accountable to an audience:

> From the point of view of the audience, the act of expression on the part of the performer is thus marked as subject to evaluation for the way it is done, for the relative skill and effectiveness of the performer's display of competence. Additionally, it is marked as available for the enhancement of experience, through the present enjoyment of the intrinsic qualities of the act of expression itself. Performance thus calls forth special attention to and heightened awareness of the act of expression and gives license to the audience to regard the act of expression and the performer with special intensity. (Bauman, 1975: 11)

This definition tells us much about the social drama of the interview. It describes its communicative norms, the burden of evaluation, the enhancement of experience, the intrinsic value of expressive skills and the intense visibility of the performing candidate. It is, above all, 'achievement focussing' (Coupland, 2007: 148). But this achievement depends on the extent to which this heightened display enhances or detracts from candidate authenticity. Is it enjoyed by the interviewers or received as false or over-egged?[11]

There is no clear distinction between the everyday and the heightened performance in many social and institutional activities. Rather, there is a continuum from a sustained heightened performance at times to a more routine and fleeting performance (De Fina and Georgakopoulou, 2012: 64). We can see this continuum in the next example, from Pippa's interview. She first responds to the competence question on customer relations with a list of activities (lines 3–5) and then shifts to a more heightened performance in line 7, with her mention of deadlines and laughter – an 'act of expression' involving the interviewers. This act leads to a more sustained heightened performance in line 9, in explicit storytelling mode, cued by the formula 'you've heard the (one about) the advert,' which is met by the interviewer's heightened response, 'oooh' (line 10):

Example 3: Pippa – White British, Successful

1. I.1: have you had any other (.) work that you've done in the past
2.   that was very customer facing=
3. C: =yeah I've worked fo:r (xxx) opticians and (xxx)
4. I.1: right
5. C: as a lab tech and a OA (.)
6.   so dealing with them on a one to one basis (.)
7.   selling them a product (3) meeting the deadlines hhh
8. I.1: hhh (2) what sort of deadlines did you have to meet then
9. C: you've- you've heard the advert (.) glasses within an hour=
10. I.1: =oooh=
11. C: =so you have to get the glasses to them within the hour (.)
12.   and it's er- slightly annoying
13.   if they actually break on the machine (.) hhh (6)

A candidate may be admired for their polished performance but – unlike the many public and formal encounters that Bauman's description rests on – the interview is also an interaction where, as in many day-to-day encounters, 'territories of the self bring to the scene a vast filigree of wires which individuals are uniquely equipped to trip over' (Goffman, 1971: 135–136). Given these unpredictable moments, performance must include the rituals to deal with and ameliorate any tumbles. So many of the small rituals of conversation – part of our everyday performance – are scrambled to deal with uncertainties, negative implications and unsettling moments, to restore equilibrium to the encounter and save face. As performance in its classic sense deals with the enhancement of experience, these small performative rituals offer 'a defence against its vulnerabilities' (Rampton, 2009: 12). So the candidates' successful performance includes the (confident) display of self and also the defensive moves that may protect them from failure.

2.7   The 'True' and 'Staged' Self

The performative self is rather an assembly of selves. There is the ongoing, 'stable,' narrated self, but also the bricoleur reaching for whatever resources are to hand to perform the moment – to manage its frames and tripwires. Then there is the staged, artful and expressive speaker, but also the subject governed by institutional and neoliberal discourses. In sum, there is not one self but a set of selves that has to manage both big and small performances. However, the ideology of psychometric tests, oral exams and interviews rests on the assumption that their objective technologies erase both the interactional self and the performed self; that only the true self is revealed. The division that Giddens asserts between the self and performance – in stating that 'all human beings, in all cultures, preserve a division between their self-identities and the "performances" they put on in specific contexts' (Giddens, 1991: 58) – is masked by the interview ideology, which does not countenance such a division. You are what you talk. So a leakage of what is seen as 'performance,' put on for the interview, leads to judgments of lack of authenticity. Candidates must be real and not actors.

The assemblage of selves suggests a more complex relationship between a sense of self and performance; between the 'true' and the 'staged' self. It is not a simple matter of a division between these two, as Giddens suggests, or of erasing the staged self. Rather, to pass easily through the interview gate, it is the fit between these different selves and how they are performed which is crucial. So the overarching rule of the interview game can be summed up as follows: come across as authentic, but hide any staged work required to do it. Only those who experience a fit between who they are and how they behave in the interview – between the self and the performer – will have 'a feel for the game' and can play with these rules (Thompson in Bourdieu, 1991: 13).

'A Feel for the Game'

Those with such a feel for the game can flout the rules and break frame deliberately and to their advantage (Seale et al., 2007). In other words they can momentarily drop their concealment of staged work and let it surface, in order to share the game-like quality of the encounter with the interviewer. And playing the game produces an overall conversational tone which is the hallmark of the successful interview (7.4). They may do this through an ironic stance which plays on the tensions between personal and official definitions of the interview (Adelsward, 1988) or display metaconsciousness about the interview game, for example in knowing jokes (Scheuer, 2001: 231). Gladston, born in Jamaica, who showed consummate mastery of the game, gives us a neat example of this:

Example 4: Gladston – Jamaican Migrant, Successful

1. I: okay (.) alright (.) er:m moving onto the next and final question
2. C: amen hhh
3. I: hhh moving onto the next and final er:m (.)
4.   can you give me an example of a time
5.   when you've had to implement (.)
6.   a course of action which was unpopular

Gladston's humorous comment and laugh is echoed by the interviewer (line 2). The candidate may also be drawing on a shared cultural reference. The interviewer is of African origin so the 'amen' could be a joking reference to the call-and-response sermons of evangelical preachers. Gladston puts himself on an informal footing, sharing an understanding of the ritual elements of the interview, and yet implicitly acknowledges who is in charge as the interviewer is imagined as preacher.

Candidates may also flout the formal constraints of allowable contributions and turn taking as in Pippa's interview where, on several occasions, she turns the interview into a more symmetrical interaction, calling up the everyday performance. The topic here is physical strength and the carrying of heavy mail bags, but the conventional turn taking and contribution structure has been replaced by a conversational one – part of the everyday performance in which Pippa asks questions and sets up a joke, which one of the interviewers caps, at lines 7–8. The two interviewers and Pippa are discussing how many bags of mail a delivery woman or man can carry:

Example 5: Pippa – White British, Successful

1. I.1:   seventeen was the highest I heard of (.) guy in Redditch (.)
2. I.2:   oof
3. I.1:   seventeen bags I believe=
4. C: =what time did he finish out [of curiosity?
5. I.1:   ooh I dunno]
6. C: [midnight? hhh
7. I.1:   I think] he's still out there hhh ((I didn't speak to)) yeah seventeen
8.   was the highest I heard
9. I.2:   okay

Such candidates may, paradoxically, be judged as more real and sincere *because* they have broken through the formal performance and let the everyday self leak out, rather than maintaining a more consistent – and supposedly truthful – role.

When the interview demands a performance which is at odds with a candidate's own narrative and self-presentation, there are implications for interviewer conduct and judgments as well as candidates' chances (and, arguably, for longer-term insecurities). A central theme of this book is the interactional production of misalignments and uncomfortable phases when there is no such fit. Talk that is considered 'staged' or unreal feeds into negative evaluations. For example, the type of confessional-eliciting question, 'Tell me about a time when things didn't work out,' can set up what is perceived as a defensive frame when the candidate denies all weaknesses. The candidate is in the frame of displaying their untarnished self, using heightened performance, while the interviewer's frame expects self-deprecatory reflection and self-awareness – an everyday performance of modesty and disparagement (10.5). Such performances feed into an overall 'effect arising diffusely from a scene' (Goffman, 1959: 253) of inauthenticity.

As well as affecting the conduct and management of the interview on both sides, a lack of fit between self and performance can manifest itself in subtle ways, based on different ways of thinking and valuing work. For example, Scheuer suggests that subtle class-based differences associated with relative success in interviews for managerial and professional posts stem from differences in how work is experienced and the extent to which candidates identify themselves and their sense of fulfilment through work (Scheuer, 2001). For migrant candidates, this blending of their work and sense of themselves into an entrepreneurial self applies particular weight (10.1, 10.2).[12]

There may also be longer-term repercussions from the negative evaluations of migrant candidates which could contribute to an undermining of a secure sense of being – what Giddens calls 'ontological insecurity,' a feeling of not being oneself. 'The individual might come to feel that the whole flow of his activities is put on or false' (Giddens, 1991: 58). This is well illustrated in the gap between many migrant candidates' perceptions of their relatively good performance at the interview and their ultimate lack of success. This can lead to both perceived discrimination and into wider processes of anxiety and uncertainty, and is a marker of the hidden processes of the job interview.

2.8   'The Quiet Sorting Process' and the Dialectics of the Interview

Power inheres in the abstractions of categories and classifications used to judge candidates, in the implicit assumptions of what makes a good performance and in rendering invisible the joint responsibility of a candidate's outcome while making the performing self startlingly visible. Power is hidden in plain sight. The wash-up sessions (the term widely used in organisations to describe the decision-making process after the interview) are the places where interviewer rationalisations bundle up the mix of feelings taken from the interview and which constitute the 'quiet sorting' process (Goffman, 1983: 8).

This sorting process has to remain quiet since making explicit 'the double binds' that it produces would weaken claims to objectivity and meritocracy (Komter 1991: 32). These 'double binds' include: being objective while involved in the intersubjectivity of talk; being informal and egalitarian, and yet professionally distant enough to be fair to all; expecting the candidate to be authentic, as a true self, and yet constantly flexible and adaptable; being entrepreneurial, and yet being institutional; being engaged in an interaction but judging the candidate as if the interview was a monologue; leaving unsaid what is politically unsayable and yet being accountable in explicit ways for the grounds on which decisions are made. In sum, these dialectics arise from the mix of neoliberal and modern/bureaucratic processes played out in the design and running of organisations and institutions generally – and the job interview in particular. Thus it is hardly surprising that the selves assembled in the moment should also be full of tensions and paradoxes (Tranekjær, 2015: 13–52). The tension between institutional norms and the interactive self is summed up in figure 2.1.

Critical sociologists argue that neoliberal imperatives, alongside new technologies, are replacing closed systems with networks and flows. Foucauldian theories of control and surveillance are now accomplished through deregulation and flexibilisation (Rampton, 2015); to look at organisations and the formal systems of selection is now old hat. But despite the new systems of flows and networks, in all but some jobs in the low-level and 'gig' economy, the job interview is still the final gatekeeping act where closed systems butt up against the entrepreneurial self.

Figure 2.1. The Dialectics of the Job Interview

	Neoliberal/Late Modern		**Modern/Bureaucratic**
The shaping discourses and interactional production of the job interview	Self-expression, authenticity, also flexibility, enterprising, sensitive to customer demand	but	regulation, standardisation, classification, rationalisation.
	Friendly, informal, egalitarian, intersubjective	but	structured, asymmetrical, defensive, objective.
	Everyday performance – the merging of self/work; more free-floating systems	but	heightened performance ('sell yourself') and a closed system.
	Indirectness, quiet processes, unsayables	but	bureaucratic explicitness.

Conclusion

We are constantly acting on and evaluating ourselves in order to be subject to wider institutional processes and regimes. This tension between institutional subjection and the self as active, self-expressing and agentive shapes the entire gatekeeping process. Faced with the dilemmas of the job interview, the candidate has to meld a range of selves into one institutional self with a performance which may be far removed from their continuous sense of self and how they conduct themselves. The quiet sorting process of the interview hides – from both those who design and run interviews and the candidates – its power to produce linguistic penalties.

A final, overarching paradox concerns the stance of us the analysts, particularly those of us who consider ourselves as taking a critical position, and this chapter is a case in point. While institutions are depicted as controlling and defensive agents, we are all part of and indeed benefit from many aspects of the institutional order: acting as gatekeepers ourselves, using it to our advantage or finding ways of relaxing its grip. What matters is the extent to which, for certain groups, this institutional order is not relaxed and indeed is tightened. And this is the theme of the rest of the book.

3 Researching Ethnic and Linguistic Penalties

In the last chapter we discussed ideologies of the self and the institutional regimes which constrain and reflect this self, leading to the dialectics of the interview. Here we turn to the research context, rationale and methods which form the basis of this book. The focus is on the ethnic penalties produced by the labour market and how these, in combination with sociolinguistic studies, lead to the concept of 'linguistic penalties.' The foundational sociolinguistic studies of 'intercultural' job interviews are considered in the light of the new sociolinguistic economy of contemporary Western society. The second part of the chapter turns to methodological issues and how linguistic ethnography provides the flexibility to look at both detailed interactional sequences and the wider institutional context. The chapter ends with a return to some of the facts of inequality in our own research data.

3.1 Employment Disadvantage and Discrimination

Inequalities in the workplace can be understood and explained qualitatively, but also need some facts and figures that show starkly the impact on significant numbers of minority group workers. Theoretical and analytical understandings can do with some numerical muscle. The context within which this study was undertaken was one in which many parts of the Western world, particularly large urban centres, are perceived as 'superdiverse' (Vertoveç, 2007; Arnaut et al., 2016). BAME groups constituted fifty-five per cent of the population in London at the last national census (ONS, 2011).

While the concept of superdiversity has been critiqued, it acts as a constant reminder of the complexity of job seekers' experiences and background, and how this contrasts with the relative uniformity of institutional procedures. Vertoveç's notion does not only refer to different ethnic and linguistic minority groups per se, but 'a dynamic interplay of variables including country of origin … legal status … migrants' human capital (particularly educational background) [and] access to employment' (Vertoveç, 2007: 3). These variables within migrant groups include reasons for entry into the UK, social and educational backgrounds, aspirations in the labour market, degree of trauma in migrating, motivation to stay, previous work experience, and training and networking.

The employment picture of these groups is increasingly complex, as no one factor or outcome for one group can be used for general explanations (Modood et al., 1997). Many of these variables – particularly in terms of social and cultural capital – are present in any cohort of job seekers in superdiverse cities, where jobs are more precarious (Del Percio, 2017; Lewis, Dwyer, Hodkinson and Waite, 2015). But what stands out from both international and UK research into the labour market is the degree of discrimination and disadvantage that all BAME job seekers face (Catney and Sabater, 2015; Pager and Shepherd, 2008) – migrants in particular. Thus, the significance of these complex variables which they bring to the search for employment cannot be underestimated.[13]

In many European countries, the aggregate unemployment rate of migrants is more than double that of the non-migrant population (OECD, 2010). As mentioned in chapter 1, most BAME workers are clustered in the low-skilled and least well-paid jobs, the lower-tier labour market and the lower end of the so-called upper tier (Brynin and Longhi, 2015). Newcomers are two-thirds more likely to be in 'elementary occupations' – the least skilled and worst-paid jobs (Migration Advisory Committee, 2014). These have come to be known as the three Ds – dirty, dangerous and demeaning – and are often described as 'migrant jobs,' not suitable for the local community.

More recent migration has produced an even more complex picture. Many new migrants are more highly educated than their UK peers and there is a significant proportion of this group in the high-skilled market, notably health and software professionals (Rienzo and Vargas-Silva, 2016). However, skilled and professional jobs are not necessarily available to this group and so it is commonplace in Western countries for migrant candidates for low-paid work to be better qualified and more experienced than their local counterparts (Moyer, 2018). For both migrants and long-resident groups, progress into higher-paid, professional and managerial jobs is still hard (Wood and Wybron, 2015). Trevor Phillips, the director of the then UK Commission for Racial Equality, referred to 'the snowy peaks' of most large organisations in 2003: while the lower slopes were becoming more ethnically mixed, the top remained white.

3.2   The 'Ethnic Penalty'

The fact that many minority ethnic groups are still disadvantaged in the labour market – and that there is a persistent gap between the success of the white majority and minority ethnic groups – has been called the 'ethnic penalty' (Heath and Cheung, 2006). This term is used to refer to all sources of disadvantage, including discrimination that might lead ethnic minorities to fare less well in the labour market than do similarly qualified whites (Heath and McMahon, 1997). This penalty refers to a package of disadvantage including education and job histories, family commitments and discrimination (among other factors listed by Vertoveç and others) and is a central concept in this book, underpinning all the linguistic analysis.

While some racism and direct discrimination undoubtedly still occurs in the workplace, much recent research emphasises that, today, discrimination most often occurs on an indirect level: we must 'look for subtle acts of exclusion rather than grand, overt forms of discrimination' (Noon, 2005: 9).[14] The assumed neutrality of selection processes and the lack of recognition of the job interview as a cultural construct (part of the taken-for-granted knowledge institutions have built) is well illustrated in two reports on widening participation in top British companies (Sanglin-Grant, 2003; 2005). The managers of the twenty-one FTSE 100 companies surveyed were confident that discrimination was not occurring in recruitment, with ninety-five per cent agreeing that minority ethnic staff were readily accepted and respected in their organisation. However, within some of these same companies, HR managers commented, 'We're struggling to convert applications from ethnic minorities into appointments.' At the level of internal progression, managers recognised that there were potential issues of cultural background, people 'identifying with their own kind' and concern over whether BAME staff would 'fit in' (2005: 8). When questioned about the recruitment process, HR managers did not reflect on the institutional processes and demands of the job interview and its relevance for posts on offer. Rather, they placed the blame on BAME groups themselves, who did not submit enough applications, had problematic accents and had 'an inability to make themselves come across well at interview, or to make themselves understood' (2005: 8).

Our research suggests that it is difficult to unpick the mix of negative attitudes and uncertainties towards BAME groups from apparently neutral recruitment and selection processes. Legal cases have shown that unconscious prejudice, if it has led to an unequal outcome, can be defined as indirect discrimination (9.1, 9.5).[15] However, interviewer responses to candidate contributions in terms of 'not meeting the standards required' (an apparently neutral judgment) may overlap with unconscious prejudices or with social evaluations based on the interviewer's own level of competence. For example, the ability to adapt to different accents or make comprehensible a range of varieties of English may relate to interviewer competence rather than attitude, or to both. While individual prejudices and competences have to be recognised, it is the taken-for-granted neutrality of interview processes that is the focus of critique here.

Equality legislation has attempted to tackle both direct and indirect discrimination but the very nature of such indirect or institutional discrimination – and the broad policy terms in which codes of practice are written – tend to lead to research and audits which show the facts of inequality, as mentioned above, but not how they have come to be produced. The UK Government's *Race Relations Code of Practice Relating to Employment* raised more questions than it sought to address in tackling inequality. It states that interviewers should assess 'solely on ability to do the job satisfactorily' (para 4.28) and that 'a language requirement for a job may be indirectly discriminatory and unlawful unless it is necessary for the satisfactory performance of the job' (para 4.51) (UK Government, 2006).

Neither statement addresses explicitly the issue that the job interview is made of talk and interaction, and so necessarily assesses linguistic competence which may or may not be relevant for the job. Nor does it acknowledge that the interview may not assess at all the ability to do the tasks required of the job. While the second statement may assume that 'a language requirement' consists of managing a job interview, again no guidance is given on how the communicative demands of the job could be fairly assessed through a job interview. While both statements are laudable, they betray a lack of understanding of language as a social practice and its complex role in constructing the interview. This lack of understanding also leads to the assumption that linguistic and cultural explanations for differential outcomes are placed outside the box called 'discrimination,' rather than tangled within it (9.1).[16]

The psychological literature, particularly in the US, has attempted to account for how inequalities in selection interviewing have come to be produced. The research has been in three key areas: the extent to which interviews are structured, the type of questions which are more likely to produce bias – whether past experience (so-called behavioural questions when candidates are asked about what they have done) or hypothetical questions (when candidates are asked what they might do in a particular situation) – and the ethnic make-up of interview panels (Palmer and Campion, 1997; Hubbuck and Carter, 1980; Huffcutt and Roth, 1998; McFarland et al., 2004). However, no clear picture emerges from these studies. This is hardly surprising since the social dynamics of panel interviews have not been addressed within the psychological literature (Maurer et al., 1999; Posthuma et al., 2002: 13), with the exception of some research comparing interviewer and candidate speaking times when interviews were first audio recorded in the 1950s. Indeed, most of the social science research on selection interviews more generally has treated the subject as a relatively straightforward 'matching' process within a technical psychological frame (Keep and James, 2010). No detailed analysis of interview context, its interactional production and the relationship to interviewer judgments has been done outside sociolinguistic research. So the conundrum of how apparently objective and standardised procedures still produce bias and unequal outcomes remains unanswered by the research in occupational psychology.

3.3   The 'Linguistic Penalty'

The particular role that language plays in the selection interview is part of its capillary role at large, in constructing difference and inequality and contributing to the production of an ethnic penalty. Drawing on this concept and the metaphor of the linguistic marketplace (Bourdieu, 1991) is the notion of a 'linguistic penalty.' This is a pack of disadvantages that relate to all groups who, in different contexts, are part of a linguistic minority. The word 'penalty' – with its punitive associations and the consequences implied from some fault or misdemeanour – also inevitably suggests football and other team sports, and the rules of the game. Like many other aspects of institutional life, the selection process has its own set of 'offside' and other expert but often-disputed rules that are easy to fall foul of.

A 'linguistic penalty' is a combination of all the sources of disadvantage which might lead a linguistic minority group to fare less well in the selection/evaluation process generally, and specifically in the labour market. Those who experience it are doubly disadvantaged, since their minority ethnic identity and experiences may already penalise them and the language-mediated gatekeeping interview adds to this penalty. This book explores some of the sources of disadvantage which make up this linguistic penalty and which include: the lack of fit between the sense of self and its required performance (chapter 2); lack of shared definitions of the interview and its practices (chapter 4); the hybrid discourses of the interview (chapter 5); the narrativised self (chapter 6); interactional constraints on candidates' self-presentation (chapter 7) and processes of evaluation (chapter 8). While any candidate may be penalised for lacking familiarity and resources for managing the interview, the linguistic penalty falls most heavily on migrants and mobile job seekers who have been educated and socialised into institutional talk in very different contexts from those of the UK (chapters 9, 10).

Aside from the sociolinguistic studies discussed in this book, the role of language in disadvantaging job seekers from minorities has been tackled, like the social psychological studies, from outside the social dynamics of the interview itself and takes a generalised and unproblematic view of 'language' (9.1). These studies, largely done by economists or social scientists from an organisational studies background, clearly show that a lack of competence in the language required of the workplace is a source of disadvantage (9.2). But again, these studies raise more questions than they answer, relating to lay assumptions of language as an undifferentiated set of skills, as something outside discrimination, as related to individual competence and as uncoupled from its contexts. By contrast, the earlier sociolinguistic studies explored some of these sources of disadvantage.

3.4   Earlier Sociolinguistic Studies of 'Intercultural' Job Interviews

Sociolinguistic studies have examined the social and cultural dynamics of the job interview at four interlocking levels: the dominant cultural ideologies of the workplace; the institutionalised definition of the interview and its special register, interactional norms and rhetorics; and multimodal ways of communicating at the microinteractional level.

1. **Dominant cultural ideologies:** The relationship between work and self, discussed in chapter 2, was given a cultural and ethnic group gloss in some of the earlier sociolinguistic studies of selection interviews. These showed that a real or perceived failure to align with dominant attitudes to work was rapidly and negatively sanctioned (Auer and Kern, 2001; Birkner, 2004).

2. **Interview definition and register:** Candidates born abroad faced difficulties in adopting the interviewer's definition of the interview situation, its purpose and allowable content, and so struggled to understand work/self relationships. They had difficulty inferring the implicit meanings of questions and successfully answering them (Jupp et al., 1982; Akinnaso and Ajirotutu, 1982; Roberts et al., 1992; Birkner, 2004). Some groups were reluctant to 'talk up' their skills and 'sell themselves' (Fitzgerald, 2003; Scollon and Scollon, 1995; Young, 1994). Where conditions for negotiating the inferred meaning of a particular question were not shared, misunderstandings and uncomfortable moments arose (Gumperz, Jupp and Roberts, 1979; Gumperz, 1982a; Roberts and Sayers, 1987; Roberts et al., 1992).

For example, Birkner – in her study of West and East Germans applying for jobs in West Germany – examines how these two aspects of work/ self relationships and interview definition work together to exclude. She looks at the metacomments about the interview process, in which interviewers defend Western interview discourse as universally valid, in opposition to the perceived transgressions of East German interviewees. Interviewers assumed ignorance of the interview on the part of East Germans, over-explained it to them, refused to tolerate attempted negotiations of what could be said and translated East German terms into those of West Germany.

3. **Interactional norms and rhetorics and the co-construction of discrimination:** The interview required candidates to infer from its interactional sequences what their roles and modes of communicating should be, both within a particular phase of the interview and in response to a particular question (Gumperz, 1992a; 10.1). Negative evaluations were the product of perceived transgressions of interactional norms affecting both overall interactional smoothness and overall emotional tone (Erickson and Shultz, 1982; Gumperz et al., 1979; Gumperz, 1982a and c). The Western problem-centred or teleological rhetorical style of interviews (Auer, 1998) was contrasted with other candidate styles (Gumperz, 1992a).

4. **Multimodal and microinteractional aspects of conversation:** Both paralinguistic features of rhythm, pitch and stress and aspects of bodily conduct were unconsciously processed and functioned as contextualisation cues to signal what was to be expected in the encounter, flagged the transition between stages of the interview, conveyed satisfaction or the opposite and initiated clarification or repair sequences (Erickson and Shultz, 1982; Gumperz, 1982b, 1996: 396–397; Kerekes, 2006; O'Grady and Millen, 1994; Roberts and Sayers, 1987; Lipovsky, 2006). Stylistic and inferential differences again led to misunderstandings and awkward moments. For example, the matching of pitch and tempo between white candidates and interviewers contrasted with the mismatches among some South Asian candidates who, despite their relevant experience, were perceived as unresponsive and slow to infer meaning (Gumperz, 1992a). Interviewers also failed to interpret many of the features of African American communicative style such as vowel lengthening and rhythmic patterning, and so misjudged candidates' intent and motivation (Akinnaso and Ajirotutu, 1982). Meanwhile, an Italian American candidate became increasingly disfluent as the interviewer failed to give him the expected active listening behaviour (Erickson, 2004).

Underpinning all these studies are two broad themes: the sense of otherness emanating from the stranger at the gate, and the interactional perturbations this sense produced and fed into. These are the key features of the original gatekeeping study (Erickson and Shultz, 1982; 2.6). Here, lack of 'co-membership' and conversational arrhythmia led to less helpful and optimistic advice for students and less chance of passing through the gate. The notion of co-membership includes shared race and ethnicity, in as far as they are more likely to reflect particular common experiences – such as being at the same school or part of the same neighbourhood community. This in turn is realised as part of the interviewee's 'performed social identity' (Erickson and Shultz, 1982: 16–17), with its associated interactional features summed up as 'cultural communication style.' These features – more recently described as 'persuasion-rhetorics of self-presentation' (Erickson, 2011) – when at odds with those of the gatekeeper, produced the arrhythmia and lack of behavioural smoothness which indexed discomfort and negative outcomes. These ideas have also been taken up more recently in cultural sociology (Collins, 2004; Rivera, 2012), but not pursued in any interactional detail.

The sociolinguistic research over the last thirty years has shown that job interviews are specific 'communicative cultures' which 'pre-structure what can or should be talked about' (Auer, 1998: 280), what interactional conventions are assumed and what styles are acceptable. This research, much of it based on case studies of simulated encounters, has identified and critiqued the particular discursive skills required in the selection interview by focussing on linguistic and cultural differences between applicants and interviewers. As a result, we have significant insights into the nature of inferential processes, contrastive social knowledge required for institutional encounters and the nature of the interview game and how these contribute to a 'linguistic penalty' through negative social categorisation and indirect discrimination.

While this research brings interaction and institutional practices together, they remain in a rather timeless, spaceless world focussed on cultural differences in the (micro)analysis of interaction – as Scollon and Scollon critique in their concept of 'nexus analysis' (Scollon and Scollon, 2007: 615–619). More recent studies (including the research in this book), while building on these earlier studies, also shift attention onto the current organisational discourses and practices around the job interview and how, in these late modern times, they are interactionally (re)produced in the moment to create linguistic penalties (Tranekjær, 2015; Kirilova, 2018; Kusmierczyk, 2014; Angouri, Marra and Holmes, 2018). This is also starkly illustrated in the regulation of migrant groups through gatekeeping encounters for the right to asylum (Jacquemet, 2005; Blommaert, 2001; Maryns, 2006), the offer of a work permit (Codó, 2008) and the selection for internship (Tranekjær, 2015). This more recent research is both set in wider ethnographic contexts and discourses and is aligned to what has been called the new sociolinguistic economy (Heller, 2010; Blommaert and Rampton, 2011; Duchêne, Moyer and Roberts, 2013).

3.5   The 'New Sociolinguistic Economy' and This Research

Examining the research data and analysis on which this book is based, it is possible to see several tensions that arise as more traditional certainties and classifications about 'language,' 'ethnicity,' 'migrant' and 'intercultural' are challenged but not always easily replaced. Recent rethinking of these traditions, the still-prevalent, common sense views of these categories and the facts of superdiversity are all in the mix. In attempting to understand the penalties that produce inequalities some classifications – although imperfect, as Douglas and others discuss – sharpen our instincts even though they may simplify an increasingly differentiated social world. Compromises must be found, as I now discuss.

In an excellent summary of the 'new sociolinguistic economy,' Blommaert and Rampton sketch out the turn towards hybridity, dynamism and historical and contextual embeddedness in our concepts of language and society (Blommaert and Rampton, 2016), critiquing traditional categories:

> Although notions such as 'native speaker,' 'mother tongue,' and 'ethnolinguistic repertoire' have considerable ideological force (and as such should certainly feature as *objects* of analysis), they should have no place in the sociolinguistic toolkit. (Blommaert and Rampton, 2016: 26)

This new economy builds on a wide-ranging critique of notions of 'culture' and 'ethnicity' (Arnaut, 2016), of idealisations of 'language' (Blommaert and Backus, 2011; Makoni and Pennycook, 2007) and 'the native speaker' (Rampton, 2016). These shifts in thinking have several consequences for the basis for classification and analysis, as well as the analyst's reach beyond the interview event itself.

Firstly, there is the problem of categorising job seekers in terms of ethnicity, language background, place of birth/nationality or length of time in the UK. Decisions about any of these categorisations are highly contested and may not correspond to ways in which people identify themselves or use these terms – such as a particular ethnicity – as strategic resources. We chose in this research to use standard categories for ethnicity used by the UK Office of National Statistics (White, 2002) combined with subcategories from self-identification by research participants. In the UK and indeed many other parts of the Western world, to ignore these distinctions would have obscured our central research interest around job interviews and how they produce a linguistic penalty. But we also needed to make a distinction within the BAME category between migrants and non-migrants, since we hypothesised that migrant candidates were the group most likely to be failed by formal selection processes. Having opted to distinguish between migrant and other categories of candidates, the problem for us was then how to categorise 'migrant.' In the literature and public discourse there are many interpretations: migrants may be 'newcomers' (Rienzo and Vargas-Silva, 2016), in the UK for five years or less or – more generally – 'foreign born' and the question remains unresolved.[17]

We have opted for a wide definition of migrant, making the somewhat arbitrary decision that a 'migrant' is defined as someone born abroad. 'Squeezing' participants into a simple dichotomy of local and migrant leaves many fuzzy edges, most obviously the degree to which anyone is a 'second language speaker' (Rampton, 2016) and where any cut-off point should be, beyond which 'migrant' cannot apply. Gladston is a good example: originally from Jamaica, he had been in the UK for over twenty-five years and worked for many of those at the company where he was now seeking promotion to management level. Thoroughly at ease with the register of the job interview, he displayed some phonological variants in this register which indexed roots in the Caribbean (Hewitt, 1986; Sebba, 1993). So while born abroad, he was clearly not a 'migrant' in the sense of newly arrived. By contrast, Sara was born in the UK but identifies her Maltese communicative resources as different from English norms and Tahir, a Bangladeshi also born in the UK, speaks the local London vernacular but has many features of self-presentation more closely aligned to the South Asian migrant candidates (10.3).

Secondly, the critiques of language, culture and ethnicity as some pure, stable and essential categories and classes thoroughly undermine the automatic assumption that all interviews between those from different ethnic backgrounds are 'intercultural.' As Auer and Kern argue, 'culture' can only be understood as part of action and interaction, rather than standing outside it. An encounter is not intercultural just because people originate from different parts of the world and belong to different races and ethnicities; it is 'brought about' and made relevant in action and interaction (Auer and Kern, 2001). Interviews become intercultural as the organisational culture of the event becomes relevant, and may be explicitly oriented to by either side. As Holmes discusses in her notion of 'culture order,' it is a question of what is noticed and how this noticing affects the interaction: 'The culture order draws attention to pervasive, hegemonic assumptions which *constrain* and *shape* social interaction' (Holmes, 2018: 33, my italics). It is the differences between the candidate's performed self and the requirements of the institutionalised workplace which might designate it as intercultural, rather than any general, ethnicised cultural 'facts.' Gladston's interview with a white British human resource manager is not 'intercultural' in that no aspect of his roots in the Caribbean were made relevant in the interview, were the cause of any difficulties or misunderstandings, appeared in any way to affect the decision to promote him or were consequential in the video feedback sessions. And yet in his second interview with an interviewer of African heritage, his jokey 'amen' when told he has reached the last question may be an explicit, momentary nod to shared cultural experiences about the role of the church in many Black communities – within an overarching British interview norm (2.3). It is also one of the very few examples in the data where vocalised co-membership between interviewer and candidate was not based on white British norms. And so while ethnicised cultural knowledge may, exceptionally, surface and become relevant in interviews, it is not helpful to start from the premise of interculturality in looking at such encounters.

Thirdly, and related to this last point, while data from early research tends to contrast white gatekeepers speaking the 'legitimate language' with minority ethnic candidates who do not, recent research based both on changing demographics and the new sociolinguistic economy tells a different story. In our data, almost one third of interviewers were from BAME groups, although only one was not born in the UK. In well over half the interviews, there was no shared ethnicity, in terms of broad ethnic divisions (sixty-one per cent), but these encounters resulted in virtually as many successful outcomes for candidates as those where ethnicity was shared. While our database was very small for any generalisations, these figures suggest that race or ethnicity *per se* were not the factors. Our data also shows that whatever their race or ethnic background, interviewers did not necessarily use the expected repertoire of English in terms of formal linguistic features, and that there was no straightforward dichotomy between gatekeeping, educated English – the 'legitimate language' – and other varieties from candidates (8.3).[18]

We are thus faced with the age-old vexation that, by classifying groups and drawing on general notions to identify inequality, we are feeding essentialism. But without this visibility, there is no evidence upon which to act. The response is to work with some telling if unsatisfactory categories, being alert to their limitations and attuned to their destabilisation in the constant interplay between habitual resources, the activity of the moment and the wider discourses and contexts which shape them and give them value or not. This discussion and the issues of context in the earlier sociolinguistic accounts of interviews, raised above, draws us into methodological debates and the hard choices to make in project design, fieldwork and analysis.

3.6 Methodological Issues

One of the key questions in current sociolinguistic practices is how we zoom out from micro to macro practices and back in again, to do justice to and make ourselves accountable to both the local and the wider discursive and historical contexts which inform and are informed by them. As well as scrutinising the front stage interview, we also have to ask how this particular interaction and its penalties come to be produced and what are its ramifications for individuals, the labour market and issues of social inequality:

> The contexts in which people communicate are partly local and emergent, continuously readjusted to the contingencies of action unfolding from one moment to the next, but they are also infused with information, resources, expectations, and experiences that originate in, circulate through, and/or are destined for networks and processes that can be very different in their reach and duration (as well as in their capacity to bestow privilege, power or stigma). (Blommaert and Rampton, 2016: 32–33)

We have come a long way since context was seen as a 'bucket' into which interaction was poured (Heritage, 1987). But having kicked said bucket, we need some analytic purchase on how to deal with the contexts that shape how people communicate in the job interview. Luckily we have sociolinguistics, linguistic anthropology and ethnography with which to understand how talk and text circulate. Much of this thinking has been drawn together into what has come to be known as linguistic ethnography (LE). The theoretical and methodological reach of LE, which is something of an umbrella term, has been discussed in some detail elsewhere (Rampton et al., 2015; Snell et al., 2015; Creese, 2008; Rampton, 2007) and so here I will concentrate only on how we can use it to research the job interview.

In an often-cited synthesis of performance studies, Bauman and Briggs argue that a performance is tied to many other events, contexts, practices and discourses (Bauman and Briggs, 1990: 74–79). These become anchored in the performance by the process of decontextualisation, which transports aspects of talk and text from a particular context, and recontextualisation, which reworks them into the new context. Developing this recent work on transcontextual analysis and the various trajectories that spoken, written and multimodal text move through (Maybin, 2017), I shall illustrate some of the 'chains of entextualisation' (Linell, 1998: 144; Park and Bucholtz, 2009) by which talk and text are decontextualised and recontextualised and move between settings.

If we think back to the example in chapter 1, where Ire is asked about repetitive work, we can trace back the interviewer's question to one of the key competences used in interviewing – that of managing oneself – and see how it has been decontextualised, taken from a written document used in interview training. It is then recontextualised in the interview and given a particular performative twist by the interviewer as she reformulates it to Ire. After the interview, in a feedback session, she defends the borderline category that Ire is given because of his performance in answering this question, thus recontextualising the question and its response as evidence of her decision. This brief example of transcontextualisation shows some of the explanatory power of linguistic ethnography, but LE research gives us some conundrums which we should at least be reflexive about, namely: where do we stop, should we be neat or messy and what might count as junk interpretation?

Where Do We Stop?

We have to acknowledge that we cannot look across all the potential contexts which may affect the performance and outcomes of the interview. When is enough, enough? Cicourel warns against trying to explore all relevant contexts:

> A nagging issue that undoubtedly remains for any readers is the familiar one that an infinite regress can occur whereby the observer must presumably describe 'everything' about a context. Such a demand is of course impossible to satisfy because no one could claim to have specified all of the local and larger sociocultural aspects of a context. (Cicourel, 1992: 309)

Agar suggests that we must decide what data are central to our ethnography and make ourselves accountable to them (Agar, 1986). If, as in the case of our projects described here, the recorded interviews are central then we may have to stop specifying all aspects of context, once we feel we have a reasonable interpretation of these data – a grasp of the 'communicative ecology' (Gumperz, 1999: 465) of the interaction. An easy example of this is in line 4 of the data example below, where Gladston speaks of 'taking ownership,' and this can be traced back to one of the competences required of managers. So there is a textual trace to institutional discourse, but also a wider trace to the current neoliberal ideologies of self and responsibility discussed earlier. These informed our understanding of the power of the job interview, but they remained a background resource.

Similarly, the analyst needs some grasp of the 'primary knowledge about the institutional order'; the sum total of 'what everybody knows' (Berger and Luckmann, 1966: 83; 2.4) in a given organisation. This may include the guidance notes, the gossip in the canteen, the informal mentoring, the shared ways of talking about other groups, the tick box forms and how to use them, and so on. What everyone knows is slowly (and always only partially) learnt by non-members of the institution through ethnographic fieldwork. But again, this has to be limited depending upon the researcher's accountability to the data. For example, in the second project – where the DWP was interested in researching the wider organisational and cultural practices which might act as barriers to promotion – we interviewed sixty-two staff, workers and trade union representatives across the board. More of this 'primary knowledge' was thus identified, but it proved difficult to trace links between the research interview and job interview data within the timetable of the project and so the research interviews also remained as a background resource. Letting go – calling a stop to collecting data and theories – raises questions about how we can make our interpretive claims convincing.

Neat or Messy?

Cicourel argues that although we cannot look at everything, the research must have 'ecological validity' convincing others of the viability and authenticity of our claims through 'the systematic ethnographic grounding of social interaction and language use' (Cicourel, 2007: 735–738). Arguably, tracing 'taking ownership' back to a competence question in the interview design is an example of 'systematic grounding,' indicating how, as with Gladston, using the institutional language of competences contributes to a high rating. But other data show that candidates who draw on the institutional terms used in the interview are seen as overtrained and not trustworthy. So more data make things messier, or less neat; this 'systematic grounding' is both necessary and problematic (Briggs, 2007: 580; Rampton et al., 2016). The inevitable variability that comes from all the grounded examples that make a study 'authentic' also prevents its systematicity. And the linkages between local stuff and big discourses become increasingly open to criticisms of implausibility as the contexts ripple outwards and back again.

What Counts as a Junk Interpretation?

We are left with the problem of how we claim interpretations as valid and convincing when trying to be simultaneously authentic, open, uncertain, systematic, neat and grounded. As linguistic ethnographers argue, we can use ethnography to open up and linguistics to tie down but it is not always easy to move between small and large scales. Sometimes, in trying to cover too much ground but be faithful to the fine-grained detail, we can end up making junk interpretations – precarious leaps from microanalysis to large social implications – without taking account of the mesoprocesses: the mid-level practices where big discourses get mediated through routine conversations and texts. For example, if we mishear a moment's talk, we can find ourselves transcribing a word which fits with a stereotyped ideology of what a bureaucrat might say. Ethnography might then help us to tie down what was actually said. A previous conversation, feedback or other fieldwork data would lead us to listen again and perhaps this time hear something more nuanced – not a case of indirect discrimination, which we had pounced on earlier with researcher enthusiasm. Done well and with sufficient reflexivity and self-criticism, we can avoid such junk interpretations and, rather, use this multiscalar analysis both to enrich and thicken up the somewhat thin gruel of some of the earlier sociolinguistic studies of interviews and also, conversely, 'trace the palpable mundane reality of wide-spread societal ideologies through close scrutiny of discursive and contextual processes' (Rampton et al., 2016: 32).

Taking one small extract from Gladston's interview, we can begin to see how it comes to be infused with voices, discourses and texts from wider social contexts – both specific to this event and circulating more widely as ways of seeing the world. In turn, this event feeds into decision-making processes and sustains the organisational discourses which shape these processes across time and space).[19] I have chosen to capture these ripples of context in a series of circles (fig. 3.1), but the lines between them are clearly meant to be thoroughly permeable.

Tracing these ripples to and fro helps to identify how microscale actions come to have much larger consequences within institutional settings and can amplify inequalities when those with little or no power are processed through the system (Maybin, 2017: 45; Maryns, 2013; Ehrlich, 2012).

This illustration draws mainly on the second of the two projects, *Talking Like a Manager*, which focuses on promotion and junior management job interviews set within ethnographic information from two contrasting workplaces. Some of the wider discourses related to internal promotion are given in circle 6. This is dealt with in somewhat more detail than aspects of the other circles, since this set of discourses are not part of the detailed analysis of this book but give some background to the promotion and junior management interviews.

Figure 3.1. Ripples of Context

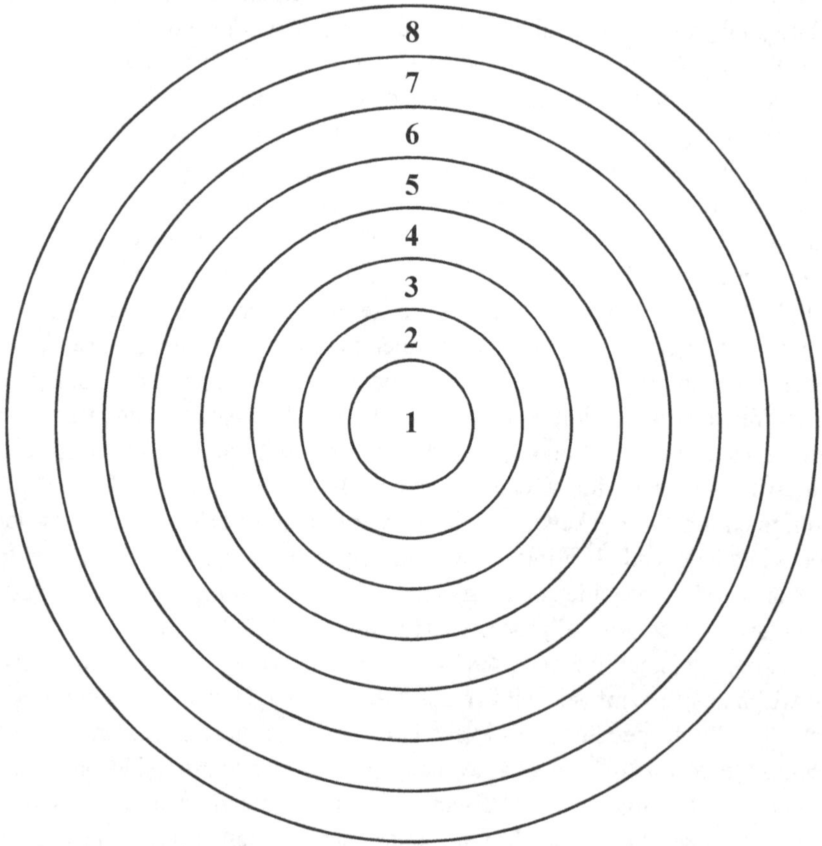

1. Bounded units	5. Wider practices
2. Resources	6. Discourses and relationships
3. Activity	7. Wider institutional discourses
4. Local practices	8. Social/historical discourses

3.7   Transcontextual Analysis: Gladston and the Bent Aerial

As mentioned above, Gladston has worked for many years in a delivery company, after having run his own garage for a while, and is now applying for a permanent junior management position. The competence-based interview has already covered several key capabilities and the next is a somewhat trickier one, about coping with mistakes. These two extracts, given in circles 1 and 2, then expand out gradually to the eighth and final circle of wider institutional discourses.[20]

The first circle is a chunking exercise, dividing phases of the interview into analysable units and allowing both sides to agree on 'what is going on here.' The second circle moves out to analyse the resources both sides use.

Circle 1: Identification of Sequentially Bounded Units

Gladston has been explicitly alerted by the interviewer to the shift to the next 'capability' – that of 'taking ownership' – and has been asked to 'give … an example of how you dealt with a mistake you have made.' He tells the story of when he owned a garage and one of the young technicians damaged the aerial of an expensive car. After the story, some seventeen minutes into the interview, he is asked: 'What goes through your mind at that moment?'

Example 6: Gladston – Jamaican Migrant, Successful

1. I: {(looks up)
2. C: yeah so I thought well the the thing to do is to be honest
3. I: (nods)
4. C: take ownership} {(I looks down, writes)
5.   it's my fault you know put me hand up
6.   and and I'll I'll ask the customer
7.   just give me a chance to put it right you know
8.   and if and if they're still not happy with it after I put it right
9.   then they can take any action that they feel [needs to be taken
10. I: okay} {(I looks up) tell me a] little bit about that conversation then
11.   that you [had
12. C: yeah]
13. I: with the [customer} {(I looks down, writes)
14. C: well] what I said to the customer was
15.   that er:m you know w:e er:m
16.   I- I- I invited him into the office and said
17.   well I'm I'm sorry but we had a little bit of erm a mishap
18.   with your vehicle those are the words I used er:m [and
19. I: mishap]}{(I looks up) [hhh
20. C: hhh} {(I looks down, writes) yeah]
21. I: [mishap
22. C: not] accident we don't like them to to get them alarmed=
23. I: =okay=

This extract can be identified as two 'sequentially bounded units,' marked off by some degree of topical coherence and by other markers, such as shifts in content and/or contextualisation cues (Gumperz, 1999: 465). There are several cues that mark off the first unit (lines 1–9): Gladston's 'yeah so' marks a shift from him telling what options he had to what action he actually took; this seems at least partially triggered by the interviewer looking up from drinking his tea. The first unit ends with the 'taking ownership' context established, before the second begins with the interviewer's 'okay' at line 10, with a shift in gaze to the candidate and overlapping question. The second unit ends again with 'okay' at line 23 and, while not finishing the story, concludes the talk about the use of the term 'mishap.'

Circle 2: Participants' Interactional, Linguistic and Cultural Resources

The interviewer's resources include the authority he has as the voice of the company to elicit competence narratives, to control the question/answer sequences and to interrupt the candidate – in sum, his institutional resources. These are combined with the conversational resources of humour and a relaxation of institutional requirements. Gladston has a range of narrative and interpretive resources which allow him to glide smoothly between institutional and personal discourses:

Example 7: Gladston – Jamaican Migrant, Successful

1.   C: =so I said we had a bit of a mishap with o- with your vehicle
2.   er:m w- we didn't realise that the your aerial was up
3.   and when one of our guys i- it was an apprentice (.) you know
4.   these young boys who just really (.) er
5.   just like to drive flash cars [and
6.   I: yeah]
7.   C: just didn't take note and as he was driving it out
8.   we we damaged your aerial (.) I says
9.   er:m (.) er it will be of no cost to you we'll fix it
10.   if you just give us the opportunity to fix it
11.   we we apol- apologise for it e:r
12.   if you just give us the opportunity to fix it
13.   is- it doesn't interfere with your rights of course
14.   if you feel that e:rm you want to do something else er:m
15.   er take it further then please do so
16.   but give us the opportunity to fix it we'll put it right and

17.   er:m whatsoever you need we'll (.)
18.   we'll we'll d- we'll get it done (.) e:r
19.   if you need a er:m a hire car we'll pay for it
20.   while it's done for the day
21.   because it won't take us more than another day to do it
22. I: okay what was the customer's reaction
23. C: er:m they in fact they they were quite taken aback
24.   that that we actually told them about it
25.   because he because he looked
26.   he went and had a look at at his car
27.   and the aerial was down (.)
28.   so er:m he- he could not have seen that it was damaged
29.   and he said I don't see anything wrong with it (.)
30.   so well I said it's not up at the moment
31.   but if you put it up you'll f- you'll soon notice it you know

Gladston's resources include the telling of narratives in an institutional context, his strengths in making inferences from abstract competence statements and his deft footing in moving from more institutional talk to personal talk – for example, in his use of the term 'mishap,' the delicacy with which he alerts the interviewer to his skills without boasting and also projects himself as an animator of the talk (Goffman, 1981: 148), distancing himself from the telling in order to show his reflective abilities. This metacommunication also brings humour into the story, showing how he juggles several frames and footings at the same time (Goffman, 1981: 155; 1.5) – firmly standing on two feet, by meeting the competence being assessed, while jumping up and down on another to provide humour, energy and solidarity. The two participants co-produce a particular environment which, at this moment, seems smooth and in tune with institutional norms.

Circle 3: The Interview as an Activity

The next two circles move out to look at this interview as token of a particular job interview type and the local practices which determine its outcome and many aspects of its conduct (although these also depend crucially on participant resources). This extract is clearly only a small part of the story and any microanalysis has to be done within the context of the whole story-telling phase, the particular competence phase of the interview (in which each of five competences are given five minutes) and the whole interview, which lasted forty-five minutes. Here we see the orthodox discourses of the gate-keeping interview at work, plus its constraints and occasional relaxation of them. There are also traces of much earlier job interview designs, which still inform the current ones and contribute to the interview dialectics described previously.

Circle 4: Local Practices Around the Job Interview

While the recorded and transcribed interviews were the core data to which we were accountable, they can only be understood and valued as evidence of institutionalised inequality within the immediate practices that inform them (this circle), from the organisations' wider practices and procedures (circle 5) and the ethnographic information about the participants and the interview outcomes. In circle 4, the ethnographic evidence is about decision-making: the written record kept in the interview, the wash-up sessions and the final outcomes for each candidate. The making of this written record (or not) and its effects on the interaction feed into the final outcome and illustrate the process of entextualisation and recontextualisation in making institutional decisions. The wash-up sessions (where they occurred and could be recorded or notes taken) give explicit insights into 'the local communicative ecology' (Gumperz, 1999: 465) of the particular workplace, already 'given off' in the interviews themselves and from which implicit criteria can be derived. They are evidence of both explicit and implicit criteria used in the evaluation of candidates.

Circle 5: Organisations' Wider Practices and Procedures

Circle 5 looks beyond the immediate interview to how it comes to be produced and circle 6 at the prevailing talk and discourses elicited in interviews and feedback sessions. In circle 5 it is possible to see how organisations design their practices and procedures, and how these are enacted and reworked in particular selection processes. In particular, the dominance of competence frameworks on interview design and interviewer and candidate behaviour can be traced in guidance notes for interviewers and candidates, in the structures for recording candidate narratives and in instructions on wash-up sessions, where candidates are often numerically graded. From these can be derived a set of explicit criteria upon which the decisions are formally based, and which interact with the more implicit criteria actually used in wash-ups.

Circle 6: Local Institutional/Organisational Discourses and Histories of Relationships

In this circle the contexts are not naturally occurring but researcher produced, looking at the wider organisational knowledge and opinions about selection and promotion. In these two studies they included ethnographic interviews, brief informational and feedback encounters with candidates, video feedback sessions with interviewers and ethnographic observations, the 'lurking and soaking' (Werner and Schoepfle, 1989) carried out in the selection sites, over-hearing informal talk and some of the off-the-record comments and explanations for decisions made. The interview data are instances of interviewers', managers', trade unionists' and workers' discourses on selection and promotion, plus candidates' responses on how they considered the interview had gone. For example, Gladston's first interviewer commented in general terms on what he was looking for in candidates (8.5), emphasised self-awareness – particularly learning from mistakes – and anticipating questions (and we could include here picking up on prompts), both of which Gladston displays in examples 6 and 7.

The ethnographic data on promotion interviews more generally under-scores some of the characteristics of our data on the internal promotion interview, such as Gladston's in the large delivery company. Candidates here were all directly or indirectly known to the interviewers; this knowledge may have infused the particular social context of each interview and contributed to co-membership or not. There were also discourses circulating both about how to position oneself for promotion and why BAME candidates might find it more difficult to achieve. Informal networks and relationships with management often led to 'the tap on the shoulder' which led potential candidates putting themselves forward and gaining help from mentors on how to 'think like a manager.' Such informal networks can bypass minority groups, particularly where 'they don't see people of their ethnic makeup in positions of responsibility' and also mirror class-based practices, where social entitlement encourages those from higher-class backgrounds to stand out and be noticed.[21]

The ethnographic interviews also gave some background into how candidates might feel about performing in the interview, and what might inhibit them. What was seen approvingly in management's eyes as 'standing out' could be seen by BAME candidates as 'selling out' to their fellow workers. So BAME staff were unlikely to put themselves forward lightly and some felt there was little chance of promotion, so did not position themselves to apply successfully. In addition, and despite the existence of equal opportunity policies, there was some cultural stereotyping evident amongst management. Some BAME staff and junior management were seen as over-conciliatory towards those senior to them ('saying the right thing not the true thing') but too harsh and hierarchical to their own staff ('too brusque in their orders') and this may have played out in individual cases (Roberts et al., 2008).

Circle 7: Wider Institutional and Organisational Discourses

The specific interview training and guidance on competence-based interviews stems from the general move towards skills and competences based on neoliberal notions and enterprising selves, and how these fit with the new discourses of 'diversity' and diversity management discussed below. This historical trajectory from informal processes to formal ones, based on sets of decontextualised values, is part of the assessment and audit culture of most institutions and produces a very specific gaze on how individuals align to the ideal culture of the workplace. While Gladston's performance suggests a thorough socialisation into this culture – in his translational work from the abstract language of competence statements to grounded stories – other migrant and BAME candidates interviewed tended to identify quite different selection criteria. They said that working hard, being willing and interested could lead to promotion.

Circle 8: Broad Social and Historical Discourses

Relationships between these outer circles and fragments of transcribed data are, of course, increasingly difficult to make and are subject to accusatory howls of determinism. Traces of these broad discourses emerge at distinct moments or act in subterranean and unnamed ways which defy precise identification or analysis, and there is an obvious overlap between circle 7 selection discourses and the wider sociohistorical discourses that may inform all other aspects of social life. In this book, I have drawn particularly on four sets of sociohistorical discourses: neoliberal discourses and discourses of power within the marketplace (1.2), notions of the self and soft skills (2.1), institutional and bureaucratic discourses of objectification and classification (2.2) and linguistic ideologies (8.3, 9.1).

3.8   The Data: *Talk on Trial* and *Talking Like a Manager*

The research originally published in the two reports *Talk on Trial* (Roberts and Campbell, 2006) and *Talking Like a Manager* (Roberts et al., 2008) stemmed from the UK government's concern to identify how the ethnic penalty was produced by the selection processes.

Since the DWP already had data on the inequalities of labour market outcomes between two broadly defined groups – the white majority and the BAME minorities – it was important to link this information to the candidates' outcomes in our own research, albeit with very small numbers and with some classificatory scepticism. Since access to job interviews was so difficult, our data collection was opportunistic and no attempt could be made to sample from different institutionally defined groups. Once we had agreement to record, candidates were asked where they were born and grew up but no additional monitoring data were collected.

In the *Talk on Trial* research, of the sixty-one candidates whose interviews were recorded, their self-identified ethnicity led to the following broad groups: twenty-one were white British, twenty-one were BAME British (with predominately South Asian and African/Afro-Caribbean origins) and nineteen were migrant. The latter group came from Bosnia, Brazil, Ethiopia, Philippines, Ghana, India, Ireland, Italy, Liberia, Pakistan, Poland, Romania, Sierra Leone, Somalia and Sri Lanka.

Figure 3.2. Differences in Success at Low-Paid Job Interviews

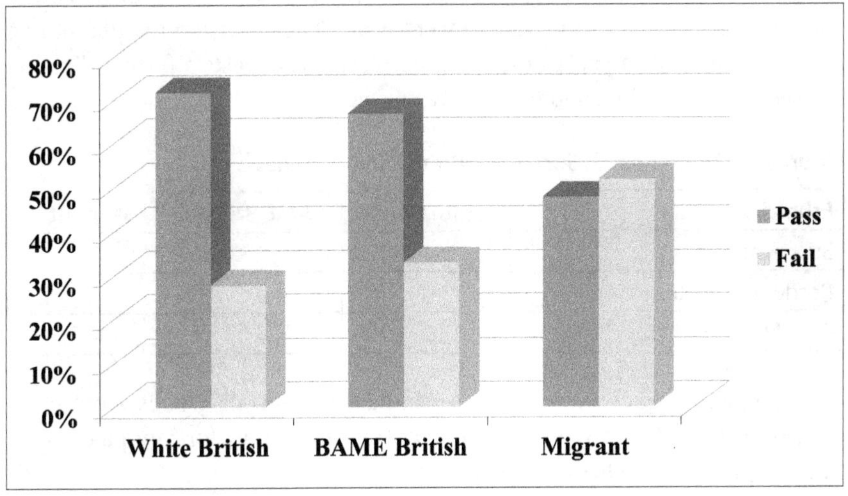

There was a clear distinction between local and migrant outcomes. The graph above shows only a small difference between the white and British BAME groups, with around seventy per cent of candidates successful. However, migrants were more likely to fail than pass. These figures must be read in the context of the assessment process. Of the eight research sites, only three were selection sites where one person is selected from a shortlist. The other five represented what is a norm for recruiting low-paid workers into large organisations. They used recruitment days where large numbers are invited to take some basic tests and then, if found acceptable in the interview, candidates would be offered a job; they were not directly competing for a single job against others on a shortlist.

In the *Talking Like a Manager* research, promotion interviews were even more difficult to record than the low-paid job interviews. And these interviews contrasted with the recruitment days in having tighter selection criteria and a much lower ratio of applicants to successful candidates. Of the seventeen candidates who consented, six were white British, five were from BAME groups born in the UK and six were migrants. Thus the same pattern as that found by earlier research can be identified, with roughly a third in each of the major categories. Within the BAME/migrant group, nine were from the well-established categories used in ethnic monitoring – African/Afro-Caribbean and South Asian – and two were from white minority groups.[22]

Only three candidates were successful: Emma, white British, who had applied for a senior operative post; Gladston, who was born in Jamaica but a long-term resident in the UK; and Junior, a British African candidate. All three were already in post and there was no external recruitment. Junior was a borderline candidate, the last to be interviewed in the assessment process, and was offered the post as the interviewers were under pressure to appoint one more candidate. Analysis of the wash-up sessions suggests a further division between the borderline and the clearly unsuccessful.

Figure 3.3. Differences in Success at Promotion Interviews

Ethnicity/history	White British	BAME British	Migrant
Successful	1	1	1
Borderline unsuccessful	3	2	1
Clearly unsuccessful	2	2	4

These figures suggest that whereas candidates from all groups were challenged by the interview process, as with the interviews for low-paid work, migrant groups were the least successful.

Conclusion

On a small scale, these data reflect the pattern of disadvantage for BAME groups found in labour market research, as noted above. But precisely what it is about the current job interview – with its coating of rationality, objectivity and formality – that produces such disadvantage can be addressed by understanding it in terms of a linguistic penalty. Rather than an analytic stance and interpretive process that looks at interaction outcomes solely within its own terms, the approach here looks beyond it. The methodology outlined above combines the facts of discrimination, conceptual understandings from the new sociolinguistic economy and knowledge from the earlier microstudies with wider ethnographic and discursive contexts. The next chapter looks at circles 4 and 5 of figure 3.1 and how the design of the job interview shapes its fine-grained interactional detail.

4　Competence Models and Covert Linguistic Penalties

This chapter looks briefly at the history of the job interview in the UK. It then considers the design of current interviews in terms of competences and their role in assessing the crucial soft skills, which have come to define what makes a successful candidate. Finally the notion of 'diversity' in the workplace is discussed as masking some of the contradictions of competence management, rather than as an enabler of BAME groups and migrant candidates.

4.1　The Early Job Interview and the Current Selection Processes

In many respects, the job interview as a selection tool in Britain in the last half of the twentieth century and into the twenty-first has followed its use and design in the US. Its widespread use in the early part of the twentieth century soon led to an increasing interest in its validity, with structured 'problem situation' questions, written records and standardised rating. In 'A brief history of the selection interview' (Buckley et al., 2000), the authors conclude that – despite some developments in structuring the interview to respond to validity and equal opportunity requirements – there has been no sustained critique of it, nor any imaginative alternatives.

There were already doubts about the interview as early as 1927, with concerns that it did little more than engage the candidate in conversation (Buckley et al., 2000); in the 1980s, some argued that the interview should only be used to evaluate those skills observed in the interview. Despite these doubts, from the middle to late 1980s onwards, in Britain and elsewhere, it became more widespread, more standardised, more textualised (Iedema and Scheeres, 2003) and longer – even for low-paid, routine work. For example, in our data, interviews lasted between thirty and sixty minutes. With the exception of small organisations, where informal techniques of recruitment are still widespread, the interview remains the most popular mode of selection in the UK (Keep and James, 2010).

The demands of the global economy require employers to hire highly skilled staff quickly and effectively, and electronic recruitment techniques such as the Skype or Zoom interview are increasingly used. There are other imagined possibilities such as smart watches, so that candidates can be interviewed with a glance at the wrist, and possibly Snapchat for screening interviews only ten or twenty seconds long. But while these future plans and the current electronic media use technology to mediate and compress interviews – or use them as a first stage process, or supplement them – they do not replace face-to-face interviewing.

As with many other aspects of the new economy, in which modes of production are increasingly mediated through technology and language (Heller, 2011; Duchêne and Heller, 2012), the role and design of the textualised job interview has also given language a new importance. This has been nicely summed up in the shift from 'workforce' to 'wordforce' (Heller, 2010). Discourses of mission statements, the regulation of human resources through competence frameworks, guidelines for the structuring and managing of job interviews and the length of such interviews are all evidence of this current languaging and textualising work, and the ideology of new capitalism and equality bureaucracy (2.1) that underpins it. Two contrasting tropes used in the prevailing discourses of job selection in the UK sum up the language loading that these processes now bear. In the mid-twentieth century, it was commonplace to hear recruiters talking of 'a pair of hands' to fill a job. By the beginning of the twenty-first century, the 'language of talent' (Brown and Hesketh, 2004) – with its celebratory image of the successful communicator – had superseded it.

4.2   Job Interviews in the UK: 1960s to the Present

As well as all the language work implicit in the interview, the other main change over the last three or four decades has been the extension of this selection tool to relatively low-paid and technical jobs. In the 1960s and early 1970s, the 'job interview' for such jobs was often not much more than checking personal details and the 'a pair of hands' criterion. Organisations often used what was called 'chain recruitment,' using informal networks of friends and relatives already employed. Even for management and professional posts, it was common to have an informal chat and for the interviewer to decide whether the applicant 'had what it takes' and 'would fit in.' This was also a period when 'political correctness' and 'glass (and class) ceilings' had not entered the vocabulary; issues of race and gender inequality were only just beginning to seep into recruitment and selection processes. It was routine at that time for women applicants to be asked about their marriage plans and childcare arrangements and I, as mentioned in chapter 1, was asked if I was 'courting' at an interview in the early 1970s.

By the late 1970s and 1980s, industry had developed more formal interviews – although these remained relatively loosely structured, focussing on motivation and other psychological attributes. Jenkins' research during the early 1980s in the Midlands, around Birmingham, showed that employers did not only check for 'suitability' in terms of previous experience and skills but also for 'acceptability,' rating highly evidence of 'appearance' and 'manner' (Jenkins, 1986) which, he argued, led to indirect discrimination. The following example is typical of the early 1980s in that it is loosely structured around the candidate's CV, their motivation and hypothetical situations. The job is that of a bus driver in a large transport company. The interviewer is local white British and the candidate a migrant from East Africa of South Asian origin:

Example 8: Rashid – Indian Migrant, Unsuccessful

1. I: why do you actually want to leave (.) it's a nice steady job
2. C: well the thing is um you know it's better
3.   to change the jobs and get other jobs
4.   I was very interested in working for (xxx) Buses you know
5.   right at the beginning
6.   because I couldn't get the job I had to take the job at (xxx)

(twenty lines deleted)

7. I: since then you have worked as a process operator
8.   what do you think (xxx) Buses will offer you
9.   that (xxx) don't offer you
10. C: well quite a lot of things (.) for example
11.   like um (.) Christmas bonus
12. I: uh huh
13. C: so many things (.) holidays and all that (.)
14.   well we get holidays in (xxx) but you er (.)
15.   get here more holidays than you get in (xxx) (hhh)
16. I: all right (.) okay (.) before you actually went to (xxx)
17.   four years ago you were in Africa

(eighteen lines deleted)

18. I: you obviously don't drive in the job you are doing
19.   what sort of driving experience have you had
20. C: in this country
21. I: uh huh
22. C: I've got light good vehicle driving licence and
23.   (.) I've- I don't think done nothing wrong

(Roberts, Davies and Jupp, 1992: 44–45)

The interview is loosely structured, moving between motivation, biographical discussion about the candidate's life in Africa, hypotheticals about what the company might be like and past experience. The candidate's failure to understand the interview game is clear in each response to these topics.

By contrast, the public sector in the mid-1980s – in response to the race and equality legislation – designed 'equal opportunities' interviews which were highly scripted and controlled (fig. 4.1). Drawing on bureaucratic ideals of objectivity and standardisation, the assumption was that talk and interaction, if sufficiently regulated, produced equality of outcomes. This type of interview was a response to the general trend, noted earlier, that increasing globalisation and diversity required more standardisation and was aligned to the modern, rational, Weberian project that differences could be controlled and managed. A version of these interviews is still used in some public sector organisations, particularly those run by local authorities, as our data show (7.2).

Since the 1990s the notion of competence has driven the recruitment and selection process; such interviews are now routine in both public and private sectors. The use of a competence framework with standard questions and training is designed to lead to the holy grail of objectivity, reliability and equality of opportunity. Some organisations follow what could be called a total competence approach in which questions are only asked of a tightly defined set of key competences, questions are behavioural – that is, asking for past experience – and interviewers are trained to drill down further with each one. But unlike the scripted equal opportunities interviews, the interviewer can build on or probe the candidate's answers. For example, the delivery company trained their interviewers in a method called 'funnelling' (fig. 4.4). As one of the interviewers explained:

Asking candidates, 'what if this, what if that,' and making it increasingly difficult to answer, you can get to the point where the candidate says 'I don't know.' If you don't reach this point then the candidate is more knowledgeable than you.

Other organisations used a mix of competence and more general motivational and biographical questions, or retained elements of the rigidly standardised equal opportunities interview. So in our data, some interviews were typical of the dominant model whereas others retained aspects of the 1960s, 1970s and 1980s alongside competence-type questions (fig. 4.1). This melding of different interview designs contributes to the hybrid discourses discussed in chapter 5.

Figure 4.1. Job Interviews 1960s to the Present

	1960s and 1970s	1980s	1990s to present
Typical of the period	Little or no formal interviewing: 'A pair of hands' Migrants often offered jobs on the basis of 'chain recruitment' Not politically correct: 'Are you courting?' Loosely structured Motivation: 'Why do you want the job?'	'Equal opportunity' interviews (in the public sector): Highly standardised No response from interviewers	Competence-based interviews and 'the language of talent' with a focus on expressivity: Highly structured but some 'wiggle room'
(Some) continuity across periods		Set questions read out Answers written down verbatim and numerically graded No opportunity for clarification	
	Biographical: working through CV		

4.3   The Competence Model of Selection Interviewing

Competences are everywhere. They are not confined to industry but are also widely used in professions such as teaching, health and medicine. Drawing on Boyatzis' model of twenty-one competences, which was based on an analysis of the characteristics of highly successful performers (Boyatzis, 1982), the term 'competence' refers to the capability to reach a specific goal (Weinert, 2001: 45; Pelsmaekers et al., 2011). The dominance of this model and the consistency of competence discourses stems largely from the neoliberal ideology of marketising the social and commodifying the self, as well as from the ideology of new capitalism. They are a response to the multidimensional changes that new or fast capitalism has produced: more diversity, more change, more legislation and more new technology – so more independent working and more cross-functional working. But they also reflect and help to construct the reflexive, always-improving self – aligning to the values of the organisation while at the same time presenting the self as an individual, authentic project (2.1) – as the competences and questions outlined below show.

Figure 4.2. Competences as Formulated in Interviewer Guidelines and Job Descriptions

---

4.2.1. Large supermarket – junior management positions

Respect for the individual:

- *Valuing other people*: Give me an example of a successful team you have worked with. Then what was your contribution to the team's success? What did you most enjoy about being in that team?

  Describe someone you found hard to get on with. What steps did you take to build rapport with them? (Interviewers have to say whether the candidate 'lives the value.')

- *Working together*: Tell me about a colleague who you had to help all the time. How did this colleague's needs affect your own job?

Service to the customer:

- *Cheerfulness*: Describe a job you have held that had a fun working environment. How did you feel working there?

- *Happy to help*: Tell me about an irritating customer you had to deal with. What irritates you about customers generally?

Strive for excellence:

- *Always improving*: Tell me about a time when you went beyond your job and more than was required of you. What is the best idea you have had implemented?

- *Successful communication*: Tell me about someone you find it hard to communicate with. What is it about their style that is challenging?

Resilience:

- Why do you feel you are suited to retail?

4.2.2. Large delivery company – low-paid delivery work			
Key dimension	**Key capability**	**Example question**	**For candidates**
Group inter-personal skills	Working with people	Tell me about an occasion when you worked with a group of people to achieve something.	Getting on with others
Customer-handling skills	Satisfying customers	Give me an example of when you have tried to help a customer.	Dealing with customers
Personal resilience	Managing yourself	At times the job involves working on fairly routine or repetitive tasks. Can you think of a recent occasion when you had to carry out a task that you thought was repetitive?	Think of an occasion when it was hard to motivate yourself.
Openness to change	Managing change	Think of a time when you had to adapt to a new way of doing things.	Did you enjoy the new experience?
Improving things	Improving the business	Can you think of an occasion when you noticed that something wasn't working well?	What did *you* do when you noticed it wasn't working so well?

4.2.3. Large London local authority – clerical work and management positions

The competence clusters: total of sixteen, each with three to five competences/sub-competences

Five core clusters

- *Reasoning*: problem solving, innovative thinking, professional expertise, organisational awareness
- *Drive*: drive for excellence, planning and organisation, service focus, business initiative
- *Personal qualities*: confidence, adaptability
- *Leadership*: developing talent
- *Interpersonal*: working in partnership, communication and influence, inter-personal sensitivity

Examples from the drive cluster: drive for excellence

- Business initiative – takes action to avoid problems, seizes opportunities, pre-pares ahead
- Planning and organisation – manages own workload: uses simple planning tools, juggles priorities, allocates time effectively, learns from planning errors

While job analysis, description and person specifications were used long before competences drove selection, the new model was rapidly embraced as a means of identifying effective staff and of meeting equal opportunities legislation (Wood and Payne, 1998) while also managing diversity. These models are used in training and both audit and human resource planning, but it is the interview – and most significantly, the selection interview – that is seen as the ideal technology for assessing the soft skills of relating, communicating and displaying the self (Reissner-Roubicek, 2017; chapter 8) as illustrated below.

These three frameworks, designed by organisations in three very different sectors, reflect slightly different ways of classifying them in guidelines for interviews. Only the second organisation – the delivery company – also has guidelines for candidates and these are included to show how, even within one organisation, the competences are described somewhat differently for interviewers and interviewees.

These three frameworks show that although the competence cake can be cut in different ways, the range is nearly identical across three quite different organisations. This also fits neatly with the top twelve identified in 1996, but with some slight difference in emphasis (Wood and Payne, 1998: 27). Similarly, our data (which included data from organisations one and two) showed that interviews were structured around the same competences, with the language of the competence statements and documents routinely appearing in the interviews. What is surprising is that this core set in the standard frameworks are very similar across all levels in an organisation; the low-paid clerical or manual worker is assessed according to the same broad criteria as managers or indeed senior executives. These all-embracing frameworks are driven by the ideology discussed in chapter 2, where even low-paid workers are expected to align themselves to the vision and mission of the organisation and become – like more senior staff – both self-managing and able to manage others.

Even for low-paid jobs, these highly abstract models and frameworks underlie the interview and have to be recontextualised in the face-to-face-encounter. It is the role of the candidate to interpret and ground the abstract framework in detailed and reflective accounts.[23] So for example, the question, 'How does an organisation manage change?' asked at an interview for a low-paid job draws directly on the competence 'open to change.' It is recontextualised as a request for an analytic response, in which the candidate should align his or her own capacity to manage change with that of the organisation. This puts a large inferencing load on the candidate, to get from this huge and complex question to the key notion of 'flexibility' or 'adaptability' which underpins the 'open to change' competence. Next there is the question of how flexibility can be demonstrated in their response, using work experience that is familiar enough to the interviewer to provide evidence of this competence.

The competence questions asked in the recorded interviews were broadly adapted from these interviewer guidelines. For low-paid, entry-level work the two questions that occurred in all our data concerned team working and organising oneself and one's time. Others that occurred frequently in our data related to customer service, learning from failures or dislikes and making improvements. Since some of the interviews were not total competence interviews but a hybrid, other topics covered concerned describing oneself, general questions about motivation and suitability, plus outlines of previous jobs. In some of the public sector interviews, there was a standard equal opportunities question and occasionally technical questions such as, 'What computer packages have you used?' – or else questions about the physical demands of the job.

For the junior management and promotion interviews, there were four overlapping sets of questions. Each main set was elicited across a range of general or more specific topics:

1. **Building relationships, teamwork and developing others:** building relationships within a team, developing a team and establishing oneself in a new team; inspiring, communicating and influencing people; keeping people motivated; giving appropriate help, development and training; managing resistance from groups and individuals; challenging unacceptable behaviour.

2. **Problem solving (often in relation to customer service or resource management):** identifying a problem and solving it; prioritising; implementing unpopular decisions, or those which have a negative effect on some or all of the team; disciplining; challenging decisions made by more senior managers.

3. **Achievement/results orientation (particularly in the face of difficulties):** going the extra mile and pushing oneself to the limit; overcoming setbacks; making risky decisions and challenging wrong ones; introducing new practices and innovations.

4. **Learning/taking responsibility (not top-twelve competences [Matthewman, 1995], but links with those of adaptability/flexibility and developing others):** self-development and self-awareness; learning from past experiences, particularly failure; willingness to take responsibility for mistakes; willingness to seek out help and advice; knowing what one still has to prove about oneself.

4.4   Competences and Skills

The discourse of competences is clearly aligned to the soft skills of communication, problem solving, motivation, judgment, leadership and initiative, and loyalty and harmony – or how to fit into the culture of the organisation – noted in chapter 2. These soft skills are deemed essential in what Boltanski and Chiapello call the 'network society':

> Transverse modes of coordination (teams, projects, etc.) place greater weight not only on specifically linguistic mastery, but also on qualities that might be called more 'personal,' more clearly bound up with the 'character' of the person – for example, openness, self-control, availability, good humour, composure – which were by no means so highly prized in the old work culture. The techniques of enterprise psychology (interviews, graphology, etc.) are used to pinpoint these propensities in candidates for a job. (Boltanski and Chiapello, 2005: 241)

In most of the English-speaking world, experience and soft skills are given the highest priority. A survey of employers in the UK showed that eighty-six per cent rated experience as the top priority. Qualifications came some way down after skills at fifty-four per cent (Keep and James, 2010). Only one-fifth of employers rated hard skills highly; four-fifths favoured soft skills.

As mentioned in chapter 2, individuals are expected to soak up the organisational discourses and come to see themselves as a 'bundle of (soft) skills' (Urcioli, 2008), aligned to the workplace culture and so transportable to new environments and conditions. These soft skills have put back into the competence model some of the more psychological dimensions that a strictly behaviourist interpretation of competences lack, but which were in the original formulation (Boyatzis, 1982).

Sociologists of work have traced the shift from expertise and technical skills to these soft skills and competences (Hillage et al., 2002; Payne, 2000), the examples above being evidence of this. Particularly noteworthy is the framework of a large local authority (fig. 4.2). The 'bedrock competences' developed in 1994 of planning, professional expertise and problem solving had been superseded – in a revised framework in 2004 – by a set of softer and more abstract skills of adaptability, innovative thinking and organisational awareness.

Two examples, one from our own data and one from Grugulis and Vincent's case studies (2009), illustrate the enormous power of competence/skills discourse in recruitment and selection. In our data, we could see clearly the contrast between the job description and what was expected in the interview. All the instructions and guidance written about the design and conduct of the job interview for the large delivery company (fig. 4.2) are driven by competences (or skills or capabilities, which seem to be used interchangeably). By contrast, the job description for the low-paid job of delivering mail – what the candidate reads and would be expected to prepare for – only has one reference related to a competence, and that indirectly: '[You] must maintain a professional and friendly attitude.' The rest of the job description is about time-keeping and a description of sorting and delivering mail. The gap between the requirements of the job and the requirements of the interview are clear. The interview follows the bureaucratised ideology of the contemporary workplace, while the job itself is a routine matter requiring some limited manual dexterity, a careful reading eye and the physical strength to shift mailbags around.

The second example is of a case study of gender disadvantage from a local authority housing department. The selection criteria were based on soft skills, especially 'attitude,' which were considered more important than technical skills in dealing with casework. Women tended to be recruited because of their 'right attitudes,' but then were disproportionately selected to work as receptionists where these soft skills were thought to be most needed. However, most of the real business of the department (and the better-paid jobs) required technical casework expertise. Once candidates were through the interview process, these soft skills were acknowledged but not valued – and women found themselves relegated to lower-status work.

The favouring of soft skills over technical and professional expertise has the potential to discriminate against migrant groups, as well as women (Allan, 2013). Attitude, character, relationship building and so on are hard to tie down, are based on norms of self-presentation and are judged by the interviewer's level of comfort in the interaction: 'Soft skills … replace the technical power of the artisan to produce with the social power of the courtier to please' (Grugulis and Vincent, 2009: 611).

The image of the fawning courtier, reliant on the particular whims of the powerful monarch, may seem far removed from the machinery of competences but the softness and indeterminacy of terms such as 'openness' or 'inspiring others' – however much they are incorporated into hard lists and models – are judged in interaction by just those subconscious processes and feelings that such frameworks are designed to erase. And it is no surprise that interviewers fall back on 'personality' as the main criterion for selection, since it is the candidate's capacity to please which ultimately seems to matter the most (8.5). To this extent, the job interview is one of the most intense tests of 'belonging' and of quite a different order from the citizenship tests, for example, which are so often used as a proxy for assessing belongingness (Roberts, 2019).

These personal qualities and the other soft skills, elicited through examples of work experience and seen as essential for any job, have to be institutionally framed. This requires a level of analytic detachment which glosses over glimpses of a personal, emotional being and the narratives of workaday skills. So the competences of flexibility, customer handling or personal resilience are brought alive through personal touches and narratives, then tamed and institutionalised through reflection and objectification. The competence model implies a hybrid set of discourses – personal, professional and institutional – critical in interview outcomes, as chapters 5 and 6 discuss. But these are never attended to in any procedures, training or preparation.

4.5   The Competence Interview: Training, Preparation and Recording

Along with the interviewer guidelines to meet criteria of explicitness and transparency go texts for training interviewers and preparing candidates, and for compiling written records of candidates' talk. Organisations vary in how far they provide documentation, but all subscribe to the interview orthodoxy that interviews should be explicitly structured and that records of some kind must be kept. The following examples come from one of our research sites and are the most transparent in outlining interviewer conduct, recommending topics for candidates to prepare and in their form for recording candidates' responses.

Guidelines for Conducting the Interview

In this set of guidelines, the topics covered are: encouraging diversity and avoiding discrimination, using the structured interview, examples of question types (e.g. open, closed and probing) through the 'funnelling' technique, and dos and don'ts of successful interviewing.

Figure 4.3. Why Use a Structured Interview

<table>
<tr><td>

Why use a structured interview

The structured interview ensures the same information is collected from all candidates, and that the questions asked are relevant to capabilities that support performance in the job.

Do not try to mark the candidate's responses as you ask the questions. Observe and record, during the interview, but do not try to judge or formally mark the response until after the interview.

Funnelling

The concept of funnelling is that through a series of questions you initially broadly identify a situation and some of the background, and then subsequently drill down into the finer detail. This technique will help you to establish the full story and get better evidence on which to make your decision.

Once you have established the situation, you should then try to pin down the details of the candidate's task including things like the objective, why the task was necessary, who else was involved, etc. It is important to find out what actions they took to complete the task; we are interested in their contribution, before asking about the end result.

</td></tr>
</table>

These instructions were then followed by a funnelling diagram, similar to figure 4.4 below.

These guidelines are followed up by the interview assessment form, in which each of the five competences to be assessed is given a separate sheet. A model question is given when the interviewer introduces the competence and asks for examples – e.g. 'Working with people: Tell me about an occasion when you worked with others.' This is followed by further questions about the example, then questions eliciting reflections on the occasion and a follow-up question probing self-reflection. This form structures the main section of the interview around these five competences and also directs the precise conduct of the interview, regulating questions and follow-ups.

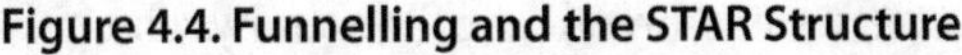

Figure 4.4. Funnelling and the STAR Structure

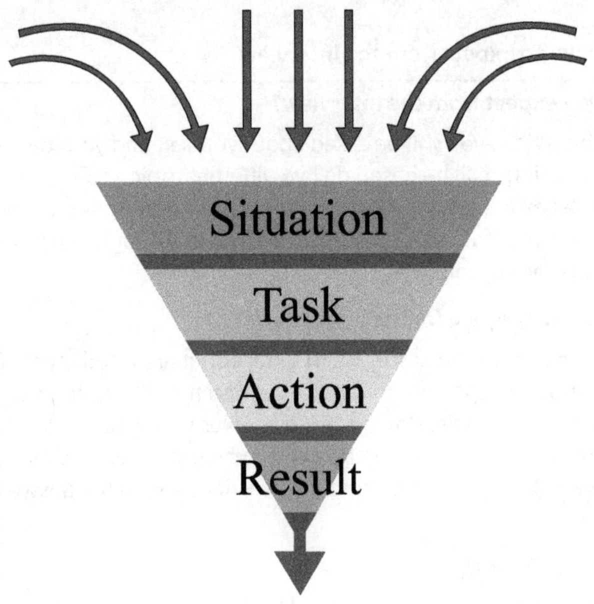

Preparation Guidelines for Candidates

The candidate is similarly directed, with a booklet on what to expect and how to prepare – although, as mentioned above, the information here is very different from the job description. After two general paragraphs, the booklet gives one page to each of the headings 'getting on with others,' 'dealing with customers,' 'staying motivated,' 'doing things differently' and 'improving things.' Underneath each explanation, blank space is provided for 'your notes.' The explanation for 'doing things differently' is given in figure 4.5.

The candidate guidelines mirror the assessment form and are exemplary in displaying what was traditionally an event shrouded in mystery. Striking is the weight given to soft skills: on being reflective about experience and the status given to such notions as flexibility, around which the narratives of the interview are organised. While it is clearly designed to help the candidate prepare, its presuppositions about competence and register remain unstated. The fact that so many candidates applying for jobs in this organisation still failed to provide adequate responses indicates that content explicitness, while helpful, leaves crucial performative components such as footing, structuring of responses and means of self-display implicit. Understanding these components is part of the linguistic penalty that migrants, in particular, face and which are not addressed in the discourses and practices of 'diversity' championed by organisations.

Figure 4.5. What to Expect from the Interview

What should I expect from the interview?

During the interview, you will be asked about yourself and your past experiences. The questions will be based on five different topics. You will be asked to give some brief examples. Ideally these should be examples from the last two to three years, either from your work life or school, although you may also use other examples as appropriate.

What can I do to prepare for the interview?

The five interview topic areas for you to think about are listed on the following pages. To help you prepare for this interview, you may like to think about the topics in advance and write down a few examples from your own experience. This is purely for your own preparation and to help you get ready for questions at the interview. No one in [the company] will need to see the answers that you write.

Doing things differently

Think about a time when you were asked to do something differently, or try out new things. How did you react? Did you enjoy the new experience? Do you consider yourself a flexible person? Think about why.

Examples might include: taking on new tasks in the workplace, doing a completely new job, being asked to change how you do something, starting a job after many years at school, changing your routine for yourself or your family, having to adjust to something new in your life.

4.6   Competences and Diversity

Competence frameworks are a response to some of the implicit dialectics of the job interview (2.9). These frameworks are seen as solving the problems of how to select the flexible, self-managing self and also provide equality of opportunity in an increasingly diverse labour market. Competence management (CM), it is argued, selects for broad capabilities which can be tuned to changing situations, while also providing a strong element of structure and regulation to meet equality requirements (Kandola, 1996). No tension is seen between the standardisation and consistency required of equal opportunities legislation and bureaucracy on the one hand, and the impact of neoliberal ideology of the new capitalism and the requirements of the dynamic, flexible, pragmatic, spontaneous and 'enterprising self' on the other.

This tension, like other tensions outlined in chapter 2, is carefully hidden. Here the seeming contradiction of standardisation and the marketisation of skills and self is managed and therefore masked by the new discourses of diversity. Discourses of equal opportunities and affirmative action of the 1980s and 1990s have shifted to discourses of 'diversity management' (DM). These are about judging everyone as individuals on the basis of their competences, within a new discourse of unity and the 'common culture' of an organisation. The DM approach stems from a neoliberal model of individual talents and close identification of the individual with the culture of the workplace. Diversity discourses no longer speak of discrimination but of individual competence which includes, unsurprisingly, fitting into the cultural categories of the ideal employee. So whatever your background, if you present yourself as a culturally appropriate team worker – and your experiences are invoked in linguistically acceptable ways – then you are likely to be successful at selection. Diversity and competence discourses are thus blended into a single discursive regime which reinforces further the competence-based interview (Scheepers, 2011). In contrast to the earlier period, where equal opportunity concerns could challenge institutional conventions, diversity discourses support them.

The argument here is that the organisation is open to selecting candidates from all linguistic and cultural backgrounds and the competence-based design ensures standardisation; the selection process appears fair on two counts. However, such fairness rests on shaky ground. It assumes that candidates can and do accept the requirement to align with an organisational culture and so, by implication, with the culture of the interview. The competences themselves, such as 'team working' or 'coping with change,' already assume an understanding and acceptance that personal attributes and attitudes must be aligned to organisational priorities. In other words, you can be as diverse as you want – as long as you are like us.

It also assumes that regulating the design of the interview means that all aspects of the interaction can be regulated. Again, this produces its own difficulties. Total regulation squeezes interaction into scripts and formulaic, conventionalised answers far removed from the discourses of variety and difference in DM – and also from the routine judgments of interviewers in wash-up sessions, where personality and how candidates 'come across' are more important criteria than any other (8.5). So CM and DM have forged an alliance that defends the institution, but only provided that the gap between these discourses and the actual linguistic practices of the job interview event is not exposed.

Conclusion

Despite different trends in interviewing styles over the years, the job interview as the ultimate form of selection has not been fundamentally critiqued. The current competence model fuses rational, objective and standardised ideals with neoliberal discourses of soft skills. Diversity discourses bolster this model and serve to hide its contradictions. The power of these selection processes to produce inequality is either denied or goes unnoticed. The appearance of objectivity, fairness and validity is maintained and routinely structured around these frameworks and interview training. But these apparently scientific discourses create their own linguistic penalties. They demand of candidates an easy familiarity with hybrid modes of talking, aligned to a given set of competences. And they set up systems to ostensibly regulate and standardise interaction which penalise many, and through which subjectivities leak in at all points. In the next chapter we see these processes at work, as these tensions are realised in the hybrid discourses of the interview.

5 Institutional, Professional and Personal Discourses

Chapters 5 and 6 focus on candidate contribution and how to perform the institutional self. They examine the ways in which the candidates' talk is inserted into the orthodoxy of the interview discourses and how these hybrid discourses are a combination of professional, personal and institutional modes of talking which judge the different selves required. While a distinction between these different discourses is useful, it is the interplay of all three in the design of questions and how candidates show alignment to them in their performance – both individually and where they are integrated – which determines the character of the interview and the decision-making process. In this chapter, institutional and personal discourses are illustrated.

As mentioned in chapter 2, a different book might look at candidates' contributions through other lenses, such as the production and maintenance of 'identity.' The central concern here is the wider question of how institutional processes create penalties, rather than an exploration of social identity through varieties in speaking practices – although this is a thread running through the study. While candidates draw on repertoires of style and interpretation in their contributions, what is thematised here is how these different modes of self-presentation are institutionally evaluated as an acceptable candidate self. In other words, it is the institutional assessment of the moment which is at issue, rather than an understanding of an assemblage of stylistic repertoires over time and space and their connection to social groupings more broadly.

5.1 Hybrid Discourses

Chapters 2–4 have examined some of the practices that make the institution. But as this chapter's title suggests, however powerful the institutional gaze, there is no one set of discourses which characterise it; personality, a range of soft skills and the institutional and bureaucratic regimes of the interview all play a part. Indeed, as critical discourse analysis has shown, most public life is colonised by hybrid discourses and their blending and recontextualisation in an interdiscursive space. Such interdiscursivity appears routinely in a wide range of institutional settings such as legal proceedings, in mediation, counselling and therapy, political rhetoric, medical settings and the workplace more generally – as well as in selection processes.[24]

Much of the sociological and sociolinguistic literature tends to make a distinction between only two large and potentially competing discourses: the institutional, organisational and professional on the one hand, and the personal on the other (Gunnarsson et al., 1997; Mishler, 1984; Holmes et al., 1999). Take, for example, Mishler's well-known distinction in medicine between the world of medicine and the lifeworld. But while there are many overlapping features of institutional/organisational and professional discourses, important distinctions between institutional and professional can be identified and indeed amplified in highly charged selection processes (Candlin and Maley, 1997; Roberts and Sarangi, 1999: 13–19; Iedema, 2007: 1–17) and strikingly so in our job interview data.

For example, Scheuer's analysis of job interviews for professional-level posts identifies certain context-specific, competing discourses which make a distinction between relatively more institutional and more professional discourse. He contrasts the 'teleological' discourses of the successful candidate with the 'school' and 'circumstantial' discourses of the failed candidate (Scheuer, 2001: 234). Teleological discourses (Auer, 1998; Scollon and Scollon, 1995: 183) are based on goal-setting theory and are presented as an agent-driven, smooth trajectory in which the candidate's past is recontextualised as continually working towards a specified set of end goals. Such teleological discourses contribute to the 'enterprising self' discussed in chapter 2 and are orientated towards the institutional demands of the interview. The alternative and less successful discourses show the candidate as inserted into typical education and career experiences; embedded in circumstances, rather than standing out from them. These circumstantial discourses are straightforward professional descriptions, lacking the knowing stance and analytic character of the institutional self.

So in gatekeeping encounters, there is some analytic purchase in identifying three, rather than two, modes of discourse at work (Sarangi and Roberts, 1999: 15). Firstly, there is the discourse mode which imagines a straighttalking, consistent and truthful world – aspects of what has been called a utilitarian discourse system of clarity, brevity and sincerity (Scollon and Scollon, 1995: 98–117; chapter 10) where you are what you talk as you describe your career and, occasionally, educational experiences. This is the professional discourse mode which people routinely use in carrying out their duties and responsibilities, and in narrating them in assessment settings.

The second mode is the performance and poetics of self, where emotions and more intimate aspects of the individual are displayed, drawing on the self outside the work role. The personal breaks through the roles that speakers enact into what we can call a personal discourse mode. Thirdly, and laminated over these two, are the institutional discourses which manage such encounters, assuming a meta level of knowledge about how institutional events should be conducted and demanding a level of analytic detachment from all parties involved. This institutional mode enacts rational accounting practices to maintain and defend institutions and organisations, and it is where the candidate displays this understanding of institutional requirements (chapter 2).

These three modes are introduced here, before the institutional and personal discourses are discussed in more detail. The professional mode, specifically how it is enacted through narrative, is the topic of chapter 6. But first, a word of warning: the distinction between different discourses are relatively defined, and often only glancingly realised in a particular utterance. There is no absolute set of discourses that constitute any one set of activities. Nevertheless, the fact that these discourses and their combinations in the interview do have a certain stability – and ultimately a degree of coercive power (McElhinny, 1997: 106–139) – is evident in the links between the candidates' talk and interviewers' responses in the interview, in feedback sessions, interview wash-ups and in the final decisions. Candidates who successfully used and synthesised these discourses were routinely more likely to be successful than those who did not.

5.2   Professional Discourse Mode

This is the discourse used in and constitutive of people's duties and responsibilities in their daily work. The descriptions of working life conveyed briefly and clearly draw on shared ways of knowing and seeing, which make an individual sound like a member of a particular profession or job community. As Charles Goodwin puts it:

> Professional vision [consists of] socially organised ways of seeing and understanding events that are answerable to the distinctive interests of a particular social group. (Goodwin, 1994: 606)

'Professional,' in the sense used in this book, refers to any type of practice which associates the individual with belonging to a work community as part of the taken-for-granted way of organising oneself and one's conduct in respect of work.

Although the selection interview is an institutional activity and it is designed to defend the institution, its taken-for-granted function is to elicit candidates' work experience, skills and potential and select for jobs on offer. While the explicit criteria of competences are abstract formulations, evidence of them is expected to be largely in professional discourse modes. Competence frameworks are designed to elicit micro-accounts of experience; the most frequent question asked is, 'Can you give me an example of ...' Narratives texture the encounter.

The following is an archetypal example of a successful narrative. Like Ire in chapter 1, Duncan is expected to interpret the repetitive work question as one about self-management in overcoming boredom and staying motivated:

Example 9: Duncan – White British, Successful

1. I: yeah so (.) what I'm looking for here is an example
2.   where you have done a similar kind of like routine (.) repetitive work
3.   o- over a period of time
4. C: well one specific agency contract I got
5.   it was only four months but it was (.)
6.   the complete mind numbingly same repetitive stuff
7. I: okay
8. C: I was working for (xxx) in (xxx)
9.   and we were building headsets for helicopter pilots
10.   and my specific task was to get this tiny little ear piece
11.   and get a little drill and glue that
12.   and that was all I had to do (.) all day every day (.)
13.   I didn't have problem with that
14.   because I was sat round a table with half a dozen other blokes
15.   and you know you don't really need
16.   to turn your brain on to do something like that
17.   you can just chat and get the job done
18.   and it's- you got to keep yourself amused for boring jobs
19.   it's as simple as that
20.   and I absolutely love working outdoors (.)
21.   I've got no problem at all with (.)
22.   doing the same round day in day out (.)
23.   I could quite easily do that

Unlike the analytic framing and distancing of institutional discourses, here there is a grounded account which rhetorically conforms to the utilitarian demands of brevity, sincerity and clarity. Topics and coding schemes centre on actual conduct, job processes and vividly described tasks, and are rounded off with personalised evaluative comments. The underlying goal of Duncan's story is to produce – through descriptive detail and evaluation – a shared vision of the work and of the importance of self-motivation, even with the most repetitive tasks: 'the complete mind-numbingly same repetitive stuff.' Yet even within the professional mode there is hybridity. Part of the evaluation of the story combines a deontic element – 'you got to keep yourself amused for boring jobs' – with a passing glance at the institutional. I return to this example and a more detailed discussion of the narratives of professional discourse in chapter 6.

5.3 Personal Discourse Mode

It is routine for interviewers to tell candidates that 'they want to get the best out of you' or 'want to get to know you,' reminding us both of the Foucauldian confessional and the market sales pitch, as the self is worked up and disclosed as a subject. While all aspects of the interview are concerned with the individual candidate and so their contributions are, arguably, all in the personal discourse mode, the prized synthesised self (Fairclough, 1992a) combines the personal with the institutional and professional.

Personal discourses consist of talk concerned with the affective self, with individuals' more intimate experiences and with feelings. Increasingly, candidates' acceptability is judged on the extent to which they are seen to display a fully rounded being, authentic and self-expressive, who can contribute personally to the organisation. They are required to perform 'new forms of participation' that 'marshal what were previously considered to be forms of engagement uniquely reserved for intimate or friend-to-friend relationships' (Iedema, 2003: 11). So the interview genre has become a site of 'personal expressivity' (Habermas, 1979; 2.1), but one which is managed structurally and in taken-for-granted ways, through professional discourses, and laminated over with the institutional. The topics and coding schemes of personal discourses relate to glimpses into people's domestic, family and emotional lives and relationships, their feelings, self-perceptions and opinions drawn from interacting with others. These also give a light touch to usually idealised personal characteristics – as one candidate, Jim, says: 'Me, being me I worked.'

The rhetorical strategies of anecdote, reminiscences and intimate chat (chapter 6) are typical of these personal discourses and are realised linguistically with vivid, affective and colloquial talk with imagery, repetition and associated rhythm. The mode is often conversational with direct and reported speech, humour and aspects of grammatical modality associated with casual conversation (Eggins and Slade, 1997; Scheuer, 2001: 236). All these can be summarised as a 'high-involvement strategy' (Tannen, 1989: 17–35) and they are frequently embedded in the professional narrative mode.

In the next example – in which Lucy, a white British candidate, is applying for a junior management position in a supermarket – the interview opens with an encouragement to talk about herself through an open question about her past:

Example 10: Lucy – White British, Borderline Unsuccessful

```
 1.  I:   (.) ahm talk me through the period
 2.       of nineteen ninety two to two thousand and three (.)
 3.       what have been the highs and lows during this time
 4.  C:   erm nineteen ninety two (.) ten years ago (.)
 5.       would b:e just before I decided probably to come to London
 6.  I:   mhm=
 7.  C:   =because [my family are
 8.  I:   what made] you come to London
 9.  C:   er- well my- well we were all originally from Essex=
10.  I:   =right
11.  C:   Clacton-on-Sea (.) and my- we came on holiday in Yorkshire
12.       and my mum instead of buying a postcard or a stick of rock
13.       bought a house
14.  I:   hhh
15.  C:   and decided that we were all moving up there (.)
16.       so we ended up living up there (.)
17.       went to secondary school up there (.)
18.       found a lot of my friends and that from school were leaving school
19.       and not really doing that much constructive
20.       other than getting boring jobs in factories and (.)
21.       it just didn't seem like a very promising future for me
22.       at that time up there
23.  C:   mhm
24.  I:   so (.) I thought if I can pack my bags and go to London
25.       and I can survive there and be okay
26.       then I can do that anywhere in the world (.)
27.       it was my quest for independence more than anything
```

The interviewer's question produces a self-revelatory, amusing and somewhat romantic account of Lucy's last ten years – her 'quest for independence' – as she aligns to the personal discourse mode of the question. A domestic and humorous self is revealed through the reminiscence about buying a house instead of a stick of rock (line 12); through the colloquial, vague language 'and that' (line 18); and in the structuring of the chronology of her school life, and the affective charge of the claim to survive anywhere in the world. The personal story is made more intimate and involving through the rhythmic repetition at lines 15–17, with each line ending in 'there.' Lucy was judged by the interviewers as 'upbeat,' 'confident' and 'prepared to muck in,' and this impression may well have stemmed from the involved style and humour she shows here. However, the criticism that 'she lacked clarity of thinking' and was 'blinkered' and was ultimately unsuccessful may have partially stemmed from this early, detailed domestic account which was not crafted to align with a potential management persona in a more institutional discourse mode.

5.4   Institutional Discourse Mode

The decision to opt for a more institutional mode is most starkly illustrated in the next example, which is taken from another assessment context: the membership examination for the Royal College of General Practitioners:

Example 11: White British, Successful

Examiner: If someone took out a personal complaint against you
           how would you react?
Candidate: That's where my personal stress management plan comes in.
           (Roberts and Sarangi, 1999: 483)

Instead of replying in a professional mode, perhaps saying how she would take action – for example, discussing the matter with a senior partner – or in a personal mode, describing her emotional reaction to the complaint, the successful candidate opts for an institutional mode. Any stress or anxiety is reified as a 'personal stress management plan,' distancing it from the personal and aligning her answer to the institutional requirement to show herself at ease with abstract organisational categories.

Some of the features of institutional discourse were introduced in chapters 1 and 2, where the requirement of displaying an 'institutional self' was discussed as a response to the coercive force of institutions. The stock of common cultural knowledge which comes to define the institution and its means of defending itself soon appear as given, unalterable and easily interpretable to those in the know. In the job interview, institutional discourses combine these subtle processes of coercion with the bureaucratic ideologies of rationalisation and detachment discussed in chapter 2, as well as in the teleological discourses mentioned above.

The particular characteristics of institutional discourse are identifiable in the topics and coding schemes which refer to competences and other management categorisations, commonplace in recruitment and selection talk and text. The ability to use such categories, what Potter calls 'category entitlement' (Potter, 1996: 132), implies an authority that stems from aligning with the category of management – as the medical candidate above does very explicitly, and as Lucy fails to do. Not all candidates were aware of the abstract categories used to define the ideology of the good worker and the structuring of work relations in the new work order: taking ownership, managing change and self-managing. Not all candidates stylised their answers to align with these assumptions, but instead drew only on 'truthful' professional discourses. For example, candidates whose talk of previous work experience positioned workers in a potentially adversarial relationship to management (and so implicated themselves in this relationship) rather than as a self-managing team, did not get the job.

The rhetorical strategies which characterise institutional discourse and distance the speaker from the palpable experience of the now are summed up as 'impartiality, symmetry, balance, propriety, decency and discretion' (Bourdieu, 1991: 130) Like legalese, these have the subtle power of being both clear and ambiguous at the same time (Allan and Burridge, 1991; Trinch, 2003). Characterised by depersonalisation (Iedema and Wodak, 1999; Iedema, 1999; Scheuer, 2001: 237), common rhetorical moves include analytic lists; general, evaluative comments on the self which recontextualise experience in the light of organisational imperatives and institutional requirements; and argumentative modes of structuring speech or framing talk with metacommunicative comments such as, 'I think there are several options here,' or 'We can identify a number of causes,' or 'That's a difficult question to answer briefly.'

The linguistic forms typically associated with the institutional discourse mode are those of the more formal, literate register (Thornborrow, 2002), tending to more abstraction with commonly occurring linguistic features which realise the Bourdieuvian rhetorics of impartiality and discretion (Morales-López et al., 2005). These are features such as nominalisations, impersonal modality and organisational and euphemised vocabulary. For example, a senior economist heard on the BBC discussing the reasons why employment might be up while production was still low said, 'These are hypotheses that merit further attention.' His personal stance is discreetly hidden by topicalising 'hypotheses' and, rather than using the modalities of urgency and action – for example, 'We need to find out why' – he chooses the more modest and cautious vocabulary of 'merit further attention.' Such language, within the linguistic marketplace, comes to be seen as the legitimate language, although by no means always used by interviewers in low-paid jobs.

In job interviews for low-paid work and junior management positions, the institutional discourse mode is relatively less marked than this summary suggests. Nevertheless, as the next examples from Sara, Jim and Sandeep indicate, there are institutional elements in their professional/personal talk. Early on in the interview, Sara is asked to give an overview of how she sees the post she has applied for:

Example 12: Sara – BAME British, Unsuccessful

1. I: so what would you s- what would you see
2.   as the key challenges of the job
3. C: well (.) (xxx) is er:m currently going through
4.   more major change (1) with a lot of the work
5.   from the mail centre actually being moved to (xxx)
6. I: mhm
7. C: er:m so obviously that's going to have a hu:ge impact
8.   on (.) what (.) is actually handled by [the
9. I: yeah]
10. C: delivery office it's going to have huge a impact (.) you know
11.   are we going to need to reduce the number of staff (.)
12.   are we going to have to have staff working at different times (.)
13.   are we going to have to have split shifts maybe
14.   which has happened in other offices
15. I: mhm
16. C: er:m there's a whole host of things there
17.   that might need to happen (.)
18.   so (.) there's going be a lot of challenges
19.   because whatever you decide on (.)
20.   you've got to put it down in a form that you can discuss
21.   not only with your your bosses
22.   but also with e:r (.) your staff and with the union

Here, Sara frames her answer in terms of organisational change, drawing on the relatively abstract terminology of 'major change,' 'impact' and 'challenges,' aligning with the institutional mode of the question. She also frames her response in terms of various institutional groups and at lines 11–13, uses rhetorical questions as an analytic list incorporating what these changes might be. As well as the institutional vocabulary of her response, plus this choice of rhetoric in these lines, she uses modalities that chime with institutional discourses, such as the impersonal and hypothetical grammar at lines 16–17. While this is not the high institutional discourse of, say, senior judges or economists – after all, Sara is applying for a junior management post in a service industry – many features of the opening turns in her interview contrast with more professional and personal modes she deploys later. While Sara's institutional mode potentially aligns well to this early question, she remains in an institutional mode and then shifts rapidly to a much more personal – and what is seen as overly effusive – mode (example 19).

Similarly, Jim combines some reflective distancing with his narrative, when asked about how he copes with changing to new shifts to demonstrate his flexibility:

Example 13: Jim – White British, Successful

1. C: you just adjust yourself to the time clock (.)
2.   you know (.) your work's more important
3.   than your social life (.) you know
4.   you can see your friends any time of the week (.) you know
5.   so it don't really matter to them (.) you just adjust yourself to it

Here, Jim stands back from the narrative he is telling to evaluate the capacity for adjustment that people (like himself) have – 'You just adjust yourself to the time clock you know' – and produces a more analytic, deontic and depersonalised style in the phrase, 'Your work's more important than your social life.' He reduces the use of the singular personal pronoun, particularly as a grammatical subject, and makes claims about his own attitude more cautious and impersonal. So like Sara, and also Sandeep below, he uses 'authorisation discourses' (van Leeuwen and Wodak, 1999) – that is, compliance to what one has to do.

Sandeep also makes frequent statements of his own attitude to work, and the norms and discourses which govern it:

Example 14: Sandeep – BAME British, Successful

1. C: you got to help the customer to make the customer (1)
2.   and if you just tell him ohh I can't do it (.) it's a- (.)
3.   it would be like an attitude problem because business only grows
4.   if like- if you if you helping the business (.)
5.   the bus- that that's what you're employed for (.)
6.   if you're not going to help the employer
7.   it's no point wo- I don't think it's worth working for them

At junior management level there is more evidence of the Bourdieuvian qualities of balance, discretion and euphemisation. For example Peter, a Black British candidate who was highly evaluated, had to euphemise his and his team's lack of knowledge about the mark-up prices of some of the supermarket products he was responsible for selling. He did this by playing down the knowledge gap, saying 'I had a little conversation with the company head buyer.'

Tim, a white British candidate, when asked about his feelings about having to redefine his role, responds in a discreet and analytical way:

Example 15: Tim – White British, Borderline Successful

1. I: they- they're clearly looking for you
2.   to almost be a floor manager you know
3.   how did you feel about that
4. C: er:m (1) I felt probably previously
5.   they hadn't had the direction maybe that they should have had (.)
6.   a:nd er:m (.) it's very easy to (.)
7.   drop into the role of actually managing the floor
8.   and taking control er:m (1)
9.   it's more difficult probably to give up control
10.   er:m a- and trust people
11. I: mhm

Although Tim is asked how he feels, he rapidly translates his feelings into institutionally expectable actions: that the team had not had the 'direction' and that the option to take or give control has to be debated. Similarly, he displays a rhetorical balance between 'it's very easy to' and 'it's more difficult to,' thus euphemising the difficulty of giving up control.

5.5   Synthesising Hybrid Discourses

The selection process constitutes hybrid discourses: a mix of institutional, professional and personal. The latter two must be recontextualised within the institutional frame, but institutional talk must itself be open to recontextualisation and movement across the other two discourses. Indeed, such hybridity is the rhetorical signature of the interview system. In chapter 2 I suggested that the interview required both an institutional and entrepreneurial self, since private sector practices of marketisation and the new work order have penetrated public sector institutions at all levels. And similarly, the private sector has become more bureaucratised. So considerable discursive work must be done to fuse into a comfortable alliance: the euphemised, analytical and impersonal institutional mode; the brief, clear and convincing accounts of professional life; and the expressivity and engagement of the personal discourse mode.

The rules of this hybridity extend across both question design and candidate contribution. Questions are often framed in one discourse mode but expect an answer in another one – as in the Lucy example above – or one mode may dominate but entail another mode. In the health setting, where we first developed the notion of three hybrid discourses in gatekeeping settings, questions drawing on professional discourses were the least ambiguous and carried the lightest inferential load. Other topics which were more removed from daily professional competence – such as values and attitudes, feelings or coping with stress – were dealt with more institutionally, despite the topics being more personal. Similarly, in job interviews, opening competence-based questions like, 'Give me an example when you had to deal with a difficult customer,' could be dealt with largely, but not exclusively, in the professional mode. But follow-up questions, designed to push the candidate to reveal their personal opinion and their ability to reflect on themselves, were more hybrid and expected synthesisation of the institutional, professional and personal.

Successful candidates are those who synthesise the three discourses in their contributions, often gliding between them, responding to questions in ways which achieve a balance between the explicit and implied discourse expectations of the interviewers and which are sensitive to the location of the question in the interview structure. They produce synthetic selves in both senses of the word: synthetic as artificial and synthesis as combination or blending. These synthetic personalisations are the product of both everyday and heightened performances, on display on the front stage. They present a consistent, measurable and continuous narrative of the self, realised in a fusion of the three discourse modes. This apparently essential (and so seemingly authentic but in practice crafted) self has become a formative myth in the discourse of institutions (Wodak, 1996) and is part of the wider discourses of the self discussed in chapter 2. Hence the teleological discourses, in which the candidate is expected to present their life as a clear trajectory from their early years, polishing up their competences as they are rocked in the cradle.

Such synthesisation is itself a form of euphemisation, since each of the discourse modes in interaction with the other two can mellow their impact. The candidate can simultaneously appear institutional, professional and personal enough, while also being coherent and whole. This euphemisation works to enforce the institutionalisation of the interview in two ways: Firstly, it is endemic to institutional discourses, as defined by Bourdieu; institutions defend themselves through euphemisation. Secondly, it masks the power of the institution by playing to the professional and personal. Both interviewers and candidates subscribe to the view that the interview is about getting to know the candidate better, rather than knowing how to play the institutional game. The institutional cards stacked against candidates not in the know are hidden behind discourses of skills and personality. Interviewers and institutions can defend their practices on the basis, as one interviewer said, that they 'got to know what the candidates were really like and chose the best.' The discursive technologies of the interview take on new and powerful meanings (Iedema and Wodak, 1999: 5) as 'getting to know you' is revalued as an abstract and institutionalised competence.

Ahmed, a successful candidate who has come from Sierra Leone, draws on both institutional and more personal discourses in this phase of the interview – although not always in conventional interview talk. He has described how he has managed the conflicting demands of work and college, and he cites the appreciation of his bosses and team mates:

Example 16: Ahmed – Sierra Leonean Migrant, Successful

1. C: that encouragement (.) it gives you the spirit of working
2. I: exactly
3. C: yeah
4. I: so when they appreciate- appreciate you then you know
5.   all the hours that you have put in is- hasn't gone to waste
6.   that it's been appreciated as well [isn't it
7. C: yes] yes exactly

(ten seconds of talk deleted)

8. C: yes my school was Monday to [Friday and
9. I: Friday and th- th]
10. C: the job was Monday to Friday=
11. I: ={(God) (lo)}
12. C: and sometimes I have to work on Saturdays

Ahmed's blending of more institutional discourse (line 1) with a personal glimpse of what his days were like jointly constructs with the interviewer a shared ideology of motivation and an empathetic understanding of what it means to study and work all week (line 12).

Pippa's hybrid discourses are well matched to a question on flexibility, where she is asked about the changes she has had to make in the different jobs she has been in:

Example 17: Pippa – White British, Successful

1. C: erm well it is I think t- m- majority of the jobs that I have worked in
2.   I have been erm customer focussed and <u>deadlines</u> and under pressure
3.   hhh erm <u>catering</u> I've m- you know
4. I.1: mhm
5. C: my family own a business and I've worked in that
6.   since the age of nine (.) you know (.)
7.   helping them out (.) erm
8.   but that that's I suppose that's a different field altogether from=
9. I.1: =yeah
10. C: customer focus but (1)
11.   I've sort of gone off on a tangent now hhh (3)
12. I.1: n- no it's (1) I mean the range of experience just [shows you
13. C: mhm]
14. I.1: in many ways that you're used to=
15. C: =yeah I'm quite
16. I.1: having new things thrown at you so (.) no I- I don't see anything (.)
17.   (turns to I.2) anything you need to add to that (xxx)?
18. I.2: no I'm comfortable with that

From line 1 to line 7 of this passage, Pippa offers a self-evaluation that connects institutional and personal self-awareness with professional experience,
linking her values and motivations to those of the company. She opens in a
more generalised, institutional mode by using competence terms such as 'customer focussed' and giving an analytic overview of a bundle of transferable
skills she has acquired. She then links the skills of customer service to her
experience in the catering industry, and then her personal history, by disclos-
ing childhood experience; there is a brief glimpse of the little nine-year-old,
perhaps staggering under a pile of plates. Following this, she moves back
to an institutional frame – 'I suppose that's a different field' (lines 6–8) – to
'apologise' for this discursive transgression; an example of metacommunicat-
ing as a rhetorical device to display propriety and discretion (5.4). This final
coda reveals a reflexive consciousness of the way in which the interviewers
might perceive her, aligned to their institutional requirements.

   From early on in the interview, Pippa demonstrates a clear awareness of
the institutional frame in her use of certain vocabulary (e.g. 'but obviously
you've got to be open for these positions (.) flexible') and later on she talks of
'implementing my own strategies.' She also describes how she would implement the policy of the delivery company by using the supplied complaint
cards to deal with dissatisfied customers. Her use of these markers appears to
reassure the interviewers that a certain institutional frame will be upheld in

the interview, and so they do less work to establish its institutional orderliness when compared with many other candidates, such as Sara (example 19).

5.6   Lack of Synthesisation of Hybrid Discourses

The linguistic capital of the job interview is assessed both within and across candidate contributions in the blending of three discourses within an answer, as well as in the overall distribution and location of the three discourses throughout the interview (Roberts and Campbell, 2006). Successful candidates illustrated above have acquired this linguistic capital and have achieved, more or less, the synthetic self which fits with the idealised notion of the fixed and continuous individual. For example with Jim, Pippa and Tim, there is no clearly demarcated entering and sustaining of one mode of discourse.

Those who have not found this synthesis have often been in low-paid, back stage jobs (Holland et al., 1998: 190), do not use their work to form a job interview identity (Scheuer, 2001) and may see little that is positive in the work they do (Evans et al., 2005). So it is more difficult to recontextualise different aspects of one's work, education and private life into the interview setting in an upbeat way. The capacity to recontextualise styles and move between them with ease, as Scheuer points out, is not equally distributed among members of different social groups and this is particularly problematic for migrant groups. They are less likely to move smoothly and fluently, gliding between topics and stances. Rather, they appear to lurch between different discourses, producing what is seen as a jarring juxtaposition (Auer and Kern, 2001) of institutional, professional and personal (9.6).

Many unsuccessful candidates, as well as failing to align to the mix of discourses within a turn or sequence, also failed to align to the different phases of the interview. They were either too institutional or too personal in their opening contributions, as Lucy seemed to be (example 10). Similarly, Nazrul's opening response to the question, 'Can you tell me what you enjoy about your current job?' consisted only of the institutional discourse of how he 'engaged with external and internal clients' and he was dismissed by interviewers as someone who 'had just been told what to say.' Endings were also problematic, with some candidates seizing on the, 'Have you any questions for us?' stage as an opportunity to be overly personal in their enthusiasm for the job, as in the case of Tahir (10.1).

Other unsuccessful candidates tended to present themselves, in all their answers, as predominately personal and involved or, by contrast, institutional and distant (10.1). For example Alison, a local white British candidate applying for a post in a hospital, is asked about data protection and the confidentiality of patient records. Instead of blending experience with her procedural knowledge of data protection and her stance on confidentiality, Alison answers this – and all questions – in the personal mode: 'I've never really disclosed too much, don't like shouting out names and things you know, so and so got this …' While a few candidates come across as consistent but inappropriate, like Alison, the great majority of failed candidates are viewed as inconsistent, untrustworthy and not fitting in to the organisation. Two case studies (discussed in more detail in Campbell and Roberts, 2007: 260–262, 256–259) analyse the problem of lack of synthesisation and misalignment to the expected discursive response.

Yohannes

Yohannes was from Ethiopia and was unsuccessful in his job interview. His persuasion rhetorics were not judged as acceptable. He shifted rapidly between different discourses, did not align to the expected discourse implied in the question and highlighted his ethnicity in his self-presentation, under-mining a homogenised institutional self. Repeatedly, he responded in terms of personal relationships and his own personal goals, rather than orienting to corporate values. So when asked about team working, for example, he describes it in terms of friendliness rather than efficiency, saying that 'you have to take life easy and cooperate with each other,' and 'we are all together, we had togetherness.' So he presents himself as a mate in a team, rather than taking leadership as part of a self-managing team. Similarly, when pushed further to talk about the advantages of working as a team, he both fails to align to the institutional motif of the question and interprets the 'advantages' in terms of his own future goals:

Example 18: Yohannes – Ethiopian Migrant, Unsuccessful

1. I: okay what would you then say the advantages are (.)
2.   by working as a team
3. C: er:m the advantage wherev- wherever you go are the e-
4.   if you apply other jobs you won't find it difficult (.)
5.   you already integrate

(nine seconds of talk deleted)

6. C: then wh- wherever you go in say (.) in (xxxxxx) job
7.   (.) or in a community job (.) and you won't get hard you

8.   won't be a- feel ashamed or if y- you ((won't feel))
9.   a shy person (.) you get more powerful a:nd (1)
10. I: yeah (.) what more would you say
11. C: e:r (1) you would be open minded you don't have [to
12. I: okay yeah]
13. C: be worried (4)

The question presupposes some kind of analytical list that relates certain qualities of a good teamworker to the effective accomplishment of tasks. But as elsewhere, Yohannes responds in a personal mode about the benefits which team working has brought to him, how it would help in future job interviews and in terms of confidence (lines 4–9).

Occasionally, Yohannes opted for institutional discourses when a more personal/professional voice was expected. So when asked, 'How do you motivate yourself?' Yohannes moves suddenly to asserting his method and his timetable but does not display his inner strategies, as the successful candidate Ibrahim does: 'I tell myself go on, go on, you can do it.' Yohannes's rhetorics are an instance of a common strategy to shift suddenly from factual lists of structures and tasks, in which he has not seemingly invested, into animated and expressive language of personal relationships. In the feedback session, the interviewer described him as 'unreliable, contradicting himself, hard to follow, mumbling, waffling, unwilling to take on responsibility.' Yohannes's unfamiliarity with the requirements of the institutional self and his unsynthesised discourses are translated into incompetence and personal deficiencies. His talk is inadequate to the task and so, therefore, is he.

Sara

The second case study revisits Sara's interview for a junior manager position (example 12). Like Yohannes, Sara is perceived as producing a 'jarring' lack of synthesis of hybrid discourses and of problematically coopting her ethnicity into her presentation of self. Her first extended response, given above, is one of many answers almost entirely in institutional discourse. In the video feedback, the interviewer criticised her in this opening phase for 'lecturing him' and 'saying what she had been told to say' (and so being too institutional), which then translates into personality judgments of arrogance and insincerity. As with many less successful candidates, institutional discourse does not readily infiltrate other more personal or professional modes and is more likely to be transmitted or merely 'animated,' coming across as trained or inauthentic (8.5).

In the latter part of the interview, Sara uses largely personal discourses when speaking about emotional reactions to colleagues and giving narrativised details of colleagues and friends. She speaks of her emotional reactions to colleagues – 'he really upset me' – and discloses aspects of the personal lives of family and colleagues. At one point she talks about the importance of knowing the correct procedures so 'that you're not being taken for a fool, taken for a ride because there will always be the worker there that says oh I know what I'm doing I don't need you to tell me you know.' In the feedback, the interviewer commented on this as 'excessive and garrulous,' 'an overly emotional reaction,' indicating a lack of professionalism and discretion. He also suggested she was 'adversarial,' possibly shifting Sara's ventriloquising of a recalcitrant worker onto Sara herself.

In another example of unsynthesised discourse, with a rapid shift from the opening more institutional lines to a markedly personal register, Sara describes an incident where she put a colleague in touch with a friend in social services to help him with childcare problems. This narrative is in response to a question about how she manages problems within her team:

Example 19: Sara – BAME British, Unsuccessful

```
 1.  C:  you can (.) I wouldn't have discussed with anybody
 2.      had he not given his permission (.)
 3.      so I contacted my friend in social services
 4.      I mean she (.) (h)
 5.      hhh contacted (.) {[ac] [lo] I gave her a ring that night (.)
 6.      and said look this situation's going on
 7.      he knows I'm talking to you about it
 8.      what can he do} (.)
 9.      she s- she said well I can't tell you give me his number or
10.      {[ac] here's my number tell him to ring me} (.)
11.      so fine and I had a discussion with my brother about it
12.      and er my brother said well
13.      give him my number and I'll talk to him
14.      so although they both put me out of the loop so [to speak
15. I:   yeah]
16. C:   I expected [that
17. I:   you] you'd sort of facilitated it (begins writing)
```

In lines 4–10, Sara uses a series of contextualisation cues – outbreath, laughter, speeding up her pace and lowering her pitch – as well as more colloquial terms like 'gave her a ring' and direct speech quotations, shifting to a highly personalised mode. This could be read as an attempt to undercut the institutionalised environment of the interview, by being ironic and attempting an affiliative alignment with the interviewer (7.3). Such discursive play seems to work with candidates who have already established an acceptable synthetic persona, and so can play with the rules of the cultural game. However, Sara's interviewer does not accept this ironic play but interprets her, in the feedback session, as contradictory and shifting from what she feels she is 'supposed to say' in the early stages of the interview (in institutional discourse) to a revelation of her 'true' feelings, her unprofessional self, in a high-involvement, gossipy style which he said 'made him uncomfortable.'[25]

Sara was seen as divulging too much personal information – the interviewer commented, 'I was wondering how many friends *has* she got?' – and so not being adequately discreet, adequately institutional. His translation of her story into institutional terms at line 17, 'you'd sort of facilitated it,' was typical of his reactions to her personal accounts. It calls into question her ability to abstract herself from the action and make an evaluative comment, and so her right to participate in the production of institutional discourse. It appears to set up a distinction between what she says and what she is 'actually doing' or 'really saying,' as he remarks in the feedback.

Later in the interview, a similar episode occurs when Sara responds to an institutional-mode question in a personal and effusive way. Here the transcription is more detailed, to show how aspects of bodily conduct feed into the negative evaluation of Sara:

Example 20: Sara – BAME British, Unsuccessful

1. I: {(looking down) how- how do you ensure (.)
2.   you know wh- when you're a manager
3.   that you (.) you learn from} {(I looks up) experience
4.   and you pick up particular lessons from past mistakes} (1)
5.   {(I looks down, begins writing)

(twenty-five seconds of talk deleted)

6.   C: I mean I'm Maltese {(C moves arms) I tend to talk with my hands}
7.   and one thing that's really brought up quite often
8.   when I'm talking in a meeting you know
9.   I'm sitting there
10.   with my {(C gesticulates with hands, I looks up and nods) hands
11.   flailing away like this} {(I looks down)
12.   which puts everybody off
13.   because they're looking at you know {(I looks up, C moves arms)
14.   what on earth is she doing} {(I looks down) doing this [business
15. I: right]

The interviewer responds to the lack of blending of discourses by shifting into an increasingly institutional mode, frequently looking down as she tries to engage him, thus emphasising his membership of the organisation and the 'outsider' status of the candidate. Sara chooses an individual and ethnicised foible, talking with her hands (line 6), rather than describing homogenised synthetic personal characteristics such as 'time management issues.' Sara, instead of displaying a reflexive awareness of self in euphemised, institutional ways, acts out her bodily conduct in a satire of Maltese behaviour and ventriloquises her colleagues in the reaction in line 14, 'What on earth is she doing.' So her overly personal style, combined with the ethnic focus, undermines the theme of the reflexive self and instead positions her as both interactionally and ethnically an outsider. In the feedback, the interviewer commented on lines 6–14 as 'highly personal, effusive and indiscreet'; Sara was not considered 'professional.' The interviewer invoked a binary opposition between her body language and style, on the one hand, and substantive points on the other.[26]

In implicitly linking her body language, speech delivery, 'garrulous' long responses and personal discourses to her ethnic identity, she comes across to him as unprofessional and her responses as insufficiently substantive. The new forms of discrimination, in which certain ethnicities are seen to be assigned a non-professional identity, have also been noted by Gaudio and Bialostok (2005). Both the initial lack of discretion and topicalising of her ethnicity lead to uncomfortable moments of heightened institutionalisation, providing evidence of her 'untrustworthiness' and the basis for her failure in the interview.

Conclusion

Different discourses are called up in the voices of the candidates in the job interview. Such 'polyphony' and 'double-voicing' – 'whereby a variety of different or competing voices enter into the struggle for influence within an individual's consciousness' (Bakhtin, 1981: 348) – is, as Bakhtin notes, a general feature of the human condition. However, in the interview such variety needs to be masked by synthesisation. This carefully crafted synthetic persona must not appear to be 'double-voicing' and borrowing the words of others lest they appear to reveal a hybrid identity inconsistent, untrustworthy and not belonging.

Candidates have to perform an institutionally recognisable synthesised self, combining the different selves discussed in chapter 2 – team worker, self-managing individual and compliant, customer-focussed assistant

– rendering invisible the inconsistencies of the new work order (Campbell and Roberts, 2007: 244). This is combined with vivid and sincere professional accounts, plus personal glimpses of what a likeable person they 'really' are. There has to be a constant dance of display and discretion which conceals divisions between work and personal life.

Whereas Bourdieu's formulation of linguistic capital, within a unified linguistic marketplace, is that of a formal register in a lexicogrammatical standard variety and associated with the dominant class, the discursive regime of the job interview blends aspects of this 'legitimate language' with more personal and narrative modes – as the next chapter discusses further.

6 Narrating the Self through Professional Discourse

'Professional discourse' was briefly introduced in the last chapter as a way of giving accounts about working life and social relations with team mates, management and customers which both display experience and are reflexive. These accounts are presented as narratives, the genre of talk most closely associated with the self and specifically with the self as a project; we are the stories we tell. Narratives are also institutional gifts for interviewers, since a well-told story is easy to attend to and memorable. This chapter first examines the relationship between narrative and institutional order. It then looks at four different aspects of the job interview narrative: structure, engagement through detail, stance and reporting talk. While the focus is on candidate contributions, as in chapter 5, these are shaped and constrained by interviewer conduct, as chapters 7 and 8 detail.

6.1 Narratives in Bureaucratic Settings

Revealing the Self through Narrative

As noted previously, the preferred candidate persona is an idealisation of the individual as utterly coherent, consistent, trustworthy and credible. The HR world widely accepts that the competence-based interview, which seeks the telling of explicit behaviours and reflection on them, can sort out the ideal candidates from the rest. So although 'narrative' is not part of the selection lexicon (too fictional and fabulous) a well-ordered, detailed and readily understandable story – one that has a strong 'authorial centre' (Holland et al., 1998: 182) – is taken to establish the likely trustworthiness and competence of the candidate in the job. The structure and texture of an acceptable narrative stands in iconic relationship to this ideal.

Narratives are now well-established resources for understanding the self as we 'construct, interpret and share experience' (Schiffrin, 1996: 167); the concept of narrative is now widely used in fields as different as political analysis, the environmental crisis and medicine. This 'narrative turn' in the social sciences (Riessman, 1993) – drawing on sociolinguistics, social and discursive psychology and sociology – tells of the self in relation to others. The main arguments from this literature are that the self is given meaning through narrative (Mishler, 2006; Ochs and Capps, 1996: 21), is performed through narrative (Bamberg, 2004; Bamberg and Georgakopoulou, 2008) and, most significantly for the context of workplace selection, the narrator will be revealed in the narrating (Johnstone, 1990; Schiffrin, 2000). Self-revelation and self-commentary are the stuff of job interviews and since narratives do this work so well, it is scarcely surprising that they should play such a central role in imagining the 'real person' inside the candidate. The story-eliciting function of so many questions also feeds into the move to 'conversationalise' institutional discourse, masking underlying relations of power.

Institutional Narratives

Stories performed in institutional settings have particular characteristics in terms of their purpose, the conditions under which they are told, the value they are given and their effects on the life chances of the narrators. They are (explicitly) elicited, shaped and judged in relation to the institution's functions (Blommaert, 2001; O'Barr and Conley, 1996; Jacquemet, 2011). For this reason, assuming that narratives are always defined as personal modes of discourse understates the professional and institutional work they have to do in the selection process. I argue here that in the job interview, stories are narrated predominantly in the professional mode, shot through with personal discourses and laminated over by institutional requirements.

Many of the features of institutional stories conform to taken-for-granted principles of early narrative research: sequencing (Labov and Waletsky, 1967), coherence and detail (Tannen, 2007; Edwards, 1991). They constitute story in Western traditions, most notably in the work of Labov (1972) and what has come to be called the big story research, or canonical or fully fledged story (Bamberg and Georgakopoulou, 2008) (example 9).

In proposing what they call an antidote to the big story tradition in their formulation of 'small stories,' Bamberg and Georgakopoulu identify precisely those features of big stories which institutions rely on in their assessments of individuals. The acceptable institutional self is largely a big story self. Three of the critiques of formulating narrative in only big story terms are particularly relevant here: Firstly, big stories have a canonical structure which produce coherence both in them and their speakers, plus a certain structure and element of distancing and detachment (Ochs and Capps, 2001; Helsig, 2010; 6.2). Secondly, and related to the first point, big stories 'focus on consistencies across time, places, and actions' (Bamberg, 2004: 355) so that the narrating self is displayed as either trustworthy if these matters are consistent and the opposite if they are not (6.3). And thirdly, there is the assumption that the 'real' self is unproblematically revealed in the story – a transparent representation, rather than being an interactionally performed self (Georgakopoulou, 2006; 6.5; chapters 7 and 8). For example, the emphasis on the referential, with each new clause matched to an event, links the sequencing and fluency of the narrative to the sense that these things actually happened (Linde, 1999).

The institutional order relies on these big stories since they provide recordable evidence and 'stress textual consistency, linearity, logic, rationality and factuality' (Blommaert, 2001: 436) in apparently transparent ways. The candidate is a 'glass citizen' or glass cabinet, the interview orthodoxy maintains, whose 'true' or 'real' self is there to be seen through the glass. Candidates who never give narratives – unstoried candidates, such as Alex – fail the interview:

Example 21: Alex – White British, Unsuccessful

1. I: what sort of experience have you had
2.   of working with groups of people
3. C: erm (.) quite a lot really mainly with em working at (xxx)
4.   really (.) (really) (.) there's been a lot of people
5.   sort of erm (1) well erm
6.   working with other people a lot really (1)

Not only is there no evidence of experience in the example above, but there is no persuasive or engaging talk to relate to. The interviewers' dissatisfaction with his responses is evident in their many reformulations, which still do not produce the expected narratives (6.4).

Job Interview Narratives in Comparison with Other Institutional Narratives

Narratives in selection interviews function in broadly similar ways to other institutional narratives, such as court or social welfare cases, where narratives are allowed or actively elicited. But there are differences in terms of criteria for final assessment and some evidentiary standards. Such differences are often a matter of degree and of the overall emotional tone of the encounter, in the significance of credibility for example (6.3).[27]

In judicial or quasi-judicial interviews, the determination of an individual's credibility is absolutely central (Jacquemet, 2011: 482; Blommaert, 2001; Maryns, 2006). In these cases, the story is judged as credible in as far as it is consistent and accurate in relation to the details of an assumed external reality. By contrast, a lively, engaging story can often matter more in job interviews than a strictly relevant answer. Narratives are a way of producing a 'thumbnail sketch' of a candidate and credibility is harnessed to other facets of character such as engagement, competence and professionalism to produce an acceptable self.[28]

Most institutional narratives are designed to recount one particular past experience at a time. Indeed, there are often constraints on narrators who urgently want to display multiple examples, as in Trinch's study of stories of domestic abuse (Trinch, 2003). To some extent, this is also true of job interviews. The single example request encourages stories of extreme experiences which are viewed as exemplary 'evidence,' such as 'the most difficult customer you ever dealt with' or 'the most difficult day on which you had to pull together as a team.' Implied here is the expected stance of the hero(ine) as a moral self, coping with adversity, but without actively claiming heroism.[29]

As hypothetical questions in the job interview go out of fashion, these experiences elicited from 'give me an example questions' are viewed as evidence of things which really happened to *you* and often, crucially, include reports of what was said on all sides at these heightened moments (6.5). The selection of an extreme case gives candidates more choice than in most institutional narratives, but this is only empowering if the value placed on the telling of extreme experiences is known to candidates and they can manage the tension between the vivid telling of the extreme case and the requirements of a relatively euphemised response (6.4).

In job interviews, other tellings of the self are also allowed. Narratives of vicarious experience (Norrick, 2013), where the talk and action of others is used to comment on and give a good impression of the candidate/narrator, can add depth to a story (6.5). Another type of narrative is also elicited in the job interview. This is the 'iterative' narrative (Baynham, 2011), where candidates describe what habitually occurs in a work setting and tends to be used to demonstrate resilience, coping with boredom and other competences which require evidence of consistency (as Duncan does successfully in example 9 and Luis less so in example 23). It can also be used in junior management roles to illustrate a methodical and systematic approach. In the most tightly structured competence-based interviews, these iterative narratives were expected to include the name of the company, the size of the team and the type of job – not only to contextualise the action, but also to check discrepancies against the application form (example 23). In contrast to extreme narratives, these iterative narratives were judged more on their rhetorical structure and less on their vividness.

Interviews are designed around the fully-fledged story, but the small stories of everyday conversation also occur and indeed complement the big ones. The small story approach 'allows for, indeed sees the need for a scrutiny of fleeting, contingent, fragmented and multiple selves' (Georgakopoulou, 2006: 128). While there is no recognition in the interview orthodoxy of 'multiple selves' – indeed the consistent, singleton self is what interviewers seek and are comfortable with – the fleeting glimpse of an aspect of the self may feed into the interviewers' summative sketch of the candidate. For example, Pippa's mention that she worked in her parents' pub from the age of nine is one such small story (example 17). These small stories are a key element in what we have called personal discourses (5.3) and are part of the hybrid discourses that need to be successfully managed. Here we focus on the canonical narratives as professional discourse and develop four different aspects of them: their structure, their means of engaging listeners through vivid detail, their function in conveying candidate stance and how reporting talk is managed. Chapter 8 deals with what happens to these stories as they are socially evaluated and turned into a written record.

6.2   Narrative Structure

The requirements of consistency and coherence are most clearly realised in the structure of the canonical narrative. It corresponds to the deductive argumentative structure, favoured in utilitarian professional discourse systems (Scollon and Scollon, 1995), which flags up the main points to be made at the outset of the turn at talk These are followed up with evidence and a conclusion, which links the claims and evidence. In competence interviews, this is called the STAR structure.

The STAR Structure

The STAR structure consists of four elements: situation, task, action and result (4.5; Byham and Pickett, 1999).[30] Any sociolinguist will recognise a close correspondence between the STAR structure and the classic Labovian account of narrative (Labov and Waletsky, 1967; Labov, 1972: 363). The definitive six-part structure – widely employed and critiqued by narrative theorists since – consists of an abstract and orientation followed by complicating action, evaluation, result or resolution, and finally a coda. It is routine for guidelines given to interviewers to set out a similar but reduced structure, and it is now commonplace for applicants for jobs across the spectrum to be told about or expected to use the STAR structure. The type of answer interviewers are looking for should first lay out the *situation* described (or the 'abstract') then the *task* which the candidate has to do (orientation), followed by their *action* (complication), and then the *result* of the events (resolution, evaluation and coda). In these guidelines, as one interviewer said, 'good evidence' is acquired by 'broadly identifying a situation' and then 'drilling down to the finer detail.' This funnelling technique stands in an iconic relationship to this deductive linear rhetorical style (4.5).

It seems very unlikely that those designing the interview were familiar with Labov's research. But they were unwittingly reproducing a crude, prescriptive and unreflective version of the big story. In one organisation's interview training literature, this narrative structure is framed as universal and obligatory – essentially allied with clear thinking, correct exposition and 'better evidence' – rather than merely being the form which canonical narratives most often take in Western cultures. And in one of our major research sites, this structure was also used in the design of the interviewers' record sheet (8.7).[31]

In many instances, candidates produce the STAR in a single turn – a linear structure, fluently performed, producing a smooth and uninterrupted story. But it was also common for interviewers to convey requirements of the structure as part of the initial question, or to intervene to pull the candidate back to the structure – with mixed results. British-born candidates draw upon this prototypical structure routinely, when asked for examples of experience to demonstrate a particular competence. In the case of Duncan, first introduced in 5.2, the competence relates to self-management and managing boredom in repetitive jobs over time. Here, unsurprisingly, Duncan responds with an iterative narrative:

Example 22: Duncan – White British, Successful
(Repeat of example 9.)

1. I: yeah so (.) what I'm looking for here is an example
2.   where you have done a similar kind of like routine (.) repetitive work
3.   o- over a period of time
4. C: well one specific agency contract I got
5.   it was only four months but it was (.)
6.   the complete mind numbingly same repetitive stuff
7. I: okay

8.   C: I was working for (xxx) in (xxx)
9.   and we were building headsets for helicopter pilots
10.   and my specific task was to get this tiny little ear piece
11.   and get a little drill and glue that
12.   and that was all I had to do (.) all day everyday (.)
13.   I didn't have problem with that
14.   because I was sat round a table with half a dozen other blokes
15.   and you know you don't really need
16.   to turn your brain on to do something like that
17.   you can just chat and get the job done
18.   and it's- you got to keep yourself amused for boring jobs
19.   it's as simple as that
20.   and I absolutely love working outdoors (.)
21.   I've got no problem at all with (.)
22.   doing the same round day in day out (.)
23.   I could quite easily do that

Duncan immediately establishes the purpose and relevance of his narrative, the 'abstract'(lines 4–6), and gains the interviewer's agreement with this (line 7). He then very quickly lays out the context, or 'orientation' (lines 8 and 9), completing the situation aspect of the STAR structure, before moving on to 'my specific task' (lines 10–12) and so directly moving into the task and action sections, 'the complication'. As Duncan's story is an iterative narrative about repetitive work, rather than an extreme case one, the task and action are merged. But he then goes on to give quite an extended 'result' or self-evaluation (lines 13–19), describing his strategies for dealing with boredom. Here he moves on to the general, extractable moral of the story – or Labovian resolution and evaluation – of 'keeping oneself amused.' It is this movement from the particular to the general which characterises deductive reasoning, and where Labovian structure and utilitarian discourse systems meet to produce a performance which can be fitted into the STAR boxes on the interviewer's form. Duncan concludes with an anchoring statement, or coda, which brings him back to the current job and interaction with the interviewer (lines 20–23) where he contrasts sitting all day with working outdoors and reaffirms his ability to manage boredom and repetition.

This neat fit with the STAR structure is a strong indicator that this candidate did well. Further evidence stems from the way his responses to this competence about managing the self in repetitive work are interactionally produced and valued. Duncan is only asked two very brief follow-up questions on the length of the shift and how he motivated himself. The interviewer in the video follow-up remarked that if the answer is good, he does little more than the basic follow-up questions which were required of the 'funnelling' design and which, in this case, seem merely formulaic.

When the STAR Structure Falls Apart

The critique of the universalisation of Labovian narrative structure (Holmes, 2005a; Baynham and De Fina, 2005; Bamberg and Georgakopoulou, 2008) highlights the gap between Western institutional narrative conventions and those used by many who come under the institutional gaze. Defendants, claimants and candidates find their non-standard narratives interrupted and dismissed as they do not conform to internalised Labovian standards (Trinch, 2003; Maryns, 2005). This narrative inequality (Briggs, 1997; Blommaert, 2001) reaches into the job interview as well, as some of the examples below show. Here, as in other research, the challenge to the unconventional and seemingly incoherent occurs during the interview and is confirmed later in what organisations often call the wash-up sessions.

For example, Luis's narrative is persistently interrupted because it does not follow the conventional structure, and so appears disorderly. Yet many of the components of the Labovian paradigm are present in his attempts to tell the story his way (9.7):

Example 23: Luis – Filipino Migrant, Unsuccessful

1. I: my first question is erm working with people
2. C: yeah
3. I: (.) could you give me an experie:nce (.) you've had (.)
4.   in the past (.) or present (.)
5.   where you have worked with a group of different people
6.   to achie:ve something (.)
7. C: [mhm
8. I: I] need to know (.)
9. C: (coughs)
10. I: the name of the company (.)
11. C: mhm
12. I: how many people were involved (.)
13.   and your main responsibility

(fifteen seconds of talk deleted)

14. C: okay (.) g- ah- here my p- ah I have a part time work

15.   as a bar staff as a bar tender (.) [sniffs] in (xxx)
16. I: mhm
17. C: i- it's a in a restaurant ba- yeah then (.) (coughs)
18.   in ah I'm [working
19. I: what is the] name of the bar
20. C: the bar- name of the bar
21. I: mhm
22. C: is it's ah the (xxx) Chargrill in- on (xxx) (.)
23. I: (xxx)=
24. C: =(xxx) [yes ma'am
25. I: spell that for me)] please
26.   (2) (looks through application for reference)
27. C: [that's it

(ten seconds of talk deleted)

28. I: okay (.) now tell me about (xxx)
29. C: oh [yeah
30. I: how] many people were there?
31. C: ah we a- I think we are (.) we only eh nine [staff
32. I: mhm]
33. C: and two managers (.)
34. I: okay [and wh-
35. C: and] working in a restaurant is er- really busy [really
36. I: what w-] what was your main role your responsibility
37.   what did you [do there
38. C: er- I am a] bar staff as I-
39. I: bar staff
40. C: yeah serv[ing-
41. I: you] sell drinks
42. C: drinks, cocktails, beverages
43. I: mhm
44. C: er at first they said I'm going-
45.   just going to serve th- some spirits and some wine
46.   but when eh I- I start the work
47. I: mhm
48. C: they just added some addition job to me er- er
49.   they giving me th- er serving the cocktail
50.   serving the beverages mhm [serving some-
51. I: serving] what
52. C: some- some soda (.) beverages some Coke some (.)

53.   Coca Cola [and fruit
54. I: Coke] see
55. C: and some coffee as in cappuccino an-
56. I: cappuccino coffee [mhm
57. C: yeah] an er an it was er you're gonna say
58.   it's gonna be a physically demanding
59.   because you have to be alert (.)
60.   you have to be always on motivated
61.   because [you're in
62. I: but could you] tell me er
63.   what do you like most about working with a team

The interviewer repeatedly cuts into Luis's speech, in an attempt to get him to conform to the narrative structure she has been trained to look for (lines 8, 19, 34, 41, 51, 62). She uses interruption, closed questions concerning trivial details and statements summarising his speech or reformulations as strategies of control and containment. Throughout the interview, she 'translates' Luis's answers with summary statements before writing them down – thus enacting the process of translating the speech of a non-member of the organisation into bureaucratically processable language. Many of these interventions are specifically related to stages in the narrative structure which she has been trained to elicit – which have become, through routinisation, linked to specific content and therefore more rigidly demarcated. So lines 19 and 30 look for contextual information which establishes the situation – in particular the name of the employer and the number of people in the team. The prompts at lines 37–8, 41 and 51 seek to elicit task- or action-related information which demonstrates his particular role and achievements. By lines 62–3, the interviewer is already seeking a result or conclusion in terms of the favoured points of this work, before a narrative about teamwork has even been elicited.

This question cuts into an attempted introduction of a new topic by Luis (lines 58–61) concerning his understanding of the physical and motivational demands of the job, which the interviewer does not sanction. Luis's contribution here is in fact a recycling of a topic which the interviewer introduced just before the extract shown above, in a segment in which she described the physical demands of the job and asked Luis if he understood these, before cutting into his response. Luis's return to this topic was, however, described by the interviewer as 'irrelevant' in post-interview feedback, as it came in the context of the new topic of team working. It might also be argued that Luis's attempts to open a narrative in line 35 – 'working in a restaurant is really busy' – does indeed offer a type of orientation, but that this is not recognised by the interviewer because it is not located in the right place, and Luis is therefore again cut off.

In sum, there is an ongoing rhetorical duel between the interviewer seeking explicit details and extreme case examples – forcing Luis into more analytic, evaluative comments – and the candidate's eagerness to provide more general, upbeat and inclusive descriptions of his working world. It must also be remembered that the job he has applied for is a delivery job where he would need to work in a busy environment, as he tries to tell the interviewer, and that the details of what drinks he served – which she elicits – are irrelevant for this post.

Reflection and Evaluation

The STAR structure ends with reflection, allowing the story to be told and then assessed. In his later studies, Labov recognises that evaluation is threaded through the whole narrative, as well as being oriented to in the later stages (Labov, 1972). In the job interview, as the STAR structure shows, it is the concluding evaluative and coda phase of his earlier work which is particularly significant. This orientates the narrator back to the interviewers and to the institutional requirements of the interview. But while there is this conventional evaluative ending to a story, there are also crucial evaluative elements woven into the whole.

The STAR structure provides the scaffolding for a blend of action and evaluation, but it is also in the detail of the performance that an acceptable self emerges or not. The action sequences of the story give the space for candidates to show agency, animate their experiences (telling what they have done), convey authenticity and credibility and involve the listener – what we can call conversational engagement. The more reflective and evaluative elements allow candidates to display how they want to be seen through self-description, opinions and the footing they establish with the interviewers; in other words, the stance they take up (6.4).

6.3   Conversational Engagement through Vivid and Detailed Accounts

The task and action phases of the story display the candidate's engagement in a particular experience, and the way this is done can also engage the interviewer. The evidence displayed provides some truth and credibility contributing to judgments of trustworthiness, although candidate responses do not have to meet strict evidentiary standards (6.1). The test is whether stories are coherent and engaging, rather than absolutely true. A persuasive story may distract the interviewer from strict relevance requirements. It can carry the listener across irrelevancies, factual inconsistencies or omissions as in the case of Sandeep, a successful British candidate of South Asian origin. Here, the interviewer is asking about the 'managing change' competence:

Example 24: Sandeep – BAME British, Successful

1.   I.1: what sort of experience of change have you had (.)
2.   either because of moving to very different jobs
3.   or changes in the job that you were doing
4.   C: (1) never had any problems (.)
5.   like yo- when you go to the job (.) you ask them
6.   wh- wh- like w- what they want done (h)
7.   and that's- and that's how you build the routine (h)
8.   not flexible hours
9.   I got nothing (.) major responsibility at home (.)
10.   the kids are grown up (.) missus working
11. I.1: (7) (interviewer writing) yeah it must have been-
12.   from being a shop owner, to [driving people around
13. C: I used to open] say from six o'clock in the morning
14.   'til half past ten at night
15.   that's one thing I would rather do a job
16.   than sit- from six in the morning
17.   from all the way to half ten
18. I.2: mhm
19. C: just by yourself

Sandeep's story of work and domestic life is not strictly relevant; it is more about working preferences (driving around rather than sitting in the shop all day) than exemplifying the 'managing change' competence. But the personal glimpses of his domestic world, his lexical choices of 'kids' and 'missus' evoke a successful portrait of a can-do candidate in an ordered and familiar world. This example contrasts with that of Luis, above, where the content of the story is more vulnerable to interrogation and both the narrative flow and potential for engagement break down.

Vividness and Detail to Align to a Shared World

The best-received stories are those that make detailed evidence vivid and involving – a mix of 'truth' and 'theatre,' as in Janet Hill's prescient discussion of American presidential elections (Hill, 2000: 263–266) – where the grounded details of an experience are enlivened by a heightened performance. These 'experientially grounded' accounts (Edwards, 1991) make use of the depiction of bodily and sensory experience, vivid and detailed description, first-person, present-tense narration and direct speech quotations. These reports engage the interviewers' attention and shared imaginative world (7.4), providing real-world evidence for the more analytic talk. They are crucial in creating and sustaining a sense of authenticity.

For example, Tom – a successful, white British candidate – describes his life as an airport construction worker by using vivid descriptions of his embodied experience. He describes how at times 'you're soaking wet … you're up to there in a trench full of water,' coordinating this physical description with bodily movement by indicating his chest as he says 'up to there.' The interviewer expresses empathy with this embodied experience in her response which echoes his speech – 'if it was pouring rain down the back of my neck it would need to be quite exceptional' – invoking Tom's involvement strategies and an easily recognisable trope of the enduring working man (6.4).

Later, Tom is asked about how methodical he is and he describes how he has to work from a method statement. His example is from digging up a key arterial road, the A1:

Example 25: Tom – White British, Successful

1. C: yeah it works (.) obviously you will come across something
2.   that's not on the statement that you –
3.   I mean when we were on the A1
4.   we dug bones up on the A1
5. I: mhm
6. C: so obviously everything's got to stop there (.)
7.   is it old bones (.) is it recent bones (.)
8.   is it a murder victim (.) is it somebody from an ancient battle (.)
9.   things like that you come across
10. I: yeah
11. C: obviously th- unforeseen
12. I: yes
13. C: you know (.) but you've got to work it all
14.   into the method statement
15.   (.) and try and progress it you know

It is the inclusion of apparently insignificant detail – such as Tom's depiction of wetness and the bones under the A1 road, or Gladston's mention that it was a Mercedes car that had its aerial broken – which can make the story. Psychological studies of witness statements have shown how persuasive these details can be. Together with 'experientially grounded' elements, they produce a scene which is both concrete and imaginable. As well as adding vividness, image-making stories are useful at times of potential conflict or strain in job interviews because they cannot be attacked on a factual basis (Drew and Holt, 1988) – rather in the ways that Sandeep carries off a not strictly relevant answer. By contrast, rather than talking vividly from their own experience to demonstrate 'this is what I did,' unsuccessful candidates often make unauthenticated claims such as, 'I'm a good communicator' or 'I've got a natural ability to learn things' – telling rather than showing (6.4).

The overall effect of performing these vivid and detailed experiences is to elicit engagement establish credibility and allow some wiggle room for possible infelicities to be overlooked. Tannen makes an argument for a structure proceeding from detail to image to scene: 'It is in large part through the creation of a *shared world of images* that ideas are communicated and understanding is achieved' (Tannen, 2007: 136). This shared world, therefore, convinces imaginatively as well as seeming coherent and relevant.

The 'shared world' is not just done through lexical choice, but also through traditional rhetorical devices. Triads, contrasting pairs and linking images, the use of repetition and speech delivery consistent with one's story are the most obvious and frequently used forms. For example, Tom's repeated rhetorical questioning in lines 7–8, 'Is it old bones? Is it recent bones?' involves the interviewer in the discovery. Repetitions are also used to display methodical, routine and repetitive work – so often the crux of the interview question. When answering the question about dealing with repetitive work, Ahmed uses repetition of words to recreate the sense of motivating oneself repeatedly to do a demanding task, saying, 'Go on, go on, go on you can do it' with increasing emphasis, evoking the almost physical goading of the self. The same rhetorical device is used by Lloyd, who uses repetition ('every day every day' and 'just chipping bricks, chipping bricks, chipping bricks'), falling intonation and a weary tone of voice to convey the routine and repetitive nature of the tasks which he enumerates – as does Joe, in describing painting large walls the same colour all day (9.6).

Candidates such as Ahmed, Lloyd and Joe, whose speech delivery is consistent with their story – what Tannen (2007) calls matching 'sound and sense' – tend to be more convincing in persuading interviewers that they possess the kind of hard-working resilience sought. This matching of story content and tone is performed across other competence-based questions, such as team working and customer relations. Lloyd uses a range of expressive features to tell the story of a hectic day in the mail delivery room:

Example 26: Lloyd – BAME British, Successful

1. I: when you worked here here at Christmas er:m
2.   can you remember one particular day for instance
3.   whe:n there was a lot of work to clear
4.   and you really had to work as a team to get it

(one minute of talk deleted)

5. C: there was a day where I remember where (.) erm (.) like (.)
6.   wi- with (xxx) they'd get piled up wh-
7.   quite kind of quickly like between- like
8.   I used to start from five 'til ten that was my shift
9.   so between like five to seven it was
10.   {(lo) quiet like always quiet} (.)
11.   so let's say we'd go on facing for a bit
12.   and after about seven it would
13.   {(ac) it would just come loads like just start rushing}

Lloyd uses pace, pausing or speeding up his delivery to convey a relatively calm or hectic work environment, and so matching his sound to his sense (lines 1–13). He builds up some dramatic tension, by the strategic use of pausing and shifts of pitch and tone after 'quiet' (line 10), which delays the introduction of the climatic 'rushing,' which is accompanied by a louder, faster and more emphatic delivery at line 13. Similarly, Ire (example 1), who has worked as a mortgage adviser but has applied for a post in a delivery company, explains how he managed to calm down and satisfy an angry customer: 'All I'll do is just calm him down, calm down, sit down have a cup of tea, make him a cup of tea alright, and make him feel relaxed. Then I asked him the questions.' The soothing, slow speech – with stretched syllables in 'calm,' pausing and repetition of 'cup of tea' and 'calm down' – both tells the story and enacts it, as he shifts from what he would do to what he actually said to the customer and back again.

By contrast Khaleda, an unsuccessful BAME candidate of Bangladeshi family background, delivers her apparent enthusiasm for her current job – 'I enjoy everything I do …. the job is brilliant. The students always come in and say hello' – in low, unvaried pitch and is hesitant and slow-paced, with pauses mid-clause and halting self-interruptions. Interviewers commented that she was too withdrawn and quiet for the position of receptionist in a college, and yet her current work experience fitted precisely the job on offer.

6.4 Stance

The action-based components of the narrative – giving convincing evidence, building a shared imaginary world and engaging the interviewer in it – form an essential part of the linguistic technology of the interview. Added to this is the reflective and evaluative work narrators do to take up a stance on this action, either explicitly or more tacitly.

Stance is the relationship or standpoint taken up by speakers towards their experiences, other people, ideas and values, and also towards those with whom they interact (Dubois, 2007: 163; Jaffe, 2009; Baynham, 2011: 70).[32] I am using it here as one of several resources to convey a particular self that manages the face and footing demands of the interview. And while doing the work of the more analytic and evaluative elements of conveying the self, stance still retains the tension between relative solidarity and distance that holds interaction together. It is the movement and blending of action and evaluation, between engagement and distancing (Linde, 1993: 105; Riessman, 1993: 2) that, like the STAR structure and the engagement through vivid detail, helps to establish an overall sense of consistency, credibility and coherence (6.4). This acceptable institutional self, as assessed by interviewers, forms the thumbnail sketch so frequently used to sum up a candidate in the final decision-making. But this is a tricky process, as Bruno Bettelheim's metaphor of two porcupines trying to mate – coming closer and then moving apart – reminds us, and this blending and shifting needs to be sustained both in the hybrid discourses already discussed and here in the candidate narrative.

This thumbnail sketching creates a simplified 'version' of the candidate, easily fitted into boxes; for example, Jim's comment of, 'Me, being me, I worked,' conveying his relationship to work and so his character as a hard worker. While the competence framework is designed to disaggregate the 'bundle of skills' that are supposed to constitute the candidate, in practice global judgments of personality are routinely made as the candidate's acceptability is summed up from the stance they take. The dilemma for the candidate is threefold: to build in an acceptable stance, either explicitly or implicitly, while keeping the stories grounded and engaging; to display an enterprising, reflexive self, while maintaining the interview on a proper footing; and to find a stance which manages explicit probes of any weaknesses or problems without losing face.

Explicit and Implicit Stances

We can see how both Duncan and Luis, with differing degrees of success, take up a particular and explicit stance about themselves: Duncan says that 'you got to keep yourselves amused for boring jobs,' while Luis says that 'you have to be always alert.' Explicit stance is most frequently displayed in two ways: through deontic statements, as just illustrated, and through self-descriptions which are bald or somewhat mitigated statements. While both are conventionalised means of performing the self, their effectiveness crucially depends on their location in the story – on how far they are embedded in or appear immediately after the task/action narrative and on the extent of mitigation. In other words, how far experiential evidence and nuanced claims ensure that the self is not too personal on the one hand, nor too distant and institutional on the other. The preferred STAR structure, as in Duncan's story of repetitive work, determines the location of explicit stance taking at the end of his story, the culmination of a grounded account. By contrast, Luis's explicit stance ('It's gonna be a physically demanding because you have to be alert, you have to be always on motivated') breaks into a narrative already fractured by the interviewer and seems to dangle unsupported, without evidence. So there is a perceived double failure: both in structure and in how his positive stance is overlooked.

Similarly, self-descriptions have to be carefully located and mitigated if candidates are not to appear boastful, too emotional or extreme; for example, 'I love this,' 'I'm too picky' or 'I'm a specialist in IT.' They are seen as too categorical or as overselling themselves, too locked into personal discourses or as not being sufficiently objective or distant about themselves (5.3, 10.1). In other words they are not self-reflexive enough. And while affect permeates all talk, too much feeling is not institutionally allowable as the euphemisation of institutional discourse shows.

Turning to more implicit stances, successful candidates manage much of the stance taking through the action of the stories. Tom the airport construction worker implicitly draws the interviewer into a shared social world, as Pippa does in her story of making spectacles (example 3). Tom glosses his story of discovering bones while drilling with the comment, 'So *obviously* everything's got to stop there,' indexing a membership of people (including himself and the interviewer) who understand the archaeological imperative of such findings. This co-membering work invokes a social world which is more about shared assumptions of moral conduct than the more specific identity recognition in Erickson and Shultz's original formulation of co-membership. As such, this tacit work can feed into those subterranean impressions that the candidate is 'one of us' or not.

The blending of detailed description with stance – summed up by Holland et al. as 'standing apart from immediate experience that yet defines it as ours by the very arrangement that relates it' (Holland et al., 1998: 182) – manages the tension between distance and involvement (which the loved-up porcupines feel). Candidates can successfully achieve this through an organising trope, linking stance and story. In the next example – a classic 'entrepreneurial self' question about how to 'improve business' in a low-paid job interview – Ahmed's initiative-taking stance is demonstrated by the actions he took (and it is no surprise that the STAR structure helps him to do this):

Example 27: Ahmed – Sierra Leonean Migrant, Successful

1. I: okay (1) the last one on there i:s
2.   improving the business (.)
3.   er:m what we looking here is (.)
4.   an example where you have come up with
5.   while you are working a- i- in any of the workplaces (.)
6.   to (.) to better things b-
7.   an idea that you have come up with
8.   to (.) improve the business (.) or better the way
9.   they wer- things being done yeah

(thirty seconds of talk deleted)

10. C: I'm working as a admin assistant (.)
11.   when I first start working it's like the
12.   files were (.) to me they were not stacked properly

(ten seconds of talk deleted)

13.   I start putting them alphabetical orders (.)
14.   which was a big er:m improvement=
15. I: =yeah yeah
16. C: a:nd they were so happy about it
17.   my line manager was just like er:m
18.   that was a test passed you know
19.   I don't know if they did that on purpose or whatever s:o (.)
20.   since that time everybody was tracing files very easy
21.   and it was easy for me as well

Here Ahmed moves from description to evaluation, objectifying and linking the manager, colleagues and himself in the overall theme of satisfaction.

Crucially, at line 12, he establishes himself as the kind of person who is not satisfied with inefficiencies: '*To me* they were not stacked properly.' And at lines 18–19 he implies that while it may have been 'a test' of his personal competence, he took the initiative to benefit his team mates, himself and the organisation.

Some candidates create their own thumbnail sketch by organising and linking a certain stance throughout all their narratives. Tom designs his narratives around the organising trope of heroism, toughness and dependability – as he says later in the interview, 'If you don't like it, there's the gate.' So consistent are these images that in the next example, at line 97, the interviewer's response of 'tough' seems to encompass both a sympathetic reaction to getting soaked and a comment on his character. Here Tom tells an iterative narrative of his job, installing fibre optic cables under an airport runway:

Example 28: Tom – White British, Successful

1. C: you know (.) that was like twelve hour shifts bu- but
2.   plus the fact you're out in all weathers=
3. I: =yes [yes
4. C: you] know
5. I: sounds ((^ ^))
6. C: yeah because once you start-
7.   you start a job there (.) you see
8.   you can't like walk off
9.   because if we cut the runway lights (.)
10.   to put new fibre optic cable
11.   I've put- we put the ((duct net)) actually
12.   what you make that green stuff
13. I: oh right ah yes uhuh
14. C: now we've got to put that in (.)
15.   now that's got to be in
16.   before five thirty in the morning obviously
17.   because the lights have got to go back on
18. I: mhm
19. C: so I mean i- if the heavens open halfway through the job
20. I: tough
21. C: tough (.) it's got to be them lights
22.   have got to be back on for five thirty (.) you know

The rhetorical device of organising the presentation of self around a dominant trope is also used by some candidates to defend possible weaknesses in their CV; for example, for presenting a rationale for various life and career changes which might otherwise be deemed as markers of unreliability – of not being what one interviewer called a 'sticker.' But like all aspects of managing the interview, too much (or too jarring a way of) structuring answers around one's life trajectory can be seen as too self-disclosing, too personal (5.3). Similarly, many candidates have to manage the problem of being perceived as overqualified or too senior for the job. This is a situation faced by many migrant candidates, but in this next case Paula is a local British candidate. She is a redundant factory manager who has to downskill to an unskilled job, as there is very little work in the area:

Example 29: Paula – White British, Successful

1. I: so (.) you were really (.) in charge of production there
2.   what- what (.) tell me what that involved

(twenty seconds of talk deleted)

3. C: what else I do in a day in that is (.)
4.   I mean if you've ever worked in a small company (Bxxx) (.)
5.   thing about when you start up something like that (.)
6.   I mean there's a lot of peaks and troughs (.)
7. I: yes=
8. C: =because these they put (.) would customers
9.   {(lo) would just come on
10.   and it would literally just be a couple of days' notice}
11. I: right
12. C: right (.) so again I could work every single machine
13.   I could do every single job in the contract packing I had to ken (.)
14. I: yes
15. C: because if somebody was off or something
16.   or s- a customer came on
17.   and there was things to be done
18. I: you just had to get on and do it
19. C: that's the name of the game yeah
20.   get on and do it and get it done um
21.   I didn't mind it to be honest (.)
22. I: so you would do all the lifting and the standing and the=
23. C: =oh God yeah
24. I: running about and all the rest of that
25. C: oh yeah oh yeah
26. I: okay so
27. C: no problem with that

To mitigate her perceptions that her past experience makes her overqualified, Paula crafts her stance in relation to the interviewer, who is the human resources manager (lines 3–20). She calls up a shared social world through a set of assumptions, looking forward to a possible social relationship with the interviewer, who she calls by her first name (Bxxx), but she is careful not to come across as overbearing or managerial. So like Gladston, she keeps the interview on a proper footing. Interactionally and stylistically, Paula manages a mix of solidarity and deference. She aligns herself to the interviewer's 'get on and do it' (line 18) assumption and uses low pitch, falling tone (lines 9 and 10) and pausing to present herself as more worker than manager. This careful re-presenting of her past to fit the requirements of the present job pays off (lines 18–27), where the interviewer's interventions serve to construct her as able to meet all the physical requirements of the packing job in a coat hanger factory.

Managing the Enterprising, Reflexive Self

Part of the enterprising qualities expected of candidates is to be self-governing – both self-aware and self-managing vis-à-vis others. Two inter-related types of stance seem crucial: how candidates compare themselves (implicitly or explicitly) with others, and the degree of authority and know-ingness they claim or are allowed to claim within the (relative) asymmetries of the interview.

In many types of narratives – for example, those embedded in research interviews, or in the narratives of those with considerable status (Dyer and Keller-Cohen, 2000) – the narrator refers to others in ways which establish his or her own rightness or expertise. In the job interview this is a dilemma, since the candidate needs to come across in positive ways but cannot assume or claim to be on an equal footing with the interviewers. Gladston, the successful candidate (3.7) who is applying for promotion to a junior management position, refers to other characters in his story in ways that present himself as a professional in the context of his previous job and simultaneously expands on the story to suggest an affiliation with the interviewer, pulling him into the narrative. Here is part of the bent aerial story again, picking up from example 6:

Example 30: Gladston – Jamaican Migrant, Successful

1. I: okay tell me a little bit about that conversation
2.   then that you [had
3. C: yeah]
4. I: with the customer
5. C: well what I said to the customer was that
6.   er:m you know w:e er:m
7.   I- I- I invited him into the office and said
8.   well I'm I'm sorry
9.   but we had a little bit of erm a mishap with your vehicle
10.   those are the words I used er:m [and
11. I: mishap hhh]
12. C: hhh yeah]
13.   not accident we don't like them- to to get them alarmed=
14. I: =okay=
15. C: =so I said we had a bit of a mishap
16.   with o- with your vehicle er:m
17.   w- we didn't realise that the- your aerial was up
18.   and when one of our guys I-
19.   it was an apprentice (.) you know
20.   these young boys who just really (.) er
21.   just like to drive flash cars [and
22. I: yeah]
23. C: just didn't take note
24.   and as he was driving it out
25.   we we damaged your aerial (.) I says

At lines 9–11, Gladston draws attention to the hedged manner in which he tells the customer of the accident and so contrasts himself – the calm professional – with the potentially agitated customer. By raising his lexical sensitivity to an explicit level, he sets off a co-membership sequence in which the interviewer is encouraged to affiliate to Gladston's customer relations practice of managing potentially angry customers. This is then reinforced when Gladston uses a side sequence at line 19 – 'it was an apprentice' – to explain to the interviewer why the accident happened, to implicitly contrast himself with irresponsible youth and co-opt the interviewer into a shared understanding of the category of young men who 'drive flash cars.' Thus Gladston deals with the tricky problem of how to demonstrate his status as an experienced professional without jeopardising his status as an interviewee, and so keeps the interview on a proper footing. He subtly presents the culpable apprentice as irresponsible and himself as the opposite.

Managing Problems and Weaknesses

As narratives can generally be used to accentuate the positive, they can also be used to talk of difficulties and weaknesses in the management of professional identity in the workplace. These may be implicit as in the case of Paula, above, who downplays her previous management experience. But they are even harder to manage when they are explicit. Asking about candidate weaknesses or failures is one of the main areas of questioning in junior management/promotion interviews where candidates have, in the words of one interviewer, to 'think like a manager,' and is one of the most difficult ways of managing the self, both performing and confessing.

These questions are always problematic, but particularly so for migrant candidates who are aware of the potential for discrimination and so talk up their achievements in 'the immigrant story' (10.3). However, many candidates manage well the tension between confession and positive self-display. The underlying cultural assumption is that the good candidate is aware of and honest about weaknesses, but has learnt from unfortunate episodes and reflecting on them (as the interviewer models in example 31 with Michael and in example 32 with Gladston). In practice, those candidates whose stance discloses too much weakness, rather than crafting a stylised honesty, tend to be negatively evaluated. For example Brian, an unsuccessful white Irish candidate applying for a junior management post, describes how he was the butt of his team's joking behaviour and that he had had to reprimand them. In the wash-up session where Brian was rejected, the comments were that he complained too much and was too personal. The narrative of weakness appeared to outstrip the measures used to deal with it.

Those whose stance admits to no weaknesses have no stories to tell of reversal and rescue. Michael from Liberia, another candidate for a junior management post, has written a CV which, according to his interviewers, 'just goes up and up and up' (10.5). In the interview, he tells the 'immigrant story' of unblemished success, without any of the mitigation necessary for an acceptable stance:

Example 31: Michael – Liberian Migrant, Unsuccessful

1. I: what- wha- what's the worst feedback
2.   you've had from that (.)
3.   the worst bit that you thought
4.   oh that's terrible
5. C: I I know what so far I've actually
6.   ((to be very frank with you))
7.   so far I've no- I've not had yeah
8.   so far I've never had [anything
9. I: there] must be something someone wasn't happy with
10. C: er:m
11. I: have you taken anything from here
12.   that that you've had for example er:m (.)
13.   I remember I had feedback that I wasn't very approachable
14.   and I was really surprised
15.   because I thought oh I I I'm no- open here
16.   I'll always listen er:m and I went away
17.   and I specifically made an effort then (.)
18.   to try and do things to (.)
19.   increase my [approachability
20. C: yeah but I]
21. I: because it's important that you learn from that feedback

When asked a typical 'extreme case' question, Michael initially denies any negative feedback (lines 7–8). The interviewer then models an acceptable narrative (lines 13–19). But even so, at line 18, Michael still fails to take up an appropriate stance. The scenario of confession, learning and improvement is of course a keystone of many religions, but the interview as a place for a carefully managed secular confession is only understood by those who can play the interview game.

6.5   Reporting Talk

Much institutional narrative is reporting talk (Holt, 1996; Holt and Clift, 2006; Tannen, 1989), and is often used to defend the speaker (Galatolo, 2006; Trinch, 2003) when some failure or weakness is exposed. Such reporting exemplifies the action and evaluation components of story discussed above, producing – when successfully performed – a blend of grounded detail and reflective speaker stance. Reporting talk also allows other voices in to enliven the narrative and, used strategically, to retell and enhance the performing self.

In most of the organisations studied, one set of follow-up questions was designed to elicit the talk that occurred in any one incident – for example, 'So what did you say?' or 'How did they feel?' This reported talk was given particular credence in the junior management interviews. Here, narratives were probed for how the candidate dealt with incidents, what they explicitly said and what they had learnt about the encounter, e.g. 'Tell me a little bit about that conversation then.' In these interviews some show of manager identity, displayed in the management of people, is essential. Even more intensively than in the low-paid job interviews, this requires both a strong sense of agency – told through events and vivid experientially grounded accounts – and a more distancing, reflexive stance.

Direct and Indirect Means of Speech Reporting

Reporting what others said of you was a more persuasive tactic than claiming positive qualities – showing rather than telling, as mentioned above. Direct speech reporting seems particularly powerful as evidence for claims, since it appears to transmit facts as they actually happened (Besnier, 1993) with no recognition that reported speech is always framed and gives new meaning and value to the speaker (Maybin, 2017). In order to persuade, Edwards argues, one has to invoke categories that are attributable to oneself 'as a matter of *disinterested description*' because, if it is only self-serving categorisation, it indexes the self and not the world (Edwards, 1991). In other words, a self-claim is no more than that. But a report of how others talked about you or how you talked to them (on the assumption that the speaker is quoting exactly what was said) indexes how you relate to others, how you are appreciated in the world of work, as other voices, including your own past voice, are co-opted to present you in the now.

There is much controversy in the speech-reporting literature on how to define and delineate how speakers use others' talk. In our data, successful candidates rely heavily on direct speech in their reporting and also, but less frequently, use more indirect means in strategic ways. But as with literature on how reported talk is used in interaction, the distinction between direct and indirect is blurred (Holt and Clift, 2006). In our data, much of the direct reported speech involves an immediate shift into the talk of others, with only prosodic features cueing the shift – such as a brief pause or change in voice quality and without the quotatives 'tell or say.' Occasionally they are framed with a filler such as 'well,' or with a false start in standard reported speech which then changes to direct speech as in Junior's line (in example 34, on page 139), 'I told the guys that, "Only empty the (xxx)."' Conventional indirect reported speech – which would render Junior's utterance as 'I told the guys that they should only empty the (xxx)' – was extremely rare and may account for the blurring of direct and indirect speech.

Embedded in the story, direct speech examples give the impression of actuality, but are not 'direct verbatim quotations' (Schiffrin, 1996) in the sense of being the exact words spoken, since the original words and how they were performed are lost and their reporting is adjusted to the very special context of the job interview. Rather, they are constructed quotes doing the work of being real (Maybin, 2017). Given the importance of self-knowing and self-reflection in the interview, many of these direct reports are selfies, where the candidates ventriloquise themselves.

In some contrast to these constructed quotes are indirect forms where a speaker's own or others' speech is summed up as 'descriptions' of 'facts' or internal states (Hickmann, 1993); for example, 'He apologised.' The direct reports provide the drama, vividness and sense of reality to social encounters and what Labov calls 'internal evaluation' of the story (1972). The indirect forms and summary descriptions can call up the speaker's stance on them, providing a more external and institutional evaluation. Together they do the work of action and evaluation discussed above. As with hybrid discourses, the precise location and blending of these two – as well as the extent to which co-membership has been developed so far in the interview – changes the footing and influences how reported talk affects the judgment of candidates.

Direct Speech and Internal States: Contrastive Examples

Gladston uses both direct speech and descriptions of internal states in blended and complementary ways. We look here at the beginning of the bent aerial anecdote (example 6):

Example 32: Gladston – Jamaican Migrant, Successful

1. I.   {(looks up)
2. C: yeah so I thought well the the thing to do is to be honest
3. I: (nods)
4. C: take ownership} {(I looks down, writes)
5.   it's my fault you know put me hand up
6.   and and I'll I'll ask the customer
7.   just give me a chance to put it right you know

8.   and if and if they're still not happy with it after I put it right
9.   then they can take any action that they feel [needs to be taken
10. I: okay} {(I looks up) tell me a] little bit
11.   about that conversation then
12.   that you [had
13. C: yeah]
14. I: with the [customer} {(I looks down, writes)

Gladston has to manage the tension between admission of a fault and his identity as an agentive, reflective manager, as noted above. He starts with a hypothetical narrative set in the past, where he talks directly to himself about what he will do, at lines 1–4. Embedded in this is a description of an internal state which implies how he will speak to the customer – 'be honest,' 'take ownership' – with a nod to the institutional competence in the original question. He then shifts to direct speech reporting – 'It's my fault … put me hand up' – enacting the more abstract competence referred to. This then smoothly sets up the interviewer's request for more information about the 'conversation.' The shifting between descriptive states and direct speech throughout this example (3.7) contributes to the management of his stance as a competent, responsible professional while establishing a light-hearted co-membership with the interviewer. Simply producing a descriptive internal state utterance – such as, 'I would apologise and take responsibility' – would not contextualise his answer in ways that would allow him to work with the tensions of the story, change footing and so manage the relationship between himself and interviewer in its telling.[33]

By contrast, both Sara and Junior have difficulties in managing appropriately the blend of direct speech and descriptive states. Sara's use of direct selfie speech has a different outcome as she talks about managing teams:

Example 33: Sara – BAME British, Clearly Unsuccessful

1. C: I mean I can be very (.) abrupt
2.   when I want something to be done (.)
3.   look I've asked you to do zone three
4.   will you go and do zone three please (1)
5.   [you know
6. I: mhm]
7. C: er we are not taking a vote on this [I've
8. I: mhm]
9. C: asked you to do s- erm

10.   I've given you reasonable request
11.   could you go and do it please
12. I: mhm
13. C: so I I c- I know I can be quite (.) intimidating
14. I: mhm
15. C: stroppy (.) direct (.)
16. I: mhm

After a compact orientation to the story at lines 1–2 – framed by the indirect comment, 'I can be very abrupt' – she switches into self-quotation, only indicating to the interviewer after the quote at line 5, 'You know,' that she is constructing the words of her narrated self. Through lines 7–11, she reverts to direct speech and then shifts to indirect forms, using her quoted words as evidence of her self-evaluation, that she can be 'intimidating' and 'stroppy' and, earlier, 'abrupt.' Whereas Gladston's self-quotation includes positive internal states – 'The thing to do is be honest' – Sara's descriptions of herself as 'stroppy' and so on fall outside her ventriloquising and are negative, undermining any presentation of a 'reasonable' stance that her direct speech reporting was trying to convey. And by re-enacting how she talked at some length she shifts the footing, implicitly involving the interviewer as the addressee of her 'abrupt' and 'stroppy' manner. As elsewhere in the interview, the interviewer later comments on the fact that she reveals her feelings too much, lacks self-awareness and is verbose. So although she does show self-awareness here, she is not 'talking like a manager.'

Junior also fails to make his direct speech and descriptions of internal states work for each other. In the same question on 'taking ownership,' he tells the story of a member of staff who was frequently absent from work. As her acting manager, he was expected to raise questions with her about her absenteeism. The interviewer then presses him on what the rest of the team thought about his action, just as Gladston's interviewer asks him about the customer's reaction:

Example 34: Junior – BAME British, Successful
(Low-rated interview. Promoted because of his track record in the organisation.)

1.   C: so I told th- the guys that only empty the (xxx) if=
2.   I: =yeah but what I'm trying to [find is
3.   C: yeah]
4.   I: how did the other members of the team feel
5.   about you challenging (1) this person
6.   C: oh ri- oh no they were pr- they were ((fine yeah))

7.   they were well pleased
8. I: okay
9. C: yeah because they said
10.   she (.) got away with (.) away with it for so long
11. I: okay
12. C: so oh yeah they were [er and
13. I: how do] you know they were well pleased
14. C: because er:m (.) a couple of guys did say to me
15.   er:m (4) well er:m (.) well the other manager
16.   let her go- get away with
17. I: okay ((^ ^))
18.   is that what happened hhh okay alright then

Junior's response to the interviewer's question is to produce a brief descriptive internal state answer at lines 6 and 7, saying that 'they were fine yeah they were well pleased,' and then a quotation framed with a quotative 'they said' at lines 9–10. However, neither are sufficiently elaborated as the interviewer's overlapping, probing question at line 13 suggests. This leads to a further framed quotation (line 15) with little new information and without any of the vivid, grounded detail of Gladston's narrative. Crucially, there is no active agency in the quote or any evaluative stance which would depict what the 'couple of guys' thought about him, in contrast to the previous manager. There is an implicit comparison between Junior and the other manager, but this is not elaborated. Later in the interview (not transcribed here), when he is asked a similar question about how he encouraged a member of staff, he again gives a general descriptive statement of 'just general talk.' So despite several attempts to elicit what was actually said, this rule of the game was not one Junior was familiar with. While the content of both Sara's and Junior's examples are less problematic than Gladston's, it is Gladston who produces the persuasive narrative. Sara positions herself too vividly within the story world while Junior is not vivid enough. It is the quality of narrating any particular competence, rather than the fact of having experienced it, which counts.

Conclusion

Narratives are so powerful in the job interview because they are the central mechanism for establishing work experience and work attitudes. The institutional good story provides evidence of conduct and character. Through familiar story structures and engaging detail, interviewers are drawn into a shared imaginary world. Similarly, invoking a shared stance and agreement on the social world produces a rapid sketch of character used in wash-up sessions to determine a final positive assessment. Storytellings, like the management of hybrid discourses, are opportunities to hold familiarity and formality in balance.

But differences in narrative performance are also amplified by the interviewers' behaviour. These narratives are joint productions. The well-told story is listened to, built on and evaluated through a jointly created smooth interaction. Candidates unfamiliar with the conventions of Western storytelling and the deft management of stance have their responses judged as incoherent, their narrative interrupted and negative assessments of character made. It is to the joint production of candidates' performance that we turn in the next chapter.

7 The Interview as a Joint Production

In chapter 3 we saw how the intersection between institutional regimentation and the neoliberal economy produced conditions for the two overarching discursive competences discussed in chapters 5 and 6: the blending of institutional, personal and professional discourses, and the conveying of an institutionally acceptable narrative self. In this chapter we look at how these competences are interactionally produced, and how this leads to relatively more conversational or institutional interviews as indicators and producers of success or failure.

7.1 The Unofficial Dialectics of the Job Interview

The two overarching discursive competences could be said to override the stated competences of the interview, since evidence of these other competences is only successfully displayed through these two unstated ones. But these competences do not stand in isolation; they are 'thoroughly a product of joint ceremonial labour' (Goffman, 1967). And while the last two chapters have been concerned largely with candidates' contributions, this is an analytic conceit allowing temporary concentration on the relatively long turns expected of candidates. The interview is a joint production (2.5) and candidates' success depends substantially on the interviewers' performance, how they govern its interactional norms and manage its paradoxes.

Interviews are designed to be rational, ordered affairs. But while grasping tenaciously onto the order and orthodoxy of the event, the interviewer is also immersed in a socially charged encounter where ongoing evaluations help to determine how this order is played out. In sum, this is an account of how the social, emotional and interactional in selection processes produce variety and, in places, instability; how interviewers shape, support or constrain candidates' performance; and the institution's attempts to render this thoroughly joint, intersubjective production invisible (2.7).

The Tension Between Order and the Socioemotional

The special interactional requirements of the job interview present a heightened version of all face-to-face interaction; namely that it is orderly enough for people to make sense of the activity and each other, while simultaneously managing the impression they convey to others. The tension between and interdependence of interactional order and emotional/moral tone has been addressed by sociologists, microethnographers, interactional sociolinguistics (IS) and in conversation analysis (CA).[34] A specific take on how this tension is played out in candidates' narratives has been discussed in the previous chapter.

Goffman's foundational work on interaction identifies two overarching elements: system and ritual constraints. The system requirements of turn taking, framing and basic cooperative principles of talk (Goffman, 1981: 14–29; 1.5) allow speakers to get on with the business in hand 'in sustained, intimate coordination of action' (Goffman, 1983: 3). Ritual constraints, drawing on Durkheim, are concerned with the moral and emotional dimensions of interaction: 'how each individual ought to handle himself [*sic*],' 'his [*sic*] claim to good character,' that individuals 'are persons of social worth' (Goffman, 1983: 16). Through ritual, Goffman argues, an emotional energy is created which keeps the relationship going between participants (Goffman, 1967). The sociologist Randall Collins, drawing on Goffman, focuses on the emotional mood of the interview, looking at the 'mutual ratification' of 'interaction ritual chains' (Collins, 2004). This mutuality, he argues, enhances well-being and self-confidence and engenders positive feelings towards self and others. But of course, this emotional energy can turn the other way if the mood darkens.

While system and ritual are introduced as separate elements, Goffman recognises them as thoroughly interdependent in noting that, 'motivated to preserve everyone's face, [participants] end up acting so as to preserve orderly communication' (Goffman, 1981: 19), as well as in his use of 'intimate' when discussing coordinated interaction. Or, as the Scollons propose, what are deemed to be system requirements of coherence, relevance and so on are just as much interpersonal requirements (Scollon and Scollon, 1995). Similarly, Erickson and Shultz define the special help given by gatekeepers as the result of 'overall behavioural smoothness and overall emotional tone' (Erickson and Shultz, 1982: 168–169); counsellor and student 'define the situation within the encounter in terms of emergent and expressive, as well as institutionalised and instrumental, aspects of status and role' (Erickson and Shultz, 1982: 37). This 'emergent and expressive' element also functions to provide crucial 'strategic leeway' (Erickson and Shultz, 1982: 37) – or what Erickson later called 'wiggle room' (2004) – in what are otherwise deemed to be highly routinised interactions.

In IS, the interactional production of inferential processes is central to our understanding of how moral and social judgments of individuals are made in institutional settings (Gumperz, 1982a: 153–171). For example, Gumperz identifies in two vignettes how the lack of shared contextualisation conventions lead to negative moral judgments in a staff cafeteria at Heathrow airport (1982a: 173) and to the increasingly negative environment of a training selection interview: 'In the cases I have examined, the interaction starts on quite a friendly note, but the atmosphere deteriorates noticeably as the interaction progresses' (Gumperz 1992c: 310).

The sociolinguistic literature on selection interviews reveals a clear relationship between the initial design of questions, the perceived quality of candidate responses, interviewer follow-up questions/responses and the developing 'overall emotional tone' of the interview, which such 'wiggle room' allows, with either positive or negative outcomes. In these studies and in the research described here, the system requirements extend beyond (but always include), maintaining enough interactional order to get on with the business in hand. The interview is represented and seemingly played out as a total system in which standardisation, objectivity and social norms coalesce. The system officially drives the encounter; unofficially, the moral and emotional requirements do. But these are sequestered away, are not actively attended to, until the decision-making stage. At this point, the moral character is outed in the final thumbnail sketch of the candidate.

Improvising Order

The convention is that decision-making is a post-hoc affair, where all the evidence from a fixed and orderly encounter is summed up. In practice it is a socially charged, malleable activity where subjective impressions feed into and alter its ceremonial trappings. Interviewers use the wiggle room afforded by the face-to-face encounter to *improvise order* in developing a rationalisation for their final decision, maintaining institutional order with a strong element of improvisation (De Certeau, 1985) – or what Garfinkel called ad hoc opportunities. The interviewers' developing rationalisation leaks out into the interaction in three ways, discussed below: the design and use of main (usually competence) questions; the follow-ups – such as reformulations and additional questions – and the extent to which candidates align to them (Linell and Thunquist, 2003); and the reactions to misunderstandings and awkward moments. Successful interviews are characterised by low levels of reformulation and awkward moments plus more opportunities to break the orthodoxy of the interview, to play with the interview game. In sum, the interview becomes more conversational and less institutional, whereas less successful interviews lead to a tightening of relevance and other institutional requirements. Chapter 6 illustrated this in the way that perceived inappropriate narratives were interrupted and often reduced to low-level, factual questioning as a form of 'talking down' (Erickson and Shultz, 1982; 6.2).

So the interactional production of candidate character and competence is a mix of improvisation and regulation. It is the subtle deviations from the conventional which, like improvisation in jazz, show up the order and regulation in the original themes (Erickson and Shultz, 1982: 8–10). These improvisations go largely unnoticed, whether they help or disadvantage candidates. This lack of attention to improvisation – to the sociality and bureaucratic intimacy of the event – is reinforced by an ideology in which the rules governing them are assumed to be fixed and strictly adhered to, so that equality can be demonstrated and not just claimed. Models, guidelines, training and highly structured design all serve this ideology (4.5, 8.5).

Interviewers and those who designed the interviews we recorded frequently described an 'ideal' interview. This consisted of an objective personality measure and a replication of all other interviews in the organisation which removed the 'room for error,' produced 'valid evidence' and promoted 'equal opportunities.' Any deviations, elaborations and other subtle changes could blow holes in an institution's defence and are erased from its formal technology and discourse. Standardisation of interaction sits within a regime of truth, as Foucault would have noted, which is not to be questioned – despite its illusory qualities as a method of achieving fairness. Before looking more closely at the subtle dynamics of the interview, it is worth comparing the explicitly standardised equal opportunities interview with the more 'wiggleroomed' mainstream alternative (4.2).

7.2 Interactional Differences in Different Types of Interviews

'Presentation' Equal Opportunity Interviews

The content of the majority of interviews are designed around some interpretation of the competence framework, but they can be differently structured. The most obvious contrast is between the highly structured – what I call the 'presentation' equal opportunities interview – and the semi-structured mainstream interview. The presentation equal opportunities interview had its heyday in the late 1980s and 1990s in public sector institutions. Some organisations still use such interviews, designed around an equal opportunities ideology which assumes that fairness is derived from total standardisation. One of the seven sites in this job interview research used this type of interview.

Their tight structure and control minimises interaction and so, it is argued, bleaches out the social and the subjective from the interview. All questions are written down and read out exactly as they are written. The candidate is not expected to clarify or negotiate the purpose or meaning of the question, but to present their answer. They are not given any cues as to how long their answer should be and there are no follow-on questions or reactions, beyond very occasional minimal backchannels (such as head nods, thank yous etc.). While the candidate speaks, the interviewers write. This presentation equal opportunities interview produces its own difficulties for candidates. It assumes that candidates will understand questions without needing to negotiate their purpose, that each response is a complete and adequate answer and that candidates should not be 'helped' to provide more, and that candidates can produce extended answers which respond to all aspects of the question. The example given below is from a presentation equal opportunities interview for a junior administrative post in a further education college:

Example 35: Binta – Ghanaian Migrant, Unsuccessful

```
 1.  I:   okay (.) um (.) please describe
 2.       the administrative experience you've had
 3.       (.) especially in devising and implementing
 4.       tracking and monitoring systems
 5.  C:   (.) (h) as a l- as a learning facilitator (h)
 6.       in tracking the students um
 7.       sometimes you look at the files (.)
 8.       if the per- person hasn't been for a while
 9.       you just go on site (h)
10.       on the ((xxx)) (h) administration section (.)
11.       and then check how many times
12.       the person has logged in onto a course (.)
13.       if the person hasn't actually accessed the course at all
14.       for about a week (.)
15.       then you give them- I give them a call (.)
16.       and I tell them you know
17.       they are- they have an obligation to meet the deadline
18.       if they are not interested or they have any difficulties
```

19.   then (.) they should let us know
20.   why they haven't been able to access the course (.)
21.   and if there's any help that we can give
22.   then we ca- we have to support them (.)
23.   so basically that's e:rm (.) what I do
24.   for the tracking and monitoring
25.   and if on a second level they are not sometimes –
26.   they tell you I got so much e:rm domestic problems
27.   I can't do the course
28.   so can I suspend it and then re enrol at a a later date (.)
29.   so they- you have to take them off the course
30.   and um (.) wait 'til they come back (.) for a re enrolment

(Interviewers give no interactional response and there is a long pause while they write.)

This example shows the difficulty the candidate has in answering all four parts of the interview in one turn. Binta does not mention any experience of devising (as opposed to implementing) tracking and monitoring systems, nor does she draw a clear distinction between the two procedures of tracking and monitoring. The lack of any follow-up means she has no opportunity to add more or reinterpret the question. Her response also illustrates the difficulty candidates have in performing without feedback or response cues from interviewers; there is no opportunity for repair or negotiation sequences for either side. Binta commented afterwards that she found the style of interview intimidating and that she felt it limited her responses, prevented a natural flow developing and stopped her from explaining herself as well as she might in a more informal, interactive interview. She said that the lack of acknowledgement and the style of the interview caused her to 'get uptight and lose her way.'

Audience response is integral to the construction of a performance, since spoken discourse is designed to create an involved response (2.2) and, in a more interactive interview, candidates can monitor their own performance. But in a presentation interview, the candidate's answer has to have the qualities of integration and detachment (the characteristics of written discourse and aspects of the institutional mode of discourse), since the candidate has to produce an extended answer with no support or display of involvement from the interviewers. This more detached style puts greater demands on the structuring and grammatical skills of the candidate. Not surprisingly, there are no full-blown narratives given by candidates in the presentation interviews (although Binta does attempt to shoehorn in some passing examples), in sharp contrast to the semi-structured interviews which are now the norm.[35]

So ironically, the very design of the interview intended to address issues of subjectivity and inequality produces a regime which prevents misalignments and misunderstandings from being repaired and denies candidates the chance to interact more freely and engagingly with the interviewers. Its standardisation with long, multi-part questions in institutional discourse mode requires a more institutional alignment, in which spoken answers are more like written ones and much time is spent in writing up answers verbatim. It becomes an almost totally textualised event. In post-interview feedback from candidates, it was migrant candidates who were most negative about such interviews (Roberts and Campbell, 2006).

Semi-Structured Interviews and the Role of Questioning

While presentational interviews explicitly attempt to render the social invisible, the semi-structured interviews do this more indirectly. Aside from one public sector site just illustrated, all the low-paid and junior management job interviews in our data set were semi-structured around several main questions, conforming to what is generally thought of as the mainstream job interview across the private and public sectors. Some – particularly in the public sector – were more presentational, with scripted questions but with some opportunity for negotiation and follow-up. But the majority of the interviews were a mix of a backbone of three to ten set competence questions, then follow-ups – either funnelling down to further detail, or a range of clarifications, reformulations or prompts.

Questions define what an interview is. The increasing interest in how questions constitute the institutional encounter has been taken up in widely differing settings including the courts, police work and other quasi-legal settings (such as asylum and domestic violence hearings), doctor-patient communication, therapy and counselling, news media settings (Freed and Ehrlich, 2010; Tracy and Robles, 2009) and of course the selection interview. These various studies demonstrate the complex forms and roles of questions and their potential for ambiguity.

While the questioning regime puts massive constraints on institutional encounters, it is relatively loose in the sense that what stands as an allowable question is rather broad. It includes the full range of interrogative forms – yes/ no, alternative choice, wh- and statement-plus-tag questions (Heritage and Clayman, 2010). These studies also show the pervasive work done by non-interrogative forms in aping the function of questioning such as statements, repetitions of candidates' words and a range of contextualisation cues – such as rising intonation on statements and backchannels – to prompt and nudge candidates towards the expected response. Whether formally interrogative or not, questions do the key organisational work and this requires them to be multifunctional. As well as eliciting, giving embedded information, exercising interactional control and patrolling the boundaries of the interview, questions can show affiliation, position candidates, request clarifications, prompt or challenge candidate responses and generate inferences (Heritage and Clayman, 2010: 22).

However, question-and-answer formats on their own do not an interview make. Within any one questioning phase, an interactional ecosystem is created. This can affect both the extent to which all required topics are covered and the overall amount of candidate talk, as well as developing a rationale for their acceptance or rejection. Frequently, misunderstandings or misalignments and protracted reformulations stall the elicitation process, so that essential funnelling down to more reflective or analytic answers are not covered in the time given for each of the main questions. Occasionally, some main questions remain unasked; interviewers cannot get through the business and boxes on their interview forms remain empty. For example Alex, an unsuccessful white British candidate, is asked what action he would take if a customer was abusive to him. His non-committal response (largely related to his lack of storytelling, 6.1) and the attempts to elicit more from him are dragged out in a long reformulation sequence over thirty transcribed lines; a similar question to two successful candidates, Pippa and Sandeep, with the same interviewers, is over in a few lines.

The bureaucratic pacing of the interview also has its own unspoken metric, which values just the right amount of candidate talk. In the low-paid job interviews, successful candidates talked on average about sixty per cent of the time. Migrant candidates talked on average seventy-four per cent of the time; unsuccessful candidates were usually at the higher end and were perceived as talking excessively. This may reflect both the actual amount and perceived quality of talk. Some of these candidates were heard as garrulous and some of their talk unprocessable, or they were seen as taking over the interview. This perceived excessive talk can be explained by interviewers' reformulation work, as well as by difficulties in reading interviewer contextualisation cues designed to finish a candidate's turn – one of many reasons for misalignments to occur.

7.3 Alignment and Misalignment

Alignment

In 7.1 I discussed the tensions between interactional orthodoxy and the emotional intensity of the interview, plus the problem for both sides of managing them. To describe this work, the sociological notions of alignment – and its counterpart misalignment – are helpful. While Goffman sees alignment as the line 'we take up to ourselves and the others present' (Goffman, 1981: 128) and the associated notion of stance as something taken up by the individual (6.4), alignment as used here draws on the definition developed by Stokes and Hewitt. This has a more dynamic and co-produced dimension, focussing specifically on the perceived norms of an activity.

Alignment identifies how speakers and listeners bring the framing work of their talk in general – and their stance in particular – into line with one another in trying to reach a common goal and sustain the flow of interaction, while achieving a normative or moral agreement with interactants on how to behave. This means managing the problem of any discrepancy between what is going on and what is 'culturally normal' – that is, 'what is actually taking place in a given situation and what is thought to be typical, normatively expected, probable, desirable or, in other respects, more in accord with what is "culturally normal"' (Stokes and Hewitt, 1976: 843). Repairing these social discrepancies means 'getting things back on track' or 'on a proper footing' both interactionally, the system element, and – arguably even more importantly – the ritual element, in terms of what is appropriate in terms of facework, role relationships, what is allowable to say and what impression is given off.

Alignment depends upon both sides agreeing on the overall architecture of the interview and managing its intimate spaces – that is, agreeing on an emerging 'interactive etiquette' (Gumperz, 1992: 307). This can then lead to what Stivers calls 'affiliative alignment' (Stivers, 2008) where interviewers overtly display agreement, sympathy and joint imaginings and stories, giving a tone of relative (although still bureaucratic) intimacy and conversational involvement. (The interviewer's comment 'tough' in Tom's airport story in 6.4 is one such example.) But much of this alignment is done indirectly through speakers' moves and countermoves. Indeed, it is the relative capacity of candidates to manage the indirectness of the interactive etiquette and make appropriate inferences and interviewers' reactions to this which largely determine outcomes, as in the following example:

Example 36: Terence – Ghanaian Migrant, Successful

1. I: right] okay (.) erm and what was you really trying to do
2. C: oh we raised money and then (.)
3.   and it was an all students association so (.)
4.   we paid visits to old school (.)
5.   donated some (.) items like sanitary (.) bins and=
6. I: =right [okay
7. C: and some]times sponsored
8.   er:m prizes for (^ ^) day and=
9. I: ={(lo) right}=
10. C: =and that kind of thing
11. I: er:m (.) did you enjoy working (.) [in the group
12. C: yes I did] yeah=
13. I: =what did you enjoy most
14. C: erm there was (.) was erm the challenge of it
15.   cos erm some- some are very critical
16.   when things do:n't go right sometimes and (.)
17.   living up to that challenge
18.   was- was- was i- interesting for me (3)

In this response to the question on teamwork, Terence responds with the detailed action he took. He then reads the interviewer's backchannels as asking for closure (the low falling tone in line 9) on this topic and sums up at line 10. Then he reads the next questions on enjoying teamwork (lines 11 and 13) as cueing a different and more institutional discourse mode (lines 14–18). The sense that Terence would maintain a professional distance is reinforced by the more analytic style of speech which he adopts. He does not mention specific individuals and his personal feelings about them, but rather uses generalised responses and reactions to them such as 'interesting' and 'challenge.' These are institutionally acceptable means of conveying contained irritation with workmates – topically/lexically aligned – and not emotional self-disclosures of the kind which some less successful candidates provide in response to questions about 'enjoyment.' Terence negotiates a successful conversation by learning on the job, so to speak. His management of the two questions suggests that he has learnt the interviewers' interactive etiquette – how detailed to be, how to pick up closing signals and how to blend professional and institutional discourses.

Misalignment

The single most significant indicator of a negative dynamic is the high number of misalignments (including misunderstandings) and subsequent reformulations. Our coded data show that there were twice as many instances of traceable misalignments among the migrant group as among the British-born candidates.

Misalignments arise when both sides fail to work towards a common stance or manage the relationship between their different stances, when interactive frames are misinterpreted, when conventional modes of behaviour cannot be agreed on and when the interaction becomes uncomfortable and fractured. Candidates are then perceived as being socially discrepant.

Misalignments occur routinely in all interviews but to very different degrees, often only fleetingly, and with very different effects. They come in many forms. Some are simple mishearings, or slips of tongue and ear with brief requests for clarification. These are brief, uncomfortable moments which are usually readily identified and resolved, and do not appear to feed into interviewer evaluation. But most misalignments are difficult to identify or repair locally, often leading to reformulations, long phases of talking past each other and other interactional discomfort. These range from the more fundamental and intractable differences in the way candidates align to the implicit requirements of the interview, to more local misunderstandings like the misreading of contextualisation cues.

Early (mis)alignments can lead, even in the opening stages of the interview, to interviewers taking a subtly different stance towards the candidate. This can lead, cumulatively, to relatively more or fewer opportunities for candidates and more reinforcement of positive/negative judgments of them. For example, early on both Sara and Iqbal are reminded that the questions will be on topics that are 'key to managers.' However, this is presented to them differently – although it is the same interviewer. In Sara's case, the interviewer says:

> You'll find very similar to the previous interview format that we've done because *these are things that [Deliveries Ltd] is saying are key to managers succeeding* so again the focus is on things that you've done rather than hypothetical situations.

With Iqbal he says:

> What I'm looking at is a general area of improving things seeking improvement which *obviously is a key thing that we want managers to do* – can you give me an example where you had to learn a new working practice or procedure?

In Sara's example, the interviewer reinforces his institutional authority in presenting what [Deliveries Ltd] want; with Iqbal he assumes shared knowledge – 'obviously' and talk of 'we' – as if Iqbal could be included as a possible manager. And whereas he then immediately asks Iqbal a question, with Sara this is delayed while he talks about the conduct of the interview, implying her lack of expertise in managing it. While the question to Iqbal is a conventional means of eliciting professional discourse, Sara is arguably already positioned as too personal and requiring more institutional control. (Mis)alignments are jointly produced through indirectness, but once successful candidates and interviewers are thoroughly aligned then more explicit negotiations over relevance requirements and other more transgressive moves are allowed. When embroiled in misalignments, such explicit negotiations reinforce the uncomfortable moments.

In our data there were four main sources of alignment and misalignment relating to discursive, topic, sequential and contextual aspects of the interaction and, in many instances, more than one source at any one moment. Below, for example, Tina and the interviewer are both discursively and topically misaligned.

Chapter 5 has discussed how alignment and misalignment arise from the challenges of hybrid discourses. The other three sources are outlined here.

(Mis)alignment About Topic

Topical relevance depends upon inferences which are either interactionally sensitive – for example, linked to the location of follow-on questions – or are determined by sociocultural knowledge about work/self relations and definitions; for example, the degree of congruity between current jobs and the one being interviewed for (10.1, 10.4). Topical alignment can also be negotiated by candidates through clarification and metacommunication.

In Rakesh's interview, the precise location of follow-on questions may be a clue to their purpose. The interviewer asks a question about teamwork, and as a follow-on to this question he asks, 'So what did you enjoy about <u>this</u> work?' Rakesh responds by speaking about enjoying sorting out parcels, which is solitary work, and the interview is thrown off course for a few turns. The source of this misalignment is twofold: Interactionally, the interviewer does not make explicit the fact that he wants to know what Rakesh enjoyed about 'this' work, team working, which is implied in the placing of the question. Secondly, in terms of assumed knowledge, there is the fact that team working is generally acknowledged as something one ought to 'enjoy' in British work culture. There may also be a third source of misalignment in Rakesh's failure to respond to the slightly extra prominence on 'this' work, which signals co-reference with 'teamwork.' This lack of shared inferential conventions at the prosodic level may suggest a lack of coherence, as well as a lack of relevance (Gumperz, 1992: 322–324; 7.3).

Examples of such topic misalignments, related to assumed knowledge, occur repeatedly in interviews with some migrant candidates when they are asked about their daily work routine. However, they can also occur with local British candidates (example 37). This topic is usually slipped into larger questions as a subtopic by the interviewer, as it no longer has a clear place in the competence-based interview. Although apparently quite routine, questions like, 'What does your job involve?' are indirectly asking for the candidate to talk about their skills and the extent to which these are transferable. These vaguer and unembedded questions provide little shared context to cue an acceptable response.

Below is an example of a deeper misalignment by an unsuccessful candidate, which is not corrected by the interviewer. This shows that, whatever the social background of the candidate, there is potential for ambiguity in the relationship between character questions and the specific context created by expectations about the job applied for:

Example 37: Tina – White British, Unsuccessful

1. I: what about being organised
2.   or possibly methodical is a better way of putting it (.)
3.   do you see yourself as being that kind of person
4. C: I'm very picky
5. I: are you?
6. C: ooh I'm such a fusspot [hhh
7. I: tell] me how that- how that works
8. C: how that works ooh [God
9. I: either] at work or home=
10. C: =it was (.) just everything
11.   I'm quite a precise person if I- I like to-
12.   once I know how I'm doing it
13.   and I've been shown and ken like that and then (.)
14. I: mhm
15. C: and then even if I do adjust it to suit myself better slightly
16.   I'm I'm very oooh and if it doesn't work right
17.   I'm kind of like ooh God (.)
18.   but I am a very precise person (2)
19.   because even though they- there was
20.   another hand sewer that used to work the same

21.   and she's was like oh God (.) what're doing
22.   and I'm like it just has to be right
23.   I says I can't leave it alone unless it's right
24. I: right
25. C: I'm not (^ ^) in the sense if I'm not happy with it
26.   I'm like oh God (h) no
27. I: right

Here Tina misaligns to the purpose of the question, which she thinks is testing her precision and quality control – skills she has developed as a machinist. In fact, the interviewer is looking to test her ability to stay calm in a crisis and methodically organise her work. So the question is not about quality standards, which would be important for a skilled job, but about the general attitude which is appropriate for the unskilled packing job on offer. Tina also – at lines 6, 8, 16, 17, 21 and 26 – talks effusively and personally when the question cues a more analytic response, like many of the unsuccessful candidates described in chapter 5 who are discursively misaligned. As this topical misalignment is not repaired, Tina's answer is viewed negatively by the interviewer and was cited as the reason she failed the interview.

Sequential and Temporal (Mis)alignment

Sequential and temporal misalignments are a failure to align to the overall sequential organisation of the interview (Drew and Heritage, 1992) and its time constraints. Candidates are expected to orientate to the particular footing, interactional conventions and timing entailed in each phase – in other words, to the system requirements of the interview. In line with other research, our data shows that the interview typically falls into four stages, although high-level, graduate recruitment interviews tend to follow a more flexible structure with more weight given to selling the firm to the candidate and on the 'cultural match' between both (Bergström and Knights, 2006; Rivera, 2012). The four stages are ice-breaking (more informal), information about the job, interviewer questions and candidate questions.

Some candidates are apparently less aware of the fact that each stage requires a somewhat different participation structure, in terms of 'reciprocal and complementary communicative rights and obligations' (Erickson and Shultz, 1982: 22). Some candidates offer responses (other than listening cues) during the second stage, ask their own questions or introduce topics in the third stage and give comments or reflections rather than questions in the fourth stage – as Tahir, a British BAME candidate, does. Such conduct can be viewed by the interviewer as showing a 'lack of respect' and often makes them feel the need to keep a tighter control over the interview. However, the enforcement of these requirements by interviewers varies between different candidates and often successful candidates are allowed to – or are even praised for – transgressing these boundaries, playing with the interview game.

(Mis)alignment also arises out of managing the constraints of time in each phase and across the main five or six questions which usually structure the interview. The candidate's reading of the unspoken metric of each episode in the encounter affects the degree of alignment. Answers are often deemed too short or too long and the accepted turn length depends upon the particular phase of the interview and the design of the question. For example, in some of the low-paid job interviews, the routine questions to elicit the situation component of the STAR formula (names of workplaces etc.) can be answered with short turns.[36]

Contextual (Mis)alignments

Contextualisation, in signalling the frame for the interpretation of any utterance, both does the local work which jointly produces the other three (mis)alignments and also has the potential to nudge the inferential process one way or another at any moment, and so affect the ongoing judgment of candidate performance (8.2). Apparently small and fleeting interviewer prompts and cues help to navigate the structure of the interview and its role/relationships – or, if misread, lead to protracted misalignments. For example, interviewer minimal responses such as 'uh huh,' 'mhm' and 'yes' are cued prosodically as 'go ons' or 'finish offs,' depending on rising or low falling tunes. Local misunderstanding of these prosodic cues contributed to interviewers' perceptions that the candidate was overtalking and not listening to them. As with temporal misunderstandings, it was therefore more difficult to 'control' the interview (examples 64, 67 and 68). Conversely, some interviewer conduct suggested that candidates were being reticent and not playing the game of providing good data for the interviewers' boxes. In the following example Renard, who was a school PE teacher in Poland, misunderstands the prompts for elaborative comment or additional information about team working (lines 6–15). He simply latches on to the prompts with minimal agreements and the interviewer responds by talking for him rather than dealing with the underlying misalignment.

Example 38: Renard – Polish Migrant, Borderline Successful

1. I: okay (.) so oh- every exercise (.) [you put forward
2. C: so after that]
3. I: as a group
4. C: yeah
5. I: you- you discuss as a group to see whether-
6.   what is good about that=
7. C: =yeah=
8. I: or what is bad about it=
9. C: =yes=
10. I: =and I take it the good ones you take it (.)
11. C: yes=
12. I: =and the bad ones=
13. C: =yeah=
14. I: =you don't=
15. C: =yes
16. I: (30) (writing) okay (.) right so I mean looking back (.)
17.   what would you say the advantages are (.)
18.   as working as part of a team

7.4   Conversational Versus Institutional Interviews

The fundamental asymmetries of the interview mean that it is the interviewers who are responsible for the overall tone of the interview through questions, follow-ups and negotiations over (mis)alignment, as discussed above. The second part of the chapter examines in some detail how the range of interviewer questions and varying responses to candidate performance are used to create environments for each other, establish the developing 'feel' of the interview – socially coherent and interactionally comfortable or not, through alignments and misalignments – and determine final outcomes. But it is also common for particularly successful candidates like Pippa and Gladston to take on aspects of the interviewers' role by using some of their strategies – for example, negotiating the relevance of a topic before launching into it or actively establishing a turn-taking etiquette in which both sides jointly construct a response, thus improvising order in another way.

In some institutional settings, interviewers have a dual role, such as both advocate and judge. In the selection interview there is no such ambiguity, and yet interviewers can act in relatively more helpful or unhelpful ways as the interaction builds, easing open the gate with special help such as extra relevance work, or closing it firmly shut as they design their turns in response to candidate performance. The occupational psychological literature suggests that judgments are made early on in the interview (Posthuma et al., 2002) and while it is difficult to establish how consistently this happens, our data suggest that interviewer conduct is responsive to the perceived adequacy of candidate answers from the opening minutes – as in the contrastive examples of Sarah and Iqbal – and that most interviews follow a trajectory which creates a relatively more conversational or institutional footing. With the former, there is some relaxation of the interview structure as alignment increases. With the latter, developing misalignments cultivate a more formal footing where responses are more controlled, relevance requirements tightened and interviewers are distanced from candidates.

In our data, interviewer follow-up to the main question consists of a range of strategies, as suggested above – from simple clarificatory questions to more indirect forms of elicitation and means of controlling the interaction or conveying its unacceptable turn (fig. 7.1). And while these are separated out for analytic purposes, they are often contingent on each other; for example, embedded follow-on questions often lead to supportive confirmatory questions and statements by the interviewer. More helpful strategies are context rich and evoke a more personal engagement on the part of interviewers, such as secondary stories and embedded questions. Less helpful ones are geared to imposing the institutional frame, such as more reformulations and translations of candidate talk.

Figure 7.1. Questions and Interviewers' Follow-up and Responses

Follow-ons:	Reformulations:	Strategies for controlling/concluding topics:
Questions which elicit more information or ask for development of a point the candidate has made. These can be either open or closed and embedded or non-embedded question, but tend to be more open ended and embedded.	Reworking of a question in a similar form, with new phrasing or as a comment, usually because the question was inadequately answered. Includes translating answers into institutionally acceptable terms.	Reformulations, interruptive questions. Minimal responses to close down candidate responses.

Secondary stories: Stories which the interviewer tells in response to the candidates' talk.	Clarification questions: Questions which ask the candidate to make clear a point or piece of information which the interviewer is unsure of.	Non-question prompts, cues: Statements which elicit further responses, often with some embedding, e.g. 'I imagine that must have involved …' Giving the first part of an oppositional pair, for example, to elicit the second part from the candidate. These prompts may also preface embedded questions and the negotiation of relevance.

No single strategy falls, self-evidently, on either the conversational or institutional side of the fence – context is everything. For example, in Renard's teamwork question the interviewer uses prompts – which usually reflect a more positive, conversational dynamic – to elicit the result section of the story, but this leads to a misalignment. Misreading prompts tends to lead to more explicit strategies, such as reformulation. But here, despite the misalignment, the interviewer makes notes on what he said of Renard, rather than any comments on Renard's apparent reticence. This is one of many misalignments in the interview and yet, exceptionally, he saves rather than sinks Renard by persisting with more conversational strategies throughout. Like Renard's, the interviews of other borderline candidates – such as Ire, Iqbal (example 39) and Mohammed (8.8) – do not follow a consistently positive or negative dynamic. However, it is striking how the interview environment becomes increasingly conversational or institutional in most of our interview data and leads to a clear pass or fail outcome (fig. 7.2).[37]

Figure 7.2. Characteristics of More Conversational and Institutional Interviews

Conversational	Institutional
Follow-on questions, cues and prompts	Reformulations
Embedded questions	Unembedded questions
Co-authoring (including secondary stories) negotiating, metacommunicating	Constraining, 'translating'
Topic choice – opening up	Topic control – closing down

7.5 Conversational Interviews

The notion of 'conversational' draws on the CA theory that ordinary talk has the foundational elements for all talk-in-interaction, so that elements of casual conversation can leak into institutional talk – except in the most scripted encounters – as discussed above. While the interview is laminated over by the institutional and candidates must serve their institutional time, particularly in the early stages, many of the linguistic and pragmatic forms of social chat (Eggins and Slade, 1997; Carter and McCarthy, 2015) and of personal discourses more generally appear in more conversational interviews.

In addition, there is a relaxation of topic control and relevance requirements both offered by interviewers and negotiated by candidates, plus an easing of interactional control and overt asymmetry in terms of turn taking. In sum, a bureaucratic intimacy develops. For example, a clear pattern emerges from a set of three successful and three unsuccessful junior management interviews (fig. 7.3).

Figure 7.3. Contrastive Conversational Help in Junior Management Interviews

Candidates	No. of relevance negotiations, with follow-on questions and prompts	No. of embedded, helpful questions	No. of unembedded and unhelpful questions
Successful	11	75	13
Unsuccessful	2	33	64

Follow-On Questions, Cues and Prompts

These are contrasted with reformulations and aim to elicit more information or ask for a development of a point. They may also include straightforward clarificatory questions which do not imply unacceptable answers. In follow-on questions interviewers build on the candidate's contribution, explain the purpose of the question and give cues or more explicit prompts on how it might be answered. Frequently, these questions are prompts, followed by confirmatory statements as in the following example. Iqbal, a Panjabi British candidate who just missed being offered a junior management post, is explaining how he had to cordon off an unsafe area of the workplace:

Example 39: Iqbal – BAME British, Borderline Unsuccessful
(Example of good performance.)

1.   C: basically er as soon as I've become aware of it
2.   you know decided that was (.)
3.   that was a really our priority (.) erm
4.   and we had to make it safe (.) erm you know
5.   er also we have to stop people working around there
6.   because it really was in a bad condition (2)
7.   I: so what did you <u>do</u> about it
8.   C: w- wh- what we er initially did was
9.   to actually cordon off the area (.)
10.   by actually (.) putting some ((containers)) round it
11.   that's the only solution we could find hhh (.) erm
12.   you know once we you know blocked off that area (.)
13.   it was a quite big area an:d you know
14. I: mhm
15. C: made sure that people still were able to go past it
16. I: sure [sure
17. C: erm] but erm er felt that that was a ((doesn't help)) really
18.   because of all the containers that we decided to put round it
19. I: mhm
20. C: people would want to use those
21. I: sure (.) no (.)
22.   people are going to take the containers away aren't they
23. C: so- so- so what I said to (xxx)
24.   because it actually affected (xxx) mainly
25.   I said to him that you need to you know
26.   erm brief his team immediately

After a two-second pause, the interviewer in line 7 asks Iqbal a follow-on
question which encourages him to give the action component of the requi-
site narrative structure and display what he has done to resolve a problem,
thus helping him to align discursively to the expected narrative structure. The
'do' in line 7 is given extra prominence, a contextualisation cue to Iqbal that
his earlier response about making the area safe (line 4) now needs elabora-
tion. So this follow-on question is both an explicit prompt to say more and
also a nudge that this additional accounting should be more grounded and
experiential.

At lines 21–22 the interviewer confirms his approval of Iqbal's answer, in a moment of co-authoring (8.9). Overall, this response is highly rated by the interviewer, who himself contributed to the outcome. Such prompts are frequently used to help candidates reach institutional completion in their next response.

Embedded Questions and Shared Contexts

Felicitous interviews depend upon calling up shared contexts and shared worlds (6.4), as well as co-membership, to establish an ongoing contextual alignment. Here co-membership often has a somewhat different force from Erickson and Shultz's definition as involving 'particularistic attributes of (shared) status,' like shared interests or being part of the same community (Erickson and Shultz, 1982: 17). In job interviews such membership is either more local or more diffuse; arising, for example, from specific things in common such as direct knowledge of the same work, or joint imaginings of what work or other experience might be like. Alternatively, it forms a more diffuse 'membership' of agreeing about the way the world works; for example, how young people can be tearaways (6.4, 6.5). Two interrelated means of establishing this loose co-membership occurred frequently in the data: the use of embedded questions and the establishment of shared points of reference.

Embedded questions call up actual or real information which helps to construct a shared definition of the work context and the purpose of the interview (6.4). So for example, the interviewer might ask for an experience of teamwork in one of two ways:

1. **Embedded:** 'When you were working in X job, how did you work with colleagues to achieve Y task?'

2. **Non-embedded:** 'Could you give me an example of a time when you worked with others to achieve something?'

Successful candidates tend to be asked more embedded questions. These questions tend to advantage the candidate because they give him or her more information about the form and content expected in their answer.

When candidates have previous experience of working in the organisation, or experience which is imaginable to the interviewers, embedded questions and shared experience become mutually reinforcing. If sufficient context is negotiated early in the interview, then the narrative becomes a 'text' which acts as a shared point of reference, with comments such as the conversational, 'You'll be used to working nights now anyway.' This text is useful as a shorthand way of calling up a raft of potentially relevant work experiences, is readily transposable into a written document and also contributes to mutual alignment and sense of sharedness. Pippa's discursive alignment to the inter-viewers has already been illustrated (5.5). So too has how she plays with the rules of the interview game (2.3). Here we see the bridging section between the story of working in opticians and the blending of hybrid discourses, which she displays in the last few lines of this extract and which were illustrated in example 17:

Example 40: Pippa – White British, Successful

1. I.1: okay that's all right erm (.)
2.   what about in oth- other jobs er were there changes
3.   ei- either because the nature of the job changed
4.   while you were ther:e
5.   or you moved into something that was very different
6.   from what you've previously had experience of (.)
7.   because your work in (xxx) opticians
8.   must have been a little bit different
9. C: mhm well what p- between the two companies or
10. I.1: yeah
11. C: or as in (.)
12. I.1: er- I mean (.) that's quite an unusual you know
13.   actually making the spectacles
14. C: mhm
15. I.1: erm (.) and the time pressure
16.   that- that you're under to achieve that
17. C: mhm
18. I.1: that must have been quite different
19.   from just about anything else you've ever worked in
20. C: erm well it is I think
21.   t- m- majority of the jobs that I have worked in
22.   I have been erm customer focussed
23.   and <u>deadlines</u> and under pressure (.)
24.   hhh erm <u>catering</u> I've [m- you know
25. I.1: mhm]

Here, a basis of shared knowledge has already been established through a series of exchanges and jokes about experiences of work in the organisation where the interview is being held – and where Pippa has been working on a temporary basis – and her work in the opticians. This is referred to by the interviewer as he imaginatively invests in how different it must have been, in lines 7–8, 12–13, and 18–19. He embeds the question in his previous knowledge of the candidate, which itself has been gained through the conversationalising of the interview. It was common in similar environments for interviewers to cue their investment with terms such as, 'I imagine.' Here, one can see the self-perpetuating nature of the overall emotional tone at work and the increasing co-membership which results.

Co-Authoring/Negotiating

Embedded questions are on a cline of helpfulness: from grounding the question in more concrete detail, to the kind of imaginative investment shown above to a collaborative, mirroring act in which interviewers reciprocate with a secondary story themselves and the interview is explicitly co-authored. Co-authoring is contrasted with 'translating,' where the interviewer draws a unilateral conclusion from the candidate's contribution (8.9). Both co-authoring and translating are 'formulations' used to summarise, gloss or develop the gist of the previous speaker (Heritage and Watson, 1979). In job interviews, however, these are not neutral turns but actively promote either a more positive and conversational or negative and institutional dynamic. In the next example, Gladston explains how he has changed the work rota form:

Example 41: Gladston – Jamaican Migrant, Successful

1. I: so] what (.) okay so you you amended the (xxx)
2.   basically [which
3. C: yeah]
4. I: sort of then told you
5.   exactly where everybody was supposed to be [including
6. C: or or] when's my rest day if another manager comes in
7.   he could just look at it=
8. I: =okay [fine
9. C: with- with]out having to=
10. I: =so on an individual basis
11.   so wh- Joe Bloggs works at ((xxx)) delivery office
12.   that told me throughout the whole week where I should be
13. C: yeah exactly=
14. I: =including [your rest days
15. C: erm who's where] who is what and [where
16. I: so] wh- why did you do that what was the purpose of doing it
17. C: er:m the purpose is is just to simplify…

At line 1, after Gladston's evaluation of his own story, the interviewer echoes Gladston's story and evaluation format. At lines 5–9 a sequence of overlaps and latches helps to co-construct the story; the interviewer takes this up at line 10 and then presents a hypothetical secondary story himself at lines 11–12, signalling his imaginative investment in the story and co-authoring it with him. The interviewer at line 16 then cues for further analysis with another overlap, which maintains the turn-taking etiquette already established. (He seems to start this cue at line 1, then delays it in order to confirm and endorse what Gladston has told him so far.) So the cue for more analysis helps the topic to develop, rather than being an abrupt switch of topic. In other words, it is more conversational. Secondary stories were usually markers of a more relaxed overall emotional tone but, with a few interviewers, were used in a more pedagogic capacity to model an expected answer (6.3).

There is a similar sequence of supportive overlaps in the following example, where the interview is for a receptionist post in a hospital medical records office:

Example 42: Natalie – BAME British, Successful (for Another Post)

1. I: okay well what about the patient who rings up
2.   and says I'm the patient can I have a photograph
3. C: (h) um (h) well I'll have to
4.   I'll have to ask the consultant or (h) um
5.   I'm not sure about I think I'll have to ask (h)
6. I: okay but it's le- [it's le
7. C: ah but it] will still remain confidential
8. I: absolutely
9. C: it would [still
10. I: yep]
11. C: remain [confidential
12. I: yep]
13. C: because=
14. I: =is [it's d'y
15. C: it would be] the property of the trust by now
16.   [wouldn't it so
17. I: yeah yeah]

The interviewer and Natalie have already established a conversational rhythm in which both sides tolerate a high level of overlapping speech, with minimal responses from the interviewer, as illustrated in lines 6–17. Natalie quickly reads line 6 as a possible objection, not just a minimal response, adjusting her response so that long reformulation sequences are prevented. Having repaired her first attempt (lines 4–5), in line 7 she reinforces her 'correct' answer – 'It will still remain confidential' – by repeating it (lines 9 and 11), and by giving a rationale for her answer (line 15). All three responses are punctuated rhythmically by positive responses from the interviewer. So although she seems a little hesitant and possibly nervous initially, as her audible breathing suggests in lines 3–5, the rhythmic coordination and speedy inferencing serve her well.

The most telling case of co-authoring occurred with Emma, a white British candidate, being interviewed for a supervisory post in a food factory:

Example 43: Emma – White British, Successful

1. I: we then ask people to be flexible you know
2.   you could cook noodles today (.)
3.   we could put you on batching today
4. C: yeah [that's not a problem
5. I: (^ ^)] there's no issue with you being flexible
6. C: no cos that comes with (xxx) though doesn't it
7.   wherever you work [you have to be flexible
8. I: yeah we- we- we'd] like everybody
9.   to be flexible yeah yeah
10. C: that's always been ((something))
11. I: ((but)) obviously some people also quote
12.   once I'm a sauce cook
13. C: {I'm a sauce cook} no [it's

(mimics the voice of a 'rigid' worker)

14. I: I'm] a sauce cook yeah exactly
15. C: no
16. I: but we expect flex- sort of flexibility
17.   do you know what I mean (.) it just helps the company
18. C: of course

As well as high levels of shared knowledge and joint contextualisation, both sides echo each other's words and rhythmically coordinate the story, with conversational overlaps. The crux of this short segment is at lines 5–10 where they jointly co-author the image of the inflexible sauce cook, with the candidate upgrading the quote at line 12 to a minidrama at line 13. So the agreement at line 18 is more than just a compliant response, since she has already acted out and distanced herself from the inflexible worker she mimics. This is in contrast to Sara's ventriloquising, which the interviewer uses to sink her (6.5).

Opening Up Topics

Successful candidates can open up the set menu of topics prescribed by the institution and go more à la carte. So, more wide-ranging discussions are a marker of success (Adelsward, 1988). Most of the relevance negotiations concern allowable topics or clarification of topics, so that candidates can align themselves more effectively to the often hidden purpose of the interview. This act of negotiation both makes the interview more conversational and elicits more helpful information from interviewers, which also contributes to a more symmetrical interaction. For example, Ahmed is asked about customer service but his only relevant experience for this delivery job has been working in a mailroom. Before detailing his experience, he negotiates the relevance of serving colleagues rather than customers: 'Where a customer in a sense is like a member of staff.' Having successfully done this, the interviewer then scaffolds the question with a series of prompts and confirmatory statements so that the flow of the interview remains unbroken. Successful interviews regularly display this relationship between negotiating relevance and supportive follow-ons and prompts, producing a cooperative environment which cushions any possible institutional blows. Negotiation of topic also helps a joint glide into new and even seemingly irrelevant topics, rather than a narrowing of topic or abrupt topic shifts common in less successful interviews.

The consummate negotiator in our data set is Gladston, who repeatedly reworks the interviewer's questions so that he can answer on his terms. Negotiating what experience could be used to answer a question, as in the next example, was quite frequent in competence-based interviews, since often a particular job could be used to illustrate a range of competences:

Example 44: Gladston – Jamaican Migrant, Successful

1. I: okay thank you very much (.) er:m
2.   going to my next question (.) er:m (2)
3.   can you give me an example (.)
4.   of when you've helped someone (.)
5.   to get appropriate development or training (1)
6.   I'm talking about inspiring people here
7. C: yeah yeah yeah er:m (2) appropriate development [er:m
8. I: yeah] or training or you know (2)

9. C: er (2) development erm
10. I: coaching [that
11. C: coaching] coaching er:m I- if (2)
12.   if you could- if I could to refer back to er gymnastics time again
13. I: yeah yeah
14. C: in my life (.) yeah like I mean I know there's other things
15.   but at the moment that's what's in my mind
16.   so I'll tell you that [(((I was))
17. I: let let's] explore it [let's see
18. C: erm we can] explore it okay I'll [see
19. I: yeah]
20. C: if it's appropriate if it [fits
21. I: yeah]
22. C: er:m basically as when when I started
23.   as as a erm a gymnast erm trainer
24. I: yeah
25. C: erm I noticed that (.)

This shows the interviewer and Gladston not only negotiating on the allowable reuse of a job experience, but also on the grounds for negotiation (lines 12–21). They treat this as if it was a discussion among colleagues in which a decision is jointly agreed, using metacommunicative resources to step aside from the moment to agree the conditions on which the topic might 'fit.'

The relaxation of the interview structure also leads to more tolerance of candidate extended narrative – allowing some digression, more examples and more contextual information, but often framed with metacommunicative work to show awareness of the institutional frame – as is the case for Pippa, Gladston and Tom. Other local transgressions include candidates asking interviewers about their work. Both candidates and interviewers also occasionally break the 'rules of the game' again by making ironic comments about the interview situation and, in the case of interviewers, apologising for having to ask an institutionally required question which seems at odds with the conversational footing established. Such rule breaking, as Bourdieu points out, is only allowed of those who are 'fish in water,' who know the rules and can break them (Bourdieu and Wacquant 1992). By raising the institutional habitus of the interview to a level at which it can be scrutinised, both sides show their recognition of its institutional order while also demonstrating their ironic reflection on it.

The structure is also relaxed and there is more improvisation at the level of the whole activity. Successful candidates are not necessarily asked all the set questions and not all questions are given the same weighting. In some cases, difficult or negative questions were not dwelt on or asked at all (see also similar findings in Kerekes, 2003: 31 and in immigration interviews by Jacquemet, 2005: 13). For instance, questions about disadvantages of team-work or boring work are often dealt with in a perfunctory way. Lacunae in interview targets arise from and are judged in very different environments, depending upon the candidate's degree of success. In successful interviews, they are passed over; in unsuccessful ones, they become problems as time runs out or misalignments remain unresolved.

7.6   Institutional Interviews

These interviews entail more following and recording of institutional proce-dures to produce defensible reasons for (possible) rejection. They become increasingly formal and tightly structured, with both topic and relevance requirements controlled more firmly. Through institutional discourses, inter-viewers position themselves as merely representatives of the institution and distance themselves from their own speech; in terms of bodily conduct, they are less socially engaged (5.6). For example, the written form of questions is more relied on and follow-up questions tend to be in institutional dis-course mode: 'How were those changes communicated to you?' or 'Before the changes were implemented, did you have opportunity to discuss them beforehand?' In sum, there is more 'animation of words [the interviewers] had no hand in formulating' (Goffman, 1981: 146–147). For example, Sara's interviewer increasingly positions himself as merely a representative of the institution by decreasing eye contact, writing more and becoming an 'ani-mator' of institutional terms rather than author or principal (5.6; Roberts and Campbell, 2005).

This heightened institutionalisation leads to more closed questions and more main questions repeated verbatim, and so more misalignments generally and discursive misalignments in particular, as Thornborrow has also identified (Thornborrow, 2002: 53). Unexpected candidate responses can also lead to interviewer lack of fluency, with hesitations and false starts which can make their questions less processable for candidates. In one respect, these interviews also fracture the interview structure and lead to sequential misalignments as well. Doubts about candidates can cause the insertion of unscheduled ques-tions focussing on motivation ('Why do you want the job?'), challenging the candidate's suitability ('Would you consider a different job?') or highlighting negatives ('Is time management an issue for you?'). Such questions often lead to topical misalignments and protracted and unresolved reformulation sequences. So heightened institutionalisation has the effect of emphasising interviewers' membership of the organisation and fluency in its idiom, as well as the outsider status of the candidate.

Reformulations

As with the 'hyper-explanations' identified in asynchronous counselling sessions (Erickson and Shultz, 1982: 121–122), reformulations are an ambiguous resource. Their surface purpose is to produce clarity and elicit processable responses. However, in contrast to the prompts and follow-ons in the more conversational interviews, reformulations occur much more frequently in institutional interviews in both low-level and promotion interviews.

In comparisons between three successful and three unsuccessful candidates for junior management posts, the number of reformulations versus follow-on questions, prompts and cues indexing more conversational interviews, is telling.

Figure 7.4. Contrastive Use of Reformulations in Junior Management Interviews

Candidates	No. of reformulations	No. of follow-ons	No. of prompts and cues
Successful	25	73	51
Unsuccessful	55	12	12

Reformulations tend to index trouble, since they occur most frequently as responses to perceived misalignments. In a sample of twenty-five interviews for low-paid jobs, there are three times as many reformulations in interviews with migrant candidates as in interviews with the two other groups. Also, the relationship between misalignments and reformulation differs between migrant candidates and others.

While the large number of reformulations is partly accounted for by the greater number of misalignments in the migrant candidate interviews, there are on average more reformulations per misalignment with this group. With white British and BAME candidates, the number of reformulations closely corresponds to the number of misalignments. However, with the migrant group there are nearly double the number of reformulations and reformulation sequences are longer. 'Short' reformulation sequences consist of three or four turns or less; any sequences longer than three or four turns are counted as 'long' reformulation sequences. With migrant candidates, there are about twenty-five per cent more long reformulations. Both these differences suggest a more generalised unease with the communicative environment which is being jointly constructed and indicate that misalignments are less quickly and effectively resolved between interviewers and migrant candidates (see chapter 9).

Routinely, reformulations lead to several other difficulties, cornering candidates into a defensive position and often doing little to repair misalignments. Most importantly, they restrict allowable answers. Many of the narrowing and closed questions in reformulations lead to more low-level questions, and these in turn restrict candidate contributions by eliciting less reflective, analytical or lively responses than the competence-based interview requires. This 'talking down' phenomenon constructs the candidate as less competent and is also less processable. For example, in Luis's interview the interviewer shifts down from a more analytic questions such as, 'What do you like most about working in a team?' to, 'What do you like, young people or old people?' In turn, these minimal responses lead to hyper-questioning as in the example from his interview below.

Reformulations, like the unscheduled questions mentioned above, are often critical questions or comments which force candidates into a defensive position – 'That would have been a better time to pick it up,' 'Is there not a danger there er that what you are actually doing is a manager doing delivery work?' 'That's debatable,' 'But that was in India,' or 'You don't' find that work boring?' for example. Candidates can either defend their position or agree, but both can lead to negative evaluation as in Brian's example, below.

When the interview is going badly, interviewer and candidate appear to have fewer interactional resources with which to repair misalignments and misunderstandings – or the very resources which caused trouble in the first place are the only ones available to attempt to repair it. Seventy-one per cent of all unrepaired misalignments or misunderstandings occurred in unsuccessful interviews. Of these unrepaired misalignments, the majority occurred in interviews with migrant candidates.

Unembedded Questions and Minimal Context

Typically in more institutional interviews, the questions are either near-repetitions or either/or questions, as in the example from Luis's interview just mentioned. Few are embedded in the candidate's story or in any jointly constructed context, and so lead to more contextual and topical misalignments. With Nanak, who is seeking an upgrade in the food factory, the lack of an agreed developing shared context leads to an extended topic misalignment and to rapid topic shifting.

Example 45: Nanak – Indian Migrant, Clearly Unsuccessful

1. I: do you understand what sauce cooking involves (.)
2.   do you know [obviously yeah
3. C: yeah] yeah I know about that every sauc- sauces
4.   about jalfrezi sauce
5. I: uhuh
6. C: madras sauce (^ ^) sauce mhm
7.   hurti masala parthi masala
8. I: right
9. C: moona sauce mint sauce=
10. I: =okay
11. C: many sauces
12. I: so you cooked all these sauces [at (xxx)
13. C: mhm] just like jalfrezi sauce
14. I: uhuh
15. C: I can cook easily no problem
16. I: okay so what what type of cooking vessels
17.   did they have at (xxx) (.)
18.   what was (xxx) factory kitchen like
19. C: yeah
20. I: what was it like (2)
21. C: mhm
22. I: how [many sauces
23. C: many] sauces has been cooked there
24. I: yeah
25. C: mhm like I work in on the (xxx)
26.   and there was cooking
27.   e- (.) has been cooked er jalfrezi sauce
28. I: yeah
29. C: madras sauce (.) hurti masala furti masala [these
30. I: so have] you seen the factory kitchen vessels
31. C: yeah [I have
32. I: you] know the pots that you cook that you cook in [are
33. C: yeah]
34. I: they similar to (xxx) or different to (xxx)
35. C: mhm I didn't see here any properly

The interviewer's two open questions at lines 1 and 18, which assume a
shared understanding of 'what sauce cooking *involves*' and 'what was (xxx)

factory kitchen *like*,' only hint that she is looking for a grounded description of the process of cooking sauces and of the equipment and practices in the kitchen. As mentioned above, general questions about work processes are not adequately framed for migrant candidates and require higher levels of inferencing. Nanak's assertion of his knowledge does not align with the institutional assumption that knowledge must be displayed and evidenced through talk. And while, at line 16, the 'cooking vessels' question is a reformulation to elicit a description of the process, both lexically and topically it appears too removed from Nanak's expectations of what counts as an acceptable response. As with many other unsuccessful candidates, misalignments and more narrow and institutional interviewer questions come in many forms and pile on each other. So reformulations, unembedded hyper-questioning and talking down work together to prevent any chance of repair.

Constraining and Translating

Constraints are relaxed in successful interviews, as we have shown, with co-authoring, rapid uptake of prompts and cues, joint context building and positive confirmatory statements. In more institutional interviews, many of the solidarity strategies common in conversational ones are replaced with distancing ones, often done indirectly with backchannels such as 'right,' 'OK' and 'I understand that.' As noted above, these can lead to contextual misalignments when interviewer intentionality is misinterpreted and 'finish-offs' are read as 'go-ons' or acceptances of an adequate response.

The inferential labour of such contextualisation cues is even harder when interviewers' dismissive stances are laminated over with additional politeness. Some interviewers, when watching extracts of their video where they were giving positive confirmatory statements such as, 'Yes, that's lovely thank you,' remarked that they disagreed with the candidates' response or it was not what they were looking for. Such overly polite or effusive comments act as compensatory, as well as closing strategies. This produces a type of Batesonian 'complementary schismogenesis' (Bateson, 1972), in which failing candidates read apparently appreciative comments as 'go-ons' when interviewers want to finish off. This in turn leads to more talk from candidates and more desire to end the interview from interviewers. Institutionalised failure requires more ceremonial work, which is face-saving for the interviewer but damaging to the candidate.

The gap between candidates' ideal responses and their actual talk is an ongoing problem for the interviewer in their task of improvising order. In increasingly institutional interviews, this gap is managed by 'translating' candidate talk into an institutionally acceptable record – 'so *this* is what you are saying.' This is contrasted with the incorporation of candidate responses, and instead initiates a sudden discursive shift to a more institutional mode. These statements are particularly powerful, since they ask candidates to confirm completed propositions rather than shape the content of what was discussed (Thornborrow, 2002: 25). When these are negative translations, as in the next example from a junior management post, they can then trigger further negative sequences in which candidates struggle to defend themselves:

Example 46: Brian – BAME British, Clearly Unsuccessful

1. C: trying to getting people to understand that
2.   you know these things need to be done erm
3.   and that we do sometimes have to look at
4.   reappraising how we do things
5. I: okay so some were reluctant to embrace it
6.   is that what you're saying
7. C: some were reluctant to embrace it er:m

Here, Brian is describing his role in introducing a new piece of software to offices. The interviewer rephrases his comments negatively, suggesting that 'some were reluctant to embrace it.' In agreeing with the interviewer, the candidate colludes in his own failure. From then on (data not shown here), the interaction revolves around whether this reluctance could be attributed to Brian's ineffectual efforts to persuade. Even when the translations are neutral or positive, their persistent use – particularly when they are quite distant from the original candidate talk – can contribute to more infelicitous encounters. Candidates who were repeatedly given such translations were criticised by the interviewer, with comments such as, 'I had to give him the answer.' These assessments could be transferred to judgments of the candidate's character – that they would require 'spoon-feeding,' or would not take on responsibility.

Topic Control – Closing Down

The high level of 'talking down' with unsuccessful candidates means that they have fewer opportunities to initiate topics, as well as being boxed in by reformulations. There is also less gliding between topics and more structured question-and-answer routines, often drilling down to an increasingly narrow focus, as a result of stricter relevance requirements – which itself can produce topic misalignment. This is in sharp contrast to the topical alignment and the kind of conversational gliding between topics and tolerated digressions seen in conversational interviews. Luis's storytelling (6.2) is an instance of sudden shifts of topic; his repeated attempts to initiate topics are disallowed by the interviewer. At points throughout the rest of this interview there are more interruptions and struggles over turns and Luis commented to the researcher at the end of the interview that he felt there were some 'time constraints' on his responses. These sudden interruptions and shifts in topic have a clear negative impact on the candidate's fluency, ability to structure turns at talk and to align to the requirements of the new topic.

Similarly, rapid topic shifts and more closed questions are frequent in Ravi's junior management interview as the interview presses for more grounded accounts and fewer responses in institutional discourse mode. In the next example, Ravi is describing how he deals with difficult customers, especially those who buy DVDs, record them and then return them:

Example 47: Ravi – Panjabi Migrant, Clearly Unsuccessful

1. C: (.) and if I find it genuine (.)
2.   I would make a refund or exchange
3.   depending on the circumstances
4.   if you have a genuine damage (.) yes you do (.)
5.   but if it comes to the younger generation
6.   you have to be a bit cautious (.) and talk to them
7. I: and wh- what would you regard
8.   the percentage of customers that are dishonest (.)
9.   if I asked you what the percentage was (.)
10.   what in your view would be the percentage of customers
11.   who are dishonest
12. C: that's a very difficult question weren't it (.)
13.   I would put it into age groups (1)
14. I: yeah (.) go on (.) yeah that's fine
15. C: er in the UK I would say the younger generation yes (.)
16. I: percentage
17. C: (0.5)
18. I: say ((our fruit bowl of customers))
19.   say average customer erm (.)
20.   no no we'll do it as a group (.)
21.   say an average customer for this store would pay (.)
22.   perhaps fifty thousand customers per week (.)
23.   how many of those do you feel are dishonest in your eyes (.)
24.   this isn't a trick question by the way

At lines 7–8 the interviewer switches from customer skills to a hypothetical question, without acknowledging or developing Ravi's previous answer, and poses a 'difficult question' which Ravi begins to answer at line 12, before pausing at line 17. The interviewer warms to his theme and presses Ravi further for an answer, with a hypothetical situation removed from the specifics of customer care and interaction. This topic switch indicates that he is not satisfied with the more organisational, general response that Ravi gives, and so starts looking for precise figures. In his evaluation, Ravi is criticised for 'no examples,' 'irrelevant answers' and speaking in 'generalisations.' But as this example shows, it is the interviewer's questions – even though they are not intended as 'trick' questions (line 24) – which contribute to these negative evaluations.

Post-hoc reactions to the more restricted institutional interviews were of two types. Many unsuccessful candidates (particularly migrant candidates) seemed unaware that the interview had gone badly. But the comments of others showed their awareness of how institutional the interview was; for example, that the interview was stiff and formal, that they could not build up a rapport with interviewers or read their responses and had little in common with them, as Binta remarks (above). Some felt they were asked negative questions because interviewers were 'unsure' of them and that they were not able to get across experiences or points they had wanted to raise because of 'time pressures.' For unsuccessful BAME and migrant candidates, both types of responses may feed into perceived discrimination.

Conclusion

Over thirty years ago, Erickson and Shultz described the paradox of maintaining standardisation, universalistic criteria and objectivity in a face-to-face interview, where all manner of information leaks in from the outside and the weight of the social encounter produces a flow of intersubjective reactions and evaluative impressions (Erickson and Shultz, 1982: 37–40). It is the nature of all gatekeeping encounters that such dialectics exist, a fact summed up in some of the oxymorons in this chapter: ceremonial labour, improvising order and bureaucratic intimacy. The wiggle room that such encounters produce easily leads to more conversationally aligned and convivial moods where both sides work up and agree on the 'cultural order' (Holmes, 2018) or, conversely, leads to more misaligned moments that trigger more institutional propriety and rigidity. Attempts to prevent the wiggles in strict equal opportunity interviews are self-defeating.

Although interviewers control the interaction, they are in many respects subject to the same communicative dilemmas as candidates. It is not a simple matter of interviewer incompetence or assumptions. Rather, it is the institutional regime and its failure to acknowledge interview dialectics that produce inequality. In the next chapter, the hidden processes of evaluation explore how these inequalities lead to final assessments which indirectly discriminate.

8 Decision-making: Institutional Evaluation, Local Practices and Writing the Interview

Understanding and critiquing the processes of job interviewing and its role in producing inequalities entails looking beyond the interview talk. While chapters 5–7 focussed on the discursive and interactional work of both interviewers and candidates in performing their institutional selves, this chapter picks up some of the themes introduced in chapters 2, 3 and 4, connecting what is brought into the interview with what is taken away from it. Accounting for how decisions come to be produced opens up the analysis to many layers of context and to how voices and texts move across and change as the context changes.

Transcontextual analysis looks at text trajectories (Mehan, 1993; Blommaert, 2001; Maryns, 2013; Maybin, 2017; 3.6). This analysis moves from the voices and resources played out in the interactional moment, through the discursive pathways that can be specifically traced from these moments, to the systems and discourses of particular institutions/organisations and then to the wider bureaucratic and post-bureaucratic discourses of the workplace. And since the selection interview is not a bounded activity, these contextual layers leak into each other at all points. For example, the note-taking procedure in the job interview both produces texts which (potentially) feed into the wash-up/decision-making stage – and even into industrial tribunal cases on unfair selection – but also creates perturbation in the interactional flow which can affect how the candidate is evaluated. Similarly, the structures of the bureaucratic workplace are routinely transformed into everyday practices such as typical and banal questions, which in turn remind interviewers of the boundaries and categories which continuously sustain the institution (2.4).

The first part of this chapter opens with a brief discussion of the intensely evaluative experience of the job interview and how the decision-making process draws on its norms and conventions to produce a highly subjective assessment of candidates. The second part connects the interactive analysis of earlier chapters to the writing process in the interview and shows how writing the interview helps to shape its conduct and sheds light on its overall emotional tone.

8.1 The Evaluative Instinct in the Interactional Moment

In chapter 1, I made the provocative statement that job interviews are designed to discriminate and of course the activity of selection is defined by its requirement to make decisions about candidates. It is thus one of the most intensely evaluative occasions experienced in a bureaucratic society and produces, in Foucault's terms, 'a certain position, a certain gaze and a certain function' (Foucault, 1984: 112). Social evaluation implies some shared level of judgment about others – both in the most ordinary and routine of encounters, and in charged and potentially life-changing events. In psychotherapy, for example, it is used to relate and understand, while in asylum interviews, the right to remain is assessed; in life-threatening assessments, the shibboleth test (McNamara and Roever, 2006) will decide if you are friend or enemy. The inherently evaluative nature of all talk – 'There is no such thing as a word without evaluative accent' (Vološinov et al., 1973: 103 [1929]) – means any interaction comes with risks.

The idea of interaction as risky has long been associated with Goffman. He talks of every social situation as 'an environment of mutually *monitoring* possibilities' (Goffman, 1971: 63, my italics) so that 'life may not be much of a gamble, but interaction is' (Goffman, 1959: 243). And the business of interaction is such high-stakes because the small things of interaction have large consequences:

> The human tendency to use signs and symbols means that *evidence of social worth* and of mutual evaluations will be conveyed by very minor things, and these things will be witnessed, as will the fact that they have been witnessed. An unguarded glance, a momentary change in tone of voice, an ecological position taken drench the talk … with judgmental significance. (Goffman, 1971: 33, my italics)

If the routine of managing the social traffic of everyday life is risky, how much higher is the risk of self-presentation in the job interview, when the smallest slip can be amplified and used in evidence against the candidate on both competence and moral grounds (7.1). Some judgments are made early on and the overall emotional tone and footing of the interview is driven by continuous assessment.

Although talk is the object of intense focus, 'communication' – despite being top of the competence hierarchy – is not thematised in the interview design nor in most wash-up sessions, with only the occasional remark about 'listening.' It is taken as a proxy for other skills and personal attributes although, with failing migrant candidates, language is frequently topicalised. So despite being taken as a bounded set of skills, communication is routinely bundled up with character and personality and implicitly assessed through the total business of the interview. Unlike the experts used in oral language testing or asylum seekers' interview, where 'language analysis' is used to test nationality claims (Eades, 2010), interviewers use 'indigenous assessments' (Jacoby and McNamara, 1999) – their own professional and common sense experience – to assess communication.

8.2 Contextualisation Cues as Evaluative Tools

These general indigenous assessments derived from the fleeting moments of interaction are theorised in Gumperz's concept of conversational inference (1.5), where every act of interpreting is an act of evaluation in which particularistic leakage is inevitable:

> Conversational inference, as I use the term, is the situated or context-bound process of interpretation, by means of which participants in an exchange *assess* others' intentions and on which they base their responses. (Gumperz, 1982: 153, my italics)

While it is theoretically possible to draw any inference from an utterance – interpretations are 'open' (Garfinkel, 1967: 301–324) – Gumperz argues that they tend to be based on interactants' communicative signs in interaction; on the framing work that contextualisation cues do. As was mentioned earlier (1.5), these cues are not subject to conscious control or awareness nor do they have stable core meanings and so can only prompt, guide or nudge. Yet they cue immediate judgments about the competence and adequacy of speakers. So their function in forming and affecting social relationships goes largely unnoticed. They are hidden in plain sight, as this next example shows. Here, Vijay and the interviewers do not share the inferential processes which depend upon 'socially constructed knowledge of what the interview is about' (Gumperz, 1992: 303). While conveying confidence, Vijay does not seem to be adequately socialised into the 'institutionalised networks of relationships'

(Gumperz, 1996: 401) where the language games of institutional life are routinely acted out.

In this short segment from Vijay's interview with two interviewers for a receptionist post in a hospital, he is asked about whether he would prefer a front stage or back stage job – that is, dealing with the public or in an office behind the scenes. He responds that he could do either because he has worked for two years as a ward clerk in India:

Example 48: Vijay – Indian Migrant, Unsuccessful

1.   C: so I'm not afraid of anything
2.   I.1: but that's obviously [in India
3.   C: right]
4.   I.1: not here hhh
5.   C: (nods) that's in India yeah
6.   All: hhh=
7.   C: =but patients are patients
8.   I.1: (clears throat loudly) (looks at I.2 still laughing)
9.   [debatable
10. I.2: well (^ ^)]
11. C: I'm not here to debate because you are more experienced
12. I.1: yeah

This interview is discussed in more depth in 10.5. Here it is interesting to see how the negative evaluation of Vijay in the wash-up session arises from the frame mismatches and other misalignments based on how different contextualisation cues provide situated assessments of intent. Gumperz argues that these are powerful cues which function in three ways (Gumperz, 1992a: 232–233): in terms of processability and perception, to segment the stream of speech; pragmatically, to interpret intentionality and be sensitive to interpersonal relations; and metapragmatically, to manage expectations of how to conduct an encounter. These surface features function metapragmatically in that they cue

> what is to be expected in the exchange, what should be lexically expressed, what can be conveyed only indirectly, how moves are to be positioned in an exchange, what interpersonal relations are involved and what rights to speaking apply. (Gumperz, 1996: 396–397)

So here we are going into more depth on how misalignments discussed in chapter 7 arise interactionally, particularly the functioning of contextual misalignments, and relate these three interlocking levels of contextualisation cues to Vijay's example:

1. **The perceptual level in which speech is chunked into manageable units and assessed for coherence and relevance.** The interactants appear to segment the stream of talk into coherent chunks and there are no obvious moments when the talk seems irrelevant at this perceptual level. No feature is unprocessable. However, although line 11 is clearly a misalignment at the level of communicative intent (the next level), it is arguably also not strictly relevant as a response to line 9. 'Debatable,' implying contentious or doubtful, is taken up as 'to debate' in the sense of a formal discussion, shifting its situated meaning to raise doubts about the candidate's coherence.

2. **The level of communicative intent in the sense of what is going on right now between speakers and listeners. This is crucially about expectations and the pragmatics of face.** Here, Vijay's opening line is responded to with the downgrader, 'But that's obviously in India.' His overlapping 'right' seems to be interpreted by the interviewer as not getting the point when she reformulates her doubts about his answer in line 4: 'Not here.' He has not inferred from the 'but' response that his opening line is too extreme – not mitigated enough, not admitting the limits of his experience – and the transgression is reinforced in line 5 when he again fails to deal with the 'but' response. The laughter is perhaps best interpreted not as a contextualisation cue that changes the footing of the interview at this point – from formal investigation to joke – but as a cue used to mask the embarrassing fact that a particularistic attribute, that Vijay is from India, has been brought into the talk and this is (potentially) a factor in his social evaluation.

   He talks over the laughter to defend his case that his overseas experience is valid anywhere, with another unmitigated and somewhat sententious remark (line 7). This is received as 'debatable' in a lowered tone, prefaced by a meaningful clearing of the throat, as an aside to interviewer two but to be overheard by Vijay. He picks up on the word 'debatable,' but not the contextualisation cues that seem intended to convey that he is not being adequately social – that he has gone off on a wrong footing, giving a mini lecture rather than concrete examples and explanations. This wrong footing is compounded by the formulaic, 'I'm not here to …' which cues the positioning of the interviewers as an audience to his lecture and could also be construed as adversarial.

3. **The level at which more general framing work is going on about the nature of the exchange and what is expectable and allowable.** This is influenced by organisational criteria for selection, discourses of competence and wider social, cultural and linguistic ideologies – such as notions of the preferred identity of the candidate as both self-motivating and compliant. Vijay's lecturing tone, for example, undermines expectations about candidate compliance. Also implicit in this short segment is the assumption that 'other' experience, namely overseas experience, is excluded or downgraded (10.6).

We can draw two crucial points from this analysis: Firstly, if interactants cannot easily agree (implicitly) on the grounds for negotiating meaning, conversational involvement and repair, then the kind of alignments and misalignments seen above and discussed in chapters 5–7 will recur throughout the interview and create an overall climate for a positive or negative evaluation. It is the taken-for-granted quality of the inferential process which allows gatekeepers to be so assertive in their judgments, when so much of this assessment is based on cues which are not noticed and only suggestive. Secondly, the ideological work of contextualisation cues is clear here. For example, the 'but' in line 2, the laughter and the comment 'debatable' – prefixed by a meaningful cough, in a low but overhearable tone – all contribute to putting the candidate's turn on trial, as viewed from the interests of the interviewers. The evaluative instinct is ideological and preys on perceived communicative differences to judge and sort:

Language functions and the way they are performed by people are constantly assessed and evaluated: function and value are impossible to separate. Consequently *differences* in the use of language are quickly, and quite systematically, translated into *inequalities* between speakers. (Blommaert, 2003: 615)

8.3 Linguistic Ideology

Linguistic ideology theorises the process whereby apparently neutral or taken-for-granted ways of interacting always come laden with values arising from specific interests (Woolard, 1998; Bauman and Briggs, 2003; Gal, 1998; Agha, 2003). Over time certain styles of speaking, registers and what are perceived as distinct 'languages' become associated with certain groups and activities, and are assigned a certain value (Kroskrity, 2010; Blommaert and Varis, 2012) related to the competence and adequacy of these groups – for example, comments from interviewers such as, 'Filipinos are poor communicators' and 'candidates are hopeless.'

As the work of contextual cues shows, even the unnoticed and banal conduct of everyday practices is ideological (Blommaert and Rampton, 2011; Silverstein, 1979). In the selection interview, talk ratchets up this ideological work so that mundane relating and communicating is judged excessively and assertively. Candidates' talk is given a particular value, based on linguistic and organisational norms, and then reified into assertions of character. Even very minor things can 'drench the talk … with judgmental significance' and the smallest deviation from the norm can 'send recipients into interpretive overdrive' (Blommaert and Rampton, 2011: 13).

As well as amplifying candidate linguistic and social discrepancies, the ideological work of talk can also erase these voices. The notion of 'erasure,' developed by Irvine and Gal, identifies many of the processes of loss and invisibility recorded in the sociolinguistic literature, where differences are interpreted as oppositional and of questionable value.

> Erasure is the process in which ideology, in simplifying the sociolinguistic field, renders some persons or activities (or sociolinguistic phenomena) invisible. Facts that are inconsistent with the ideological scheme either go unnoticed or get explained away. (Irvine and Gal, 2000: 38)

The role of the interviewers is to simplify, reduce and then sort into 'one of us' and 'the others.' So erasure is procedurally necessary and operates in several ways in all interviews. First, there is the reduction and recontextualisation of voice into written texts and wash-up sessions. An iconic example of this is the equal opportunities interview (7.2), where candidates' response to each topic is rated with a number and the highest-scoring candidate is offered the job. Nothing of what the candidate said remains.

Second, how performance is jointly produced and shaped in the now of the interview is erased – or rather, conveniently overlooked (7.1). In addition to being subject to these processes of erasure, linguistic minority candidates are penalised in other ways. As some examples in chapters 5–7 have illustrated, their voices are less listened to (even though they may talk relatively more than other candidates) and less understood during the encounter. They are interrupted more (6.2), experience more misalignments with interviewers (7.5) and there is also less of a written record of their voice. So they experience these first two erasures more intensively than other candidates.

A third erasure stems from the simplifying and stereotyping of this group as more likely to have poor English and for this to be, in some instances, explicitly commented on in wash-up sessions (9.3) so that relevant experience and other social capital is ignored. Finally, the fact of multilingualism is erased. All the candidates in our data who were born abroad brought other languages to the interview. However, the idea of valuing other languages spoken was never mentioned; 'English only' ruled (9.1).

A significant theme in linguistic ideology has been the contrast between the national or 'standard' language and all other varieties. The debates about what James and Lesley Milroy have called 'standard language ideology' tend to centre around the social value or linguistic capital given to speakers of a literate, educated, institutional (Bourdieu, 1991) or 'posh' (Rampton, 2006) variety of a language and the consequent devaluing of other forms.[38] This educated variety of language is associated with institutional representatives. But in the type of interview discussed here, there is no straightforward contrast between the language variety spoken by interviewers and some other variety spoken by the majority of candidates.[39]

It was commonplace for interviewers to speak a 'non-standard,' local variety of English. For example, subject-verb agreement did not necessarily follow standard forms – 'you was' occurred quite frequently – and many of the candidates sounded more 'posh' than their interviewers. So standard grammar was not a marker of good communication. The situated assessment of differences and discrepancies used to mark down candidates arose not from grammatical anomalies and differences in accent (with a few exceptions from migrant candidates), but from the norms and conventions of the interview and the lack of fit between these and the candidates' overall communicative style. No mention was made in any wash-up or feedback sessions to 'proper' English or 'well-spoken' candidates.

Turning now to these norms and conventions, we can trace the paths travelled from the formal decision-making criteria to the subjectification process which determines final outcomes.

8.4 Decision-making in the Interviews

Management textbooks present decision-making as the endgame (chapter 7). Information is collected and then there is a decision-making event, such as the wash-up sessions, where evidence is analysed and a final position taken on the facts; rational, linear and objective. However, ethnographic and ethnomethodological studies tell a different story. The moment at which a decision is made by any individual is always 'elsewhere' (Boden, 1994). In other words, decision-making is distributed through text and talk in many different phases (Briggs, 2005; Mehan, 1993) – from the opening stage of the interview to wash-up discussions. And the processes of evaluation are done in largely hidden ways, moving from an objective rhetoric – through the situated subjectivities of the interview and its 'wiggle room' – to a decontextualised subjectivity of the candidate on which a final decision is made. Drawing on Foucault's notion of the subject as a product of power, constructed by evaluative statements (1.4), Blommaert describes this as a 'pure' subjectivity (Blommaert, 2005).

What appears as a lean and streamlined trajectory from standardised procedures of interview design to final decision is thickened up by layers of local practices which rationalise the shift from objectivity to pure subjectivity. These practices are worked up from an array of informal activities, impressions and everyday knowledge (Suchman, 1987; 2.4) which gradually become sedimented into traditions of arguing, reasoning and categorising (Mäkitalo and Säljö, 2002; 2.4); a set of rationalisations, not formally documented but which do the business. And as Goffman says, 'the mix of considerations' that lead to final decisions are concealed from those who make them (Goffman, 1983: 8; 1.7).

But while the ad hoc and improvisatory measures invoked become taken-for-granted categories, the formal, standardised procedures remain the ultimate reference point. Managing the dialectic between, on the one hand, formality and objectivity in increasingly abstract and decontextualised processes and texts and on the other, informality and subjectivity – as we saw in chapter 7 – can lead to interactional problems and the quiet shifting of categories and changes in structure. The rest of the chapter outlines two of the ways in which interviewers move from the set procedures to a pure subjectivity: the shift in evaluative criteria and the writing of the interview.

8.5   The Shift in Evaluative Criteria

Institutions defend and look after themselves by documenting the criteria required for a post and in the associated interview design. In 4.3 and 4.5 I outlined the criteria and question topics used in low-paid and junior management interviews; the universalistic attributes looked for, in Erickson and Shultz's terms (1982). To sum up, the two key criteria in interviews for low-paid work were teamwork and self-organisation/management. Others were customer service, learning from mistakes, making improvements and – in less competence-driven interviews – more general questions on motivation and suitability. For junior management posts, two criteria were similar to those in the low-paid work interviews: teamwork and learning. And the other two – problem solving and achievement orientation – were not dissimilar. A fifth area was commercial/business awareness.

The assumption in guidelines for interviewers is that the competence framework will determine the decision-making. However, the grounds for decision-making do not always map onto these competences. There is a shift in these wash-up and feedback criteria from the original set of questions, to concentrate on a more general and implicit formulation of attributes and personality. Some of these new attributes are only voiced outside the formal structure and constraints of the interview, and appeared to contradict the explicit criteria – and indeed, contradict each other. These implicit criteria were voiced in the wash-up sessions and were also derived from the interactional analysis of the interview data (9.2) as well as interviewer feedback on the videos. They can be summarised as follows:

Figure 8.1. Implicit Criteria in Low-Paid Job Interviews

> **Obedient:** Willing to 'please the bosses,' as successful candidate Ahmed said.
>
> **Honest:** Often judged on the basis of whether the candidate was consistent in their presentation, or over claimed their skills and experience.
>
> **Strong personality:** Ability to hold your own, deal with back room banter etc.
>
> **Bland:** Ability to fit themselves into broad, homogenising categories and not be too idiosyncratic.
>
> **Shared perspective on work experience:** Expectations that candidates share common sense assumptions about work, e.g. that repetitive work is boring.
>
> **A certain (unspecified) level of ability in English:** A general deficiency – or lack of 'clarity of voice' – was quoted (for some migrant candidates), but no specific examples ever cited as evidence of this and, as mentioned earlier, communication was not an explicit theme.

A similar process occurred in the junior management and promotion interviews, with a disjuncture between competence themes and implicit criteria:

Figure 8.2. Implicit Criteria in Junior Management/Promotion Interviews

Themes covered in the interviews	Criteria used in wash-up and video feedback
Building relations, teamwork and developing others	The main focus was a much narrower one: on motivating people to manage change.
Problem solving: identifying and solving problems, implementing unpopular decisions	Again the main focus was narrower: on 'being tough'; 'it's not good to be liked too much.'
Achievements/results orientation: 'going the extra mile'	Although 'getting results' was often seen as a core value in the competence themes, it was rarely mentioned. More general attributes were cited, e.g. 'seeing the bigger picture.'
Learning/taking responsibility: self-development and learning from mistakes	Rarely mentioned, except in the context of a vague notion of 'self-awareness.'

The implicit criteria here, even more than those used in low-paid job interviews, centred almost entirely on personal attributes and how candidates managed the interaction. The only other theme that arose in the interviews – apart from the four just mentioned – was commercial/business awareness, though this was surprisingly not mentioned in feedbacks or wash-ups.

By far the most frequent comments in the wash-up sessions, in both levels of interviews, concerned personality. In the case of positive attributes, these were divided into characteristics such as courage, resilience, drive and toughness (particularly for the management posts), as well as personality traits identified through interviewer/candidate social relationships such as likeable, engaging, confident and humorous. Similarly, negative attributes were the product of candidates not being adequately social – including 'patronising,' 'garrulous,' 'out of control,' 'laid back,' 'overconfident' and 'cocky' – or were criticisms of their authenticity or honesty: they were 'not being themselves,' 'blaggers,' 'just saying what the interviewer wanted to hear,' 'just using buzz-words.' Aspects of speech delivery were also translated into personal characteristics. For example, hesitations were proof that 'candidates could not think on their feet' and those who sounded 'flat' were considered to lack dynamism (9.9).

Much of the institutional decision-making process, therefore – from 'objectivity' to a situated subjectivity in performance, and then to a fixed and pure subjectivity – is partly done by this shifting of ideologically informed evaluative criteria. The candidate is summed up not so much as a 'bundle of skills,' but a bundle of personal attributes. This transformed bundle shifts the classification system up a scale to large character judgments which, like other aspects of abstraction in institutional discourse, float free from actual conduct.

Unsurprisingly, this institutional sleight of hand was not acknowledged by interviewers. They erased from their comments any recognition of the complexity of the interview, both in the dialectics of its design (2.6) and its discourse modes, and their role in making it so complex. Interviewers often commented that they were surprised at how poorly candidates generally performed, since there were standard questions and often they could only produce 'half-baked' or 'superficial answers.' A 'half-baked' answer was one in which individual agency was underplayed, with the self hidden behind general and deontic modes of talk; by contrast, it could also be one where too much was claimed for the self, in extreme and unhedged ways. In both instances, the self was not heard as inhabiting action and reflection in grounded experience, as an authentic self (10.2).

In many cases, even when pushed in feedback sessions, interviewers were unable to give detailed explanations or evidence for their summative assessment and, as has been widely noted in the Western world (Rivera, 2015), gave general emotional responses. They also fell back on well-worn, visceral reactions: 'gut feelings' or 'unhappy with the candidates' body language' (Roberts and Campbell, 2005). While the underlying neoliberal and entrepreneurial discourses create an environment, structure and rhetoric for selecting ideal candidates, the absolute subjectivity and totalising gaze of the interview exercise an even stronger power. Facework trumps form every time (7.1) and this is instantiated in the writing process, which also contributes to the trajectory from objective criteria to pure subjectivity.

8.6   Writing the Interview

This second part of the chapter examines the writing done by interviewers in the job interview. It looks at the institutional work texts do, their specific purpose in job interviews, how writing is interactionally managed and how notes from the interaction write the candidate as relatively successful or not.

The Work Texts Do

The increase in the amount of writing in the interview reflects a more general trend towards more text – both more tick boxes and more writing – in most institutions and organisations, with more accountability and auditing as part of neoliberal influences and increasing defensiveness (Jönsson and Linell, 1991; Iedema, 1999). In her work on institutional ethnography, the sociologist Dorothy Smith discusses the significance of texts in the objectification of organisations: 'They provide for the standardised recognisability of people's doings as organisational or institutional as well as for their coordination across multiple local settings and times.' But they are worked up in local practices so that, 'from a particular text, it is possible to trace sequences of action through the institutional paths, identifying where and how the institutional text produces the standardised controls of everyday work activities' (Smith, 2001: 160).

From a similar perspective in anthropology and sociolinguistics – and particularly in the idea of text trajectories – texts are seen as not only portable but produced in and out of local interaction (3.6). Here the focus is on how 'institutional memory' (Linde, 1999: 139–141) is worked up rhetorically – particularly from narratives – and fitted into institutional categories, rather than being a close record of what was said. Particular emphasis in these studies has been put on what is lost in writing through the process of erasure. When talk is not considered bureaucratically processable, it either never appears in the record and so is institutionally erased or is so thoroughly reworked as to be a 'disappearing discourse' (Trinch, 2003: 121–154; Maryns, 2013; Ehrlich, 2012).[40]

Whether talk is lost in the written record or worked up and reframed, in all cases it is the manipulation of the incommensurability between speech and writing which contributes to a 'pure subjectivity' (Park and Bucholtz, 2009; Mabyin, 2017). But there are some differences between job interviews and other institutional encounters and I focus here on the gap between the official purpose of writing and interviewers' local practices.

The Purpose of Writing

There was some slippage, in the interview and then the wash-up, from the institution's stated purpose of writing to the interviewers' local situated practices. Those designing the interviews emphasised the potential for writing to lend 'objectivity' and 'validity' to the interview. One official company policy document frames the writing as a four-stage process of observation, recording, classification and evaluation. The underlying logic here is that the writing offers a space between observation and judgments so that interviewers do not make decisions based on first impressions, but rather use the notes as an aide-memoire for considered decisions in the wash-ups. So the official focus was on the good practice of using writing to make valid decisions.

But interviewers took a more practical approach. This was influenced by the time and interactional constraints of the interview, the conduct of wash-ups and the need to answer for their own conduct if under scrutiny. The writing process, rather than preventing snap judgments, seemed to encourage them. Because interviewers were required to make a written record, they sought to form a judgment early on, which could be backed up throughout the interview. But these notes were not the focus of decision-making; the wash-ups were face-to-face conversations and written records were marginalised. The interviewers we observed rarely looked over their notes before making a decision but, arguably, the fact of writing a judgment seemed to fix an impression voiced in the wash-ups. For example, the writing of a comment such as, 'Very unclear as to what he understood to be the position,' immediately after the candidate's turn – while not specifically referred to in the wash-up – clearly fed into the negative impression of Brian as an unsuccessful candidate (8.8).

They also saw writing as a means of structuring or controlling the interview and the candidate performance. Where the STAR structure (or slight variants of it) were used, the notes could be fitted neatly into this structure

– as one interviewer, using the SOARRR (situation, objective, action, result, reaction, reflection) structure explained, summarised below:

- situation should be given quantitatively – time, date, location etc.;

- objective and action should be 'what the interviewee themselves actually did' as an individual;

- result – for the organisation, e.g. profit;

- reaction/reflection – aware of how others react to you, build on and learn for the future.

The same interviewer outlined in more detail how he used note taking:

Example 49: Interviewer on Note Taking

1. I: yeah I mean I think it erm erm it d- it serves two purposes I think
2.   it provides some structure for me for the interview
3.   so I'm clear about where I am
4.   so I'll- I'll you know very- on a very basic level
5.   I'll set down that i.e. SOARRR sort of-
6.   sort of down the left hand side you know
7.   and then I'll be dropping information into that (.)
8.   cos you can get a little bit lost at times
9.   about exactly where you are (.)
10.   so there's a kind of point of reference on the page right
11.   where am I what do I need to do what have I got to get

Both the summary and the interviewer comments show clearly how the interview in this organisation is driven by the STAR structure, and so how narrative inequality is produced by the structuring of the notes. The act of writing, officially undertaken to provide an objective and valid outcome, has the potential for discriminating against those not familiar with Western narrative structures. In a further irony, the interviewers were very conscious of the defensive role of their texts in cases of appeal by candidates, and even in industrial tribunal cases, when their notes could be used to challenge accusations of discrimination. As one interviewer related:

Example 50: Note Taking as a Defensive Act

1. I: when I write up the feedback I've got that basis to say
2.   okay these are things I want to pick out
3.   because these are the key things in terms of the evidence

4.   and they are obviously useful in terms of if there are any challenges

(some lines deleted)

5.   [appeals] yeah people have the right of appeal against sort of failure

(some lines deleted)

6.   you can use to demonstrate how you arrived at your decision

So although the interviewer's text does not stand straightforwardly for the whole performance, it works quietly alongside the moment-to-moment interactional judgments to help produce a character assessment – a thumbnail sketch that is reductive, fixed and complete, a pure subjectivity – to back up decisions and defend them.

8.7   The Interactional Impact of Writing

The written record of the interview transforms the interaction from a two-way to a three-way encounter, as both sides are required to orient to the written text. This orientation affects both the interactional (dis)comfort of the interview and indexes the degree of institutionality created by interviewers. This section will consider some of the problems – but also some of the occasional help – produced by the task of writing, echoing many of the institutional constraints discussed in previous chapters (5.6 for example). In more successful interviews, the management of writing becomes an aspect of the 'special help' given to the successful candidate. In less successful interviews, where institutional procedures are enforced (7.5), the role of written record keeping is magnified.

The extent to which candidates are written as successes or failures depends upon their ability to manage the writing demands of the interview, part of the metacriteria that feed into overall evaluation, as the following two contrastive examples show (Roberts and Campbell, 2005). Both candidates are interviewed by the same interviewer who uses a version of the STAR structure mentioned above, SOARRR, which he writes in the column of his notepaper to use as a guide to structure each question and the notes taken.

Managing Writing: the Successful Candidate

Lloyd, a British-born African-Caribbean candidate (example 26), has already done some work in the delivery company and the interviewer asks him to give an example of an experience he gained of teamwork in this position. Lloyd talks about sorting mail for the different districts of London e.g. EC1, EC4:

Example 51: Lloyd – BAME British, Successful
(Extended and more detailed transcription of example 26.)

1. I: when you worked here here at Christmas er:m
2.   can you remember one particular day for instance
3.   whe:n there was a lot of work to clear {(looks at C)
4.   and you really had to work as a team to get it (.)
5.   get it a- I know every day is [like that at Christmas
6. C: yeah yeah]
7. I: but is there one particular day (.) when (.) you know y-
8. C: there we- there were- there were
9.   a couple of like you said a little bit because
10.   it was around the Christmas period
11.   there were a couple of days tha- that there was
12.   there was a day where I remember where}
13.   {(I starts writing)
14. C: (.) erm (.) like (.) wi- with EC}
15.   {(I looks up briefly)
16.   with EC1 to EC4} they'd get piled up wh-
17.   quite kind of quickly like between- like
18.   I used to start from five 'til ten that was my shift
19.   so between like five to seven it was
20.   {(lo) quiet like always quiet} (.)
21.   (I looks up briefly, nods)
22.   so let's say we'd go on facing for a bit
23.   and after about {(I looks up, smiles, nods) seven
24.   it would {(ac) it would just come loads like just start rushing}

Lloyd's interactional work involves a double alignment to both the textual and social aspects of the interview. Throughout the interview, Lloyd manages to maintain the interaction during the writing in various ways: using pausing, word stress and repetition. In lines 14–16 his pausing and detail, 'With EC' catches the interviewer's attention. In line 20, Lloyd repeats, 'Quiet like, always quiet' in a lower pitch, in response to which the interviewer looks up and nods (line 21), engaging in a shared construction of climax which comes in line 24 with the words, 'It would … just start rushing.' Lloyd is able to read these minimal responses as cues to continue speaking or begin concluding his talk. This elicitation and reading of interviewer responses by Lloyd ensures that interaction is maintained during the writing, and that Lloyd is given cues of when to stop and start, how much is enough to say, and whether his answer is acceptable.

As well as his deft interactional management of the writing – and adaptation of his talk to it – Lloyd's response here is also made easily processable by the fact that it markedly corresponds to the variant of the STAR structure used. The interviewer's easy recognition of the markers which indicate the opening of a narrative are evident; in lines 10–12, Lloyd marks the beginning of the narrative with the formulaic, 'It was around the Christmas period' and 'There was a day I remember where,' at which the interviewer begins writing, confident that he is about to hear an easily processable narrative. This mutual understanding of rhetorical markers means that Lloyd is given more freedom to construct his answers as he wishes, and the interviewer is easily able to categorise and note down his responses.

Alignment to the writing task is achieved implicitly, through subtle cues, thus marking Lloyd as one who 'understands without having to be told' (Bourdieu, 1991). The only mention of the writing in Lloyd's interview comes much later where, following a co-authored segment, he makes a comment about the weather and jokes, 'Are you not going to write that down?' – to which the interviewer responds with laughter. This implicit understanding between them – that the interview is more conversational than institutional – is fostered by the interviewer's instances of special help and nods to the bureaucratic game. For example, at line 5 ('I know every day is like that at Christmas') he acknowledges that the question is itself rather problematic, positioning himself as an intermediary for Lloyd. So both the questioning and the management of note taking index a successful interview.

Rescuing the Less Successful Candidate

Lloyd's easy management of the writing in the job interview contrasts with the experience of Mohammed. Born in Somalia and moving to the UK when he was eleven, Mohammed had also worked on a temporary basis in the same organisation where the interview was held. The following sequence occurs near the beginning of the interview and is relates to the competence of team working:

Example 52: Mohammed – Pakistani Migrant, Borderline Successful[41]

1. I: {(writing, looking down)
2.   where you worked for us before at (xxx) (2)
3.   sorry I forgot to explain} {(I looks up)
4.   I am going to be taking some notes
5. C: no problem
6. I: so from time to time I have to stop and scribble away and}
7.   {(looks down) get ev- get all the notes down erm (10) (writing)
8.   so when you worked for us at (xxx) (.) how many people} were
9.   {(looks up) you working with in your area
10. C: er- there was a lot of people in my area actually
11.   but roughly I would say about}
12.   {(I looks down) (2) over twenty people
13. I: (4) (writing) okay and wh- what type of erm}
14.   {(I looks up) sorting were you- were you doing there
15. C: er letter sorting} {(I looks down) (.) cages (.)
16.   and sometimes I had to do tipping for the (firm) (.)}
17. I: {(looks up) e- emptying the mail [bags}
18. C: yeah]
19. I: (8) {(writing) okay so you d- you did a few different things}
20.   {(looks up briefly) while you were there okay} {(looks down)
21. C: also we had to unload and load lorries (C looks down)
22. I: {(looks up) right okay}{(I looks down, writing) (12)
23.   and what er- what did you enjoy about working in-}
24.   {(looks up) in a- a- as part of that team}{(looks down)
25. C: I enjoyed most- mostly
26.   working with the people (C looks down) (6) (writing)
27. I: and erm (.) what was it about working wit- with people}
28.   {(looks up) that y- you- that you actually enjoyed}
29.   {(looks down)
30. C: a lot of support and [(2)
31. I: {(begins writing) (.)] yeah
32. C: it is good} {(I looks up)
33.   to work with people you know} {(I looks down)
34.   get to know them and
35. I: (10) (writing) okay (4)
36.   and can you tell me any ways that erm} {(looks up)
37.   you used to help your colleagues
38.   and even if it is just little things that you used to do
39.   any ways that you helped each other
40.   to get the job done {(looks down, writing)

41. C: (3) er what do you mean (.)} {(I looks up)
42.   what do you mean by that
43. I: erm anything that you did to help erm [other- other
44. C: colleag-]
45. I: people with what they were [doing
46. C: yeah]
47. I: t- t- to get the task done quicker=
48. C: =er there was some time I was working in
49.   for example (I nods) in party shop in Chelsea}
50.   {(I looks down, writing) Kensington there was a customer who
51.   ordered the balloons (.) five year old balloons=
52. I: =yeah
53. C: she ordered twenty balloons over the phone (.)}
54.   {(I looks up briefly, nods)
55.   and she came to collect the balloons}
56.   {(I looks down, writing) (2)
57.   but my (1) colleague g- got the o- order wrong
58.   instead of four and five year olds
59.   he put- he put plain balloons=}
60. I: {(looks up briefly, nods)=right}
61. C: {(I looks down, writing) it was plain-
62.   it was supposed to say five year olds- five (.)}

In contrast with Lloyd's interview, the burden of writing is explicitly addressed (lines 3–7) and this explicitness about interview procedures – as with other unsuccessful candidates such as Sara and Luis – seems to index discomfort and low expectations of candidate's management of the interview. It can also affect how the interviewers feel about their own performance. In the video feedback, the interviewer talked of feeling his own 'lack of professionalism' as he watched this extract. Unlike Lloyd, Mohammed has difficulty in managing the writing: looking down, stopping talking or trailing off when the writing begins, for example lines 26 and 30. There are longer writing pauses than in the interview with Lloyd and, in an earlier part of this interview, the interviewer writes in silence for as long as a minute. While Lloyd encourages the interviewer to punctuate the writing with looks up and nods, Mohammed is left with few responses as the interviewer looks down at the paper and begins writing immediately after asking his questions in lines 24, 29 and 40. This gaze avoidance writing also occurs with Sara (5.6). This minimising of the social, interactive aspects of the interview and the long writing-only phases magnifies the role of written record keeping and the shift to increased institutionalisation.

The silences and disfluency affect both participants as the institutional work at hand seems to override the task of communication. Not only is the interactional smoothness jeopardised, but the story structure is ruptured. The sudden shift at lines 23–28 to the result and reflection aspect of the story disturbs the SOARRR sequence, which the interviewer tended to prompt for in most of his interviews, and leads to misunderstandings and further discomfort. So we see here misalignment to both the textual and social aspects of the interview by both sides – but of course, it is only the candidate who is penalised.

However, a quite different interactional dynamic begins to be established in the latter part of this extract. The interviewer and Mohammed begin to engage in some joint production and negotiation of the writing, so that some substantive responses are generated. Mohammed starts to tell his story which illustrates how he helped his colleague to sort out the right balloons (only the beginning of the story appears in this extract) and contributes to his likely success. At line 36 the interviewer gives a more open question about team working, but again immediately begins writing after asking the question. However, Mohammed re-elicits his attention at lines 41–42 by asking him for clarification. When he begins his answer in line 48, the interviewer does not immediately look down to write, but maintains eye contact for longer and nods in ratification of Mohammed's opening to a narrative. After this point, Mohammed continues his narrative despite the writing and perhaps strategically uses pausing – in line 53, for example – to elicit the interviewer's attention at key moments, to confirm that he is following and that the answer is along the right lines. Through this process, Mohammed begins to align to and gain more control over the writing. Later in the interview, Mohammed starts to take the beginning of the writing itself as a cueing continuer, so that the rhythm between writing and speaking begins to be established.

The written record helps to determine the relative interactional smoothness of the encounter. Successful candidates monitor the talk/writing relationship indirectly, reduce the weight of the writing on them and produce responses that are recordable as both sides then draw on shared knowledge and viewpoint. Unsuccessful candidates experience the weight of the writing more heavily. There are longer silent writing episodes when candidates are not given – or fail to read – the subtle encouragement cues, and the narrative structure is broken as interviewers attempt to fit stories into boxes. So writing leaks into the interaction at all points thereby affecting the outcome, whatever is written. But it is equally important to examine the actual notes taken, even if they are not referred to explicitly in any decision-making, as evidence of how the candidate is being evaluated throughout.

8.8 The Written Record

A detailed analysis of exactly what is noted or not shows the transformation from the elicitation of information to a loaded and selective account, ripe for a specific and defensible set of interpretations, as other studies of writing the interview have shown (Rock, 2001). To this extent all such written records are jointly authored but here, as in 7.4, I use the term 'co-authored' for the successful interview only; the co- prefix implies a sense of mutual and often equal accomplishment, whereas note taking can be highly debilitating for the less successful candidate, as we have just seen. This section draws on both the interactional work and writing of mainly junior management interviews, where the fixing of personal attributes drawn from the later stages of the STAR structure are particularly significant.

Co-Authoring: the Successful Interview

Co-authoring – producing a joint oral statement – is a marker of a successful interview, as we have seen in 7.4. Here we see the written co-authored text. The blending of candidate and interviewer voice in the text is just one common strategy used by both sides. In the next example, Gladston is asked to evaluate a new procedure he introduced two weeks ago (the second *R* of the STARRR).

Features used in writing the successful interview are well illustrated in this co-authored exchange:

1. Verbatim or close paraphrase or summarising of the candidate's account, e.g. 'I know.'

2. Verbatim noting of positive self-evaluation, e.g. 'very effective.'

3. Summaries of the candidate response with few erasures of their voice, and so more sense of internal structure and logical progression in the notes. Here some of the conversational detail is omitted, which serves to highlight this as a reflective section.

4. The flexible use of the STAR structure and its variants to support the candidate's own structuring.

5. The strategy of selecting and summarising the key evaluative themes, as the notes focus on *how* the candidate knows the procedure was effective and helps to characterise the candidate as active and purposeful.

6. Candidate's rhetorical devices such as foregrounding, emphasis and repetition taken up in the notes, indicating some candidate control over what is written, e.g. 'I know.'

Example 53: Gladston – Jamaican Migrant, Successful

1. I: okay so how how (.) how effective has that been
2. C: oh it's been ***very effective***
3.   I have I have no problem with that [I- I-
4. I: ho-] how do you know that it's been effective
5. C: er:m in the sense because
6.   ***as soon as* somebody's absent *I <u>know</u>** (.) [**as**
7. I: okay]
8. C: *soon as* somebody hasn't turned up
9.   I erm *I know* what duties not covered
10.   and ***what* duties to be covered**
11.   so when my (x senior managers) phone me up
12.   ((and says erm)) are you covered
13.   I can say no he hasn't turned up yet or he's on his way

Interviewer notes for this section:

> ***Very effective as soon as***
> **people are not in – *I know* how what to cover (provides)**

Key to examples 53–56:

Bold refer to words which are paraphrased in the notes:
Bold italics refer to words which are directly quoted in the notes

Another strategy not shown here is the offer of second chances, where notes taken from an inadequate response are crossed out and the candidate is given a second chance to respond, with this response becoming the authorised one.

Success Both Interactionally and in the Writing

The successful co-authoring in a longer segment of Gladston's interview is analysed below, to see how these strategies are sustained over time and work to produce a successful interview. Again the bent aerial story is revisited, with Gladston's 'take ownership' response reflecting a competence at team leader/ junior management level which the delivery company describes as:

1. Taking responsibility for my impact on my team's performance.

2. Displaying high personal standards.

3. Being honest about my strengths.

4. Being open about my mistakes and learning from them.

Example 54: Gladston – Jamaican Migrant, Successful
(Extended and more detailed transcription of 'bent aerial' examples 6, 7, 30
and 32.)

1. I: {(I looking up) okay I'll stop you for a moment
2.   just going to take you a little bit back [in
3. C: yeah]
4. I: terms of sort er:m (.) I guess the incident itself
5.   so you'v:e damaged th:e aerial
6.   of a expensive vehicle that you [obviously
7. C: yeah]
8. I: f- I think you said fitting the brakes of [changing the brakes
9. C: yeah that's right yeah] I was doing the brakes
10. I: or repairing the brakes er:m yeah
11.   and one of the mechanics was reversing (.) bends
12.   the the aerial and you're kind of faced with a bit of a
13.   you know (.) do I own up to this [or do I not own up to it
14. C: I know yeah and] it's my garage
15. I: and it's your garage so
16.   what what goes through your mind in that moment
17. C: **er:m if it was my car**
18. I: **yeah**
19. C: **er:m and I brought it in there with the aerial working**
20. I: yeah} {(I looks down, writes)
21. C: a:s I come back and the aerial is not working you know}
22.   {(I looks up) er:m wait a minute would I (.) would I then}
23.   {(I looks down, writes) and I went to find that it's bent
24.   you know it's quite easy to work out} {(I looks up)
25.   that it it was done at the garage
26. I: yeah} {(I looks down, writes)
27. C: o- ev- and if they come back to me
28.   I **I have a choice I *can either deny it***
29.   **that I know nothing of it**
30.   **or or say that it was my fault** (.)
31.   now e- the owner of course is going to even if I deny it
32.   he's going to work- he's going to work it out} {(I looks up)
33.   soon sooner or later it's my- it's our fault
34. I: yeah} {(I drinks tea)
35. C: yeah because it was working when he got there }
36.   (.) er:m it wasn't bent so how did it get bent} {(I looks up)
37.   yeah so I thought well the the thing to do is to *be honest*
38. I: ((nods))

39. C: *take ownership*} {(I looks down, writes)
40.   it's my fault you know put me hand up
41.   and- and I'll I'll ask the customer
42.   just give me a chance to put it right you know
43.   and if- and if they're still not happy with it after I put it right
44.   then they can take any action that they feel [needs to be taken
45. I: okay]} {(I looks up) tell me a little bit
46.   about that conversation then that you [had
47. C: yeah]
48. I: *with the* [*customer*} {(I looks down, writes)
49. C: well] *what I said to the customer* was that er:m you know
50.   w:e er:m I- I- I invited him into the office and said
51.   well I'm I'm sorry but we *had* a little bit of erm a *mishap*
52.   with your vehicle (.) those are the words I used er:m [and
53. I: *mishap*] }{(I looks up) hhh
54. C: hhh} {(I looks down, writes) [yeah
55. I: [*mishap*
56. C: not] accident we don't like them to to get them alarmed=
57. I: =okay=
58. C: =so I said we had a bit of a *mishap* with o- with your vehicle
59.   er:m w- we didn't realise that the- your aerial was up}
60.   {(I looks up) and when one of our guys I-
61.   it was an} {(I looks down) *apprentice* (.)
62.   you know these *young* boys who} {(I looks up)
63.   just really (.) erm just like to drive flash cars [and}
64. I: {(looks down) yeah]
65. C: just didn't take note and as he was driving it out
66.   we- we damaged your aerial (.) I says er:m (.)
67.   erm it will be of no *cost* to you we'll fix it if you just give us the}
68.   {(I looks up) opportunity to fix it}
69. I: {(I looks down, nods)
70. C: we- we apol- apologise for it e:r
71.   if you just give us the} {(I looks up) opportunity to fix it is-
72.   it doesn't interfere with your} {(I looks down) rights of course
73.   if you feel that e:rm} {(I looks up) you want to do something else
74.   er:m- erm take it further then please do so} {(I looks down, writes)
75.   but give us the *opportunity to fix it* we'll put it right
76.   and er:m whatsoever you need we'll (.)
77.   we'll- we'll d- we'll get it done (.) e:r
78.   if you need a er:m a *hire car* we'll pay for it
79.   while it's done for the day
80.   because it won't take us more than another day to do it}

81. I: {(I looks down) okay what was the customer's reaction
82. C: er:m in fact} {(I looks up) they- they}
83.   {(I looks down, writes) were quite *taken aback*
84.   that **that we actually told them about it**
85.   because he- because he looked
86.   he went and had a look at at his car and the aerial was down (.)
87.   so er:m he he could not have seen that it was damaged
88.   and **he said I don't see anything**}
89.   {(I looks up) wrong with it (.)
90.   so well I said it's not up at the moment
91.   but if you put it up you'll f-} {(I looks down, writes)
92.   you'll soon notice it you know (.)
93.   er:m because it wouldn't have come up now
94.   once we forced it down you'd- you'd have to
95.   literally physically pull it up by hand}
96.   {(I looks up) it's not electric anymore
97. I: yeah} {(I drinks tea)
98. C: so I said er:m so I *explained* him that
99.   **erm we made a mistake and that we'll *put it right*}**
100.   {(I looks down, writes) er:m I didn't mention cost to him
101.   at the time (.) of what it's going to cost
102.   but **I know it's going to *cost*}** {(I looks up, nods) *me*}
103.   {(I looks down, writes) er:m (.) quite a lot to pu-
104.   to- to do it (.) but we done it and er he was quite happy
105.   and he was er:m in fact he didn't even need a hire car
106.   in fact he said just leave it to the next day
107.   and he'll come pick it up the next day (.)
108.   and e:rm he was **quite *happy* wi- with the *result***
109.   **we *fix* it repaired it** and er:m (.) [re- re
110. I: okay]
111. C: and erm disciplined the young man
112. I: okay (2)

Interviewer notes for this section (**A** = action and **R** = result):

A   Considered empathy – works out can ***deny*** or:
own up. *Be honest & take ownership.*

Spoke to customer & explained had *'mishap'* young apprentice.
   ***opportunity to fix it* and met costs/hire car.**

R   *Taken aback* that explained – hadn't noticed.

Explained* would *put it right
knew it would *cost me – happy result fixed &*
       ↑

In the opening section, nothing is written until line 20 while the interviewer summarises and so co-authors the situation Gladston has portrayed. He then notes down a mini-evaluation of the action element of the narrative as 'empathy.' This is key to summarising and evaluating the moral of the story, and to recording the 'inner self' which serves to establish credibility and the tellability of the story (Trinch, 2003). With this tacit agreement of Gladston's moral self, most of the note taking then uses Gladston's voice. From line 27 onwards there are only two small utterances that are paraphrased; the rest of the notes are quotes or near-quotes as the italicised, bolded words indicate. As elsewhere, selective note taking helps to focus on the function of the particular phase of the narrative. Off-the-cuff remarks which could be interpreted negatively are not recorded (e.g. 'young boys who like to drive flash cars' [lines 62–63]), but can be used informally to maintain co-membership.

In lines 51–58 the co-authoring becomes a humorous, ironical and mutual metacommentary on the business of writing the interview. The 'mishap' exchange – also in quote marks in the interviewer's notes – is taken both as a joke about the euphemised ways in which one must deal with customers and as an ironic comment on the process the participants are engaged in: of creating and editing institutional memory, producing and recording acceptable management talk. So it is a comment on the storytelling/co-authoring/writing process itself, playing upon and bridging the gap between the sober, official 'taleworld' (Georgakopolou, 2007) and the present circumstances and personal interaction of Gladston and the interviewer. The latter's simultaneous laugher and writing (lines 53–54) shows how in successful interviews, the institutional process of writing is seamlessly blended with the professional/personal.

Both participants use their interactional and rhetorical resources to accomplish a smooth talk and writing encounter. As well as actively writing Gladston in a positive light, the interviewer supports him interactionally. He repeatedly looks up at Gladston before he begins writing in lines 26, 36–38, 45, 53–54, 73–74, 82–83, 89–92, 96–100 and 102–103. Gladston is equally facilitative. He makes his speech easily recordable by recycling fragments of the narrative – for example, 'opportunity to fix it' (lines 68 and 71) – and providing extractable and pithy phrases such as, 'be honest take ownership' and 'taken aback' (line 83). Together with these resources and the conversational tone of this part of the interview, the notes exemplify the internal logic of the story, its moral import and the accepted structuring of the narrative into the STAR boxes. The interviewer can be both institutional and engaged in a valued performance, as Bauman suggests:

Through his performance, the performer elicits the participative attention and energy of the audience, and *to the extent that they value his performance*, they will allow themselves to be caught up in it. (Bauman, 1975: 305, my italics)

8.9   Writing the Unsuccessful Candidate

In the unsuccessful interview, the conduct on both sides amplifies the encounter as institutional and uncomfortable. The note taking from these interviewers stands in iconic relationship to the environment produced. It features:

1. considerable erasure of the candidate voice;

2. little or no co-authoring and high rate of interviewer translations;

3. interviewer-based evaluative framing, including specific negative comments on candidates;

4. apparent inconsistency, incoherence and even contradiction in the notes on the candidate voice;

5. more mundane, easily recordable facts and figures written down as the product of interviewer 'talking down';

6. misalignments leading to protracted questioning and no notes recorded, or disruption of the STAR structure so notes do not fit easily into boxes; and

7. more rigid use of the STAR structure.

In the following example Brian, an unsuccessful candidate from Ireland, answers the competence question about learning from mistakes. His story is about some mail stolen from a van and the action he took, which was to counsel the worker rather than administering harsher discipline. This transcript is from the result phase of the narrative STAR structure and is noted as such by the interviewer:

Example 55: Brian – BAME British, Unsuccessful

1. C: it transpired from from that that erm
2.   **the decision that I took was the wrong one**
3.   **because it was out of step**
4.   **with erm (*xxx's*) er notion of zero tolerance really er:m**
5.   **he wanted to see me take more *firm action* (.)**
6.   in dealing with individuals who for whatever reason
7.   found themselves in that position (.)
8.   **I did *argue the point* (.) e:rm and I challenged back on that**

9.   and I did- I did identify the fact that you know
10.   whilst this chap had (.) kept his duty erm
11.   continued to use the van to make his delivery
12.   or to attempt to make his delivery in the morning
13.   e:rm that the plusses were
14.   that **I'd** *saved* the *unit budget* erm in terms of cost
15.   because that would have gone out on overtime (.) er:m
16.   **I potentially** *saved* **e:rm someone from** *losing* **their job** (.)
17.   erm and someone who's actually a good postman (.) [er someone
18. I: (tell me a little bit)] about the incident
19.   without getting into the details of the case
20.   but (.) tell me a little bit about what happened with this guy
21.   and how he ended up getting his registered items stolen
22. C: right well the details of the case itself were that …

(forty seconds of talk deleted)

23. I: how might you have (.) avoided that situation
24.   or put yourself in a more informed position
25. C: good question er:m and something which er
26.   I- I did subsequently- actually I did subsequently take
27.   on the following Monday
28.   was to *seek advice from the (xx manager)* who had returned
29.   however the advice that was given from the (xx manager)
30.   was *the same* (2) **action that I had** *in principle* erm
31.   decided to take before erm the action taken
32.   was confirmed as being the right course of action (.)
33.   it was at area level (.) at (x senior manager) level
34.   that it became an issue [er:m
35. I: yeah okay]

Interviewer notes for this section (**R** = result and reflection):

R *Decision* took outside of area policy:
(Manager x) want to see *firmer action taken.*
Argued the point. Saved unit budget,
Saved employee from *losing* role.
R *Seek advice from (xx manager)* –
this *was the same as in principal* –

Mails Integrity briefing.
Very unclear as to what he understood to be the position

All but the last two statements of these notes refer to lines 1–35 of the interview. These last two statements sum up the rest of this 'learning from mistakes' question, which continues for nearly five more minutes. Up to these last two statements, the notes show a similar level of co-authoring as with Gladston (example 54). But the last two comments are summaries of a long exchange, end on a very negative tone and erase Brian's voice; there are several minutes when no notes are taken and the interviewer shifts away from what the candidate might have learnt to hyperquestion his knowledge of the policy, which causes an extended misalignment (not shown here) where Brian attempts to defend his position on the policy.

In contrast with the Gladston example, the interviewer does not make a written prompt of the points Brian is making in order to follow them up. Instead, engaging with the misalignment leaves no space for writing and he only summarises his negative perception of Brian at the end of the notes. And this negative assessment seems at odds with the earlier noting that Brian saved money and someone's job. In addition, in his first note the interviewer has translated and upgraded Brian's 'notion of zero tolerance' (line 4) to 'outside area policy,' which then produces the extended misalignment. Unlike Gladston, Brian has no control over the topic choice or what is written down. A lack of detailed notes usually signals negativity.

Later, in the feedback session, the interviewer commented that he thought Brian was untrustworthy, tried to put up an 'impressive facade' and that, in this example, was 'being disingenuous and arguing on a semantic point.' Brian's attempts to defend his position are erased, since they are not recorded. This erasure – combined with the recorded lack of clarity – allow the interviewer to claim him as something of a 'blagger' and therefore untrustworthy, despite his frankness and honesty in the opening lines (1–12).

One other feature of writing the unsuccessful interview relates to the lack of tolerance of unofficial remarks. While both Lloyd and Gladston make off-the-cuff remarks which are not recorded but are treated as part of the social business of the interview, Brian's comment later in the interview of, 'You'll have to forgive me I'm getting a little bit tired' is recorded as 'said he was tired' and used against him in the wash-up session. When a negative dynamic is well established, interviewers may cherry-pick remarks to reinforce it. To sum up, we see the opening up of a gap between the interviewer's assessment of Brian and his own account of himself. The notes do the judgment work. The gap between Brian's claims, as noted in the result section and the criticism of him as 'very unclear,' encapsulates the final thumbnail sketch of incompetence and untrustworthiness.

Lack of Success Both Interactionally and in the Writing

In the next example, the interactional weight of note taking, which some candidates experience much more heavily than others, is combined with an analysis of the notes taken and serves as a contrast to Gladston's interview above. Although Junior is successful in being promoted to a junior management position, this is in spite of rather than because of his interview performance. He came with a positive reputation of being an active manager; this trumps his rather poor performance and the lack of any other highly rated candidate to fill the final post (example 34). The interviewer is the same as Gladston's. Junior is asked a question about the competence 'seeks improvement,' for an example where he has adopted a new practice which has affected the way he works. The first part of his response is given here:

Example 56: Junior – BAME British, Successful
(Low-rated interview performance.)

1. C: yeah it was a- well we had a ***mail sort*** work ***plan changed***
2. I: right} {(looks down)
3. C: it had come in at different times (.)
4. I: okay} {(begins writing) (.)
5.   ***so the mail sort work plan changed***
6. C: yeah (.)
7. I: okay how had it changed
8. C: we used to get (.) e:r
9.   before mail sort comes in in the morning ***two mail sort***
10.   ***two's two lorries and two lo- mails sort three lorries*** (.)
11. I: so two mail sort two
12. C: yeah
13. I: a:nd two mail sort three
14. C: yeah
15. I: these are lorries yeah
16. C: yeah of lorries yeah coming in
17. I: coming in to where
18. C: er:m the mail centre
19. I: which mail centre=
20. C: =(*x*)- (***xxx***) ***mail centre***
21. I: ***into*** (***xxx***) ***mail centre***

The notes cover the situation and opportunity components of the SOARRR (the variant of STAR used in this organisation) and this situation and opportunity (seventy-three transcribed lines in all) took over three minutes of the allotted five minutes per competence question, leaving little time for the crucial result and reflection sections. Line *a* and the first part of line *b* of the notes cover the segment given here. (Lines *c* to *e* cover the remainder of this section not shown here.)

Interviewer notes for this section (**S** = Situation and **O** = Objective):

a　**S**　***Mailsort Plan*** (^^^) ***changed*** **2 M2 + 2M3 lorries**
b　***into*** (xxx) **_Mailcentre._** Prior to 9am. 2 came before 9am 1M2

c　**O**　1 M2 @ 11am – M3 @ 3pm　　　　　　　1M3
d　　　→ staffing level changed: 24 people – 16
e　became staggered

Although Junior's information is summarised in these notes – the two sets of lorries bringing the mail to be sorted and the effect on staffing – his voice is not present. And while the SOARRR structure is expected to elicit some detail, this terse list of facts comes without the narrator's viewpoint or moral self. Both sides seem to struggle over the labour of writing, simultaneously investing in its importance while inhibiting its value. And this stems from the interviewer's interactional conduct – both his more universal behaviour (the need to take notes and stick to the STAR structure) and his more particularistic behaviour (his unease in an interview that is not going well, shown in extended lack of eye contact) – and Junior's misinterpretation of this conduct.

While the situation component has been routinised into a set of features – when, where, numbers involved and so on – the extended elicitation of these facts, as in this case and in others given earlier, is often a marker of troubled encounters with the interviewer 'talking down' to focus on increasingly easily writeable items (6.2). Both sides seem to become locked into closed questions and minimal answers, which amplifies the significance of detail. For example, the interviewer re-dictates to himself at lines 5, 11 and 13, thereby increasing interviewer control over topic and interaction. This tight control may have fed into judgments made about Junior in the wash-up that he 'needed spoon-feeding,' 'needed a lot of assistance', needed to be 'weaned' and wouldn't be able to 'stand on his own two feet.'

This pattern of closed questions and brief responses continues throughout the interview and tends to break up the narrative flow so that the moral heart of the story is not clearly reached. The concentration on detail is interpreted by Junior as being significant and he continues to give exact times and numbers later in the interview (see lines *b*, *c* and *d* of interviewer notes). At this later point, the interviewer does not write down most of what Junior says and interrupts him to summarise. These inappropriately staged details suggest that Junior is unaware of the SOARRR structure being cued for and the need to frame his responses differently if they are to be processed onto the form. There are several other moments in the interview (not illustrated here) where misalignments and misunderstandings occur because of the need to fit Junior's story into the form's schema.

A lack of familiarity with the interview design is not the only weight of the interview for Junior. As with Mohammed, the act of writing seems difficult to manage, particularly picking up on the interviewer's writing behaviour. At line 2 the interviewer looks down as soon as Junior responds, and at lines 4 and 7 cues Junior to expand while still looking down. This encourages the pattern of hypercueing and 'talking down' which develops, and throughout the interview a lack of eye gaze leads Junior to be more hesitant and to trail off. Again, in contrast with the successful and more conversational interviews, the writing seems to inhibit talk, rather than being seen as an affirmation that what is spoken is recordable. Perhaps less successful candidates are not simply misreading the cues, but are alert to the possibility that writing can also be used as a mode of disengagement. Interpretations are open and meaning comes from local social relations as they are enacted, so writing can be a positive or negative act for the candidate.

Conclusion

As Goffman says of the 'quiet sorting process' of the interview, it conceals from both those being sorted and from the interviewers themselves the basis for decision-making. The ideological work done to move from perceived objective and standardised decision-making, through local practices to a pure subjectivity is hidden in plain sight. The shifting in evaluative criteria and the amplification/erasure of the candidates' voice in the talk and text of the interview simultaneously provide defensive evidence while covering up the processes that determine it. So the basis of decision-making is concealed not only from those in the interview room, but from the institution at large.

This concealment is most clearly realised in writing the interview, where candidates have to quietly but actively manage the process, yet the interviewers' power to select and record cannot be scrutinised; their notes reflect the overall emotional tone of the interview. The co-authored notes imply a mutuality in talk captured in writing. In these successful interviews, the version of the self given off is, among other things, structurally appropriate and so smoothly processed. And this in turn allows transgression of the institutional frame to be accepted, occasionally. As well as voicing much of the text, candidates are permitted to digress and to joke about the writing.

In contrast, the institutional character of notes from unsuccessful interviews are less tuned to the candidates' voice, index more of the interviewer's voice and are less coherent. In sum, they represent a more fractured encounter and a less pleasingly holistic sketch of the candidate. Writing fixes the linguistic penalty of candidates whose communicative resources do not meet institutional standards. The contexts and text trajectories that surround and are produced in the interview show that this penalty results not so much from individual choice or prejudice, but from institutions' processes and the interviewers' local practices in adhering and responding to them.

Chapters 5–8 have looked at candidates from local white British and BAME backgrounds, as well as migrant candidates. It is to the communicative resources of this latter group specifically that we turn in chapters 9 and 10, and to the penalties that can face any candidate in an interview – but are amplified in the case of linguistic minorities.

9 Migrant Candidates and the Linguistic Penalty

Over the last chapters, I have discussed how all candidates are required to perform a particular institutional self through the linguistic technologies of the interview. Chapter 8 looked at how the institutionalised processes hide the subjectivity of assessment behind them. Here and in chapter 10 I will draw together how these processes of social evaluation produce the special weight of the interview for migrants. These are not the candidates who are like 'fish in water' (Bourdieu and Wacquant, 1992: 127), swimming in their natural environment, but those who feel the weight of the water. The linguistic penalties of such gatekeeping encounters as job interviews are clear from their outcomes: migrant candidates do much less well and British BAME groups do slightly less well than local white British candidates (3.8). This stratified outcome has also been widely reported in other institutional assessment settings, such as medical education and licensing exams (Woolf et al., 2013; Roberts et al., 2014).

The norms and conventions of the job interview produce discursive tripwires that can make any candidate tumble. But as we have seen, migrants are more likely to be detected and alarms set off than other groups of candidates. As well as the assessment of hybrid discourses and extended narrative skills, social evaluation depends upon the processability of candidate talk (sometimes explicitly mentioned) and social judgments about accent and other aspects of communicative style (never mentioned). For many of this group, talk becomes alarming and burdensome.

It is difficult to address the linguistic inequalities built into selection processes because there is no analytic public discourse about language, and the line of judgment is often hidden from the decision-makers themselves, as chapter 8 discusses. The stratified outcomes – in which migrants routinely fall into the lowest rank – induce easy and general explanations of cultural difference and linguistic deficit. Such simple and dismissive assessments are based on a mix of ideological formations, some of which are easier to identify than others. As a backdrop to summing up the particular weight of the job interview on migrant candidates, it is worth revisiting some of the hegemonic, common sense ideologies of language and their palpable but largely unspoken effect on workplace selection decisions – and the potential for indirect discrimination.

9.1 Common Sense Ideologies of Language

In chapter 8.3, some of the key ideas of language ideology were briefly discussed when considering how social evaluation is carried out. These included notions of standardisation, and so the noticing of discrepancies from the standard. Here we look in more detail at how these ideological formations have an incisive role in the penalties faced by migrant candidates, even in the banal conduct of the interview (Blommaert and Rampton, 2011). These formations, or indigenous assessments, assume three things: that everyone knows what it means to speak a language, and there is one correct and aesthetically pleasing way to speak; that anyone can assess someone's language ability and value it and the speaker; and that it is common sense to read off from someone's talk bold statements about general competence, personality and social adequacy. This is the proxy work that language does. It is also assumed that linguistic ability is pretty much fixed, whatever the situation and corresponds to a 'level' based on the first few minutes of talk – and as such, is readily measurable (Budach, et al., 2003; Heller, 2003). Such assumptions are then associated either with particular ethnic groups or with migrants and 'others' more generally.

What stands out from the public discourses is the common sense assumption that failure is a matter of individual incompetence rather than, as Bourdieuvian analysis identifies, structural inequalities. To work with Bourdieu's metaphor a little more, it is the choppy conditions of the interview water that cause the fish to struggle and fail, not the fish's inability to swim in other conditions. Or to put it more prosaically, language proficiency is interactionally produced (Fosgerau, 2013; Tranekjær, 2015: 179–193). And since this water is made up of the flow of talk and interaction, this final stage of the selection process always has the potential to produce a linguistic penalty for migrant groups. Language as a cultural resource is the ultimate capital – and all the more powerful for its capacity to work as both a covert and overt mechanism, as the critical sociolinguistic literature has vigorously debated.

The discriminatory force of these common sense ideologies is not easy to identify in the data. For example, the erasure of any notion of multilingualism in interviews (9.5) at the lower end of the UK job market is clear in the data, but it is more difficult to establish the reach of other common sense ideologies about language and negative ethnic stereotyping in institutional contexts, where such stances are usually rendered invisible or euphemised. (In our data there were only two mentions of a link between interactional conduct and a particular minority ethnic group, in all the recorded wash-up and feedback sessions). The reach of these linguistic ideologies in job interviews can be better understood by looking outside the conventional job interview – in both non-linguistic and sociolinguistic studies – at research on language and employment (the effect of what is called 'low levels of language' on access to the labour market), plus language attitude studies. We will also look at two critical sociolinguistic areas which have an impact on practice: the legal aspects of language discrimination and special programmes aimed at job-seeking migrants.

9.2   Language, Access and Attitudes

Language and Access to the Labour Market

The research on race, ethnicity and the labour market in the UK has been carried out largely by economists and other non-language specialists in the social sciences. These studies, mentioned in 3.1 and 3.3, show a persistent gap in employment rates between the majority and BAME groups. Other studies specify that competence in English is a factor. A gap of about twenty to twenty-five per cent has been identified, between 'fluent English speakers' and those 'who struggle with English' (Chiswick and Miller, 1995; Wood and Wybron, 2015).

Sociolinguists would rightly critique aspects of the methodology used in these studies, particularly around issues of categorisation, how language levels were assessed and the common sense ideologies that underpin them. These few studies alone exhibit a flurry of different ways of categorising this migrant group as 'immigrants,' as well as those with 'low English proficiency,' who 'struggle with English,' 'do not have a good command of English' or are 'not fluent English speakers.' They also describe the 'native-immigrant gap,' having 'English as an additional language' and 'non-native English speakers.' These studies of migrants in the labour market establish unequivocally the persistent disadvantage migrants face, but it is framed as a matter of individual competence, with an on-off switch: having enough English, or not. This unwittingly feeds into an automatic association of migrants with language problems and does not address any of the structural reasons for this substantial gap.[42]

Social Judgment of Accent

By contrast, the literature on social assessments of language in social psychology and sociolinguistics shifts the responsibility onto those making judgments. The social psychological literature on language attitudes – both the general literature and that related specifically to employment (Ball and Giles, 1982: 101–122) – is concerned with the negative effects of 'non-standard accents' based on the widely used (and more recently modified) matched-guise technique (Gardner and Lambert, 1972), including the assertion that such accents are noticed more, categorised on ethnic lines and affect judgments more than the physical appearance of BAME groups (Rakić et al., 2011).[43]

While the sociolinguistic literature critiques the 'mentalist' approach of these studies and instead discusses the social judgment of accent in naturally occurring social interaction (Lippi-Green, 1997; Stroud, 2004), it also acknowledges the pervasive effects of accent at the institutional gate where social evaluation is crucial (Spotti, 2016). Drawing on the history of shibboleth tests to classify individuals as 'one of us' or 'other' in any assessments directly or indirectly testing language, McNamara discusses 'the pervasive phenomenon of monitoring the social significance of accent' in every day institutional interactions (McNamara and Roever, 2006: 158). So from different methodological perspectives, the studies of access and attitude are broadly aligned in recognising that accents are noted and habitually rated – although rarely explicitly (Dragojeviç et al., 2013).

Occupational psychologists and others in the HR field, involved in selection and diversity matters, may well be aware of the general findings on language attitude – or at least familiar with the emotional public discourses that associate sound with stereotyping and 'accent' with negative ethnic stereotyping (Crystal, 2018). The guidance and training given to HR professionals to guard against bias suggests that they acknowledge that interviewers may hold such negative attitudes. It seems plausible that the general judgments of the competence and personal characteristics of migrant candidates were influenced by these commonplace attitudes. However, equal opportunity policies and training against bias regularly police what is allowable to be given as a reason for rejection. There was no explicit discussion of accent in our data of informants' talk.

9.3 Legal Aspects of Language-Based Discrimination

Common sense ideologies of language may leak in everywhere, yet language as a topic escapes in the cool, evidentiary world of legal action. Language is a powerful discriminator, and yet powerless as a reason for discrimination. Given the fifty or so years of anti-discriminatory legislation in much of the Western world, the fact that language-based discrimination is so rarely the subject of any judicial process might seem surprising, until we take account of common sense ideologies of language which suggest two main reasons for such a modest number of successful cases. Firstly, when issues of fairness arise, language tends to be put in a box separate from discrimination. It is seen as a matter of competence. Linguistic discrimination is deemed acceptable because it is transformed into language incompetence.

Secondly, people's variable use of language is not subject to hard evidentiary standards. In her study of language-based discrimination in the USA, Lippi-Green (1997: 147–181) discusses some of the forty language-focussed employment cases in the US between 1972 and 2007. While equality legislation includes certain protected classes such as race, gender and religion, language is given much more latitude for the reasons noted above: no clear definitions of what the language/communicative demands of the job might be, a general reliance on commonly held beliefs about language (assumed expertise) rather than relying on language experts, erasure of the jointly produced intelligibility of the speaker and little consistency in the way courts approach issues of language and communication. Where there were direct associations between negative social evaluations and stigmatised uses of language, the burden was on individual incompetence, e.g. 'The appellant's accent was undesirable' (Lippi-Green, 1997: 170). Language evidence does not stand up in court, so language escapes from the legal process.

In other countries apart from the US, there is a similar dearth of legal judgments which expose and penalise language discrimination. In the UK there is a legal requirement only to use language selection criteria appropriate for the job, but no specificity of what this might be (Roberts et al., 1992; 3.2). For example, in 2017 the London branch of Uber (the international taxi service) was told it could only license drivers if they could pass a written English test. Subsequently a court ruling upheld the requirement that in order to be licensed in the UK, drivers must take an English language test which requires them to write a short essay on a subject such as river pollution or festivals (*The Guardian*, 4 March 2017). How an essay on the environment might help Uber drivers communicate with passengers was not raised.

It is difficult to establish the gap between selection criteria and what is actually required in terms of communicative ability in the workplace, because there are few ethnographic studies which observe unremarkable language use in the contexts of low-paid work. The workplace studies undertaken[44] suggest that the work environment routinely either limits communication to minimal functional exchanges – often because of the noise of such places (Holmes and Woodhams, 2013) – or allows for work units to operate in the preferred language of the unit. These studies indicate that shop floor communication is far removed from the deft footwork, engaging stories and institutional discourse mode of the routine job interview.

As well as the covert selection criteria which are the subject of this book, there are other conditions and processes in the workplace which produce linguistic inequalities but are rarely challenged in the courts (Piller, 2016). These include language practices in factories which exclude minority workers from access to where power is exercised and language (the dominant language) is most intense (Goldstein, 1997; Duff, 2008), plus requirements for a 'pure' standard variety of a language – in Canadian call centres which exclude vernacular speakers, for example (Roy, 2003; Budach et al., 2003). Another covert but seemingly overt employment policy in Australia, discussed by Piller and Lising (2014), lets employers off the discrimination hook. It is made quite explicit that there are no English skills required to do butchering work in a meat packing factory. However, proficiency in English is used to ensure flexibility in this labour market, since migrant workers have to score Band 5 in the IELTS (International English Language Testing System) examination in order to get a visa extension or apply for permanent residency. These unremarkable acts of language discrimination, in job interviews and elsewhere, only tend to surface when they are the focus of attention in what have been called 'migrant events.'[45]

9.4   'Migrant Events' as a Window onto Job Interviews

The sociolinguistic studies of institutions and migration tend to fall into two broad categories: those which – like the job interviews analysed here – are open to all job seekers, and those which are 'migrant events' (Louise Tranekjær, 2015: 6–8) where (entirely or very substantially) migrants are the object of the institutional gaze.[46]

While both are concerned with processes of classification, regulation and legitimation, it is the status, competence and personality of applicants as migrants – where they are the objects of specific policies and practices – which give a window onto the linguistic penalties in general selection interviews. 'Migrant events' help us to reach plausible conclusions about what lies behind the judgment of migrant candidates in general job interviews.

Most importantly, they elucidate the language/cultural weight on migrant candidates and also the hiatus between these events and the actual language requirements of a particular job.

The programmes that are designed for migrant integration into the labour market – such as those in Belgium, Denmark, Italy and Switzerland – do the specific job of producing commodifiable labour power (Del Percio, 2016, 2017; Flubacher et al., 2017; 2.1). Where such state-designed work integration programmes include selection interviews, we can see a specific focus on language/cultural differences. Although not designated as language tests, language is topicalised together with other categories – namely religion, nation and culture – as recent studies in Denmark discuss. In interviews for internships, for example, there is an explicit orientation to candidates as low-proficiency speakers of Danish with frequent, 'Do you understand?' questions (Tranekjær, 2015).

The everyday stereotyping that these categories evoke makes them powerful players in the interview process (Tranekjær, 2015: 238–249), where their use and the negotiation of their meaning in the context of the workplace serve to reproduce power asymmetries and differences. They also demonstrate the wiring together of language and cultural processes in identifying and amplifying differences, as well as in producing a particular interview register. These processes of 'ethnification' (Day, 1994, 2006) arise from the interaction between the use of specific categories such as 'Danish' or 'Muslim' and the rhetorical strategies used by interviewers to set up contrasts between 'Danish ways' and 'others.' (Tranekjær, 2015: 127–162; Kirilova, 2013: 113–140). For example, the specific skills of applicants are backgrounded and more abstract and general practices of the host country's 'ways' and 'systems' are foregrounded, to contrast them with the cultural differences the applicants are assumed to have (Tranekjær, 2015: 161).

The upshot from this type of intervention comes with a terrible irony: just those types of provision set up to shape and integrate migrants as employable workers are the ones where a lack of cultural and linguistic fluency is most attended to. Interviewers tend to reject precisely those migrant candidates whom the special work integration projects have been set up to support, and accept those who are already most culturally attuned to the majority workplace culture. In employment-orientated 'migrant events,' there is a shift from liberal practice – providing opportunities for linguistic minorities – to neoliberal ones, in which the burden falls on constantly improving individuals (Martin-Rojo, 2016; Allan, 2016) whose ability to culturally align is intensively scrutinised, and where flexibility in the labour market overrides migrants' self-identified needs.

The argument is that many of the stereotypes that coalesce around and are made explicit in these migrant events – and are highlighted in other research – may well also be in place in gatekeeping events such as the job interview, which are open to applicants whatever their background and status. However, in these non-migrant events the stereotypes remain implicit – except for occasional comments in the wash-up sessions about language competence. Migrant candidates have to respond, defend and account for the type of assumptions made more explicit in the 'migrant event' interviews. It would seem that whether cultural/linguistic matters are made explicit or not, there is always the potential for talk and interaction to index perceived social differences and social discrepancies arising from interviewers' normative assumptions. And while in migrant events candidates can be discussed in terms of language and ethnicity, in job interviews set within an equal opportunities framework the discourses are euphemised through proxies, and the weight of the interview water is not attended to. So as I have done here, analysts must draw on indirect means of understanding decision-making processes as well as the talk and text data.

In the second part of the chapter, the weight of the interview on migrants – the linguistic penalties they face – will be considered in five different areas, drawing together analysis from previous chapters and its implications specifically for migrant candidates in the context of some of the public discourses touched on above. These areas are the erosion of migrant capital, metapragmatic fluency and coherence, cohesion and processability, heightened institutionalisation and how any aspects of these may be used as proxies for competence and personality.

9.5   Erosion of Migrant Capital

The design and evaluative criteria of the job interview erode the capital of migrant candidates. The valuing of soft skills and competences and the event's unspoken linguistic weight foregrounds just that capital which candidates are least likely to have amassed, while backgrounding their professional and technical expertise and qualifications.[47]

Multilingualism has been given some new value in the globalised marketplace, but such value depends upon the linguistic economy of the state, current public and employment discourses, the changing labour market and the social class and professional background of the speakers. In mainland Europe and Canada, for example, late capitalism and globalisation have led to the commodification and valuing of minority and lingua franca languages (Heller, 2003; Duchêne, 2009; Budach et al., 2003) which can also be used to manage the macro 'one language' policy within the realities of everyday working practices (Angouri, 2013; Apfelbaum and Meyer, 2010). However, even on the promising terrain of globalised economies only certain languages, certain language speakers and certain standards of language are valued – or given distinction, in Bourdieu's terms (DuBord, 2010; Flubacher et al., 2017; Lorente, 2017; Moyer, 2018).[48]

In those countries where English is the dominant and state language (so-called English-speaking countries, or the Anglosphere), the fact of multilingualism is largely ignored despite its functional exploitation when necessary in workplace settings. This 'banal multilingualism,' where any languages other than the state language(s) are taken to be 'natural' and not valued (Duchêne and Heller, 2012), reflects 'the monolingual mindset' (Clyne, 2005) and decapitalises both less-skilled migrants and those with professional backgrounds (Martin-Rojo, 2015, chapter 8).

All the migrant candidates in our data brought other languages to the interview, but they were never acknowledged at any time either in the interviews or in the subsequent decision-making process. These resources were not capitalised, despite their potential value in the workplace. For example, the selection process for promotion to higher-grade operatives in a food factory in the Midlands ignored the multilingual skills of some candidates, despite the fact that our ethnographic studies in the factory showed that there were many so-called 'ethnic lines' where both workers and supervisor routinely used languages other than English and communication with management was with a bilingual 'go-between' (Roberts, Campbell and Robinson, 2008; Roberts et al., 1992). The English-only rule means that migrants are seen as having a language problem, but the institutionalised workplace is not.

9.6 Metapragmatic Fluency and Coherence

The soft skills and competence model at the heart of interview design depend absolutely on discursive resources. Unsynthesised accounts are judged as too 'lecturing' (Nazrul, Vijay or Ravi, for example) or, by contrast, too 'emotional' (for instance Sara, Yohannes, Tahir or Bruno). Similarly, a story perceived as incoherent is rapidly interrupted and the candidate is talked down to (for example Luis). These hybrid discourses and narratological skills are culturally normative, have stable and recognisable indexical meaning and form a central part of the linguistic capital required of the job interview. But the relative success of candidates depends also upon the conversational resources called up in the moment – the highly localised inferences made and responses offered. And we have seen that the legitimacy of talk in interviews at the lower end of the market does not conform to the 'legitimate or official language' (Bourdieu, 1991: 130) but is part of a different linguistic economy where certain types of dysfluencies are tolerated, provided other rhetorics of engagement and persuasion are present (6.3), and where sense-making rather than some strict notion of 'fluency' is what matters.

Both these more stable elements and the conversational resources scrambled for the fugitive moment depend upon a series of metapragmatic functions and cohesive features which make no real distinction between language and cultural processes and are used, through contextualisation cues, to frame and govern and make processable and engaging what is going on. For example, metapragmatic functions, as well as including what moves are to be expected in an exchange and how to sequence them (the system requirements, 8.2), crucially help to realise the appropriate footing – in particular when to use involvement strategies such as imagery and humour – and facework, or knowing when to display aspects of the self explicitly or convey them indirectly (as Gladston does in 6.3, 6.5). This is evident in the following example from Joe, a local white British candidate:

Example 57: Joe – White British, Successful

```
 1.  I:   so all we're looking for here is er:m
 2.       an example where you have done
 3.       similar type of routine repetitive work
 4.  C:   painting magnolia for three weeks hhh
 5.       that was the most (.) painting (.)
 6.       you couldn't get anything more erm repetitive (2)
 7.       walls with nothing (.) just walls the size of hhh
 8.       just giant walls in a warehouse say fifty feet high (.)
 9.       painting one colour (.)
10.       day in and day out day in and day out hhh
11.       there ain't nothing more repetitive than that (.)
12.       you'll be pleased to be paint- (.)
13.       white ceilings was- was a bit of a pleasure (2)
14.       and with printing as well (.) it's d- I'll let write (5)
15.  I:   hhh (3) and this this what you're talking about
16.       except you ((was)) seven hours a day as well
17.       [(((that long))
18.  C:   yeah you we're] talking r- half hour- half hour lunch
19.       and it's- (.) wouldn't even class it as lunch (.)
20.       eating on the job (.)
```

In Joe's story of painting a warehouse, we can see how he structures and progresses his narrative account through a series of vivid images and repetitions so that it hangs together without being formally fluent.

Joe infers from the question that while routine work is boring, the story about it can be engaging and humorous and he immediately responds with a set of conversational involvement strategies which are far removed from the impersonal and discreet institutional mode that Bourdieu describes. The emotional tone of this interview is startlingly different from that of almost all migrant candidates – even the successful ones. Like some of the most successful candidates, Joe plays with the rules of the game, talking humorously, vividly and without formality. These strategies include deleting any preface to the story in line 4, playing with the normative rules of storytelling and so establishing a relatively intimate footing, and then a set of repetitions, formulaic expressions, metaphors and ellipses which progress the narrative structure and lead to the interviewer's involved and detailed response (lines 15–17). For example, the repetition of 'painting' and 'walls' (4–12), the formulaic expression 'day in and day out,' the ellipsis of 'magnolia' (a well-known, off-white colour of paint) and the metaphor of 'giant walls.' All these strategies cohere rhythmically into a narrative of repetitive work. Indeed, the 'experientially grounded,' vivid detail of the account is not only acceptable and easily processable but persuasive and credible (Edwards, 1991; 6.3).

But Joe also has many features that might be called dysfluent in a formal setting: unfinished sentences (line 7, line 12), some ambiguity over relevance (line 14) and false starts (lines 18 and 19). Neither the overall outcome for Joe nor any local interactional conduct from either side suggest that these features contributed to how he was assessed. What might objectively be called dysfluencies such as false starts, unfinished utterances, pauses and stammerings – and which might be perceived as lacking cohesion or coherence – appear to be widely tolerated, both with Joe and other successful candidates such as Sandeep, Lloyd and Gladston, provided other strategies of engagement and intelligibility are present. In other words, 'non-incoherence' (Silverstein, 2003) is good enough to let through a candidate's linguistic capital. However, when a lack of coherence is perceived as an issue, then common sense ideologies of language kick in as institutional constraints, discursive and narrative differences and perceived lack of clarity are bundled up together. Some speakers' dysfluencies matter more than others' and some speakers' utterances are more listenable to and acceptable than others:

> The competence adequate to produce sentences that are likely to be understood may be quite inadequate to produce sentences that are likely to be listened to, likely to be recognised as acceptable in all the situations in which there is occasion to speak. (Bourdieu, 1991: 55)

Those who were overtly judged as linguistically incompetent, both in the wash-ups and feedback sessions, were all migrant candidates. Any doubts about the processability of their talk became part of an overall assessment of their lack of competence or unacceptable personality. At this point, the differences in ways of speaking sometimes become the focus and interviewer discomfort coalesces around undifferentiated statements of 'poor English' or 'hard to follow.' As I have suggested, this is not a matter of 'fluent,' expert English speakers on the one hand and migrant learners of English on the other, as Ben Rampton has elegantly shown in his case study of Mandeep (Rampton, 2016: 104). In other contexts, such 'hard-to-follow' moments might not have arisen at all. Nevertheless, for some migrant candidates the lack of surface cohesion in performing extended utterances led to such negative judgments, and it is important to analyse these responses in understanding some elements of the linguistic penalty.

9.7   Cohesion and Processability

Identifying characteristics of speakers' non-expert language use can build up a deficit picture of migrants and their limitations. However, the purpose of such analysis here is to show how the activity of the job interview creates conditions for speaking which put particular and unnecessary demands on candidates' linguistic resources. Linguistic limitations are interactionally produced and amplified by interviewer conduct and communicative problems should not be interpreted as matters of individual or general incompetence:

> Although the problems we have described are communicative in nature, the question is not one of appropriate discourse styles. Misunderstandings are mutual and *they are as much due to the nature of the situations in which interaction takes place, and to the standards by which words are evaluated, as to linguistic or cultural facts as such.* (Gumperz, 1982b: 195, my italics)

The 'difficult-to-follow' moments tended to occur in extended answers, either narratives – large or small, both one-offs and iteratives – in response to a request for an example or when candidates chose to illustrate more analytic answers with an illustration. These are both cognitively and linguistically complex. The speaker has to recall several incidents to exemplify a theme (such as being good at teamwork), locate them in time and space, show how they are relevant to the question and tie them together into a cohesive whole; all this to be done without benefit of the immediate workplace context and its material/semiotic potential for supporting talk, and under the intense gaze of the interviewers. As Linde says of narrative performance, what is actually a 'temporally discontinuous' set of events has to be made into a linked narrative – consecutive, but also related causally and/or metaphorically (Linde, 2000), as Joe's story is.

The problem of comprehensibility in extended institutional encounters, as Gumperz argues, is primarily one of conversational cohesion (and the related notion of conversational inference in processing potentially cohesive utterances): how surface syntactic, grammatical, lexical and prosodic features help us to read between the lines so that a speaker's turn can be processed into manageable chunks which hang together, make sense and fit with listeners' metapragmatic expectations (in other words, how to segment speech so that it becomes processable). This is explored in some detail in his analysis of speakers of South Asian and Filipino backgrounds (Gumperz, 1982b: 22–56, 163–195).

Gumperz argues that for discourse to be cohesive the following must be clear:

- the main message and what is less important (topicalisation, relativisation and emphasis);

- that which is assumed to be shared, including implicit knowledge of what makes discourse cohesive (such as the use of ellipsis, anaphoric and deictic pronouns, conjunctions, repetition, associated metaphors);

- the distinction between old and new information;

- the anchoring of the messages in time and space;

- the progression of utterances and some sense of completeness;

- speaker perspective (the speakers' own point of view as relatively personal or impersonal and how they distinguish between theirs and others' voices and the deft movement between positionalities).

As we have seen, Joe produces enough of these surface features – such as topicalisation, ellipsis, deictic pronouns, repetition and speaker perspective – for them to carry him through the story and elicit an involved response. His talk is engaging and processable enough and the less cohesive features are tolerated.

While prosody and word stress figure as elements in cohesion, the notion of accent in terms of segmental features – how vowels and consonants sound – was never mentioned by interviewers in any wash-ups or video feedback sessions, as I have previously said. Rather the negative comments listed above appear to link to discursive, conversational and cohesive differences and not to how they sounded (although, as discussed above, there may be unarticulated ideologies at play). So the analysis here concentrates on the lexicogrammatical, syntactic and prosodic oddities which seem to affect cohesion and the ways information is located in time and space.[49]

The performance of two candidates, Luis and Yohannes, are used here as case studies of the problem of conversational cohesion. While they are both candidates whose relative incompetence is commented on, these features can also appear in candidates' talk that is readily processable most of the time, such as Vijay's (8.2, 10.5).

Luis

Luis, a Tagalog speaker from the Philippines, was introduced in example 23. The data from his interview show how rhetorical and narratological differences lead to interactional difficulties and a shutting down of opportunities for him. All these uncomfortable moments would seem, unsurprisingly, to put additional stress on his linguistic resources. While there are hesitations and small grammatical slips, these are less likely to affect comprehensibility and Luis is able, when he has the chance and is not cut off, to convey his main ideas (9.8). However, if we look again at the teamwork question (analysed from a different perspective in chapter 6) and then his response in example 59 to part of the repetitive work question, certain cohesive links are not clear:

Example 58: Luis – Filipino Migrant, Unsuccessful
(This example picks up from the last few lines of example 23.)

1. C: yeah] an er an it was er you're gonna say
2.   it's gonna be physically demanding
3.   because you have to be alert (.)
4.   you have to be always on motivated
5.   because [you're in
6. I: but could you] tell me er
7.   what do you like most about working with a team
8. C: ah- yeah ah (.) on- on the restaurant I work it-
9.   I like to work it because er of er ahhm some er (.) ah
10.   working on an- on young people and on older people
11.   because you'll get to know ah ah
12.   s- you know ah y- o:h about some (clicks tongue)
13.   because you know some young people are some-
14.   some high temper and y- you'll never know [how
15. I: yeah what] do you like about working
16.   in the team [is that
17. C: ah]

Example 59: Luis – Filipino Migrant, Unsuccessful

1. I: what do you dislike about a repetitive job=
2. C: =oh no e:r I- ther- there's nothing I dislike in repet-
3.   repetitive job it's j- it's only i- it's a new-
4.   it's a great chance for me
5.   because (.) I think some [new work
6. I: you don't] find it boring and eh-
7.   you don't find it boring
8. C: but- I find it boring but sometimes but sometimes erm
9.   the manager ask me for some- yeah some- yeah (.)
10.   at first you're going to find it boring
11.   but when you get used to and you know the-
12.   you handle the job eh properly (.)
13.   then- then ah then th- then there's a time
14.   that you're going to ask the manager
15.   just there's some you have to give me
16.   because I finish here already
17.   and the manager going to- you finish already
18.   okay you- you can rest now
19.   sometime is that [hhh
20. I: okay]
21. C: because I do it- I do it ah g- ah ah
22.   one by one and it's straight an- I ha-
23.   I want it to be finish and that's it
24. I: right [okay
25. C: th- th]
26. I: now (.) let's go to the next question

The following outlines the 'difficult-to-process' utterances in Luis's interview:

1. **Pronoun use:** Shifts between 'you' and 'I' make it hard to determine
    whether he is talking about his personal action or a more general, deon-
    tic statement about workers in general (for instance, example 58 at lines
    8–12 and example 59 at lines 9–18). This affects the listener's judg-
    ment of speaker involvement and perspective, and thus assessments of
    agency. There is also a vague anaphoric reference in example 58 lines
    8–9; what does 'it' refer to?

2. **Grammatically cued expectations which then are not met:** Luis sets
    up causality with 'because' in example 58 at lines 9–13, but this list-
    ing of reasons gives no sense of completion. Similarly, in example 59

at lines 10–13 we expect completeness in the idea of 'at first … but then.' Luis does convey this idea, but there is a long qualifying utterance between the 'but' and the 'then' and no clear prosodic contrast in terms of perceptual stress either in time – before and then later – or in the progression of the theme that once you are experienced, then you can perform better.

3. **False starts and reformulations, but no evidence that this is a restart rather than a continuer:** Elsewhere in the interview, where he is allowed more interactional space, such false starts are not problematic; he manages a rhythmic repetition which carries him over the false start in a way that is commonplace in those speaking English as their expert language. But elsewhere – as in example 58 at lines 9–10 and example 59 at line 13 – it is difficult to disambiguate whether the incomplete phrases are starting a new topic, or are used to come to a reformulation and so continue on from what has just been said.

4. **Shifts in tenses between past/present and future:** In example 58 at lines 8–11, Luis shifts from present to future and it is not clear whether he is using 'working' to indicate aspect. There is also a lack of temporal anchoring with 'sometimes' in example 59 at lines 8–12, and then the shift to a specific moment in the past with 'at first.' It is also not clear whether 'ask' refers to the unspecific present or is setting up the moment in the past when the manager told him, 'At first you're going to find it boring' (in which case 'ask should probably be 'told'). It is difficult to follow the progression in Luis's narrative at this point and there is less of a sense of 'here and now,' which other candidates convey when quoting others. Lack of clear temporal anchoring occurred quite often in Luis's speech; when asked in the early stages about his visa giving him the right to work in the UK, he says: 'I assure you that we got it already,' when he means that in December he *will* assure them that he has got it.

5. **Rapid shifting between speaker voices (and so production formats):** In particular, a lack of clarity as to when the candidate is using his own voice or quoting someone else. Quoting others is generally a successful strategy amongst candidates. It can add vividness to an account and also allows candidates to show their positive side through someone else's voice (6.5). However, some migrant candidates do not differentiate clearly between themselves as narrators and quotes from others: in example 59 at lines 10–12 ('At first you're going to find it boring') Luis appears to shift to quoting the manager, but it is difficult to establish when he shifts back to his own voice in the narrative. Then,

at lines 16–17, he quotes both himself ('I finish here already') and the manager ('You finish already? Okay'). This rapid switching between voices is coupled with the undifferentiated use of 'you're' (meaning 'one') in line 14, in the habitual sense, and the lack of specificity in time mentioned above. The interviewer's lack of understanding and failure to prompt is evident in the fact that she does not write anything down here or pursue any of his responses, but interrupts him at line 26 to move rapidly on to the next question. This is relatively late in the interview and, in the feedback, the interviewer indicated that she had decided to reject him well before this point.

In the feedback session, when Luis's video was played back to the interviewer for comment, she said that she was 'confused within forty seconds of the opening of the interview,' that he was 'telling me a story but I couldn't follow it' and that 'he knew what he wanted to say but lacked the vocabulary for it.'

What is not clear from this analysis is the extent to which these issues of comprehensibility are the result of a lack of lexicogrammatical knowledge of English or a reliance on a system of Filipino English influenced by Tagalog. In a very high-stakes encounter, where a Filipino doctor is required to give testimony in a child abuse trial, Gumperz (1982b: 163–194) discusses how elements of the doctor's English appear to be systematically related to Tagalog grammar and syntax. For example, tense is not grammatically marked in Tagalog, which might account for the difficulties in temporal ordering and anchoring illustrated above. Similarly, differences in interclausal syntax between Tagalog and English may also account for expectations not being met as to where the speaker's theme is going – as in the 'because' and 'at first' examples above. In highly stressful situations such as a difficult job interview, it is very likely that Luis's linguistic resources are under strain and also that he is more likely to be influenced by Tagalog and the English he used in the Philippines, when put on the spot in this way.

Yohannes

As already discussed in 5.6 (example 18), there were many misalignments between the interviewer and the Ethiopian Yohannes, whose expert language is Tigrinya. As well as 'jarring' shifts between institutional and personal discourses, there were also some 'hard-to-follow' episodes in this interview. As in Luis's interview, there are times when the interviewer stops writing, apparently unable to process his talk. This occurs from line 9 onwards until, at line 23, the interviewer interrupts to ask a series of simple, factual questions. The extract opens with the habitual competence question about teamwork:

Example 60: Yohannes – Ethiopian Migrant, Unsuccessful

1. I: an example where you been working as part of a team=
2. C: =mhm
3. I: to achieve something

(twenty seconds of talk deleted)

4. C: and we were friendly we were not er:m bothering to argue
5.   this is your- your job is my job
6.   we are all together we had togetherness (.)
7.   they are very helpful (.)
8.   they are a lot of integration each other
9.   e:rm if something happen we have to sort it out ourselves (.)
10.   instead of complaining to each other
11.   we have to (.) know (.) the first thing
12.   whoever comes first mhm say for example
13.   if you have a job today interview
14.   and then he offer the job in that place
15.   we tell that person if he doesn't understand
16.   he asks he can ask us five to six times
17.   doesn't matter=
18. I: =mhm
19. C: er:m because he is new
20.   at least for one month he might get confused
21.   he might=
22. I: =what to do- has to do- okay
23.   ho- how many of you in th- in that team
24. C: e:r we were (.) me (xxx) about five people (3)
25.   that was in valet service [and that was in
26. I: right okay]
27. C: was in public [area
28. I: how] many rooms would you be covering
29.   on a- any given date
30. C: er:m (.) one room we had- we had guests' laundry
31.   to bring it from the floors
32. I: okay
33. C: then we have to wash them in e:r machine
34.   or if not we send them to l- er dry cleaning (1)
35.   and we have to do- go and get that erm but
36.   th:e how much it costs (5)
37.   and then we have to give them back to the customers (6)

Yohannes's response between lines 11 and 17 displays some of the problems of cohesion identified in Luis's performance, such as pronoun ambiguities, shifts in tenses and anchoring in time and space:

1. **Use of pronouns and other references:** Ambiguity occurs in lines 13–15, as 'you' suggests the impersonal 'one' rather than the you in 'Your job.' The 'he' in line 14 has no clear anaphoric reference – it is presumably the manager, but may refer to the newcomer – while the 'he' at lines 15 and 16 clearly refers to the newcomer. Similarly, there is ambiguity in line 14 where 'in that place' suggests a location elsewhere rather than in Yohannes's own workplace.

2. **Shifts in tenses:** There are several shifts in tenses throughout this example – past, present and conditional. These do not raise issues of comprehensibility, but do not express the temporal drive of the successful narratives illustrated in chapter 6. The original question at line 1 asks for 'an example,' but Yohannes remains in a more generalised temporal world where no one action led to a particular achievement. So the ambiguous references and shifts in time and mood may make it difficult to process his talk as anchored in a specific time and space.

3. **Stance and voice:** Although his personal stance clearly centres around integration and cooperation, he does not take up an unambiguously fixed vantage point from which he looks back and forwards. Like Luis, he shifts between his own voice and quoting others at lines 4–5, and slightly later in the interview – 'If they phone us down er to the valeting department erm good morning or good afternoon sir' – where there are no obvious cues that he is shifting the narrator's voice. This reporting talk, where there is no clear sign when the speaker is quoting others or not, is in contrast to the successful use of quoting others discussed in 6.5.

As in Luis's examples, the discursive discrepancies and cohesive ambiguities appear to reinforce each other. Yohannes's focus is on interpersonal relationships and general practices; while he gives details of helping newcomers and the processes of doing the laundry, there are frequently no clear consequences or conclusions or a clear logical progression. For example, it is not clear how the cost of dry cleaning relates to teamwork or any decisions *he* had to make. The lack of apparent relevance is compounded by the ambiguities and breaks in cohesion mentioned above. And, as in Luis's interview and many other unsuccessful interviews, the interviewer's interventions at lines 23 and 28 – talking down with low-level questions – ruptures the overall line of questioning and leads to an extended misalignment. These misalignments and 'hard-to-follow' moments act as proxies for incompetence or poor attitudes such as unwillingness to take on responsibility, unreliability and lack of credibility.

9.8   Heightened Institutionalisation

For both these candidates, 'difficult-to-follow' moments only happen occasionally. But because of misalignments arising from discursive and narrative requirements – and the interactional discomfort that can arise from both – cohesive oddities are writ large and used to judge candidates as limited both in attitude and language skills. Heightened institutionalisation is even more evident where conversational cohesion appears to break down, since it is a marker of interpersonal failure as well as some surface language difficulties. This burden of interactional discomfort and the subsequent heightened institutionalisation falls particularly heavily on migrant candidates (3.7): there were twice as many traceable misalignments and the reformulations triggered by these difficulties were both more frequent and longer, within this group (7.3).

The weight of the institution fell on migrants in four main ways: more control over candidate talk, such as tightening the structure and raising relevance requirements; more negativity and less helpfulness; higher levels of conversational inferencing required from candidates, as interviewers' registers became more formal and indirect; and stricter alignment to formal participation roles (7.5; Campbell and Roberts, 2007). Such conduct was a response to local interactional difficulties but also, crucially, served to construct what was perceived as less-than-adequate overall performance which could, in turn, be used defensively to justify rejection.

It is the interactional behaviour of the interviewers which can fracture the attempts to produce extended, cohesive utterances. Repeated interruptions and reformulations are often a strategy for talking down to candidates to elicit short, factual and banal answers which are processable enough to be recorded but do not display the competences required. At worst, they lead to interactional bullying which makes candidates even less fluent, as we have seen in Luis's interview (chapters 6 and 7). Those candidates with somewhat fewer conversational resources for the interview context are the ones who have to deal with this heightened institutionalisation, try to identify and manage problems of understanding and rework their responses.

So the ideology of a fixed notion of 'good' or 'fluent' English is thoroughly undermined in the jointly produced, improvised order of the job interview – and indeed any other institutional setting (Gumperz, 1982a and b; Linell, 2015; Bremer et al., 1996; chapter 6). Language competence is a volatile thing, with candidates' performance massaged or fractured by the discursive regimes and interactional orthodoxy of the interview, where the problems of creating shared meaning are routinely handed over by interviewers to candidates.

Even within one encounter, both candidates' and interviewers' abilities to communicate vary depending on topic, opportunities to structure their own accounts and amount of misunderstanding, misalignment and attempted repair. This is well illustrated by the increase in fluency as the interview progresses of Luis, who is 'talked down to' early on in the interview (examples 58 and 59) and then allowed more space to structure responses for himself later (example 61). Early on, the interviewer's cues constantly interrupt Luis's talk so that he has to put a lot of focus on the interactional work, to the detriment of his fluency and relevance. He hesitates as he struggles for an appropriate discourse and footing, and each attempt is found wanting. By contrast, later in the interview, he is given more space to develop his story when asked about his flexibility:

Example 61: Luis – Filipino Migrant, Unsuccessful

1. C: as a bartender sometimes I do handle the waiter job (.)
2.   when the- during the manager told me (xxx) can you er
3.   after you do the cocktails can you do the waiter (.)
4.   then you go back to the bar
5. I: mhm
6. C: then I do that yeah because
7.   it's a new challenge for me and-
8.   but if I think it's not m- it's not on more
9.   my job description any more
10.   because I work as a bartender (.)
11.   my work is a- a bartender
12. I: mhm
13. C: but- waiter is a new ch- a new job for me
14.   and a new challenge (.) a new experience (.)
15.   so (.) I work as a waiter to some
16.   yeah m- most of the time because eh-
17.   there's only that the manager ask me
18.   because if I see my colleague which is er which er
19.   they are hardly er enough to handle some customer(.)
20.   they're busy they're s- m- there's more customer
21.   coming inside the restaurant (.)
22.   there's (.) there's no more question
23.   that I-I-I didn't make more question ah-
24.   any question to my colleague they need help-
25.   I just take (.) I just take some menu book
26.   and I'm going to the customer ready at the front door
27.   and- and I'm g- and serve him- their serve them their drinks

Here Luis has more opportunity to structure his response for himself and to develop a rhythm and narrative flow, which results in a more fluent answer – despite some cohesive oddities (Gumperz, 1982b: 173), e.g. 'which' instead of 'and' in lines 18–19, leading to some confusion about relativisation. The interviewer just gives minimum feedback in appropriate places (lines 5 and 12). Unfortunately, the reason Luis is able to do this is that the interviewer, as she informed researchers in the feedback, had already decided that he had failed by this point. She was no longer asking follow-on questions or making notes, thus illustrating the point made in chapter 8 that decisions were made based on overall impressions at any stage of the interview, and often early on, rather than assessing each competence separately.

9.9 Language Differences as a Proxy

The notion of language differences or difficulties as ideological proxies for moral or social inadequacies has a long history (Cameron, 1995: 77; Milroy and Milroy, 1999; Allan, 2013). In high-stakes gatekeeping, any aspects of language and interactional conduct may be implicitly used to pass judgments on personality and social competence – such as 'being unprofessional' or 'not able to take on responsibility' – as several of the case studies here have already shown. In an interview, you are what you talk. So interruptions could lead to an evaluation of 'too controlling,' or sudden shifts in topic or footing were translated as 'inconsistency.'

Even where there was talk about talk – for example, 'It sounded scripted' or 'words that were not their own' – the judgment concerned trust or authenticity, not communication; styles of talk were used as the DNA of character. Similarly, when there were explicit comments about language such as, 'hard to follow,' these were packaged up with broader personality comments based on discursive and narrative differences. For example, in the video feedback after Yohannes's interview, the interviewer criticised the overly institutional moments in his responses as a lack of personalisation and interpreted these as evidence of unwillingness to take on responsibility. And the 'hard-to-follow' examples above may also have been a proxy for such a negative comment.

The complex set of features of language which lead to negative assessments are difficult enough for analysts to identify, let alone interviewers. We cannot pull out one element and isolate it from the 'multi-channelled' nature of all conversation. So figure 9.1, which sums up the many examples given throughout this book, is suggestive only.

Figure 9.1. Assessments Made of Migrant Candidates

Criteria	Interviewer comments	Features of talk
Personality	Domineering, lecturing, cocky, controlling, overconfident, timid, not able to organise herself, not enough personal input, not creative enough, had to spoon-feed him, lacking dynamism and initiative	Long turns/interruptions (misreading context-cues signalling turn taking), extreme case formulations, low levels of hedging, overly formal lexis, assertive talk, low pitch register, low use of 'I', lack of extended responses, misreading of contextualisation cues
Trust and authenticity	Didn't think I could trust him, not consistent, not being themselves, not real, he just said what we wanted to hear, used buzzwords, no substance, claiming without backing it up, lack of self-awareness, not credible, unreliable, words that were not their own	High frequency of formulaic interview lexis, rapid shifts between formal/institutional register and personal one, little prosodic embedding of formulaic utterances in more conversational style, extreme case formulations, rupture between sound and sense, overuse of deontic modes (e.g. 'we should be very polite'), lack of clear temporal anchoring
Professional/ workplace characteristics	Not able to fit in, uncompromising, not flexible, not adaptable, unprofessional, not able to take responsibility	'Jarring' shift between topics and registers, lack of hedging, personal discourses too prosodically 'emotional' and conversational, use of stylistic features such as proverbs, lack of progression
Explicit comments about language (only made with some migrant candidates)	Poor English, mumbling, hard to follow, waffling	Shifts between past and present so no clear temporal ordering, differences in prosodic conventions when changing speaker perspective and position (e.g. when quoting another character in the narrative), unclear deictic marking, lack of grammatical completeness, markers of dysfluency such as false starts

Conclusion

The linguistic capital of the job interview endorses the conversational resources learnt by local candidates as part of their early language socialisation and amplifies the communicative differences of migrant candidates, their linguistic and cultural otherness. Its discursive regimes, interactional constraints and intolerance for certain types of non-coherence – bolstered by common sense ideologies of language – put an unnecessary interpretive and cohesive burden on this group. Judgments about communicative competence are always relative and ideologically bound.

So language is both an overt and covert mechanism for assessing candidates, but cannot be pinned down to be tackled in the courts as a source of discrimination or understood as a complex, context-bound resource by HR professionals. For this reason, this chapter has also considered some of the unspoken negative judgments which influence the interactively produced misalignments and other difficult moments and lead, ultimately, to candidate failure. In the final analytic chapter, the other sources of knowledge and experience which inform the talk and interactional conduct of migrant candidates are discussed.

10 Knowledge and Experience Brought into the Interview

This chapter focuses on those aspects of the linguistic penalty which stem from migrants' different experiences of work, of selection processes and of presenting the institutional self, linking these to the discursive and communicative regimes of the interview. These different experiences produce asymmetries of knowledge, both as a result of direct experience and from the social stock of knowledge about work and the labour market in other societies (Günthner and Luckmann, 2001). They are brought along to the interview and, together with experiences of living in the UK as minorities, affect the construction of subjectivity in the encounter while producing additional communicative requirements in making the strange familiar. This assemblage of linguistic, social and cultural capital must be transferable if migrants are to achieve social mobility, since what is considered as capital in one society may not be in another. These different aspects of (de)capitalising the self are variously realised through different rhetorics of the institutional self, assumptions about selection and the interview brought in from previous experience, the 'immigrant story' and foreign work experience.

10.1 Different Rhetorics of the Institutional Self: the Narrow Gate

The narrow gate through which candidates must pass requires governing the self to produce a coherent, crafted, corporate being. In earlier chapters I have illustrated how the performative self is expected: to be engaging, but not 'too personally involved'; self-managing and forward thinking, but also compliant and controllable; humorous and confident, but not garrulous and cocky; displaying skills, but not overclaiming; reflexively aware and strategic, but not too distant (and, for management positions, be tough without being 'harsh').

Many of these seemingly irreconcilable differences are built into the competence framework, since the personal qualities required in one competence may conflict with another (Wood and Payne, 1998); hence the centrality of hybrid discourses and also well-structured, engaging narratives which may distract from some of the dialectics of the interview. In the last chapter I discussed how these institutional norms are realised in terms of a set of conversational resources used to create involvement through metapragmatic fluency and cohesive strategies (9.6 and 9.7). Here we sum up how the linguistic economy of the interview is set against the different rhetorical traditions – illustrated throughout the earlier chapters – brought into it, and how such traditions further erode the linguistic capital of migrant candidates.

Rhetorics of Personhood

The extent to which the convincing self is brought about or not depends in part on the different rhetorical traditions and experiences brought into the interview, including how much the neoliberal discourses which permeate it have been internalised. In low-paid job interviews in particular, there is a constant tension between the interviewer's expectations of a crafted, corporate self governed by new work order competences and the candidate's sense of the individual as a sentient, communal being. Themes such as 'teamwork,' 'managing repetitive work' and 'making improvements' were frequently oriented to by migrant candidates in personal discourses, taking a common sense, emotional and self-protecting stance. For example Yohannes, as discussed earlier, does not pick up cues about team working as a self-managing process. Instead, he positions himself very much with his team and against the management. This stance is explicitly criticised by the interviewer in the feedback session.

Luis also falls foul of the new work order notion of 'teamwork' in some of the same ways as Yohannes. Luis views it as sharing work, saying that he enjoyed opportunities to help colleagues out when he was not busy and do their work for them. This leads to a descending spiral of questions in which the interviewer asks why Luis did not report his teammates for not doing their own work; the implication is that he is not able to manage them.

Bruno, from Italy, also organises much of his discourse around the self as an emotional being. While he is ultimately successful, the interviewer is quite critical of aspects of his stance. In the interviewer feedback on the video, during a detailed emotional response by Bruno on the hardships of working in the London catering industry, the interviewer ironically remarked of a gesture when he puts his hand to his face, 'I think that's me wiping a tear away.' As with Yohannes, Bruno does not align himself to the corporation and speak from a position of reflexive self-awareness, but rather talks about what he wants from his employers.

Rhetorics of Distance

By contrast, migrant candidates were also often criticised for being too distant, not grounded nor problem-centred nor narrative enough; in Foucauldian terms, not adequately self-governing. Instead of showing their understanding of how they act on themselves – as Pippa, Tom and Jim do – they often rely on an 'authorisation' discourse (van Leeuwen and Wodak, 1999; Günthner and Luckmann, 2001). Talk is authorised through well-known 'truths,' conveyed in an assertive mode. This assertive strategy was realised through maxims, proverbs and general truths which are seen as making one's talk more authoritative. But in the job interview these have to be used in a nuanced and strategic way, anchored in individual experience, if they are not to be taken as mere sententious-sounding aphorisms – as telling rather than showing – or merely animating others' voices. This assertive mode tends to produce negative evaluations of being 'distant,' 'controlling,' 'untrustworthy' or seeming like one who 'had been told what to say' (fig. 9.1). Typically these candidate assertions were made in a deontic mode, a sense of compliance to what one has to do, as in, 'When we are approaching a customer we should be very polite,' or 'You should be always alert.'

Such perceived assertive talk was often combined with extreme case formulations (ECFs) as part of the 'immigrant story' (10.3). These formulations – consisting of superlatives and other extreme terms, being used to defend, justify and promote the self – were common amongst most migrant candidates. And while they claim a personal stance, these extreme cases gloss over the detailed and individual experience. Examples include: 'If you don't like your job, there's no way you can work there,' 'It's exactly the same job' (as I'm currently doing), 'I know everything about business management,' 'I'm particularly good at everything,' 'I can do anything,' 'I never have a problem,' 'I don't mind anything,' 'I was the main head solely' and 'I know everything about management and organisation behaviour.'

ECFs are routine fare for interviewers, with questions such as, 'What's been the most … thing you've had to …' or as in Ravi's interview (example 62), 'What's been the golden moment?' They are designed to elicit a dramatic albeit reflective and nuanced performance of a particular incident, but not an ECF response. Candidates hear these extreme cases and may feel encouraged to use them, but when they do they are sanctioned. And so this is another

example of the joint interactional production of failure for many migrant candidates. Luis, for example, is asked six times, 'What do you like most about
working in a team?' since none of his responses are deemed adequate. The
'extreme case' environment created by the interviewer does not travel across
well to migrant candidates' reflection on the self.

Even in promotion interviews for junior management posts, where candidates are expected to be more analytical, migrant candidates who failed were
criticised for being too 'distant' or 'studied.' This was the case for Ravi:

Example 62: Ravi – Sri Lankan Migrant, Unsuccessful

1. C: er (.) achieving targets (.)
2.   that's what I was talking about (.)
3.   and customer service is number one (.) er (.)
4. I: you mentioned that before didn't you
5. C: I did (.) I did
6. I: and I was intrigued because I wanted you to-
7.   because I didn't know I'd be interviewing you
8.   but one thing I was- I was going to ask you-
9.   for you to clarify that (.)
10.   it seems to be a massive thing for you
11.   in terms of the customer number one (.)
12.   what do you perceive by the (.) for- for (.)
13.   two things that are most important
14.   about customer service to you
15. C: the first thing is your listening skills (.)
16.   you listen to the person (.)
17.   and then erm (.) how you get that service back again (.)
18.   and the feedback you have after that (.)
19.   over there you (.) try to build the customer to have a base (.)
20.   once they get used to it you-
21.   they come back to you over and over again
22. I: right
23. C: that's of a paramount importance
24. I: mhm
25. C: a group of people coming down last year (.)
26.   you should be able to retain them
27.   rather than going- them going to another store (.) to do that
28.   that all comes in
29. I: right
30. C: and erm I've taken it very very seriously (.)
31.   especially on the customer service desk

32. I: so what's been your golden moment
33.   in terms of customer service (.) for you personally
34. C: satisfaction
35. I: ok (.) you satisfied or the customer
36. C: the customer satisfied I'm satisfied (.)
37.   if not then there's something wrong
38. I: right
39. C: that's the way I look at it
40. I: ok (.) alright (.) we'll move on

Ravi's opening statement is a well-known maxim. When the interviewer (lines 6–14) asks for clarification and his personal view on customer service, Ravi responds with an analytic list using 'you' rather than 'I' or 'we,' speaking in generalisations and well-worn evaluations such as, 'That's of paramount importance,' and making unmitigated assertions like, 'They come back to you over and over again' (lines 15–23). At line 26, instead of following through with a specific example, he uses the deontic mode ('You should be able to retain them') and a general assertion at line 30. Again, at line 32, the 'golden moment' question designed to produce a concrete example is responded to with a general assertion, 'satisfaction,' and with a cliché at line 36. Ravi also uses repetition with the two connected themes of listening and customer retention/satisfaction throughout this sequence. Ravi was strongly criticised in the wash-up for having no examples and using generalisations and buzzwords.

Ravi's talk appears 'studied,' distancing and academic because of both the impersonal features of his language and because he frames his talk as if it was a presentation or lecture, again using repetition and listing to convey authority rather than engaging the listener through stories. This lecturing mode inhibits any lively, detailed, engaging talk which would give him authenticity in the interviewers' eyes (10.5). And yet this is a rhetorical style that would be persuasive in many other cultural contexts, where narratives would be seen as not adequately institutional.

Footing in the Interview

These rhetorical differences affect the overall interview footing as candidate stance is routinely interpreted from them. This in turn is judged as relatively aligning (or not) to the interview's stance. An unacceptable stance is amplified when it stands outside a narrative and is baldly stated, as in the case of ECFs. So the unstoried self is particularly vulnerable to misalignments since it is often through the story and candidate reflection on and evaluation thereof that the stance can be nuanced, dynamic and engaging in multiple ways. This reminds us of Goffman's metaphor of sustaining multiple footings, as the speaker stands firmly with two feet on the ground while jumping up and down on a third. Gladston is a master of the art of sustaining a viable image of the self or selves, which the interview game requires.

In the next example he is asked to give an account of a mistake that he made and to say what he learnt from that. In contrast to Michael (examples 31 and 65), he manages the difficulty of displaying a weakness without being assessed negatively. He narrates a time when a documentary was made of his organisation and he was filmed apparently not following procedure. While this retelling could have created a serious loss of face for him, he and interviewer collude in playing with the rules of the game:

Example 63: Gladston – Jamaican Migrant, Successful

1. I: thanks for that (.)
2.   I think I recognise you from the vid- I'm only joking
3. C: hhh superstar my fifteen minutes of fame [hhh
4. I: hhh]
5. C: what do they say no publicity is bad publicity
6.   [hhh that is
7. I: hhh] well yeah not all [of it is true
8. C: not always] bad don't believe that
9. I: okay [e:r
10. C: I got] a lot of stick so I know

Gladston aligns to the jokey footing established by the interviewer, managing to be both self-deprecating and ironical by exaggerating his role in the film ('Superstar my fifteen minutes of fame') and so together they move away from the serious import of the question. But Gladston deftly keeps one foot on the institutional turf by recontextualising the jibe, humorously given to him in line 2, in terms of the institution's characteristic attitude to misdemeanours, saying. 'I got a lot of stick.' In addition, the rhythmic overlapping of laughter and near repetition (lines 3–4 and 6–7) maintains the informal footing throughout. Unsurprisingly he is judged as 'engaging,' 'relevant,' 'ready to make changes' and with 'good experience.'

It is getting onto the right footing that seems to count in the end. Early wrong-footedness can rapidly transform the interview into one of heightened institutionalisation (7.5 and 9.6) and interviewers' attempts to recalibrate relationships along more conventional lines are too indirect to be readily interpreted. Lack of familiarity with the interview and the candidates' 'immigrant story' (10.3) help to explain how elusive the right footing can be, even when interviewers attempt to nudge the inferential process along.

The least successful candidates are those who appear to take up a stance as equal to or in some way superior to the interviewer. While local British candidates can get themselves on the wrong footing (10.2), it happens more often with migrant candidates and relates to issues of control and of their stance towards the interviewer and themselves (6.3). Candidates such as Ravi position the interviewer as less knowledgeable than themselves, or like Sara they try to claim solidarity through a cosy knowingness. Others take up a stance as if outside or above the typical situations and expectations of workers in low-paid jobs (10.5).

While migrant candidates were particularly challenged when attempting to put themselves on the right footing, there was no absolute distinction between this group and local British candidates. Tahir, of Bangladeshi origin, applied for a job as a receptionist in a college in East London. There were five candidates shortlisted – four local candidates of Bangladeshi origin and one other British candidate of South Asian origin (but not Bangladeshi) from another part of London. This latter candidate was the successful one.

Many of Tahir's rhetorical and positioning strategies show similarities with unsuccessful migrant candidates. He shifts between a 'lecturing' and familiar register, uses ECFs such as, 'I'm an expert in IT' and attempts to control the interviewers by speaking over them or using phases of the interview unconventionally. He positions himself as superior to the interviewers in a question about cash handling by asking them: 'Do you know what reconciliation is?' but also, contrastively, in his attempts to collude with them in talking about the students in his current job, he is judged as overly personal and too effusive. The relationship tripwires set by the cultural norms of the interview can bring down local British candidates as well as migrants if they are not at ease with the interview game.

10.2 Lack of Familiarity with the Interview Game

Both brought-along and brought-about aspects of self-presentation depend on how familiar candidates are with the interview game and its regulatory discourses. For many migrant candidates, what counts as capital and how it should be displayed is far removed from their own experiences of selection processes. The added weight for migrant candidates is interviewers' taken-for-granted, normalising attitudes towards the interview (8.5): their surprise that so many candidates did badly since 'all they had to do was talk about themselves.' These negative comments about candidates contrasted with the latter's perceptions of how the interviews had gone.

Although many candidates were initially surprised that they were required to go through a formal interview, most of them – whether successful or not – considered the interview had broadly met their expectations and that it had been 'relaxed' and 'friendly' (with the exception of 'equal opportunity' interviews, chapters 3 and 7). However, migrant candidates were more likely than other candidates to misread the surface behaviour of interviewers. The fact that the interview was perceived as 'friendly' was interpreted as an indicator of good performance, which led to many unsuccessful candidates misconstruing their chance of a job.

The Cultural Rules of the Game

On the surface, comments from both sides about 'talking about themselves' seem nicely aligned and would appear to leave little room for hidden misunderstandings and wrong footing. Yet the narrow gauge through which only acceptable responses flow shows how highly constrained and culturally specific the communication of subjectivity must be. The candidates who are clearly successful know the cultural rules of the game, what makes them an acceptable player and – in collusion with the interviewers – are allowed to play with these rules.

Candidates such as Gladston or Pippa are allowed (or indeed encouraged) to digress, to joke and tell secondary stories – as do the interviewers with certain candidates. Bourdieu calls this the 'ultimate privilege of membership' which, 'by conferring an undeniable and indelible essence ... authorises transgressions which would be otherwise forbidden.' In this way, 'the person who is sure of his cultural identity can play with the rules of the cultural game' (Bourdieu, 1991: 124). But migrant candidates have no easy access to membership of the cultural game, as their insecurity in establishing a proper footing has shown. They are disadvantaged by lack of familiarity with its rules and then further excluded from membership since they therefore cannot play with them (10.4). Nevertheless, there were a few white British candidates who were not allowed to transgress because their performance has not produced an 'insider' (Silverman and Jones, 1976). For example, Alex responds to a question about uniform by saying, 'It's okay, I've looked like a jerk before.' This comment is taken as an affront by the interviewer, who views it as disrespectful mockery by an outsider of the institution of which he is a part.

However, such mistimed humour was rare among local white and BAME candidates. In a terrible irony, when candidates draw explicitly on job and person specifications and more general guidelines in attempts to align to the stated requirements, they are seen as lacking authenticity. In the equal opportunities question, Tahir aligns to the institution very overtly, saying, 'I was reading your brochure, and it states …' This open reference to the preparatory work which he has done disadvantages him because it makes reference to the fact that he is making certain claims and playing a role *in order* to align himself to institutional objectives, and so be successful in the interview. This unmasking of the pretence of the interview orthodoxy – that Tahir should really be giving the interviewers a description of his own deeply held convictions – means that Tahir is stepping outside the interactional moment of the interview game. This is, inadvertently, a risky move which he does not carry off successfully.

Migrant candidates, in feedback after interviews, as well as misreading the degree of comfort and friendliness in interviews, often displayed a mismatch between their assumptions and those of the interviewers. They expected the latter to orientate to their background and achievements generally – a more personal (10.1) and career-based emphasis – and not to limit the interview to standard questions. They also mentioned 'qualifications,' 'working hard' and 'good manners' as criteria by which they would be judged. Comments such as, 'I enjoy talking and was able to give examples' showed no realisation that the amount of talk is constrained. And 'the purpose of the interview is to prove that what you said on the application was true' suggested little appreciation that application forms and CVs play a minor role in competence-based interviews.

To migrant candidates, the objective value of external and authorised cultural capital such as qualifications contrasts with the intense subjectivity of the interactional performance used by institutions to rate them. Luis remarked that 'in the Philippines if you had a degree in a subject then you would be successful in the interview,' while a candidate from India said that 'you could forecast what questions will be asked, they would be about your qualifications.' In the more traditional interviews (rather than the dominant competence-based ones), where a candidate can summarise their personal trajectory, candidates may wrongly assume that they can talk about their qualifications. The opening lines of Vijay's interview show how powerful this assumption could be:

Example 64: Vijay – Indian Migrant, Unsuccessful

1. I.1: can you tell us about your skills and experience that you've got
2.   erm that's useful for the job that you've applied for
3. C: right (h) first of all
4.   I would like to t- tell you about my qualifications
5.   that I'm a master graduate (.)
6.   I've got a master's degree in information technology
7.   and business administration

Other Experiences of Job Selection

In many parts of the world, what might be seen as the standard job interview does not exist – or did not when migrant candidates left the country
they had been working in. Also, several candidates in our data reported that
'most jobs were found through friends.' Bruno from Sicily had experienced
only informal interviews, often 'chats' arranged through social networks. He
brought this assumption of the interview as a conversation into his British
interview and unintentionally overrode the formal interview design by treat-
ing it as a chat. Candidates, particularly from professional backgrounds, may
have experienced some type of formal job interview. However, international
comparisons of selection interviews offer only broad brushstrokes of how
they differ – for example, the degree of standardisation of questions (Ryan
and Ployhart, 1999) – and use generalised and decontextualised cultural traits
to contrast different countries. So it is difficult to assess what brought-along
knowledge candidates bring from the experiences of selection outside the UK,
apart from the sociolinguistic studies that identify interactional differences in
the interview (chapter 3).
    One telling example is a guide to good interviewing in India published in
the 1970s or 1980s. It is aimed at those applying for government administrative jobs and similar administrative posts, such as with Indian Railways:

> Apart from wide and varied information obtainable through constant study
> of new literature, a sweet, amiable and cheerful disposition is unquestion-
> ably the greatest and most valuable asset in the expression of the personal-
> ity of the candidates. (Vohra, n.d.: 6)

One candidate in this guide talks about what makes for an impressive interview and identifies expressing one's ability as an important component. He is
asked how he can do this:

I: How can you express your ability at the time of the interview?

C: Whatever we may say, tailor does make the man. Smartness in clothes is very impressive ... The next important thing is speech. If the speech is well cultivated ... the interviewers would be agreeably impressed. Next comes knowledge ... But more important than any of these is personality. (Vohra, n.d.: 220).

While the content is not so very far from the today's implicit criteria relating to communication and personality, the style is totally different. Here 'impressive interviews' require a display of wide knowledge, a 'cheerful' disposition and a cultivated and sententious manner. Proverbs, sayings and assertive generalisations are highly praised and seen as part of collective wisdom but, as mentioned above, are all sources of misalignment for migrant candidates in the UK context.

10.3 The 'Immigrant Story'

In addition to the only partially overlapping stocks of cultural knowledge about self-presentation that this group brings to the interview, they also have to manage the social pressures resulting from immigration. Experience of discrimination and failure – and the racialised language of the media, the workplace and the streets – requires a counternarrative where they can defend themselves against categories, assumptions and processes of 'ethnification' in which their identity is ascribed rather than inhabited (Blommaert, 2006: 238). We have called this counternarrative the 'immigrant story.'[50]

In this story, everything about the individual must be as positive as possible: attitudes to work ('You feel happy to come to the job,' as Ire remarks in chapter 1), willingness to work hard, an impeccable CV and all the required skills and knowledge for the job on offer, often conveyed in extreme case formulations. Afram, a borderline Ghanaian candidate, can give no example of when a customer has been angry with him and claims that this has never happened. Commenting on his performance in the feedback afterwards, the interviewer used this moment in the interview to illustrate her lack of trust in him.

Striving to be perfect to counter negative ethnic stereotyping is itself counterproductive in a communicative environment where the self must be euphemised, responses hedged and balanced and weaknesses acknowledged and then used positively. Although crafted to please the organisation, the immigrant story fundamentally misaligns with the institutionalised neoliberal paradigm where self-understanding regulates and improves the self.[51]

Many questions in the competence-based interview are about how to cope with difficulties and manage and learn from negative experiences. 'Immigrant story' responses are particularly vulnerable as answers to these questions, with candidates denying that there have been any negative experiences. Michael's CV of unblemished success has been mentioned in 6.3. In this organisation, part of the interview is structured around timelines, an autobiographical form filled in before the interview in which candidates had to summarise their working lives:

Example 65: Michael – Liberian Migrant, Unsuccessful

1. I: let me- let's start off first of all so talk me through
2. C: yeah
3. I: your timelines (.) this is quite an unusual one hhh
4. C: hhh
5. I: it just goes up and up and up

The interviewer's comments at lines 3 and 5 imply some incredulity at this consistently upward trajectory, further reinforced later in the interview when Michael initially declares that he has never had any negative feedback and does not display any shortcomings (example 31).

The negative value given to the 'immigrant story,' as in Michael's case, is often reinforced by other misalignments. At this point, the interviewer models an acceptable answer from his own experience, showing his own weakness and how he was helped to overcome it. But Michael fails to make the appropriate inference from the interviewer's prompting example. So Michael is marked down on two counts: he does not interpret the underlying assumption of the question that he is to admit some weakness then show how he overcame them (6.3) and he also fails to learn from the model answer supplied by the interviewer to help him. He misses both the competence requirement (learning from mistakes) and the metacriterion of this type of interview that candidates should be able to respond to interviewers' modelling of their own experience as a nudge to the expected inferential process.

The other side of the 'immigrant story' is about the attributes associated with their ethnicity. Here candidates explicitly use their 'inhabited' identity to present aspects of their national or ethnic identity. On the few occasions when this occurred – for example with Luis, Yohannes, Sara and Bruno – this was not successful. In taking a stance as foreign or from a particular country outside the UK, an implicit dichotomy was set up between the characteristics expected of candidates in aligning to the organisation's values and behaviour and their ethnic identity. Examples include Bruno's comment, 'I am Italian and I'm not used to live in a – in a multiracial city like London' and Yohannes's reference to 'my community, Ethiopian community' when talking about his community work.

These markers of idiosyncratic personal identity and specific group membership do not sit comfortably with the synthetic personality of current organisational ideology, as some of the explicit statements in the interviewer feedback convey. Bruno's interviewer commented that he didn't like this, or the position it put him in as interviewer. He was uncomfortable with such remarks from Bruno because 'it's not like that at [this company].' He said that this made him worry that Bruno might make ethnicity/racism an issue where it was not one. In this way, the interview creates a double bind for migrant candidates: they must not align themselves too superlatively to the British workplace, nor must they identify too clearly with their own ethnic background. For this group, work experience examples – which form the greatest part of any job interview – almost invariably require some reference to or comparison with their lives outside the UK, as the next section discusses. Yet these references, called up to translate and convince, tend to focus and reinforce an outsider status.

10.4 Foreign Work Experience

More time was spent on narrating past experience elicited from competence questions than any other component of the interview (chapter 6). So the management of foreign work experience (FWE), by both interviewers and candidates born abroad, is a significant feed into the evaluation process and highlights the 'othering' of this group on several levels. In sum, the lack of recognition of FWE – along with the soft skills focus – is one of the major contributing factors to their downward mobility, as identified by economists and sociolinguists (3.1 and 9.3).

There are several problems for both sides in dealing with FWE, notably the assumptions about it brought into the interview and the lack of fit between local and foreign experience. The impact FWE has on the narratological requirements of the interview and the additional linguistic capital needed to deal with it alongside all the other regime requirements have already been illustrated throughout the book, particularly in chapters 6, 7 and 9. Translating global work experience into the institutionalised models of competence (see Roberts, 2016 for a more detailed discusison) requires FWE to be topicalised, communicated within the linguistic economy of the job interview and defended within the new work order assumptions of the organisation.

Assumptions About FWE Brought into the Interview

Both interviewers and candidates bring to the encounter orientations to FWE which make it problematic. One of the failures of the selection process is the erasure of FWE from most paperwork and training, as well as the interaction itself. Where it is raised by candidates, interviewers respond differently – occasionally building on it, but more frequently dismissing it (examples 66 and 67). Where there is no space made for it, some candidates shoehorn it in, even if its sequential location is inappropriate. Nanak, who works on a food processing line and is applying for an upgrade, is told he must pass a literacy test. He responds that he was a maths teacher:

Example 66: Nanak – Indian Migrant, Unsuccessful

```
1.  I:   also need to tell you that all A (.)
2.       this is an A grade job okay
3.       with A grade jobs now
4.       everybody will be put forward
5.       for a (.) for a literacy and a numeracy test
3.       so English and maths test
7.  C:   yeah
8.  I:   okay if you shouldn't shouldn't=
9.  C:   =I was a mathematician in the India [maths master
10. I:   oh was you]
11. C:   yeah=
12. I:   =okay good (.) good
13.      so everybody will be put forward for this test
14.      if you- if you don't pass this test
15.      then unfortunately we wont be able to offer you the job [okay
16. C:   alright]
17. I:   but- but everybody will go through the same test
18. C:   alright
19. I:   er:m and that is the next stage of the interview stage [so
20. C:   alright]
21. I:   if you get through this stage
22.      we'll then put you forward for your English and maths test (.)
23.      if that's okay then we'll- we'll call you back
```

At line 9 Nanak interrupts the interviewer, latching onto what he may anticipate is a negative outcome – that he may not pass – to interpolate new information: he was a maths teacher in India. The interviewer's apparently positive evaluation at line 12 is rapidly followed by a twice-repeated assertion that 'everybody' will take the test. The new candidate information is now treated as irrelevant since, whatever his experience and competence, he will be treated the same as all other candidates. There is no extended token of acknowledgement of his experience as a teacher, nor any comment during the interview or in the wash-up session afterwards that he might have skills more relevant to office work than cooking sauces.

The inclusion of FWE by candidates is also hedged around with difficulties realised through hesitations and comments that frame its inclusion as potentially inappropriate (e.g. 'But that was a bit different'), or explicit checks with interviewers on acceptability. Such experience is already tagged as lacking the necessary symbolic or human capital, and so feeds into the existing discursive regimes about allowable contributions.

The Lack of Fit Between Local and Foreign Experience

While work experience is routinely used to forge some solidarity and familiarity, FWE can produce the opposite result, creating interactional asynchrony and problems with fitting stories into boxes. The additional work and resources required to make FWE comparable with jobs in Britain falls into two broad categories: the contextual burden and the equivalence burden.

To connect their experiences to the competence framework requires considerable contextual explanation which relates to values, relations, ideologically based working practices, professional categorisation and wider sociopolitical forces. As Maryns shows in asylum interviews, the greater the difference between interviewer and interviewee, the more discursive effort is necessary (Maryns, 2006). And this is also reflected in our data where migrant candidates took on average seventy-four per cent of the talking time, suggesting that, among other aspects of the linguistic weight of the interview, they had to spend more time contextualising their experiences. But unlike the 'home narratives' of asylum seekers (Blommaert, 2001: 428), where detailed accounts of their lives and politics can provide convincing contextualisation, the time and design constraints of the interview penalise candidates' attempts to contextualise their very different work experiences.[52]

For example, the Polish candidate Renard had to do a lot of contextualising work to relate his own work as a teacher and in a distance learning company to the competence of 'satisfying customers.' The interviewer is looking for evidence of how he 'went the extra mile' in doing this. However, the distance learning company is state owned and staff are expected to follow standard procedures and not stand out as doing exceptionally well (Kulessza, 2002)

– in contrast to the neoliberal, marketised discourses of the West. While the East German candidates studied by Auer and Kern orientated to and tried to compensate for the relative lack of individual decision-making in their work experience (Auer and Kern, 2001), Renard and his interviewer never agree on the grounds for negotiating this stand-out trait. In the video feedback, the interviewer commented:

> In customer service, Renard generalises a lot – he doesn't use the personal pronoun enough, and while he explains the reasons why customers might be upset, he doesn't explain what *he* would do about this. I feel that Renard is repeatedly missing the point as he explains about the book company he was working for and their policies, but doesn't realise that I am trying to look at how he has gone *beyond* this.

The burden of trying to establish equivalences between FWE and British jobs requires other additional communicative resources. On occasions, whole categories of work have no clear equivalence in the UK, as in the case of Luis. He was a type of civil engineer in the Philippines whose job combined being an engineer, draughtsman, surveyor and tax inspector in the land tax department of the national government. Many migrant candidates from a professional background, like Luis, find little similarity between the low-paid job competences such as 'customer service' and their more complex dealings with people. In addition, they tend to talk about their work in terms of general processes and in the more abstract registers of institutional discourses, rather than concrete examples.

The outcome from these FWE differences is highly consequential for migrant applicants. The normative interactional structures – particularly narrative structures – are ruptured, work experience becomes untranslatable and evaluations of personality and communicative abilities are negative. More speculative is the profound challenge to the sense of self in the interview when a candidate's professional identity is ignored or downplayed – when their capital is eroded in the quest for a display of soft skills.

All candidates were expected to talk about their current low-paid jobs, where work is not routinely used to talk about identity. As Evans et al. noted in their survey of low-paid Londoners, ninety per cent of whom were migrants, about a third 'found nothing in particular they liked about their job, considering it "just a job"' (Evans et al., 2005: 19–22). The disjuncture between migrant candidates' earlier selves and their 'just a job' selves could undermine the ongoing narrative of the self and produce 'ontological insecurity' (Giddens, 1991: 58; 2.1). This sense of self is to some extent distinct from performance, but Giddens argues that a close fit between the continuous, coherent self and the performance is crucial both in doing well and in maintaining a secure sense of being (1991). While the labour market studies identify the gaps between migrants and locals in gaining employment (3.1 and 9.5) in terms of skills and competences, the felt experience of failure and its longer-term consequences must also be added to these more objective factors.

The four different areas described – different rhetorics of the institutional self, different assumptions about selection and the interview, the 'immigrant story' and foreign work experience – along with the other differences in social and linguistic capital brought along to the interview, are illustrated in the extended case study below where they are amplified by the interviewers' conduct.

10.5 Vijay Case Study

Vijay has already made an appearance in chapters 5, 7 and earlier in this chapter. Part of the transcript below was used to show the three levels at which contextualisation cues work to produce and sustain (or not) conversational involvement through mutual inferential processes (8.2). Here it is revisited with some additional examples, to act as a telling case for many of the main arguments in the book.

Vijay has considerable experience of administrative work in hospitals, which is highly relevant for the receptionist post in a medical photography department in the hospital where he already has a temporary job in the X-ray department. Just before this extract begins, he has told the two interviewers that he worked as a medical clerk in India for two years and in a one year administrative post in a management college in London. Although the interviews for this job are not explicitly designed around a set of competences, the implied competence of the next set of questions is to do with customer relations and satisfaction. He is asked what transferrable skills he has acquired from this work and his response focuses on his ability to prioritise and work independently. This may have triggered the subsequent question, asked in this first example, about possibly doing a backroom job, which is where this extract begins. Arguably, the interviewers are signalling their disquiet with his front stage performance so far:

Example 67: Vijay – Indian Migrant, Unsuccessful
(Extended version of example 48.)

13. I.1: um (.) can I a- ok questions I want to ask you
14. C: yep
15. I.1: if you was not successful in this position (.)
16.   would you work somewhere else (.)
17.   doing a very similar position what you've got-
18.   what you're doing now
19. C: [mhm
20. I.1: which is] the- (.) working in x-ray
21.   because obviously you're dealing with (.) behind the scenes
22. C: mhm
23. I.1: a:nd obviously the position that you've applied for is actually (.)
24.   get in there sit there (.) t- handle the patients face to [face
25. C: mhm] mhm
26. I.1: if you weren't successful would you (.) um (.)
27.   like to be considered for (h) a position behind the scenes
28. C: well [f-
29. I.1: or] are you [specifically
30. C: for me] it's not [very important
31. I.1: patient okay]
32. C: whether I'm working behind the scene or in front of the scene (h)
33.   actually speaking because I worked as a ward clerk
34.   I've handled the reception I've got two years working=
35. I.1: =yeah I [understand that
36. C: experience also] so I'm not afraid of anything
37. I.1: but that's obviously [in India
38. C: right]
39. I.1: not here hhh
40. C: (nods) that's in India yeah
41. All: hhh=
42. C: =but patients are patients
43. I.1: (clears throat loudly) (looks at I.2 still laughing)
44.   [debatable
45. I.2: well (^ ^)]
46. C: I'm not here to debate because you are more experienced
47. I.1: yeah
48. C: so I don't because (.) obviously I mean I- I'm here to give my best=
49. I.2: =mhm=
50. I.1: =[yeah I appreciate that]
51. C: [and I'm here to convince you]

52.   if I if I'm able to convince you I'm fortunate
53.   if I'm- I cannot convince you I'm [unfortunate
54. I.1: yeah]=
55. I.2: =mhm=
56. C: =alright (.) I- I can say my confidence says=
57. I.1: =u huh=
58. C: =that you'll be unfortunate hhh
59. I.2: [mhm
60. I.1: yeah]
61. All: hhh
62. C: [right]
63. I.1: [oo:h] (looks at I.2)

General Framing Work: Different Assumptions About the Interview and the Role of FWE.

While Vijay appears to align to the overall design of the interview and so the candidate role (display your experience and show that it is relevant), he is not helped to align to the metacriteria by which this design needs to be read. The interviewers expect him to demonstrate the specific skills, motivations and experience which has led him to do *this* job, through grounded competences. Vijay strikes a different note: speaking generally about his work history, making general but somewhat puzzling claims about his confidence and structuring his narratives around his career trajectory rather than his tasks and how they are relevant. (Like Bruno, he is criticised for trying to control the interview, where the relationship between lack of relevance and lack of control is mutually reinforcing.) For example, when asked about his transferrable skills (just before example 67 begins) Vijay says:

Example 68: Vijay – Indian Migrant, Unsuccessful

1.   C: so what is required out of the person is natural ability
2.   to prioritise your workload which I've g- got (^ ^)
3.   right what is more important is (.)
4.   the person should be (h) prudent enough
5.   to work on his own initiative
6.   because there can not be one person sitting always over you
7.   and guiding you (pointing) do this do that
8.   no that's not o:n (.)

He tends to say, 'This is what x is/should be like' in deontic mode, rather than 'This is what I did,' and to claim his 'natural ability' rather than illustrate it.

In example 68, relationships with teammates or customers or ability to self-manage are not dramatised or described in any detail – so the interviewers are left with little sense of his lived experience. Just at the point when he should be emphasising his personal agency, he – like Renard and many of the highly educated, professional candidates – distances himself to ventriloquise a classic job description.

Returning to example 67, Vijay (like many migrant candidates) is penalised for his FWE and his orientation to the immigrant story, since in neither case does his talk conform to the evidentiary rules of the interview (lines 36–46). Although not stated in any institutional texts, transferrable skills from previous work experience are presumed to be familiar and imaginable in an interview and part of its implicit framing. As discussed in 8.2, there is a highly charged set of contextualisation cues where the first interviewer attempts to collude with the second interviewer in dismissing Vijay's bid for the transferability of his skills. Vijay then inadvertently ratchets up the awkward moment by commenting on the interview process, thus exposing the game for what it is: an examination and not a friendly chat (lines 46–51). He thus amplifies the wrong footing that he has already established, presenting himself as commentator on the interview process rather than a contributor to it. In narrative analysis terms, he has shifted himself from the storied or narrated self to the narrating self, commenting on both the interviewers and his possible success.

Communicative Intent: Rhetorics, Footing and the 'Immigrant Story'

The expected rhetorics and footing of the interview – to be personally engaging but also institutionally appropriate – must be realised linguistically. But Vijay is penalised for not being personal and institutional in the right way. This is most marked in the ways in which he shifts the rhetorical grounds of the interview at different stages of it and within a particular sequence, so that there is an uneasy footing – jointly created but rarely stable. This in turn means that he appears to be personal when a more institutional response is expected and too institutional when a more personal and grounded account is required.

In trying to convince about his transferrable skills – at line 36, when he says, 'So I'm not afraid of anything' – he uses an ECF, claiming too much for the self when a more analytic and euphemised response would fit better. Similarly, when a more detailed and grounded account is required, as he still tries to convince, he opts for a rather gnomic expression: 'Patients are patients' (line 42). In the space of a minute he introduces much more of himself, and yet removes himself from being the active storyteller. As with his comments on the interview mentioned above, he shifts here to podium talk (Goffman, 1981: 137–140), appearing to put himself on an equal with or superior position to the interviewers (as he also does at the beginning of the interview with, 'First of all I would like to tell you'). But then reverses this footing at line 31, saying, 'You are more experienced' (as he does earlier in the interview, when he claims, 'You are my superiors'). While Gladston's deft footwork allows him to be both personal and institutional, Vijay's jarring shifts in footing – stating his lowlier position but also, by the act of claiming it, assuming some sense of superiority – produces more uncomfortable moments.

These extracts jointly produce misalignments which characterise the interview throughout, but cannot be judged as incoherent. However, there are also moments of difficulty where candidate lack of discourse cohesion (9.7) feeds into unresolved misunderstandings. We see this in the last few lines of example 67 above – and particularly in, 'My confidence says you'll be unfortunate' (lines 56–58). Is he saying that he is not confident that he will be fortunate, and has simply used the second person pronoun rather than the first ('I'll be unfortunate')? Or is he saying the opposite in a jokey way – that he is confident that the organisation will have the bad luck of taking him on? Interviewer one's look at interviewer two may suggest this. Or is it simply not clear at all and the laughter is there to mask the confusion?

Similarly, immediately after this laughter sequence, interviewer two asks how Vijay would deal with a phone request for a medical record when the caller is ringing up on behalf of a patient.

Example 69: Vijay – Indian Migrant, Unsuccessful

1.   C: I'll just apologise] I'll say I'm very sorry
2.   I can't do anything
3.   because confidentiality means confidentiality (.)
4.   I can't disclose anything which is (.) confidential (.)
5.   because that's part of my job (h) and (.)
6.   if I'm (.) if I'm given a job
7.   first thing is I'll be asked and I'll be expected (.)
8.   to maintain confidentiality
9.   which at any cost I can't leak out
10. I.1: mhm
11. C: I can't disclose anything
12.   which is (.) not related to you directly
13.   unless my superiors=
14. I.1: =mhm
15. C: they- because they have got more experience
16.   and they know all the things are-
17.   unless they ask me to do it (.)
18.   I won't do it (shakes head) [no

Vijay's footing appears to shift between narrating what he would say to the caller and justifying his action to the interviewers (lines 1–10), and then at lines 11–12 to addressing the caller. The rest of the example seems to shift back to self-justification. But these shifts are not clear. Unlike Gladston and other successful candidates (6.5), there are no contextualisation cues which mark who his addressees are and the aphorism 'confidentiality means confidentiality' could be addressed to the interviewers or the narrated caller. If it is addressed to the interviewers, then it may well be interpreted as sententious and as if he is lecturing them on confidentiality, rather than demonstrating his understanding of it in a specific situation.

To sum up, both interactional dissonance and a perceived lack of convincing, relevant work experience prove Vijay's downfall. In feedback immediately after the video, he considered he was 'ninety per cent likely to be successful.' By contrast, the interviewers scored him well below the successful candidate. In the video feedback session, they remarked that he seemed to be 'trying to take control of the interview,' seemed somewhat 'overbearing' and was perhaps overeducated and overqualified for the job; although acknowledging he had done a similar job in India, he had shown no transferrable skills:

Example 70: Interviewer Wash-up Sessions

1.   I.1: because I didn't feel (.) that he told me enough
2.   about his skills and experience
3.   I.2: mhm

(thirty seconds of talk deleted)

4.   I.1: apart from the fact that yes he could do it (.)
5.   because he worked as a ward clerk (.) in India (.)
6.   but there was no transferrable skills
7.   abo:ut (.) what he'd learnt from working as a ward receptionist
8.   to what he's worked as a (.) as a in heal- in erm x-ray filing
9.   I.2: mhm
10. I.1: there was no transferrable skills
11. I.2: yep

Vijay, a fluent and educated speaker of English with highly relevant experience for the job, singularly failed to impress the interviewers. So what makes for his lack of convincingness? Chapters 9 and 10 suggest that a candidate must meet the criterion of plausibility, consisting of three broad elements:

firstly a sense of connection, or right footing, with speakers and their expectations; secondly a sense of authenticity, of interactional realness, in terms of shared framing and imaginability about candidates' work experiences; and thirdly the processability and reasonableness of their responses. Vijay seems to be judged wanting on all three counts. But when candidates do meet these criteria, the interviewers often describe this in terms of trust.

10.6 Harmonía

In the sociolinguistic literature, it is commonplace to write about 'trust' in gatekeeping interviews (Kerekes, 2003, 2006; Linell and Marková, 2013). While many of the features which led to mistrust in Kerekes' analysis are similar to the features of talk and interaction analysed in this book – such as not knowing the rules of the game, dysfluency, overclaiming and misunderstandings – the notion of trust, similar to notions such as empathy and rapport, is a highly subjective inner feeling. Interviewers may dismiss candidates as 'untrustworthy,' but this is not illustrated in any way and it is not clear precisely what interviewers mean by a lack of trust in a workplace context.

In the ethnomethodological tradition, Garfinkel sees trust as a precondition to unproblematic interaction whereby interactants show adherence to what he calls the constitutive practices of a particular event (Garfinkel, 1963). So a lack of trust is a non-adherence to these practices, leading to bewilderment or frustration. The notion of non-adherence to the norms of an event is clearly a factor in failing candidates, but as a proxy for such a large and internal and emotional concept as trust it is rather limited. So 'trust' is either too pinned down (and perhaps too regimented – for example, where does playing with the rules of the game come in?) or is too general and diffuse a concept to explain the complexities of success or failure in gatekeeping processes.

A concept that is more inclusive and also more associated with the details of interaction is *harmonía* or when things go wrong, *dys-armonía*. The original Greek terms contain both the elements of concord, symmetry and agreement which come with the plausible candidate as described above and also the elements of music so closely associated with talk: pitch, rhythm and attunement (Erickson, 2012). The rhythmic coordination of interaction, its melodic joyfulness which acts subliminally and gives a sense of well-being and, by projection, of likeability of the other – a sense of acceptance, of fit and fitness – remains unspoken. But together with the more institutionally accountable elements of plausibility, *harmonía* must surely contribute to the success of such candidates such as Gladston, Pippa, Ahmed, Sandeep, Terence, Tom, Paula, Lloyd, Emma and many others. Likewise, its opposite – where neither plausibility nor a sense of attunement is present – is decisive in failing candidates. Interruptions, reformulations and translations rupture their stories and produce a jarring arrhythmia, which destabilises a potentially coherent self-presentation.

Conclusion

The linguistic and cultural norms of the interview are wired together into the institutionalised processes of judging people talk. They are the structures of selection which are institutionally defended and embodied in the conduct and values of the interviewers. The linguistic penalty resulting from *dys-armonía*, experienced by migrant candidates, is a structural matter created by institutions – the production of different linguistic economies – rather than a general and objective matter of inadequate or inappropriate communicative resources. There is no fit between the demands of the interview game, constructed out of the different kinds of capital discussed throughout this book, and the demands of the job.

Like many other institutional events, there is a social gradient built into the job interview – a penalty which disadvantages and indirectly discriminates between those whose talk is plausible and convincing and those whose talk is not. It is surely time for talk to be put on trial; not only to understand how candidates are tried and often found wanting through talk, but also to put talk on trial more widely as a central and pervasive means of producing and reproducing inequality at work. The final chapter discusses some of practically relevant action that we can take to address linguistic penalties.

11 Linguistic Footprints

This final chapter is about practical relevance and the influence of research on aspects of institutional life. 'Not another book with such matters bolted on at the end,' would be a reasonable reaction. But I hope to show that the research discussed throughout the book has, from the start, been leaning out to address practical matters. There is also a red thread running through this book that relates to my own frustration at the continued supremacy of the job interview, its powerful role to exclude the many candidates who, given different opportunities to display their abilities to do the job, might well succeed and thrive, and the reluctance of institutions to pursue change.

A critical take on the institutionalised workplace can include any setting where institutional and organisational systems, policies and practices produce social and linguistic inequality. This challenges the usual distinction between workplace studies and other fields such as medical, educational and legal contexts. But of course, all these fields carry out their business through institutionalised workplaces. Even within this broad definition of workplaces, only some figure with any regularity in the current literature on application. So after a brief discussion on the current debates on practical relevance and application, I will concentrate on industrial and service sector examples from the institutionalised workplace – in particular, the employment and medical fields.

While the main context for these reflections is based on a critical sociolinguistics of the workplace, many of the themes in this chapter are relevant for any practical research and the discussion reaches out to aspects of applied linguistics and discourse studies, as well as to sociolinguistic studies which might not be defined as critical. But this chapter will not explore the recent emancipatory applied research, working directly with migrant and BAME groups and practitioners associated with them, since this is outside the scope of the book.

While the focus is on the potential for institutional change, it is important to include the possibility of influencing the public understanding of language more generally, since institutional representatives are ordinary folk too. Much of the decision-making in institutional gatekeeping processes is steeped in common sense ideologies about language, as has been discussed earlier, so sociolinguistic application in organisations may well have a broader impact on a public understanding of language and vice versa. Thus it is not only, as Rampton (1997: 8) says, a matter of 'persuading people about the significance of research findings but also in coming to understand linguistic objects and processes themselves.'

11.1 Current Debates on Application and 'Impact'

After a long period when discourse and sociolinguistic studies paid little attention to practical relevance in institutionalised workplaces, the twenty-first century has seen some transformations. Both research policy and recent discussions within the fields of UK sociolinguistics and applied linguistics have energised the debate about application and impact generally (Lawson and Sayers, 2016: 1–22; Stracke, 2014; McIntyre and Price, 2018), so I do not intend to go over this in any detail.

What stands out are two major concerns: Firstly, there is the tension between academic independence and application (particularly the freedom to take a critical stance, for example Cook, 2011), the implication being that impact and criticalness cannot be bedfellows. Secondly, the sclerotic stance taken until recently by the institutions of academia towards engagement – and now the rather limited and bureaucratic position taken on impact – still leave much policy- and practice-orientated research on the back foot.

While the discourses of impact bind application more tightly to research, this top-down approach seems to fail such research on two counts. Firstly, impact is rightly seen as yet another institutional requirement – and so done grudgingly – and its narrow cost-benefit image can tarnish any application-oriented research. Secondly, the design and systems of academic establishments – despite these impact discourses – do not readily support and account for the strategic thinking, time, effort and often psychological well-being of those who undertake this engagement research.

So it is not surprising that, as Lawson and Sayers (2016) observe, sociolinguistics is not widely known outside academia. If impact is about dissemination, reach and significance – as the current discourse emphasises – then we are not doing so well. But if our work is about linguistic inequality in the broadest sense, then surely not taking action that could see some effect on inequalities is a dereliction of duty? Certainly, that is the position taken up by some action-orientated sociolinguists. As Cameron et al. assert in their groundbreaking work on the ethics of researching language: 'If knowledge is worth having, it is worth sharing' (1992: 24). Easily said but not as easily done, as they would be the first to acknowledge. And 'sharing' becomes considerably more problematic when, as critical sociolinguists in the workplace, this knowledge is a critique of the systems and processes designed or used by those we are sharing it with.

Rather than taking up an oppositional stance – independent, excellent, long-term research versus cost-benefit, easily measured, short-term and institution-dependent research – it is worthwhile to analyse the possibilities of independent research which can also influence and change, neatly summed up in what Wolfram calls 'the scholarship of engagement' (2016: 97). Such analysis requires a reflexive approach and one which documents some of the struggles researchers have in doing, communicating and embedding good research in (sometimes) hostile institutional environments.

Characteristics of Engagement and Influence

The whole endeavour of engagement and influence is framed by our motivation to build on, extend and rework our expertise in communicating with those in our own field, in order to influence those outside it. Each characteristic, described below, leaks into any of the others and is primarily determined by the audience with whom we interact. In some respects, suggesting that categorising research projects in terms of three dimensions – how the research originates, how to be practical and critical and what capacities are needed – is arbitrary and foolish. But let us treat it as an heuristic, an anvil on which we can beat out some of the ideas and consequences of our linguistic footprints on the world outside our own field.

Figure 11.1. Characteristics of Engagement and Influence

Characteristics	Implications
1. Origin of the research (i) Researcher: discovery-based inquiry (ii) Policy/institution: including the determination of problem solving (iii) Partnership: academic/non-academic joint problematising and problem solving	(i–iii) Where the research originates from is likely to affect the ecology of the whole project and its values and priorities throughout

2. On being critical	
(i) Creating curiosity – with communities	(i) Degree of outreach possible
(ii) Relatively more servicing – with practitioners	(ii) Degree of responsiveness of non-specialists to new knowledge
(iii) Relatively more critical – with institutions and their policies	(iii) Degree of institutional defensiveness
3. Capacities	
(i) Our strengths	(i) The necessary personal resources and resourcefulness to engage others and develop partnerships, including reflexivity, discursive negotiation and resilience
(ii) The academic institution	(ii) The extent to which the institution is bound by existing priorities and categories

11.2 Origin of the Research

Just where and how any research project is incubated and hatched will of course determine its design, content and outcomes. The three categories of researcher-, institution- and partnership-initiated research may well overlap, but each has distinct features which affect the degree of collaboration – and indeed all decision-making.

Researcher-Initiated Projects

All research is discovery-based inquiry. In sociolinguistic and applied linguistic research, discovery is joined by usefulness to form two main axes (Rampton, 1997). Researcher-initiated research has a tradition of reaching out to the communities with whom researchers have worked (Trudgill, 1984) and giving back to them: not so much researching *on* or *for*, but *with* (Cameron et al., 1992). This is usually taken to mean a lockstep process whereby researchers 'discover' first and turn to usefulness later. As teachers, we are continually communicating our discoveries to students who are relative non-specialists; in some ways, usefulness in terms of engagement and outreach is a case of building on this capacity to communicate beyond our fellow researchers. However, engaging with wider publics is not a matter of running a few public seminars to show 'impact.' In an excellent chapter on how to engage both institutions and the wider public in understanding language variation and its consequences, Wolfram states that

> the broader social consequences of sociolinguistic research are not insignificant afterthoughts. In fact, thoughtful consideration and strategic planning related to outreach engagement should be integral to any research project, particularly those related to the role of language in society. (Wolfram, 2016: 87)

Wolfram goes on to describe the considerable investment in such engagement and argues that this must be designed into the project from the start, along with a range of collaborative relationships and entrepreneurial skills. While he discusses the success in engaging the wider public, he hints at more intransigence when seeking to make a difference to the educational establishment, its institutions and policies (2016: 89).

Increasingly, sociolinguistic projects are planning in opportunities to use the settings and the data collected to translate research outputs into outcomes geared to practitioners and the wider community, based on training and materials, and several of these workplace projects are mentioned below. These show how practitioners can be encouraged to consider their own practices and how service users and others in the community at large can be advised and prepared for institutional encounters. However, these projects still leave open the question of if and how to affect change in systems, practices and values at the institutional level. So we now turn to the other types of research initiation, where engagement is directly with institutions.

Policy/Institution-Initiated Research

Within sociolinguistics, there has been a degree of scepticism about – if not downright discomfort with – the business of doing policy-orientated and institution-commissioned research. This may involve research funded by and partnered with institutions such as government departments, the public services or businesses, of the type which forms the basis of this book. The classic response to policy-driven, institution-commissioned research is that it undermines academic freedom and therefore by implication the scope, quality and independence of the research. I argue in this chapter that this need not be the case. However, to research with independence and also to contribute to institutional change is tremendously hard labour, and remains largely unnoticed by the universities which employ us.

Engagement is built into the design of the institution/policy-initiated project since there can be struggles over the precise terms of the research, aspects of its methodology (such as what counts as enough data), degree of access to the naturally occurring events in institutions which usually form the core of our data and, most profoundly, over different ways of seeing and categorising the world – amongst other things. Members of steering and advisory groups from the organisations which have initiated the research can appear to be doing surveillance work, as much as being supportive. And such struggles can continue throughout the project; the extent to which the research is problem finding or awareness raising rather than producing the clear answers and neat solutions to meet institutional expectations, for example, or indeed researchers being critical of the initial research question asked in the first place, as outlined in the case studies (below). However, if we are concerned with how social and language inequality is produced and challenged, the usefulness of our research will depend upon how persuadable we can be. This in turn depends upon our capacity to work *with* institutions.

Research Initiated Through Partnership

Many of the themes just raised are relevant for a partnership-based research. Both commissioned and partnership research create a specific ecology for the researcher in terms of opportunities that these types of research offer, as well as emergent issues to do with researchers' own subject positions and some inherent conflicts. Many lead to collaborative relationships with their connotations of a joint vision and working towards consensus. But with institutions and government departments, language workers often find themselves going against the grain at the same time as being thoroughly implicated in the organisation's goals for the research. In such instances, a more formal partnership that goes beyond collaboration and establishes a more equal relationship between researchers and the organisation can help to maintain researcher independence. Partners can be in a formal agreement to work together and relationship building and outcomes are structured by this agreement. They need not rely all the time, as collaborative work does, on goodwill and co-membership.

Partnership research – for example, the UK Government-funded Knowledge Transfer Partnership scheme[53] – at best involves 'joint problematisation' (Luhmann, 1990) and then follow through to a set of proposed solutions. Much policy-orientated research, by contrast, leads to reports and some dissemination work, but often the buck stops there. The mode is transmission but not translation. Recommendations are communicated, but whether they are translated into practical action is – with some outstanding exceptions – unlikely to be the concern of researchers. With partnerships, translation work is crucial.

Partnerships do not necessarily require a formal agreement, particularly in the case of long-term, inter-professional relationships. For example, Sarangi discusses some of the interpretive tensions which can arise and also be resolved where there are 'communities of interest' (Sarangi, 2015: 26) amongst different professional groups. In some contrast to 'communities of practice,' what brings people together as a 'community of interest' is a common concern with a particular phenomenon (as the case studies below discuss), even though these groups may have substantial differences in ways of looking, interpreting and classifying – in sum, in their discursive habits. Partnership arrangements, whether formal or not, offer the spaces to work with and resolve some of the differences in these discursive habits – if both sides can acknowledge and acclimatise to them.

These three ways of initiating research (researcher, policy/institution and partnership) may well become increasingly integrated as the implications of change-orientated research are built into the overall design of projects. Like any good ethnography, such projects need to begin long before the research proper starts and continue long after it ends. Too many projects are time-poor. The long nose and long tail of the applied research animal need to sniff out and sweep up the institutions, groups and individuals with whom researchers aim to raise curiosity, establish good working relations and commitment to invest in the time, new ideas and reach that collaborative and partnership agreements require (Holmes et al., 2011). But this ethnographic and commitment work does not fit easily into the timetable for research established by funders.

11.3 On Being Critical

The critical perspective of this book – that the social meaning of language and its role in the contemporary world is always ideological and examining this role is always a critical endeavour – is widely shared by those who see themselves as 'critical sociolinguists.' As I have argued, much of the language inequality that migrants experience is a hidden process in which language is rarely topicalised but permeates the everyday ideologies of institutional practices. It is a matter of the extent to which these social ideologies are made explicit and link to wider settings, discourses and so forth (chapter 3) which defines critical sociolinguistics. But arguably, most applied research in language and discourse is on a cline of criticalness, and engagement with non-specialists outside the academy will continually raise questions about how critical our positioning, analysis and institutional reach can and should be. We are faced with the conundrum of working *with*, *for* and *on* institutions, managing the tensions in communities of interest, learning from and with each other while challenging existing practices and systems. Such engagement is demanding in ways which require our learnt capacities to be at full stretch.

Creating Curiosity

Arguably, we have a responsibility to take our critical stance on language out into the public domain for two main – and sometimes contradictory – reasons: firstly because there is a lot of general interest out there and secondly because there are a lot of uninformed and unhelpful views about language use. Outreach work can address both by creating spaces to be curious about language. A third and important reason is giving back to society; having taken data from people, we owe a debt to return something to them.

This can be done in many ways: through face-to-face talks, more formal presentations and an ever-increasing range of media outlets, including national TV channels and printed media as well as social media, blogging and so on. While audiences are often intrigued and researchers receive a warm welcome, being critical with audiences who hold deeply oppositional views based on uninformed generalisations can subject researchers to personal attacks, as well as attempting to undermine their expertise and standing. Academic debate can be scarring, when disagreements turn into turf wars and attempts at new paradigms are constantly rejected. But such debate is within certain professional parameters; engagement with the wider world can be much tougher and curiosity harder to create.

Critiquing Practice and Taking a More 'Servicing' Role

Recent sociolinguistic research in workplaces and looking at professional practice has led to engagement with practitioners as well as those needing to access services and employment. Investment in workplaces has both a 'servicing' and a critical role. Servicing is used here not in the sense of a slavish offering up of institutionally required 'fix it' solutions, but rather in the gradual and emergent overhaul and joint repair of aspects of professional conduct. This also implies a critique of current practice and may face institutional resistance to any change brought in from outside. The investment in time and psychological energy required depends upon an ethnographic instinct of lurking around and soaking up organisational practices, learning aspects of its culture and environment, understanding the interests of the group and the ideological underpinnings of conduct which may appear natural and neutral to them (11.4).

Many of the characteristics of this approach are present in ongoing applied sociolinguistic research on the workplace. For example, the New Zealand Language in the Workplace Project (LWP)[54] was founded by Janet Holmes in 1996; twenty-five years later it is still an active force in workplace communication, a remarkable example of sustained investment in understanding and joint accomplishment with the public and private sector. The success of these long-term relationships depends upon the applied aspects of the project, focussing on what was going well and developing mutually beneficial goals with partner organisations (Vine and Marra, 2017: 181–201), and possibly tempering critical stances to sustain such relations.

LWP-research-based materials on workplace communications – aimed at both managers and migrant employees – are easily accessible through government websites, in collaboration with the Ministry of Business, Innovation and Employment. These include guides for migrants and those working with them on living and working in New Zealand[55] – including materials on job interviewing (Riddiford, 2017) – and are complemented by ESOL materials based on naturally occurring audio recordings and emails (Riddiford and Newton, 2010). The Australia-based Language on the Move Portal, co-founded by Ingrid Piller and Kimie Takahashi, is similarly outward facing.[56] Along with many other issues on language, globalisation and migration, it is a discussion centre for workplace and gatekeeping activities and reaches out to both academics and the professions more widely.

Other applied sociolinguistic and interactional research has focussed on the direct training of practitioners through partnering up with professional bodies – both practitioners and policy makers – for example, with the police (Stokoe, 2014; Stokoe and Sikveland, 2017; MacLeod and Haworth, 2016: 151–170) and with health professionals (Roberts and Moss, n.d.).

Despite the rising number of cases of long-term, sustained applied sociolinguistics, one aspect of this work remains underdeveloped in the general debates about applied research. This relates to the lack of published articles and books translating research into practice. There are notable exceptions but, on the whole, academic journals want research findings and not the narratives of doing change-orientated research. Such limited recognition and output by the academic media means that the academic community is rarely alerted to the reach of such practical application and its trials and tribulations – as well as the contributions to change that such labour can produce.

Taking a More Explicitly Critical Role of Institutions

As the projects referred to above show, a critique of existing practices and professional conduct is possible even while working closely with organisations. Indeed, the fact that workplaces are open to possible change implies that there is at least some willingness to be critical of the status quo. Engaging with professionals to look at their own conduct from a new perspective takes linguistic inequality into the workplace and, whatever the response, has created some ripples both ways. Janus-like, workplace professionals may be consumers of research but can washback their own reactions to the research, which can in turn lead researchers to self-critique (Sarangi 2015). Working for some change with practitioners and feeding back their own concerns and perspectives to researchers in a mutual way is one of the most important things we can do; a different order of achievement from publications in high-rated journals, but one that should be properly valued.

However, as Cook says (2011: 35), part of the job of academics is to be fundamentally critical of establishment values and this goes further than suggesting changes to professional conduct or supporting those accessing services and employment. Seeing equality only in terms of improving conduct and access but not addressing the values and systems of institutions in a more fundamental way has been termed, in feminist theory, 'uncritical equality' (Plumwood, 1993). The argument here – played out in the two case studies below, warts and all – is that high-quality research, critique of institutional values and partnership with these institutions can go hand in hand, even if the hands are twisted some of the time. Nobody ever said that taking linguistic inequality beyond the academy would be easy!

This more overtly critical role can span role relationships from collaborative to agonistic, or even dismissive (see 11.5). Taking this more explicit stance has an effect on researchers' identity, role, authority and credibility and can produce some quite profound struggles. For example, in institutions and organisations where, as outsiders, our own expertise can be marginalised, *evidence*-based recommendations may have less credibility than *eminence*-based ones. Here, the authority of eminent players in a field to which we do not belong trumps the sociolinguistic evidence that we have laboured over. Even where the core of the work relates to language, ill-informed and sceptical reactions based on everyday ideologies of language are commonplace and language research findings often dismissed: '[These] ideologies are so powerful that language research which challenges them is not only *discounted* but is often *suppressed*' (Gumperz and Cook-Gumperz, 2005: 286, my italics). So being reflexive about this process and communicating it to an academic audience can help to inform the debate about critical engagement with institutions, as in the following example.

In an earlier study with the Royal College of General Practitioners (RCGP), Srikant Sarangi and I were asked, as 'transcultural discourse analysts' (it seems that some institutions know about discourse analysis but not sociolinguistics), to review the college's oral membership examination because of their concerns about the high failure rate of overseas-trained doctors. Soon afterwards, we wrote a reflexive account of our relationship with the RCGP and its examiners (Roberts and Sarangi, 2003), concentrating on role relations between ourselves and the college in discussion about articles arising from the research, where contrasting epistemologies (sociolinguistic and medical) were debated.

While the college was persuaded by our techniques, pathologising language and interaction for close scrutiny, the interpretive methodology left them queasy. We tried to illuminate and stimulate through our classificatory systems and metaphors, while they wanted evidence and hard recommendations. But while analysing the unintended consequences of the exam, it was also possible to maintain a dialogic relationship which resulted in a general acknowledgement that we had encouraged a critical debate. As two readers of our college/researcher co-authored article in the *British Medical Journal* observed:

> The importance of this study is twofold: Firstly, it shows the value of discourse analysis in understanding how human interactions go wrong, leading to the entirely unintended potential for discrimination … Secondly, and equally importantly, the paper raises some fundamental questions about the use of the oral examination as an assessment tool. (Esmail and May, 2000: 375 quoted in Roberts and Sarangi, 2003)

The first part of this comment relates to professional conduct and a lack of language awareness. The second part suggests a more fundamental critique of the exam, where we were seen to be 'raising questions' about the exam.

Arguably, our joint working with the college allowed for such a critical take. The franker, more explicitly negotiated footing and debate that had developed contrasts with what we might experience when handing over recommendations from policy-orientated research commissioned by the state. In this latter instance, contributions might well be formally received but their 'impact' not visible at all.

However, the good relationships worked out more at the academic end of our partnership (co-authoring journal articles) rather than at the action end, in terms of overhauling or even abandoning the oral exam. 'Raising questions' may just be an institutional fudge, but it is also possible that the changes in the exam system some years later were influenced by this research. At this point, we were not in close touch with the RCGP and so never knew quite what our 'impact' was. And this diffuse, possibly unrecognised, possibly very limited influence may often be a reality for many research-based applied projects, and so beyond bureaucratic scrutiny.

11.4 Capacities

Some of the unease expressed about taking practically relevant research 'out there' relates to our capacities as academics: whether we should stretch existing talents, skills and sociopsychological strengths to go there and whether we can. There is similar unease about the extent to which academic institutions and those which fund them have capacity – in terms of the understanding, flexibility and values – to acknowledge the demands and investment in attempting to make a social difference. In a heartfelt reflection on his institution's indifference to the time and effort spent on the significant social outcomes from his research on refugee status determination, Patrick observes: 'This time has been unrecognised and unrewarded within the university's view of my activities.' But on a more positive note, he adds that

> the more linguists are deeply involved in cross-disciplinary long-term work which produces significant social impact, the easier it may become to argue our profession should value it and our universities reward it – regardless of whether it produces traditional research outputs. (Patrick, 2016: 245)

That being said, application and 'impact' present a seismic shift in the academic regimes, discourses and decision-making which determine most of academic research life. There is still much to think and write about here, not least how PhD programmes and training can reflect this shift and how articles and other publications outside the traditional academic, high-rated journals can be given parity in any research assessment exercise.

I would also add that part of the argument about being valued and rewarded depends on us providing the institutional discourses and categories necessary to make a realistic assessment of this work, and to challenge the institution's defensiveness towards narrow academic success on the one hand and the audit culture on the other. This would involve defining what capacities we have to develop and what resources to draw on to do this work. These capacities would encompass:

1. The ability to communicate in a range of media to non-specialist audiences. Developing rhetorics and registers which don't lose or fudge the research, but are communicable and persuadable. This would include (amongst many other things) writing in the media about public debates, writing papers and reports jointly with practitioner partners, presentations to government departments and professional bodies and so on, using real data (subtle examples, as naturally occurring ones often are, rather than over-egged simulated ones) in training materials, and other appropriate and sustainable means of building practitioners' awareness of and capacity to innovate institutionalised communicative practices.

2. The patience, resilience, social and ethnographic skills to learn from, work with and persuade those outside the sociolinguistic community of the value of linguistic evidence and to develop and maintain long-term relationships and build our authority through extended dialogue – often up against professional resistance and everyday prejudices. This is well captured in Jacob Mey's clever metaphor (1987): feeling like poets one moment (when the cleverness and line of beauty of our analysis is appreciated) and like peasants at the next (when our work is not heard or openly dismissed or derided and we feel humiliated). As Patrick pointed out, 'Experts are representing their entire field to decision makers unfamiliar with it, and must expect that their evidence or opinions will be scrutinised or challenged by even more capable and respected colleagues – a lesson I learnt early' (Patrick, 2016: 243).

3. The capacity to identify and work closely with national and local broadcasters and with technical experts, film editors etc. as well as the ever-increasing numbers of self-taught videographers and self-publishers who can produce multimedia, multi-channelled resources for social media.

4. The imagination, entrepreneurial and networking skills to seek out avenues of communication with community groups, sections of organisations and professional bodies that can act as bridges to decision makers etc. To devise ways to make accessible all the outputs from applied research which do not flow through the usual channels of communication used by academics, and so remain undervalued.

5. Being reflexive about the whole process of engagement and generally investing more in the processes hidden from the usual academic discourse.

The next two sections are two case studies which illustrate some of these issues. The first one is a reflective account of the two DWP projects.

11.5 Case study 1: Job Interviews, Ethnicity and Disadvantage

This first case study is a descriptive reflection on the two projects on which this book is based, and which spanned six years. In both this and the next case study, the focus is on attempting to persuade organisations that sociolinguistic knowledge is relevant, useful and change-making; both also describe how any success in achieving it is hard to come by. As I mentioned above, organisations and their eminent representatives may readily dismiss the findings of linguistic scrutiny, even when the context and problems relate to language, as in the case of refugee status determination. In the workplace and in health settings, where language is rarely mentioned, the task may be even harder.

Before

The research was commissioned by the Ethnic Minorities Employment Unit of the DWP, triggered by concerns over the employment gap between white and BAME workers and the view that employment practices – specifically the interview – contributed to this outcome. We were alerted to this research possibility through a piece of luck. The DWP project manager was an ex-academic sociologist, who was familiar with the sociolinguistic work being carried out at King's College London. His background had led him to the early sociolinguistic research on job interviewing which was highlighted in the research specification, along with the much more widely known occupational psychology literature. So the original concerns that were framed by issues of racial discrimination and by the psychological literature were recontextualised as matters of interactional (and so sociolinguistic) importance. Luck allowed us to swim into focus and circumvented the extensive hard work in becoming known to government departments and other policy units, which would have been the only alternative. The second of the two projects arose out of the first, which had triggered an interest in internal promotion. This second project also provided funding for a DVD on entry-level recruitment good practice, to be used both as a training tool in its own right and as an instrument for eliciting issues and resistances to change in recruitment interviewing.

The research specification for the first project made it clear that there was to be practical application, but this was to be limited:

The Department for Work and Pensions (DWP) wishes to commission research on the interaction between interviewers and candidates in job interviews. The aim of the research is to obtain a better understanding of how interaction is managed in job interviews, to determine whether ethnic minority candidates are systematically disadvantaged in these interviews and to understand how job selection decisions are made by employers. The Department hopes to use the findings from the research *to develop job interview skills training courses for jobseekers* (my italics).

This aim reflected a hierarchical relationship between power and impact, also present in the second case study and in other applied projects: those with the least power are targeted with the greatest amount of change and those with the most power, the least amount of change. Here, those deemed disadvantaged or least competent would have this fixed through training. The next group up – professional interviewers not initially subject to change – also became the focus of attention after the first tranche of research. At the highest level, the policy makers and designers of interviews would not be asked to undertake any institutional critique of their own values and practices. These were all matters that were not addressed at the start of the research.

During

At the beginning, the priorities were getting access to organisations to collect video data of real job interviews, and early partnership building and nego-tiation with colleagues in the DWP and the Jobcentre network. Our initial concerns did not always match those of the DWP, as became clear during the steering group meetings. Our energies were focussed on getting *any* real data, as we knew how difficult it would be to get near the promised sixty-to-eighty examples, and we also knew that our methods could not encompass a large data set; their concerns centred on gaining representative samples from all the main BAME groups and on how 'ethnicity' should be categorised, reflect-ing the research paradigms and big policy focus of the Ethnic Minorities Employment Unit.

As sociolinguists working on refugee status determination have also found, communicating to government departments and other decision makers is 'often at the level of introductory linguistics' (Eades, 2010: 37 quoted in Patrick, 2016: 241). With the sociologist DWP project manager acting as mediator, we needed to persuade the steering group that small-scale interpre-tive research using sociolinguistic tools would provide new knowledge which more traditional methods would not. We also started our outreach work early with the professional body for human resource staff, the CIPD, since this is the only organisation that communicates widely to businesses on the issue of job selection and has charter status. Initially we wrote a short report for their newsletter, with the hope of recruiting organisations to the project and to provoke some general interest.

As the project progressed it became clear that any training for job seekers and professional interviewers needed to be based not on simulated examples but on our data, so that real life could come rampaging into the training room. This involved negotiating more funding for DVDs. It was also clear that we needed the resources and contacts to produce professional materials that were engaging and analytical, directed and produced by professional filmmakers using video clips from the original interviews, as we had done with DVDs for the health service (and involved informed consent from participants at the first stage of data collection). The second of the DWP projects included funding for the two DVDs: one for job seekers (funded by Jobcentre Plus – the national employment agency) and a second targeted at interviewers (funded by the DWP). The latter of these had several functions. It was piloted in focus groups and simultaneously used to elicit views on selection interviewing, and so combined training and research elements. It was also a means of disseminating our approach and critique to a larger group of organisations.

In this way, application and influence was built into the research from relatively early in the project. The piloting of the interviewer DVD was led by Joanna Channel, who combined applied linguistics with expertise in organisational training. Five workshops were held: one each with two of the key participant organisations, one with Jobcentre Plus and two with groups of interviewers/trainers (one of which was organised by the CIPD). The DVD was also evaluated by the Equality Division of Jobcentre Plus. Interestingly, these front-line professionals identified more readily the complexity of job interviewing and raised more questions about the interview as a selection process than did more senior managers and policy makers. For all groups, this was a new way of looking at interviews and most could see value in using it in training contexts to disturb the prevailing habits and discourses around interviewing. However, their comments that the DVD was too 'subtle' or 'analytic,' or that it should address 'deeper issues of power differences and racism' suggested a desire to escape from interactional detail and return to general (and perhaps more comfortable) exhortations and advice.

After

As the projects reached their final stages, we developed the outreach work further at four different levels: with Jobcentres and job seekers, with the workplace equal opportunities 'community' (including the government's Race Relations Advisory Board), with the CIPD and participant organisations, and with government policy makers – with varying degrees of success. The DVD and training guide for job seekers (*Frequently Asked Questions*) was sent to all Jobcentres and widely used in local authority ESOL classes (Roberts et al., 2007; Roberts and Cooke, 2009). This was the most effective aspect of our applied research.

It was also useful to link up with a lawyer and human rights specialist, Fernne Brennan, to co-author an article in the *Equal Opportunities Review* to reach the equal opportunities community. This helped us to give some grist to the language and discrimination mill and to raise such questions as whether this 'linguistic penalty' counts as evidence of indirect discrimination. Here is a short extract from the article:

> A selection system that favours candidates who can 'tick bureaucratic boxes' and produce 'verbal artistry,' and in which interviewers listen for and elicit certain narrative structures potentially places foreign-born candidates at a distinct disadvantage compared to others. The linguistic penalty that is 'hidden' from some candidates during the interview process may be construed as a subjective employment practice. Subjective employment practices, whilst having no discriminatory intent may have discriminatory effects (*Watson v. Fort Worth Bank and Trust*). This may lead to subconscious stereotypes and prejudices about applicants' 'downcast eyes,' 'stiff delivery' or 'waffling' that put foreign-born candidates at a disadvantage compared with other persons on the grounds of their racial group. Moreover, where linguistic capital is used to determine employability this may be a subjective hiring practice that is a disproportionate means to achieving the legitimate aim (Section 1 (1A) (c) Race Relations Act 1976). (Roberts, Campbell and Brennan, 2006)[57]

The third and fourth elements of our 'impact' strategy – what we can call the 'critical equality' dimension – were much less successful with senior staff from a range of private and public sector organisations, as with policy makers. We had attempted to highlight this critical aspect of our research over the course of the project and in the final report: namely, that the job interview had the potential for indirect discrimination. For example, in our presentation to the delivery company featured in this book, we stressed that there were implicit assumptions about the job interview unfamiliar to many candidates, that 'evidence' might only be the rhetorical ability to sound convincing, that job interviews had a dynamic which undermined equal opportunities requirements, that there was a lack of fit between the language requirements of the job interview and that of the job and that, in short, the job interview was not fair. Unsurprisingly, we received a hostile reception from the senior management and occupational psychologists, who were heavily invested in the current design.

While the response to our CIPD presentations for senior HR staff was not hostile, they were met with some bewilderment and indifference. Our anatomy of the interview contrasted with other presentations given by invited HR specialists at a conference of the CIPD's special interest group on selection. Here, job interviews were discussed in the lofty terms of organisational development strategies and framed in the positivistic terms of occupational psychology: 'defined behaviours were identified in terms of sixty-four competences, grouped into competence clusters' (my notes from the meeting). The focus was on structure – specifically, more structure – in interviews, application forms, interviewer worksheets and feedback to candidates. Again, the abstraction and bureaucratisation of the process removed the interview designers from looking at what goes on in human interaction and from realising that the very procedures that can produce inequality – more structures, more text – are tightened up even more. We had taken the steering group through our analytic processes and they had accepted our final reports, but for other audiences our conclusions remained opaque or even unfounded and irrelevant.

At the level of policy making within the DWP, the reaction was stronger. We heard that the department was reluctant to publish the reports and that the findings were thought to be 'anti-business.' Since they had commissioned the research, the reports were eventually published – but the press release was not given the oxygen of publicity and was not reported in the media. At a meeting with the senior minister in the DWP, it was made clear to us that any disadvantage faced by migrant job seekers was a matter of individual competence and remedial training, rather than to do with any systemic problems with the selection process.

What were the lessons from this case? On the one hand, we could be found guilty of hubris, going beyond our research brief to critique a whole system deeply embedded in organisational values and practices and doing this on very little evidence. (If we were to take on such a task, perhaps the whole endeavour would have to be scaled up into a major programme of research.) On the other hand, helping to fix things for disadvantaged job seekers seemed, in Bloor's terms, a useful bit of 'engineering' (Bloor, 1997) within a system which, our evidence suggested, was unfair and needed to be critiqued. If we had our time over again – and if the university funding regime had been more open to research application and impact – we could have greatly increased our outreach work with occupational psychologists and with some of the organisational representatives involved in the original research projects. This would have given opportunities to negotiate a joint way of critiquing the job interview and considering fairer means of recruitment and selection – an approach that would have been closer to a form of partnership research described in our second case study.

11.6 Case Study 2: Knowledge Transfer Partnerships and the RCGP

The focus in this case study is on the partnership arrangement and the constant dialogue that this fostered between the RCGP senior representative Kamila Hawthorne and researchers at King's College – namely my colleague Sarah Atkins and me. While such formal arrangements are not so common – and certainly not the way the DWP project was structured – there is a striking similarity between the two case studies in terms of the tense reaction to our institutional critique and relative enthusiasm for the 'engineering' elements in producing materials and training for those disadvantaged by the system.

This partnership project was initiated jointly in 2011 by our two institutions as a knowledge transfer partnership (KTP) funded by a quasi-governmental body called The Technology Strategy Board. My own engagement with the RCGP since 1995 had consisted of two sets of research consultancy work, ten presentations at RCGP conferences or seminars and a jointly authored paper (Roberts et al., 2000); such long-term engagement helped to promote the partnership process. As with our first case study, the initiative arose from the clear gap in formal gatekeeping events between British and transnational candidates. In this case, it was the ongoing concern (which had rumbled on since our first consultancy in 1995) that overseas-trained doctors – now widely known as international medical graduates (IMGs) – had consistently and substantially lower pass rates than British-born candidates (and particularly white British-born candidates) in the membership and now licensing exam of the RCGP (11.3). The current element of the exam which was causing particular concern was the Clinical Skills Assessment (CSA), set by the RCGP and similar in many respects to other medical colleges' licensing exams. The RCGP was once again trying to tackle one of the most profound and difficult areas in institutional life: how to be fair and set and meet standards in a highly diverse society. It remains the only UK medical royal college to do so systematically and over time.[58]

This KTP was established to 'identify linguistic/cultural factors contributing to poorer performance of IMGs in the RCGP membership examination, and develop new tools to aid training and preparation for it.' Like the DWP project, we interpreted such factors as those stemming from the design and implementation of the exam at least as much as from IMG differences in communicative style. This was to test the partnership relationship, especially as during the life of the project a judicial review of the RCGP membership examination – requested by one of the associations of overseas doctors to examine its fairness – was to put particular strains on the bridging role of Kamila Hawthorne. And it is a salutary example of how easy it is for added dimensions to send shockwaves through the envisaged stable progress of making useful knowledge together.

The rest of the case study will take a reflexive turn with the following themes: politicised ethnography, dialogues and persuasion, and a sociolinguistics of the self.

Politicised Ethnography

The close partnership with another organisation required, as I have already suggested, an ethnographic stance: a degree of embeddedness within its structures and activities while making sense of it from without. As Rampton describes:

> [Ethnography] tries to enter the informants' life-world and to abstract some of its structuring features, and this entails a process of continuing alternation between involvement in local activity on the one hand, and, on the other, an orientation to external audiences and frameworks beyond. (Rampton et al., 2015: 15)

In our case this meant interacting with a roll call of RCGP members and many others affected by the membership exams, both formally and informally, and as frequent overhearers of RCGP-related debates and discussions. At the centre was the CSA group of examiners who designed and oversaw the exam, including the chief examiner, whom we met regularly. Beyond them was the entire examiner team, the assessment board and the assessment development team, the GP trainers and the deaneries, the candidates and the trainees. In addition to the regular core group meetings, we presented our work at ten conferences, workshops and formal meetings of the assessment teams.

A summary of our jointly authored report (Roberts et al., 2014) was sent to all CSA examiners and posted on the RCGP website. A jointly authored book for all candidates sitting the RCGP membership exams was published by the RCGP (Rolfe et al., 2015). An e-learning course (Atkins, 2016) was also accessed by over a third of all candidates who sat the CSA (some nine thousand candidates in total) between 2015 and 2018. The report, book and e-learning materials were all discussed by the exam lead groups. We also published several joint articles (Atkins et al., 2016; Hawthorne et al., 2017) as well as articles and chapters specifically for a sociolinguistic audience (Atkins and Roberts, 2018; Atkins, 2019).

But the ethnographic stance also meant standing back from being embedded in the system and the local politics of the college's assessment regime, returning constantly to our sociolinguistic habitus and from there taking a critical stance, in order to manage and sustain our insider/outside sensitivities. So to keep the duality of the project we set up regular team meetings between King's College and Kamila Hawthorne of the RCGP, writing what we called 'think pieces' to help push forward the critical agenda.

Dialogues and Persuasion

The political and critical dimension of our work was always interwoven with the descriptive and pedagogic. Kamila Hawthorne acted as the bridge between the official college position and what may have been seen as iconoclastic sociolinguistics. The attempts to reframe and disturb current 'truths' and discourse habits met with resistance from some of the core group of examiners and our think pieces – constituting a kind of sociolinguistic diary for ourselves, in the spirit of the ethnographic diary – became a way of working on how to persuade, and of talking together outside the sacred norms of a widely acclaimed assessment regime. These think pieces were reflexive discussions on (among other issues) our different epistemologies and ways of classifying, recent formal events of which we were a part – including joint analysis of video recordings, presentations, examiner video feedback sessions, joint team viewing and feedback of videos of cases – and catch-up sessions which included informal conversations and events within the RCGP, of which the King's College team was not a part.

Excerpts from these think pieces show certain strategies at work, all of them linked from the beginning with Eades's formulation of an 'introductory linguistic course' and with a critical approach. Firstly, we wanted to show that language and sociocultural processes are wired in together; that 'culture is a verb' (Street, 1993) and language is social action. For example, after a joint viewing session with the chief examiner of some of the hundreds of video recordings of the CSA data, the think piece began to raise questions about the additional penalty of the exam that IMGs faced. Here we were looking at the assumed cultural knowledge built into the CSA exam and the inferences that candidates were expected to draw from it, as in the following extract:

> What now seems to be the difficulty, as we saw yesterday, is that candidates must not only pick up cues but need to be able to reciprocally build on them with shared cultural knowledge. They can still be graded lower for 'technical reasons' i.e. not picking up cues and so socially evaluated as not connecting enough when the problem is not having the experience or not being able to imagine the experience of the patient (an overweight teenager who felt unhappy about doing PE at school because of the gym kit) [some lines omitted]. With any diverse population, the local British GP who did not align to the cultural/linguistic background of the patient would be in the same position. In other words, more demands are put on IMG candidates than the rest of the candidate cohort, as the latter do not have to imagine what they cannot imagine! Perhaps, rather, all candidates should have to work with a patient whose life they cannot imagine and the criteria in all cases should be about eliciting without expecting active building from shared experience? (Roberts, C., Atkins, S. and Hawthorne, K., personal communications, 2011)

'Picking up cues' and 'connecting' were part of the current discourse of the exam – we wanted to raise consciousness of how these were assessed in culturally-specific ways in the exam, and how they did not take account of the realities of a superdiverse patient population.

Secondly, we discussed from the start sociolinguistic concepts and their relevance to our project, building into the final report an ongoing glossary of key concepts as a result. We also wanted to persuade the RCGP that general descriptions of competences masked the detail of interaction where the judgments were being made. And we wanted to convince them that sociolinguistic method could link current institutional processes and categories on the one hand with concepts that would be 'good to think with' and detailed analysis on the other. We used the think pieces to test out how to put our key analytical points to an expert medical audience, unfamiliar with and potentially sceptical of our conclusions; for example, that interpersonal skills are unwittingly overassessed in the exam and indeed are not best assessed in standardised, role-played assessments where IMGs face an unfair disadvantage.

For example, we drew on Goffman and the sociolinguistics of style to tease apart performance and acting, showing how acting in a standardised exam way comes readily to the British-born candidates. Some examiners justified the role-playing setting because doctors have to perform, as Goffman would argue, when they are front stage in the consulting room. While as sociolinguists we would agree with Goffman, it was important to look at the greater distance that IMG candidates were likely to experience between acting in a standardised exam and doctorly performance in a consultation. We reported:

> The irony is that those who find acting the easiest are those for whom the simulation is closest to their own practice, sense of self and presentation of self. They can be friendly, charming and at ease because they are not having to recalibrate themselves for the exam. Personal 'voice' and professional style coalesce in the successful candidates. The examiner comments – that failing candidates (largely IMGs) are clunky, unnatural and not flowing well – are partly the product of the modelling and standardisation of the exam. (Meaning and sociality are largely communicated indirectly and grounded in background understanding.) The more distant the models and assumptions of the exam, the more explicitly they have to be called up and used. This leads to what we can call over-modelling, and in doing this, there is less indirectness and so less sociality and more sense that the candidates are not drawing on a shared background with the patient. (Roberts, C., Atkins, S. and Hawthorne, K., personal communications, 2012)

Similarly, Goffman's notion of alignment and its subsequent interpretation by Stokes and Hewitt was drawn on to suggest a shift from charged, culturally specific or idealistic terms such as 'rapport' or 'empathy' to looking at professional performance. This argument was illustrated through a specific video-recorded case, where the role-playing patient asks the doctor if he can have a vasectomy without his partner knowing:

> A good example of alignment as an idea, and of misalignment in practice is the vasectomy case. The candidate asks the role-playing patient how he will 'disguise' any medical effects of his requested secret vasectomy. 'Disguise' is a discrepant word in this context since it has face-threatening force for the 'patient' and means that temporarily the patient's act of wanting treatment (i.e. a vasectomy) and the doctor/candidate's act of advising are not brought into line. The successful candidate rapidly manages to deal with this misalignment by metacommunicating on the inappropriacy of the word i.e. she brings to the surface an account of what she said and that she had selected the wrong word in order to restore alignment. Clearly, she does not agree with his decision but needs to align with him in order to conclude the consultation amicably while maintaining her stance.

Alignment deals with behaviour not putative patient satisfaction, and that is all the Clinical Skills Assessment can do. It repositions the consultation as a goal-oriented encounter in which being in line, coordinating action and showing respect are more important for appropriate diagnostic reasoning and patient-oriented clinical management than simulated warmth, empathy etc. (Roberts, C., Atkins, S. and Hawthorne, K., personal communications, 2012)

Thirdly, as well as being able to test out together what the three of us thought we were learning from each other, the think pieces gave us the opportunity to be 'off-mic' when we found ourselves unable to convince and could vent our frustrations to each other. After the project had officially ended, the RCGP documented how the partnership had worked and its outcomes. We wrote about and discussed both of these and our disappointment that the they did not take up some of our major recommendations.

The two most important of our rejected suggestions were, firstly, that an exam was designed for GPs to consult anywhere in the UK did not have role-players who represented communicative styles from a range of linguistic minority groups. Secondly, the interpersonal skills (IPS) element was unwittingly overassessed, and so produced a linguistic penalty for IMG candidates:

What exactly is meant by IPS has still not been clarified. It is a conflation of many behaviours – which you list in your email – and until there is some clarity about what is necessary in order to consult adequately, simply claiming that 'IPS is important' masks its potential for inequality. As we make clear in the report, IPS is about manner and affect and empathy which, as we say, cannot be assessed from outside and is highly culturally and linguistically sensitive. This is the issue about standards in a superdiverse society which came up a lot in the IPS seminar but was never resolved. IPS is assessed both explicitly, and also implicitly throughout the transaction i.e. by judging if candidates *sound* caring, can verbalise empathy convincingly etc. Rather shouldn't something more modest be expected i.e. being safe, being clear and showing respect, as you outline. Again, is there any evidence that this has been properly discussed? (Roberts, C., Atkins, S. and Hawthorne, K., personal communications, 2013)

This think piece revisits the IPS problem, among ourselves, taking up Kamila Hawthorne's understanding of the issue. This illustrates well the time it takes for professionals from very different discipline backgrounds to find common ground. As with the DWP steering group, while an inner core of those we were researching with often found our arguments persuasive and useful, the wider professional group were less impressed. Of course, the goal of common ground depends as much on sociolinguistic researchers' openness to working with very different priorities and ways of seeing, articulated by those we are researching for and with. And such flexibility depends on being reflexive about ourselves.

A Sociolinguistics of the Self

A reflexive account of a project draws us into a sociolinguistics of applied sociolinguistics. Much of the everyday stuff through which we define our disciplinary selves seems to be at the core of what works or not in a partnership of this kind. Most evidently, we are struck by the sheer amount of time and energy spent on struggling over differing discursive habits. The last think piece (above) reiterates what we had said two years before, and what we said again some two years later in a final meeting with another senior member of the RCGP. In the event, only some aspects of the interpersonal skills debate were accepted and led to change.

We can also be reflexive about how we can use our expertise. Drawing and expanding on the second strategy of the think pieces (integrating sociolinguistic thinking into our developing understanding of partner workplaces), we can trace a language socialisation process in which we aimed to introduce 'good to think with' sociolinguistic concepts but also worked within and borrowed the language of clinical skills assessment, stretching these terms to take on a sociolinguistic dimension while respecting the values given to them in the world of health professional assessment. For example, terms such as 'signposting' – widely used in health professional communication – we expanded to include the whole dimension of metacommunication. And similarly, as the think piece above illustrates, we introduced concepts to reinterpret heavily invested words such as 'interpersonal skills' and 'empathy' with a more sociolinguistic topography, such as 'alignment.'

This two-way language socialisation process seems both more and less than 'an introductory linguistics course'; it seems 'more' in that new sociolinguistic concepts had to be reframed and embedded in other dominant discourses and not just explained as I have just discussed, but 'less' in that many of the terms used in sociolinguistics simply do not travel. Looking back over many years, I can recall numerous examples of disciplinary-based concepts being misinterpreted or indeed ridiculed and having to look for more engaging terms: being put on the spot with the use of 'reification' and 'teleological' with medical academics, having 'social action' interpreted as some form of activism and – most shamefully – reading one of my own paragraphs in the satirical magazine *Private Eye*, which delights in a 'Pseud's Corner' (where absurd jargon is aired and laughed at) for my use of the word 'affordance.'

But while helpful, finding more persuadable terms and integrating them with the current professional language of the workplace can still feel like surface work, with a fundamental tension beneath it about what language is and can do. The kind of gatekeeping events described in this book (except for 'migrant events' and occasionally with migrant candidates) are experienced and discursively negotiated in terms of personality, general conduct or other generalisations about design, systems and procedures – or in umbrella terms such as 'subjective bias,' 'standardisation' and so on. Language escapes as an irrelevance, or reduced to a few words as jargon, or as an unmentionably sensitive subject. As we have seen, when the outcome of these events is externally judged in terms of individual success or failure, the linguistic penalties produced by them are suppressed and other reasons for the assessment are called up. This in turn often leads to a dismissal of sociolinguistic methodology and its detailed analysis of interaction as too small and subtle – or just plain wrong. Generalisations and common sense ideologies are more readily available, comfortable and less hard work. Such a stance is understandable from the perspective of busy professionals, who may be intrigued by a sociolinguistic perspective but have their own professional world to attend to. Nevertheless, a critical take on what language is and can do must be part of a sociolinguistic endeavour which aims to make a difference beyond the academy.

Lastly, the struggles over language and discourse seep into one's sense of self and identity as a sociolinguist. To have careful microanalysis dismissed as 'bits and pieces' swiftly diminishes the glow from having a paper published on the same analysis; the latter savoured as poetry, the former as peasant work, in Mey's terms. Selling ways of looking and thinking in a very different linguistic marketplace from our own can easily undermine our own professional authority and legitimacy as speakers. It can create an 'ontological insecurity' that questions the value of what we do, and so perhaps who we are as academics. For this reason, if 'impact' is to remain a significant criterion in research funding, then research training needs to include building resilience to withstand and/or learn from these slings and arrows.

I have tried to outline some of the challenges of this work so that academic institutions can think more about how to value research aimed at addressing workplace inequality but also, I hope, to persuade more early researchers that it is exciting and even sometimes change-making. To end the case study section on a relatively high note, here are some reflections from Kamila Hawthorne (vice-chair for professional development at the RCGP 2015–18 and now a trustee on the RCGP Board) on the effect of our research over the last three years:

> I think our research had a marked effect on the exam – and that the Leads [lead managers of the Membership of the RCGP exams] paid a lot of attention to it, even if they didn't do it in the way we had anticipated. I know that all cases have now been scrutinised for overlap between marking domains, and that elements of our advice have been incorporated into examiner training. There are also more BAME examiners. However, I don't think that the role-players are that different in their acting roles, even though they are quite diverse. There hasn't been a new framework for considering interpersonal skills, which is disappointing. …
>
> [Overall the Leads are] very aware of Ethnicity and Diversity issues and ensure that the examiner panel all receive training annually. The paper we wrote for *BJGP Open* was one of the '10 most read papers' of the year! And the feedback from the book has been quite positive too. …
>
> What I think is very surprising is that outside organisations haven't really picked up on what we have published or tried to use it. I suspect this is because it is quite 'niche' and complicated to analyse and apply to the case specific situation. (Kamila Hawthorne, personal communications, 2018)

The research has also had an effect on academic medical educators and may in turn seep through to other royal medical colleges, as Kamila hopes. The concluding paragraph on research by psychologists on the CSA exam, written by a psychologist, ends as follows: 'We would recommend that efforts directed at reducing these group differences should focus on "sociolinguistic" factors, rather than on clinical knowledge' (Patterson et al., 2018: 744).

11.7 The Sense of an Ending?

The quotes from Kamila Hawthorne feel more like unfinished business than an ending. Contributing to change means building in a much longer, adequately funded post-research phase. It is hard to say when research has 'ended.' It is fitting that any critical sociolinguistic research on, for and most importantly with institutions should also be a critique of our own academic institutions, which have produced a discourse of 'impact' without fully acknowledging the practical, social and emotional realities of doing it.

Todorov's image – of the fish in water that is not aware of the water it swims in – is a good analogy for the lack of awareness of the language water we all swim in. Institutions and their selection/assessment specialists are hardly aware of this linguistic pond, since so much of its effect lies below the level of consciousness and is seen as small stuff. This book has been about some of the small tragedies of everyday life produced by these hidden linguistic penalties. But these can have large consequences and, cumulatively, shore up the inequalities in assessment and selection – and indeed similar gatekeeping processes – which are part of the increasing and widespread disparities between those who are entitled and those who are not. For this reason, these everyday small tragedies need to be addressed through the same resource, namely language, which has produced them.

The interview and other gatekeeping assessments create a narrow gate, through which only some can pass. The currency of standardised assessments and competence frameworks leads to taken-for-granted assumptions that it is fair. In the neoliberal marketplace, any failure is the problem of the individual and their need to acquire more linguistic capital. The power of the interview to penalise migrant applicants (and others who cannot culturally align) remains largely unscrutinised. 'You are what you talk,' in the now of the assessment, and this remains the ultimate linguistic penalty for large numbers of migrants. But this is a penalty of context rather than conduct. The structures and practices which maintain this ideology persist. Yet like any game, the rules of the interview game may eventually change and, perhaps quite soon, this particular game will have passed its sell-by date.

Endnotes

1   Much recent work on language and migration has focussed on the small encounters of everyday life: how people get by and get on with whatever language resources seem to work at the time. These studies of ordinary multilingualism and its associated conviviality in routine and passing encounters are an important counterbalance to the well-established research on language and inequality in institutional life. However, this book is a reminder that access to jobs, training, rights to reside/work and citizenship are processed through formal interviews where talk is scrutinised and where differences are not accepted or ironically played with, but are amplified and judged. Getting along together in the context of the park or the market has a different value from getting along in the context of the job interview.

2   The debt to Durkheim, Weber and Douglas is the focus of much work in cultural sociology, in particular the notion of 'symbolic boundaries' and the role of cultural processes in creating inequality (for example, in the studies by Lamont et al. [2014], Collins [2004] and DiMaggio and Garip [2012]).

3   While Foucault's work does not address centrally how such power feeds into discrimination against certain groups, feminist theory has drawn on Foucauldian concepts to address patriarchy (Hartsock, 1990).

4   But see Riggins (1990), where Goffman is criticised for being a bourgeois apologist or mere functionalist.

5   This research was funded by the DWP, managed by its Ethnic Minorities Employment Unit and consisted of two projects entitled *Talk on Trial: Job Interviews, Language and Ethnicity* (Roberts and Campbell, DWP Research Report number 344, 2006), and *Talking Like a Manager: Promotion Interviews, Language and Ethnicity* (Roberts, Campbell and Robinson, DWP Research Report number 510, 2008).

6   Taken as a whole, BAME groups have a higher rate of unemployment, are more likely to be overqualified and less likely to be promoted than their white British counterparts (McGregor-Smith, 2017). And there is a long-standing pay gap between British-born groups compared with all migrants (Longhi and Brynin, 2017).

7   The National Centre for Industrial Language Training (ILT) was set up by the then Department of Employment in 1974 and coordinated thirty ILT units throughout England. Its original purpose was to teach English to newly arrived migrants in the industrial and service sector. But it soon took on a wider remit to address communications and relationships within the workplace, and to contribute to combating racial disadvantage and discrimination. It was an early example of combining ethnographic research with educational interventions and, with the influence of John Gumperz and his active participation in our work, became a focal point for developing interactional sociolinguistics in workplace settings. The national scheme was closed down by the Conservative Government in 1989. The role of ILT, its objectives and theoretical backdrop are described in Roberts, Davies and Jupp (1992).

8   There are some significant exceptions to the general trend of undertaking little research on and with low-paid workers in manufacturing and service jobs (chapter 11). Notable ones include the New Zealand Language in the Workplace Project (Holmes, 2005b; Holmes and Stubbe, 2003; Holmes, Marra and Vine, 2011) as well as research conducted in Australia (Piller and Lising, 2004), in Scandinavia (Kraft, 2017) and in the US (Kleifgen, 2013).

9   At the time of this research, in the first decade of the twenty-first century, the design and implementation of selection interviews was influenced by the discourses and practices quoted in this section. For this reason, I have focussed on the studies from this period.

10   Arguably, activity types are close to the notion of communicative genre (Günthner and Knoblauch, 1995). See Hanks (1987), Bauman (2001) and Rampton (2006) for discussions of genre over the last thirty years.

11   This artful performance calls up Wittgenstein's notion of language games, Goffman's (1981) 'expression games' and Bourdieu's (1991) notion of the 'feel for the game.'

12   This relationship between self and work has been studied in terms of social class – for example Adelsward (1988), Silverman and Jones (1976) and Komter (1991) – and more generally in the sociological literature, as by DiMaggio and Garip (2012). The undervaluing of professional competence and the focus on the interpersonal in a social class context is well illustrated in Friedman et al. (2015) and Friedman and Laurison (2019).

13   There have not been significant improvements, over the last fifteen years, in the extent of employment disadvantage and discrimination amongst BAME groups (Frijters et al., 2005; Clark and Drinkwater, 2007; Berthoud and Blekesaune, 2007; Wood and Wybron, 2015; Wadsworth, 2017; McGregor-Smith, 2017).

14   These subtle acts work through apparently objective and neutral workplace cultures and relations, such as the competence model described below and indeed the whole linguistic technology of the selection interview.

15 'Members of racial groups need protection from conduct driven by unconscious prejudice as much as from conscious and deliberate discrimination.' (*Swiggs v. Nagarjan*) (FN 1999 IRLR 572; 1999 EOR 51, HL)

16 The assumption that a job interview is an acceptable way of testing English has recently been encoded in law in the Immigration Act 2016. This includes a new code of practice (available from the Equality and Human Rights Commission) on the English language requirement for public sector workers, in which all staff in 'customer-facing' jobs are required to speak English fluently. The language competence required for this 'fluency duty' can be tested by 'competently answering interview questions.'

17 The distinction between migrant and non-migrant in other places could not be justified. For example Vigouroux, in the South African context, quotes Cornwell and Inder's research (2008) which shows that migrants may have as good or better access to the formal economy than locals, if the former have a high level of proficiency in English (2013: 242–243). 'Such findings point out that the issue of socioeconomic integration goes far beyond the context of migrations and should be investigated without preconceived social categories (e.g. locals versus migrants) to whom it may apply' (Vigouroux, 2013: 243).

18 Clearly discrimination still persists (as referenced above) and may have been underestimated in our research since our findings are the product of particular organisations that agreed to allow us in, who had implemented equal opportunities policies and had clear instructions on interviewing.

19 The method described here owes much to the interdisciplinary research training programme initially funded by the Economic and Research Council and led by Ben Rampton at King's College London since 2007 and, in particular, the use of transcontextual analysis developed by Adam Lefstein for this programme (Rampton et al., 2016: 32–37).

20 This eighth circle has no direct link to the eighth circle of Hell in Dante's *Inferno*, where institutional life and language are seen as fraudulent and corrupt!

21 For further discussion see Wyatt and Silvester (2015) 'Reflections on the labyrinth: Investigating Black and minority ethnic leaders' career experiences,' *Human Relations* 68(8): 1243–1269.

22 Both the research on equal opportunities in medicine and our own research on fairness in assessment in simulated consultation exams (Roberts et al., 2014; 11.6) identify broadly the same proportions in samples of candidates – i.e. one-third local white British, one-third British BAME and one-third overseas-trained doctors – with the same hierarchy as in the research described in this book.

23 These abstract frameworks form clusters of terms which become 'mutually enregistered' (Silverstein, 2003). That is, each set of terms is used in certain ways, which in turn calls up other uses and interpretations so that, together, they make sense to those who are in the know in a given organisation.

24 In addition to the job interview, interdiscursivity has been identified in: legal proceedings, in the use of both judicial and common reasoning (Maryns, 2013);

the use of mediation that blends law and counselling (Candlin and Maley, 1997); enterprise and consumerism on the one hand, and counselling and therapy on the other (Fairclough, 1992b; Sarangi and Slembrouck, 1996); medical and psychotherapy domains, with the blending of narrative and institutional reporting (Ravotas and Berkenkotter, 1998); political rhetoric (Hill, 2000: 263–266); a range of selection and licensing assessments in medical settings (Roberts and Sarangi, 1999; Atkins and Roberts, 2018; Atkins, 2019); across a range of professions (Linell, 1998) and in the workplace more generally (Holmes, 2007).

25   While the interviewer did not use the term 'gossip,' some of the features of Sara's talk are similar to gossip with its high-involvement style and the dissection of situations, people and feelings (Coates, 2011) as well as divulgence of personal details, the assessment of motivations and emotions, digression and rapid and emphatic delivery. The problem is that many interviewer questions seem to ask for gossip-type answers (for example, Pippa is probed about what people are saying about the new workplace changes), but they need to be euphemised with professional and institutional discourses if they are to be acceptable.

26   Sara, like other female candidates such as Alison and Lucy, are assessed as emotional and limited. Their personal discourses are not reined in by the institutional. Drawing on feminist theory exploring how institutions are based on the implicit masculinity of the rational subject – as outlined in classical Greek philosophy – it is possible to see the 'othering' of female candidates and their association in Plato's terms with slaves, barbarians, emotion and domesticity.

27   The issue of credibility is also linked to Schiffrin's (1996) 'self-portraits' and to Ochs and Capps (1996), on ways of getting to the bottom of things.

28   UNHCR regulations make explicit the relationship between coherence, consistency and fluency in the telling and judgments of credibility during asylum interviews (Jacquemet, 2011: 482). In the job interview, this connection is there but more implicit.

29   This is similar to the heroic stories told in medical accounts (Erickson, 1999).

30   The STAR schema was invented by a US company called DDI, and is now widely used in the UK. There is another acronym, CARL, which stands for circumstance, action, result and learning. Many companies use this (some informally) or adapt it slightly for their own purposes.

31   Clearly the reductive way in which the Labovian structure is used is well illustrated here. But this is less the fault of the original model and more to do with its recontextualisation into a form which suits institutional functions and classifications well.

32   In narrative theory, the third of three levels of positioning indicate how the narrator positions a sense of self/identity with regard to dominant discourses (Bamberg, 1997). While Bamberg uses 'positioning' rather than stance, and it is not always easy to differentiate between the two terms, positioning theory as developed in the social psychological literature is used in a more abstract and technical sense than in this book (Davies and Harré, 1990: 43; Harré and van Langenhove, 1992).

Schiffrin (2006) suggests that, from a sociolinguistic perspective, it is possible to see positioning as a more durable form of Goffman's footing. However, here I use stance (rather than positioning) as one of many resources that an individual uses to show their judgments about themselves. These in turn feed into the overall footing (or set of footings) which develop between interviewers and candidates and which come to characterise the interview environment. So footing in these contexts is arguably more durable than stance.

33   I am grateful for Sarah Helsig's comments on this section of the data.

34   While the focus in CA is on how organisations are constituted as ongoing accomplishments through the procedures and patterns of talk, recent CA studies of workplace talk indicate more of an interpersonal perspective, allying orderliness with more moral and improvising behaviour (Stivers, 2008; Stivers et al., 2011). For example, in a study of graduate recruitment interviewing, interviewers latch on to one aspect of an answer rather than another as part of a moral assessment of the candidate's talk: a gap year expedition does not count as evidence of 'achievement' when the interviewer focuses on the fact that selection onto the expedition depended only on having the funds to pay for it, suggesting that the candidate could buy the experience rather than obtain it through merit (Llewellyn, 2010: 74–95).

35   These findings support the occupational psychology literature's critique of the taken-for-granted value of the highly structured interview; for example, Blackman's (2002) claim that less structured interviews can produce more accurate perceptions of the candidates' job-related personality traits, since they provide more opportunities to relate to the interviewers. They also support Posthuma et al.'s (2002) contention that structured interviews are not free from conflict and prejudice. However, this literature does not provide a more fundamental critique of the job interview.

36   This is not unlike the diagnosis phase in simulated family doctor consultations where highly-rated doctors speed through a set of model questions (Roberts et al., 2014).

37   See similar contrasts in studying social workers (Svennevig 2001, 2004).

38   For the debate on standard language ideology, see Coupland, 2003b; Milroy, 2004; Gal, 2005; Eckert, 2008; and Lippi-Green, 2012: 67.

39   There is an acknowledged difficulty among sociolinguists about critiquing the notion of a standard when it is so much part of the sociolinguistic repertoire. Lippi-Green, in her study of 'standard language ideology' in the US (2012), sidesteps this dilemma by looking at general dictionary definitions of the standard. Overwhelmingly, these are social definitions drawing on education and class, assuming that the standard is 'educated speech,' and synthesising these definitions she describes the 'standard' model as one 'drawn from the spoken language of the upper middle class' (2012: 67).

40   For example, Trinch's analysis of Latina narratives of domestic abuse (2003) led to changes at the lexical and organisational level, which in turn produced a

focus on linearity, temporal sequencing and concrete detail to make the report authoritative.

41   At the outset of this interview, quite a different dynamic has been established between the interviewer and Mohammed from that in Lloyd's interview. The interviewer's position as a representative of institutional authority has been established quite strongly in an opening sequence in which he probed Mohammed about his national insurance documents and right to work in the UK. These situational roles are reflected in example 52, in the reduced co-authoring, responses and eye contact which the interviewer gives to Mohammed, when compared with Lloyd.

42   Studies – which are subject to the same critiques as others mentioned in the main text – have found that fluency in English improves chances of employment by twenty-two per cent (Dustmann and Fabbri, 2003), that the native-immigrant wage gap in the UK attributable to having English as an additional language is about twenty-six percentage points for males and twenty-two percentage points for females (Miranda and Zhu, 2013), and that non-native English speakers with a good command of English are three times more likely to work in higher professional jobs than those who struggle with English.

43   Similar studies include Hansen et al., 2014; Fuertes et al., 2012; and Gluszek and Dovidio, 2010.

44   Studies of language use in contexts of low-paid work: Roberts et al., 1992; Goldstein, 1997; Duff et al., 2002; Kleifgen, 2013; Strömmer, 2015; Cuban, 2013; Pillar and Lising, 2014; and Lønsmann and Kraft, 2017, 2018. Studies looking at how migrants fare in workplace internships: Sandwall, 2010.

45   As with language and citizenship (McNamara and Shohamy, 2008), what counts as acceptable levels of language in employment tests and interviews varies considerably over the years, as noted in chapter 3. Whereas the focus here is on relatively low-paid work, there is also a clear gap between the idealised language test and real workplace interaction in certain while-collar and professional demands – albeit different standards of communicative ability apply (McNamara and Roever, 2006: 188–190).

46   But see note 16 where Vigouroux (2013) makes the point that, in certain settings, such a distinction between migrant and non-migrant is not justified.

47   See also Kerekes, 2018; Bauder, 2003; and Currie, 2007 on the deskilling and devaluing of migrant labour.

48   In the Philippines there is a strong government steer to mobilise workers to work abroad, since remittances from overseas represent a significant element in the country's GDP. In preparation courses before working abroad, workers are encouraged to have 'national mobile identities' which are categorised according to their profession/skills. Those with fewer skills are encouraged to become 'supermaids' and are trained in 'scripts of servitude.' For example, they are taught how to respond to Arabic imperatives for work in the Middle East. This

group experience a double penalty: they not only have to learn the language of servitude, but they are often expected to learn such scripts in several languages. Professionals, on the other hand, only need English. So the lower a worker is in the labour market, the more they are expected to be multilingual – albeit in a very limited and subservient register (Lorente, 2010 and 2017).

49   See similar language differences in asylum seekers' stories (Blommaert, 2001: 419) and professional jobs (Lipovsky, 2006: 1157).

50   The 'immigrant story' term was originally coined by Roxy Harris, who was part of the King's College advisory group for the two DWP projects.

51   Arguably, from an organisational theory perspective, the notion of compartmentalisation may contribute to the 'immigrant story.' Bell applies Du Bois' notion of 'double consciousness' (Du Bois, 1989) to the argument that 'compartmentalisation appears to be a strategy for maintaining two distinct cultural spheres so the dynamics of one do not spill over into the other ... as a strategy, it may reduce the stress deriving from the bicultural experience' (Bell, 1990: 474). This may partly account for the idealised good candidate, who separates their actual experiences of work from their assumed institutional self (Campbell and Roberts, 2007).

52   This is not to underestimate the difficulties faced in immigration control interviews by migrants who, Jacquemet argues, must 'manipulate their experience – inevitably messy, complicated and confusing – to provide a straight, simple narrative reality perceived to fit the requirements of the asylum process' (Jacquemet, 2005: 200; Maryns, 2005). However, for the majority of migrants seeking work it is not the experience that is messy, but the way it appears to the interviewer.

53   Knowledge transfer partnerships were set up some forty years ago to help businesses solve problems by teaming up with an academic institution. More recently, they funded social science-based projects in the public sector – see www.ktp.innovateuk.org.

54   The New Zealand Language in the workplace Project (LWP). For more information, see www.victoria.ac.nz/lals/centres-and-institutes/language-in-the-workplace.

55   Examples of the LWP research-based materials and guide can be found at www.newzealndnow.govt.nz and www.worktalk.immigration.govt.nz.

56   The Language on the Move Portal is a discussion centre for workplace and gatekeeping activities for academics and professionals. For more information, see www.languageonthemove.com.

57   The Race Relations Code of Practice relating to Employment 2006, published by the Commission for Racial Equality, states that a language requirement may be indirectly discriminatory (3.1). The requirement that candidates possess a specific kind of 'linguistic capital' may constitute indirect discrimination if it amounts to a provision, criterion or practice that is applied to all applicants but has an adverse impact on a person from a particular racial group – including ethnic group – and is not a proportionate means of achieving a legitimate aim (section 1 [1A] Race Relations Act 1976). However, case law suggests that

there has to be a direct link between ethnicity and language for this ruling to apply.

58   Over the period of the research – despite some small fluctuations – IMGs had a fifty per cent pass rate, compared with UK graduates who had a ninety-two per cent pass rate (RCGP).

Bibliography

Adelsward, V. (1988) *Styles of Success: On Impression Management as a Collaborative Action in Job Interviews*. Linköping: University of Linköping.

Agar, M. (1985) Institutional discourse. *Text and Talk* 5(3): 147–168. https://doi.org/10.1515/text.1.1985.5.3.147

Agar, M. H. (1986) *Speaking of Ethnography*. Newbury Park, CA: Sage. https://doi.org/10.4135/9781412985895

Agar, M. H. (1986) *Independents Declared: The Dilemmas of Independent Trucking*. Washington: Smithsonian Institute Press.

Agha, A. (2003) The social life of cultural value. *Language and Communication* 23(3–4): 231–273. https://doi.org/10.1016/S0271-5309(03)00012-0

Akinnaso, F. and Ajirotutu, C. (1982) Performance and ethnic style in job interviews. In J. J. Gumperz (ed.) *Language and Social Identity*, 119–144. Cambridge: Cambridge University Press. https://doi.org/10.1017/CBO9780511620836.010

Allan, K. (2013) Skilling the self: The communicability of immigrants as flexible labour. In A. Duchêne, M. Moyer and C. Roberts (eds) *Language, Migration and Social Inequalities: A Critical Sociolinguistic Perspective on Institutions and Work*, 56–78. Bristol: Multilingual Matters. https://doi.org/10.21832/9781783091010-004

Allan, K. (2016) Going beyond language: Soft skill-ing cultural difference and immigrant integration in Toronto, Canada. *Multilingua* 35(6): 617–648. https://doi.org/10.1515/multi-2015-0080

Allan, K. and McElhinny, B. (2017) Neoliberalism, language and migration. In S. Canagarajah (ed.) *The Routledge Handbook on Language and Migration*, 78–101. New York: Routledge. https://doi.org/10.4324/9781315754512-5

Allan, K. and Burridge, K. (1991) *Euphemism and Dysphemism: Language Used as Shield and Weapon*. New York: Oxford University Press.

Anderson, B., Ruhs, M., Rogaly, B. and Spencer, S. (2006) *Fair Enough? Central and East European Migrants in Low-Wage Employment in the UK*. York: Joseph Rowntree Foundation.

Angouri, J. (2013) The multilingual reality of the multinational workplace: Language policy and language use. *Journal of Multilingual and Multicultural Development* 34(6): 564–581. https://doi.org/10.1080/01434632.2013.807273

Angouri, J., Marra, M. and Holmes, J. (2018) Introduction: Negotiating boundaries at work. In J. Angouri, M. Marra and J. Holmes (eds) *Negotiating Boundaries at Work*, 1–8. Edinburgh: Edinburgh University Press.

Apfelbaum, B. and Meyer, B. (eds) (2010) *Multilingualism at Work: From Policies to Practices in Public, Medical and Business Settings*. Amsterdam: John Benjamins. https://doi.org/10.1075/hsm.9.01apf

Arnaut, K., Blommaert, J., Rampton, B. and Spotti, M. (eds) (2016) *Language and Superdiversity*. New York: Routledge. https://doi.org/10.21832/9781783096800

Atkins, S. (2016) [Online] *Clinical Skills Assessment*. Available from: https://elearning.rcgp.org.uk/course/view.php?id=182.

Atkins, S. (2019) Assessing health professionals' communication through role-play: An interactional analysis of simulated versus actual general practice consultations. *Discourse Studies* 21(2): 109–134. https://doi.org/10.1177/1461445618802659

Atkins, S. and Roberts, C. (2018) Assessing institutional empathy in medical settings. *Journal of Applied Linguistics and Professional Practice* 13(1–3): 11–33. https://doi.org/10.1558/japl.31861

Atkins, S., Roberts, C., Hawthorne, K. and Greenhalgh, T. (2016) Simulated consultations: A sociolinguistic perspective. *BMC Medical Education* 16(16): 1–9. https://doi.org/10.1186/s12909-016-0535-2

Atkinson, J. M. and Drew, P. (1979) *Order in Court: The Organisation of Verbal Interaction in Judicial Settings*. London: Macmillan for the Social Science Research Council Centre for Socio-Legal Studies, Wolfson College.

Auer, P. (1998) Learning how to play the game: An investigation of role-played job interviews in East Germany. *Text* 18(1): 17–38. https://doi.org/10.1515/text.1.1998.18.1.7

Auer, P., Heller, M. and Roberts, C. (2014) John J. Gumperz. In J. Östman and J. Verschueren (eds) *Handbook of Pragmatics 18*. Available from: https://benjamins.com/catalog/hop.18.gum1. https://doi.org/10.1075/hop.18.gum1

Auer, P. and Kern, F. (2001) Three ways of analysing communication between East and West Germans as intercultural communication. In A. Di Luzio, S. Günthner and F. Orletti (eds) *Culture in Communication: Analysis of Intercultural Situations*, 89–116. Amsterdam: John Benjamins. https://doi.org/10.1075/pbns.81.08aue

Bakhtin, M. (1981) *The Dialogic Imagination: Four Essays*. Austin, Texas: University of Texas Press.

Ball, P. and Giles, H. (1982) Speech style and employment selection: The matched-guise technique. In G. M. Breakwell, H. Foot and R. Gilmour (eds) *Social Psychology*, 101–122. London: Macmillan. https://doi.org/10.1007/978-1-349-16794-4_6

Bamberg, M. (2004) Considering counter-narratives. In M. Bamberg and M. Andrews (eds) *Considering Counter-narratives*, 351–371. Amsterdam: John Benjamins. https://doi.org/10.1075/sin.4.43bam

Bamberg, M. and Georgakopoulou, A. (2008) Small stories as a new perspective in narrative and identity analysis. *Text and Talk* 28(3): 377–396. https://doi.org/10.1515/TEXT.2008.018

Bateson, G. (1972) *Steps to an Ecology of Mind*. Chicago: Chicago University Press.

Bauder, H. (2003) 'Brain abuse,' or the devaluation of immigrant labour in Canada. *Antipode* 35(4): 699–717. https://doi.org/10.1046/j.1467-8330.2003.00346.x

Bauman, R. (1975) Verbal art as performance. *American Anthropologist* 77: 290–311. https://doi.org/10.1525/aa.1975.77.2.02a00030

Bauman, R. (2004) *A World of Others' Words: Cross-Cultural Perspectives on Intertextuality*. Malden: Blackwell.

Bauman, R. and Briggs, C. (1990) Poetics and performance as critical perspectives on language and social life. *Annual Review of Anthropology* 19: 59–88. https://doi.org/10.1146/annurev.an.19.100190.000423

Bauman, R. and Briggs, C. (2003) *Voices of Modernity: Language Ideologies and the Politics of Inequality*. Cambridge: Cambridge University Press. https://doi.org/10.1017/CBO9780511486647

Baynham, M. (2011) Stance, positioning, and alignment in narratives of professional experience. *Language in Society* 40(1): 63–74. https://doi.org/10.1017/S0047404510000898

Baynham, M. and De Fina, A. (eds) (2005) *Dislocations/Relocations: Narratives of Displacement*. Manchester: St. Jerome Publishing.

Bell, E. L. (1990) The bicultural life experience of career-oriented Black women. *Journal of Organisational Behavior* 11(6): 459–477. https://doi.org/10.1002/job.4030110607

Berger, P. L. and Luckmann, T. (1967) *The Social Construction of Reality: A Treatise in the Sociology of Knowledge*. London: Allen Lane.

Bergström, O. and Knights, D. (2006) Organizational discourse and subjectivity: Subjectification during processes of recruitment. *Human Relations* 59(3): 351–377. https://doi.org/10.1177/0018726706064179

Besnier, N. (1993) Reported speech and affect on Nukulaelae Atoll. In J. Hill and J. T. Irvine (eds) *Responsibility and Evidence in Oral Discourse*, 161–181. Cambridge: Cambridge University Press.

Birkner, K. (2004) Hegemonic struggles or transfer of knowledge? East and West Germans in job interviews. *Journal of Language and Politics* 3(2): 293–322. https://doi.org/10.1075/jlp.3.2.08bir

Blackman, M. C. (2002) Personality judgment and the utility of the unstructured employment interview. *Basic and Applied Social Psychology* 24(3): 241–250. https://doi.org/10.1207/S15324834BASP2403_6

Blommaert, J. (2001) Investigating narrative inequality: African asylum seekers' stories in Belgium. *Discourse and Society* 12(4): 413–449. https://doi.org/10.1177/0957926501012004002

Blommaert, J. (2003) Commentary: A sociolinguistics of globalization. *Journal of Sociolinguistics* 7(4): 607–623. https://doi.org/10.1111/j.1467-9841.2003.00244.x

Blommaert, J. (2005) *Discourse: A Critical Introduction*. Cambridge: Cambridge University Press. https://doi.org/10.1017/CBO9780511610295

Blommaert, J. and Backus, A. (2011) [Online] Repertoires revisited: 'Knowing language' in superdiversity. *Working Papers in Urban Language and Literacies, Paper 67*. Available from: https://www.kcl.ac.uk/ecs/research/research-centres/ldc/publications/workingpapers/abstracts/wp067-repertoires-revisited-knowing-language-in-superdiversity.

Blommaert, J. and Rampton, B. (2016) Language and superdiversity. In K. Arnaut, J. Blommaert, B. Rampton and M. Spotti (eds) *Language and Superdiversity*, 21–48. New York: Routledge.

Blommaert, J. and Varis, P. (2012) [Online] Culture as accent. *Tilburg Papers in Culture Studies, Paper 18.* Available from: https://pure.uvt.nl/ws/portalfiles/portal/30332592/TPCS_18_Blommaert_Varis.pdf.

Bloor, M. (1997) Addressing social problems through qualitative research. In: D. Silverman (ed.) *Qualitative Research: Theory, Method and Practice*, 221–238. London: Sage.

Boden, D. (1994) *Business of Talk: Organizations in Action.* Cambridge: Polity.

Bolander, P. and Sandberg, J. (2013) How employee selection decisions are made in practice. *Organisation Studies* 34(3): 285–311.
https://doi.org/10.1177/0170840612464757

Boltanski, L. and Chiapello, E. (2005) The new spirit of capitalism. *International Journal of Politics, Culture, and Society* 18(3–4): 161–188.
https://doi.org/10.1007/s10767-006-9006-9

Bourdieu, P. (1991) *Language and Symbolic Power.* Cambridge: Polity in association with Blackwell.

Bourdieu, P., Passeron, J. C. and Saint Martin, M. D. (1994) *Academic Discourse: Linguistic Misunderstanding and Professorial Power.* Cambridge: Polity Press.

Bourdieu, P. and Wacquant, L. J. D. (1992) *An Invitation to Reflexive Sociology.* Cambridge: Polity Press.

Boyatzis, R. E. (1982) *The Competent Manager: A Model for Effective Performance.* New York: Wiley.

Bremer, K., Roberts, C., Vasseur, M. T., Simonot, M. and Broeder, P. (1996) *Achieving Understanding: Discourse in Intercultural Encounters.* London: Longman.

Briggs, C. L. (1997) Sequentiality and temporalization in the narrative construction of a South American cholera epidemic. In M. Bamberg (ed.) *Oral Version of Personal Experience*, 177–184. New Jersey: Lawrence Erlbaum Publishers.
https://doi.org/10.1075/jnlh.7.21seq

Briggs, C. L. (2005) Communicability, racial discourse and disease. *Annual Review of Anthropology* 34(1): 269–291.

Briggs, C. L. (2007) Anthropology, interviewing, and communicability in contemporary society. *Current Anthropology* 48(4): 551–580. https://doi.org/10.1086/518300
https://doi.org/10.1146/annurev.anthro.34.081804.120618

Brown, P. and Hesketh, A. (2004) *The Mismanagement of Talent: Employability and Jobs in the Knowledge Economy.* Oxford: Oxford University Press.
https://doi.org/10.1093/acprof:oso/9780199269532.003.0003

Brown, P. and Levinson, S. C. (1987) *Politeness: Some Universals in Language Usage.* Cambridge: Cambridge University Press.
https://doi.org/10.1017/CBO9780511813085

Brynin, M. and Longhi, S. (2015) [Online] *The Effect of Occupation on Poverty among Ethnic Minority Groups.* Joseph Rowntree Foundation, UK. Available from: http://www.jrf.org.uk/publications/effect-occupation-poverty-among-ethnic-minoritygroups.

Buckley, M. R., Norris, A. C. and Wiese, D. S. (2000) A brief history of the selection interview: May the next 100 years be more fruitful. *Journal of Management History* 6(3), 113–126. https://doi.org/10.1108/EUM0000000005329

Budach, G. Roy, S. and Heller, M. (2003) Community and commodity in French Ontario. *Language in Society* 32(5): 603–627. https://doi.org/10.1017/S0047404503325011

Button, G. (1992) Answers as interactional products: Two sequential practices used in job interviews. In P. Drew and J. Heritage (eds) *Talk at Work: Interaction in Institutional Settings*, 212–234. Cambridge: Cambridge University Press.

Byham, W. C. and Pickett, D. (1999) *Landing the Job You Want: How to Have the Best Job Interview of Your Life*. New York: Three Rivers Press.

Cameron, D. (1995) *Verbal Hygiene*. Abingdon: Routledge.

Cameron, D. (2000) *Good to Talk: Living and Working in a Communication Culture*. London: Sage.

Cameron, D., Frazer, E., Harvey, P., Rampton, M. B. H. and Richardson, K. (1992) *Researching Language: Issues of Power and Method*. London: Routledge.

Campbell, S. and Roberts, C. (2007) Migration, ethnicity and competing discourses in the job interview: Synthesizing the institutional and personal. *Discourse and Society* 18(3): 243–271. https://doi.org/10.1177/0957926507075474

Candlin, C. N. and Maley, Y. (1997) Intertextuality and interdiscursivity in the discourse of alternative dispute resolution. In B. L. Gunnarsson, P. Linell and B. Nordberg (eds) *The Construction of Professional Discourse*, 201–222. London: Longman.

Carter, R. and McCarthy, M. (2015) Spoken grammar: Where are we and where are we going. *Applied Linguistics* 38(1): 1–20. https://doi.org/10.1093/applin/amu080

Catney, G. and Sabater, A. (2015) *Ethnic Minority Disadvantage in the Labour Market: Participation, Skills and Geographical Inequalities*. Joseph Rowntree Foundation, UK.

Chiswick, B. R. and Miller, P. W. (1995) The Endogeneity between language and earnings: International analyses. *Journal of Labor Economics* 13(2): 246–288. https://doi.org/10.1086/298374

Cicourel, A. (1992) The interpenetration of communicative contexts: The example of medical encounters. In A. Duranti and C. Goodwin (eds) *Rethinking Context*, 291–311. Cambridge: Cambridge University Press.

Cicourel, A. (2007) A personal retrospective view of ecological validity. *Text and Talk* 27(5–6): 735–752. https://doi.org/10.1515/TEXT.2007.033

Clark, K. and Drinkwater, S. (2007) *Ethnic Minorities in the Labour Market: Dynamics and Diversity*. York: Joseph Rowntree Foundation.

Clyne, M. (2005) *Australia's Language Potential*. Sydney: UNSW Press.

Coates, J. (2011) Gossip revisited: Language in all-female groups. In J. Coates and P. Pichler (eds) *Language and Gender: A Reader*. (2nd ed.) 199–223. Chichester, England: Wiley-Blackwell.

Codó, E. (2008) *Immigration and Bureaucratic Control: Language Practices in Public Administration*. Berlin: De Gruyter Mouton. https://doi.org/10.1515/9783110199086

Collins, R. (2004) *Interaction Ritual Chains*. Princeton University Press. https://doi.org/10.1515/9781400851744

Cook, G. (2011) British applied linguistics: Impacts of and impacts on. In J. Angouri, M. Daller and J. Treffers-Daller (eds) *The Impact of Applied Linguistics: Proceedings of the 44th Annual Meeting of the British Association for Applied Linguistics*, 35–58. University of the West of England: Scitslugnil Press.

Cook-Gumperz, J. and Gumperz, J. J. (1976) Papers on language and context. *Working Papers of the Language Behavior Research Laboratory, No. 46*. Berkeley: University of California.

Cook-Gumperz, J. and Gumperz, J. J. (1994) The politics of a conversation: Conversational inference in discussion. In A. D. Grimshaw (ed.) *What's Going on Here? Complementary Studies of Professional Talk*, 373–395. Norwood NJ: Ablex.

Coupland, N. (2003a) Introduction: Sociolinguistics and globalisation. *Journal of Sociolinguistics* 7(4): 465–472. https://doi.org/10.1111/j.1467-9841.2003.00237.x

Coupland, N. (2003b) Sociolinguistic authenticities. *Journal of Sociolinguistics* 7(3): 417–31. https://doi.org/10.1111/1467-9481.00233

Coupland, N. (2007) *Style: Language Variation and Identity*. Cambridge, UK; New York: Cambridge University Press. https://doi.org/10.1017/CBO9780511755064

Coupland, N. (ed.) (2010) *The Handbook of Language and Globalization*. Malden, MA: Wiley-Blackwell. https://doi.org/10.1002/9781444324068

Coupland, N. and Jaworski, A. (2009) *The New Sociolinguistics Reader*. Basingstoke, England; New York: Palgrave Macmillan. https://doi.org/10.1007/978-1-349-92299-4

Creese, A. (2008) Linguistic ethnography. In K. A. King and N. Hornberger (eds) *Encyclopedia of Language and Education. Vol. 10: Research Methods in Language and Education*. (2nd ed.) 229–241. New York: Springer Science and Business Media LLC.

Crystal, D. (2018) *Sounds Appealing: The Passionate Story of English Pronunciation*. London: Profile Books.

Cuban, S. (2013) *De-skilling Migrant Women in the Global Care Industry*. Basingstoke: Palgrave Macmillan. https://doi.org/10.1057/9781137305619

Currie, S. (2007) De-skilled and devalued: The labour market experience of Polish migrants in the UK following EU enlargement. *International Journal of Comparative Labour Law and Industrial Relations* 23(1): 83–116.

Davies, B. and Harré, R. (1990) Positioning: The discursive production of selves. *Journal for the Theory of Social Behavior* 20(1): 43–63. https://doi.org/10.1111/j.1468-5914.1990.tb00174.x

Davies, R. (2017) [Online] Uber loses court case to block English-language written test in London. *Guardian*, 3 March 2017. Available from: https://www.theguardian.com/technology/2017/mar/03/uber-loses-court-case-english-language-test-london.

Day, D. (1994) Tang's dilemma and other problems: Ethnification processes at some multicultural workplaces. *Pragmatics* 4(3): 315–336. https://doi.org/10.1075/prag.4.3.02day

Day, D. (2006) Ethnic and social groups and their linguistic categorization. In K. Bührig and J. D. ten Thije (eds) *Beyond Misunderstanding: Linguistic Analyses of Intercultural Communication*, 218–244. Amsterdam/Philadelphia: Benjamins. https://doi.org/10.1075/pbns.144.10day

De Certeau, M. (1985) *The Practice of Everyday Life*. Berkeley: University of California Press.

De Fina, A. (2003) Crossing borders: Time, space and disorientation in narrative. *Narrative Inquiry* 13(2): 367–391. https://doi.org/10.1075/ni.13.2.08def

De Fina, A. and Georgakopoulou, A. (2012) *Analyzing Narrative: Discourse and Sociolinguistic Perspectives*. Cambridge: Cambridge University Press. https://doi.org/10.1017/CBO9781139051255

De Keere, K. (2014) From a self-made to an already-made man: A historical content analysis of professional advice literature. *Acta Sociologica* 57(4): 311–324. https://doi.org/10.1177/0001699314552737

Del Percio, A. (2016) The governmentality of migration: Intercultural communication and the politics of (dis)placement in Southern Europe. *Language and Communication* 51: 87–98. https://doi.org/10.1016/j.langcom.2016.07.001

Del Percio, A. (2017) Engineering commodifiable workers: Language, migration and the governmentality of the self. *Language Policy* 17(2): 239–259. https://doi.org/10.1007/s10993-017-9436-4

Del Percio, A. and van Hoof, S. (2017) Enterprizing migrants: Language, education and the politics of activation. In M. Flubacher and A. Del Percio (eds) *Language, Education and Neoliberalism: Critical Studies in Sociolinguistics*, 140–162. Bristol: Multilingual Matters. https://doi.org/10.21832/9781783098699-010

DiMaggio, P. and Garip, F. (2012) Network effects and social inequality. *Annual Review of Sociology* 38: 93–118

Doeringer, P. and Piore, M. (1971) *Internal Labor Markets and Manpower Analysis*. Lexington, MA: Heath.

Douglas, M. (1986) *How Institutions Think*. Syracuse: Syracuse University Press.

Dragojeviç, M., Giles, H. and Watson, B. (2013) Language ideologies and language attitudes: A foundational framework. In H. Giles and B. Watson (ed.) *The Social Meanings of Language, Dialect and Accent: International Perspectives on Speech Styles*, 1–25. New York, NY: Peter Lang.

Drew, P. and Heritage, J. (eds) (1992) *Talk at Work: Interaction in Institutional Settings*. Cambridge: Cambridge University Press.

Drew, P. and Holt, E. (1988) Complainable matters: The use of idiomatic expressions in making complaints. *Social Problems* 35: 398–417. https://doi.org/10.1525/sp.1988.35.4.03a00060

Du Gay, P. (1996) *Consumption and Identity at Work*. London: Sage.

Du Gay, P. (2000) *In Praise of Bureaucracy: Weber, Organization, Ethics*. London, Thousand Oaks, CA: Sage.

Dubois, J. (2007) The stance triangle. In R. Englebretson (ed.) *Stancetaking in Discourse: Subjectivity, Evaluation, Interaction*, 139–182. Amsterdam: John Benjamins. https://doi.org/10.1075/pbns.164.07du

Dubois, W. E. B. (1989) *The Souls of Black Folk*. New York: Bantam. First published 1903 by A. C. McClurg and Co.

DuBord, E. (2010) Conflicting discourses of rapport and co-membership: Multilingual gatekeeping encounters at a day labor center in Southern Arizona. In B. Meyer and B. Apfelbaum (eds) *Multilingualism at Work: From Policies to Practices in Public, Medical and Business Settings*, 187–209. Amsterdam: John Benjamins. https://doi.org/10.1075/hsm.9.11dub

Duchêne, A. (2009) Marketing, management and performance: Multilingualism as a commodity in a tourism call center. *Language Policy* 8(1): 27–50. https://doi.org/10.1007/s10993-008-9115-6

Duchêne, A. and Heller, M. (eds) (2012) *Language in Late Capitalism: Pride and Profit*. New York: Routledge. https://doi.org/10.4324/9780203155868

Duchêne, A., Moyer, M. and Roberts, C. (eds) (2013) *Language, Migration and Social Inequalities: A Critical Sociolinguistic Perspective on Institutions and Work*. Bristol: Multilingual Matters. https://doi.org/10.21832/9781783091010

Duff, P. A. (2008) Language socialization, higher education, and work. In P. A. Duff and N. Hornberger (eds) *Encyclopedia of Language and Education, Vol. 8: Language Socialization*, 257–270. New York: Springer.

Duff, P. A., Wong, P. and Early, M. (2002) Learning language for work and life: The linguistic socialization of immigrant Canadians seeking careers in health care. *The Modern Language Journal* 86(3): 397–422. https://doi.org/10.1111/1540-4781.t01-1-00157

Duranti, A. (1997) *Linguistic Anthropology*. New York: Cambridge University Press. https://doi.org/10.1017/CBO9780511810190

Dustmann, C., Fabbri, F. and Preston, I. (2003) Language proficiency and labour market performance of immigrants in the UK. *The Economic Journal* 113(489): 695–717. https://doi.org/10.1111/1468-0297.t01-1-00151

Dyer, J. and Keller-Cohen, D. (2000) The discursive construction of professional self through narratives of personal experience. *Discourse and Society* 2(3): 283–304. https://doi.org/10.1177/1461445600002003002

Eades, D. (2010) *Sociolinguistics and the Legal Process*. Bristol: Multilingual Matters. https://doi.org/10.21832/9781847692559

Eckert, P. (2008) Variation and the indexical field. *Journal of Sociolinguistics* 12(4): 453–476. https://doi.org/10.1111/j.1467-9841.2008.00374.x

Edwards, D. (1991) Categories are for talking: On the cognitive and discursive bases of categorization. *Theory and Psychology* 1(4): 515–542. https://doi.org/10.1177/0959354391014007

Eggins, S. and Slade, D. (1997) *Analyzing Casual Conversation*. Washington: Cassell.

Ehrlich, S. (2012) Text trajectories, legal discourse and gendered inequalities. *Applied Linguistics Review* 3(1): 47–73. https://doi.org/10.1515/applirev-2012-0003

Equality and Human Rights Commission. (2010) [Online] *Employment Statutory Code of Practice*. UK: The Stationery Office Limited. Available from: https://www.equalityhumanrights.com/sites/default/files/employercode.pdf.

Erickson, F. (1975) Gatekeeping and the melting pot: Interaction in counseling encounters. *Harvard Educational Review* 45(1): 44–70. https://doi.org/10.17763/haer.45.1.g2x156r1k00w5037

Erickson, F. (1979) Talking down: Some cultural sources of miscommunication in inter-racial interviews. In A. Wolfgang (ed.) *Research in Non-Verbal Communication*, 99–126. New York: Academic Press. https://doi.org/10.1016/B978-0-12-761350-5.50013-6

Erickson, F. (1999) Appropriation of voice and presentation of self as a fellow physician: Aspects of a discourse of apprenticeship in medicine. In S. Sarangi and C. Roberts (eds) *Talk, Work and Institutional Order*, 109–144. Berlin, Germany: De Gruyter Mouton. https://doi.org/10.1515/9783110208375.2.109

Erickson, F. (2004) *Talk and Social Theory: Ecologies of Speaking and Listening in Everyday Life*. Cambridge: Polity Press.

Erickson, F. (2011) The gatekeeping encounter as a social form and as a site for face work. In C. N. Candlin and S. Sarangi (eds) *Handbook of Communication in Organisations and Professions*, 433–454. Berlin: De Gruyter Mouton. https://doi.org/10.1515/9783110214222.433

Erickson, F. (2012) Rhythm in discourse. In C. A. Chapelle (ed.) *The Encyclopedia of Applied Linguistics*. n.p.: John Wiley and Sons. https://doi.org/10.1002/9781405198431.wbeal0391

Erickson, F. and Shultz, J. (1982) *The Counselor as Gatekeeper: Social Interaction in Interviews*. New York: Academic Press.

Esmail, A. and May, C. (2000) Commentary: Oral exams – get them right or don't bother. *British Medical Journal* 320: 375.

Evans, Y., Herbert, J., Datta, K., May, J., McIlwaine, C. and Wills, J. (2005) *Making the City Work: Low Paid Employment in London*. London: Department of Geography, Queen Mary, University of London.

Fairclough, N. (1992a) *Discourse and Social Change*. Oxford: Polity Press.

Fairclough, N. (ed) (1992b) *Critical Language Awareness*. London: Longman.

Fitzgerald, H. (2003) *How Different Are We?* Clevedon: Multilingual Matters Ltd.

Flubacher, M. (2020) Selling the self: packaging the narrative trajectories of workers for the labour market. *International Journal of Multilingualism* 17(1): 30–45

Flubacher, M., Coray, R. and Duchêne, A. (2017) *Language Investment and Employability*. London: Palgrave Pivot. https://doi.org/10.1007/978-3-319-60873-0

Fosgerau, C. F. (2013) The co-construction of understanding in Danish naturalization interviews. *International Journal of Bilingualism* 17(2): 221–236. https://doi.org/10.1177/1367006912441421

Foucault, M. (1977) *Discipline and Punish: The Birth of the Prison*. London: Penguin.

Foucault, M. (1984) [1971]. The order of discourse. In M. Shapiro (ed.) *Language and Politics*, 108–138. London: Basil Blackwell.

Foucault, M., Martin, L. H., Gutman, H. and Hutton, P. H. (1988) *Technologies of the Self: A Seminar with Michel Foucault*. Amherst: University of Massachusetts Press.

Freed, A. F. and Ehrlich, S. (eds) (2010) *Why Do You Ask?: The Function of Questions in Institutional Discourse*. Oxford: Oxford University Press. https://doi.org/10.1093/acprof:oso/9780195306897.001.0001

Friedman, S. Laurison, D. and Miles, A. (2015) Breaking the 'class' ceiling? Social mobility into Britain's elite occupations. *The Sociological Review*, May 2015. https://doi.org/10.1111/1467-954X.12283

Friedman, S. and Laurison, D. (2019) *The Class Ceiling: Why it Pays to be Privileged*. Bristol: Policy Press, University of Bristol. https://doi.org/10.2307/j.ctv5zftbj

Frijters, P., Shields, M. and Price, S. W. (2005) Job search methods and their success: a comparison of immigrants and natives in the UK. *The Economic Journal* 115(507): 359–376. https://doi.org/10.1111/j.1468-0297.2005.01040.x

Fuertes, J. N., Gottdiener, W. H., Martin, H., Gilbert, T. C. and Giles, H. (2012) A meta-analysis of the effects of speakers' accents on interpersonal evaluations. *European Journal of Social Psychology* 42(1): 120–133. https://doi.org/10.1002/ejsp.862

Gal, S. (1998) Multiplicity and contention among language ideologies. In B. B. Schieffelin, K. A. Woolard and P. V. Kroskrity (eds) *Language Ideologies: Practice and Theory*, 423–442. Oxford: Oxford University Press.

Gal, S. (2005) Language ideologies compared: Metaphors of public/private. *Journal of Linguistic Anthropology* 15(1): 23–37. https://doi.org/10.1525/jlin.2005.15.1.23

Galatolo, R. (2006) Active voicing in court. In E. Holt and R. Clift (eds) *Reporting Talk: Reported Speech in Interaction*, 192–220. Cambridge: Cambridge University Press.

Gardner, R. C. and Lambert, W. E. (1972) *Attitudes and Motivation in Second Language Learning*. Rowley, MA: Newbury House.

Garfinkel, H. (1963) A conception of, and experiments with, 'trust' as a condition for stable concerted actions. In O. J. Harvey (ed.) *Motivation and Social Interaction*, 187–238. New York: Ronald Press.

Garfinkel, H. (1967) *Studies in Ethnomethodology*. Englewood Cliffs, NJ: Prentice-Hall.

Garrido-Sardà, M. R. and Sabaté-Dalmau, M. (eds) (2019) Transnational trajectories of multilingual workers: Sociolinguistic approaches to emergent entrepreneurial selves. *The International Journal of Multilingualism* 17(4): 1–10. https://doi.org/10.1080/14790718.2019.1682245

Gaudio, R. P. and Bialostok, S. (2005) The trouble with culture: Everyday racism in white middle-class discourse. *Critical Discourse Studies* 1(1): 51–69. https://doi.org/10.1080/17405900500052119

Gee, J. P., Hull, G. and Lankshear, C. (1996) *The New Work Order: Behind the Language of the New Capitalism*. St. Leonards, Sydney: Allen and Unwin.

Georgakopoulou, A. (2006) Thinking big with small stories in narrative and identity analysis. *Narrative Inquiry* 16(1): 122–130. https://doi.org/10.1075/ni.16.1.16geo

Georgakopoulou, A. (2007) *Small Stories, Interaction and Identities*. Amsterdam: John Benjamins. https://doi.org/10.1075/sin.8

Giddens, A. (1991) *Modernity and Self-Identity: Self and Society in the Late Modern Age*. Stanford, CA: Stanford University Press.

Gluszek, A. and Dovidio, J. F. (2010) The way they speak: A social psychological perspective on the stigma of nonnative accents in communication. *Personality and Social Psychology Review* 14(2): 214–237.
https://doi.org/10.1177/1088868309359288

Goffman, E. (1959) *The Presentation of Self in Everyday Life*. London: Penguin.

Goffman, E. (1967) *Interaction Ritual: Essays on Face-to-Face Behaviour*. London: Pantheon.

Goffman, E. (1971) *Relations in Public: Microstudies of the Public Order*. London: Allen Lane.

Goffman, E. (1974) *Frame Analysis: An Essay on the Organization of Experience*. New York: Harper and Row.

Goffman, E. (1981) *Forms of Talk*. Oxford: Basil Blackwell.

Goffman, E. (1983) The interaction order: American Sociological Association, 1982 presidential address. *American Sociological Review*, 48(1): 1–17.
https://doi.org/10.2307/2095141

Goldstein, T. (1997) *Two Languages at Work: Bilingual Life on the Production Floor*. New York: De Gruyter Mouton. https://doi.org/10.1515/9783110815221

Goodwin, C. (1994) Professional vision. *American Anthropologist* 96(3): 606–633.
https://doi.org/10.1525/aa.1994.96.3.02a00100

Grugulis, I. and Vincent, S. (2009) Whose skill is it anyway?: 'Soft' skills and polarization. *Work, Employment and Society* 23: 597–615.
https://doi.org/10.1177/0950017009344862

Gumperz, J. J. (1982a) *Discourse Strategies*. Cambridge: Cambridge University Press. https://doi.org/10.1017/CBO9780511611834

Gumperz, J. J. (ed.) (1982b) *Language and Social Identity*. Cambridge: Cambridge University Press. https://doi.org/10.1017/CBO9780511620836

Gumperz, J. J. (1992a) Contextualisation revisited. In P. Auer and A. Di Luzio (eds) *The Contextualization of Language*, 39–54. Amsterdam: John Benjamins.

Gumperz, J. J. (1992b) Contextualization and understanding. In A. Duranti and C. Goodwin (eds) *Rethinking Context*, 229–252. Cambridge: Cambridge University Press.

Gumperz, J. J. (1992c) Interviewing in intercultural situations. In P. Drew and J. Heritage (eds) *Talk at Work*, 302–327. Cambridge: Cambridge University Press.

Gumperz, J. J. (1996) The linguistic and cultural relativity of inference. In J. Gumperz and S. Levinson (eds) *Rethinking Linguistic Relativity*, 374–406. Cambridge: Cambridge University Press.

Gumperz, J. J. (1997) A discussion with John Gumperz. In S. Eerdmans, C. Previgagno and P. Thibault (eds) *Discussing Communication Analysis 1: John Gumperz*, 6–23. Lausanne: Beta Press.

Gumperz, J. J. (1999) On interactional sociolinguistic method. In S. Sarangi and C. Roberts (eds) *Talk, Work and Institutional Order*, 453–472. Berlin: De Gruyter Mouton. https://doi.org/10.1515/9783110208375.4.453

Gumperz, J. J. and Cook-Gumperz, J. (2005) Language standardization and the complexities of communicative practice. In S. McKinnon and S. Silverman (eds)

Complexities: Beyond Nature and Nurture, 268–286. Chicago: Chicago University Press.

Gumperz, J. J. and Hymes, D. H. (1964) The ethnography of communication. *American Anthropologist* 66(6): 1–34. https://doi.org/10.1525/aa.1964.66.suppl_3.02a00010

Gumperz, J. J. and Hymes, D. H. (1972) *Directions in Sociolinguistics: The Ethnography of Communication*. New York/London: Holt, Rinehart and Winston.

Gumperz, J. J., Jupp, T. and Roberts, C. (1979) *Crosstalk*. London, National Centre for Industrial Language Training.

Gunnarsson, B., Linell, P. and Nordberg, B. (eds) (1997) *The Construction of Professional Discourse*. London: Routledge.

Günthner, S. (1997) The contextualization of affect in reported dialogues. In S. Niemeier and R. Dirven (eds) *The Language of Emotions: Conceptualization, Expression, and Theoretical Foundation*, 247–276. Amsterdam: John Benjamins. https://doi.org/10.1075/z.85.19gun

Günthner, S. and Knoblauch, H. (1995) Culturally patterned speaking practices: The analysis of communicative genres. *Pragmatics* 5(1): 1–32. https://doi.org/10.1075/prag.5.1.03gun

Günthner, S. and Luckmann, T. (2001) Asymmetries of knowledge in intercultural communication: The relevance of cultural repertoires of communicative genres. In A. Di Luzio, S. Günthner and F. Orletti (eds) *Culture in Communication: Analyses of Intercultural Situations*, 55–86. Amsterdam: John Benjamins. https://doi.org/10.1075/pbns.81.06gun

Habermas, J. (1979) *Communication and the Evolution of Society*. Translated by Thomas McCarthy. London: Heinemann.

Hanks, W. F. (1987) Discourse genres in a theory of practice. *American Ethnologist* 14(4): 668–692. https://doi.org/10.1525/ae.1987.14.4.02a00050

Hansen, K., Rakić, T. and Steffens, M. C. (2014) When actions speak louder than words: Preventing discrimination of nonstandard speakers. *Journal of Language and Social Psychology* 33(1): 68–77. https://doi.org/10.1177/0261927X13499761

Harré, R. and van Langenhove, L. (eds) (1999) *Positioning Theory*. Malden, MA: Blackwell.

Hartsock, N. (1990) Foucault and power: A theory for women. In L. J. Nicholson (ed.) *Feminism/Postmodernism*, 159–175. New York: Routledge.

Harvey, D. (2005) *A Brief History of Neoliberalism*. Oxford: Oxford University Press.

Hawthorne, K., Roberts, C. and Atkins, S. (2017) Sociolinguistic factors affecting performance in the Clinical Skills Assessment (CSA) of the MRCGP: A mixed methods approach. *BJGP Open 2017* 1(1). https://doi.org/10.3399/bjgpopen17X100713

Heath, A. and Cheung, S. Y. (2006) *Ethnic Penalties in the Labour Market: Employers and Discrimination*. Research Report 341. Department for Work and Pensions.

Heath, A. and McMahon, D. (1997) Education and occupational attainments: The impact of ethnic origins. In V. Karn (ed.) *Ethnicity in the 1991 Census. Vol. 4: Education, Employment and Housing*. London: HMSO.

Heller, M. (2003) Globalisation, the new economy, and the commodification of language and identity. *Journal of Sociolinguistics* 7(4): 473–492. https://doi.org/10.1111/j.1467-9841.2003.00238.x

Heller, M. (2007) Distributed knowledge, distributed power: A sociolinguistics of structuration. *Text and Talk* 27(5–6): 633–653. https://doi.org/10.1515/TEXT.2007.029

Heller, M. (2010) Language as resource in the globalized new economy. In N. Coupland (ed.) *The Handbook of Language and Globalization*, 349–365. Oxford: Blackwell. https://doi.org/10.1002/9781444324068.ch15

Heller, M. (2011) *Paths to Post-Nationalism: A Critical Ethnography of Language and Identity*. New York: Oxford University Press.

Helsig, S. (2010) Big stories co-constructed: Incorporating micro-analytical interpretative procedures into biographic research. *Narrative Inquiry* 20(2): 274–295. https://doi.org/10.1075/ni.20.2.03hel

Heritage, J. (1987) Ethnomethodology. In A. Giddens and J. Turner (eds) *Social Theory Today*, 224–272. Cambridge: Polity Press,

Heritage, J. and Clayman, S. (2010) *Talk in Action: Interactions, Identities, and Institutions*. New York: Blackwell. https://doi.org/10.1002/9781444318135

Hewitt, R. (1986) *White Talk, Black Talk: Inter-racial Friendship and Communication Amongst Adolescents*. London: Cambridge University Press.

Heydon, G. (2005) *The Language of Police Interviewing*. Basingstoke: Palgrave House, Kasper and Ross. https://doi.org/10.1057/9780230502932

Hickmann, M. (1993) The boundaries of reported speech in narrative discourse: Some developmental aspects. In J. A. Lucy (ed.) *Reflexive Language: Reported Speech and Metapragmatics*, 63–90. Cambridge: Cambridge University Press. https://doi.org/10.1017/CBO9780511621031.006

Hill, J. (2000) Ideology, complexities and the over-determination of promising in American presidential politics. In P. V. Kroskrity (ed.) *Regimes of Language: Ideologies, Polities, and Identities*, 1–34. n.p.: School of American Research Publications.

Hillage, J., Regan, J., Dickson, J. and McLoughlin, K. (2002) *Employers Skill Survey 2002. Research Report 372*. Nottingham: DfES.

Holland, D., Lachicotte, W. J. R., Skinner, D. and Cain, C. (1998) *Identity and Agency in Cultural Worlds*. Cambridge: Harvard University Press.

Holmes, J. (2005a) Story-telling at work: A complex discursive resource for integrating personal, professional and social identities. *Discourse Studies* 7(6): 671–700. https://doi.org/10.1177/1461445605055422

Holmes, J. (2005b) Relational and transactional functions of workplace discourse: A socio-pragmatic perspective. In B-L. Gunnarson (ed.) *Communication in the Workplace*, 7–27. Uppsala: Universiteitstrysckeriet Ekonimikum.

Holmes, J. (2007) Monitoring organisational boundaries: Diverse discourse strategies used in gatekeeping. *Journal of Pragmatics* 39(11): 993–2016. https://doi.org/10.1016/j.pragma.2007.07.009

Holmes, J. (2018) Negotiating the culture order in New Zealand workplaces. *Language in Society* 47(1): 33–56. https://doi.org/10.1017/S0047404517000732

Holmes, J., Joe, A., Marra, M., Newton, J., Riddiford, N. and Vine, B. (2011) Applying linguistic research to real world problems: The social meaning of talk in workplace interaction. In C. N. Candlin and S. Sarangi (eds) *Handbook of Communication in*

Organisations and Professions, 533–549. Berlin, Germany: De Gruyter Mouton. https://doi.org/10.1515/9783110214222.533

Holmes, J., Marra, M. and Vine, B. (2011) *Leadership, Discourse, and Ethnicity*. Oxford: Oxford University Press. https://doi.org/10.1093/acprof:oso/9780199730759.001.0001

Holmes, J. and Stubbe, M. (2003) Doing disagreement at work: A sociolinguistic approach. *Australian Journal of Communication* 30(1): 53–77.

Holmes, J., Stubbe, M. and Vine, B. (1999) Constructing professional identity: 'Doing power' in policy units.' In S. Sarangi and C. Roberts (eds) *Talk, Work and Institutional Order: Discourse in Medical, Mediation and Management Settings*, 1–35. Berlin: De Gruyter Mouton. https://doi.org/10.1515/9783110208375.3.351

Holmes, J. and Woodhams, J. (2013) Building interaction: The role of talk in joining a community of practice. *Discourse and Communication* 7(3): 275–298. https://doi.org/10.1177/1750481313494500

Holt, E. (1996) Reporting on talk: The use of direct reported speech in conversation. *Research on Language and Social Interaction* 29(3): 219–45. https://doi.org/10.1207/s15327973rlsi2903_2

Holt, E. and Clift, R. (eds) (2006) *Reporting Talk: Reported Speech in Interaction*. Cambridge: Cambridge University Press. https://doi.org/10.1017/CBO9780511486654

Hubbuck, I. and Carter, S. (1980) *Half a Chance?: A Report on Job Discrimination Against Young Blacks in Nottingham*. London: Commission for Racial Equality in association with Nottingham and District Community Relations Council.

Huffcutt, A. and Roth, P. (1998) Racial group differences in employment interview evaluations. *Journal of Applied Psychology* 83(2): 179–189. https://doi.org/10.1037/0021-9010.83.2.179

Hymes, D. H. (1964) *Language in Culture and Society: A Reader in Linguistics and Anthropology*. New York: Harper and Row.

Hymes, D. H. (1996) *Ethnography, Linguistics and Narrative Inequality*. Taylor and Francis.

Iedema, R. (1999) Formalizing organizational meaning. *Discourse and Society* 10(1): 49–65. https://doi.org/10.1177/0957926599010001003

Iedema, R. (2003) *The Discourses of Post-bureaucratic Organization*. Amsterdam: John Benjamins. https://doi.org/10.1075/ddcs.5

Iedema, R. (2007) Communicating hospital work. In R. Iedema (ed.) *The Discourse of Hospital Communication*, 1–17. London: Palgrave Macmillan. https://doi.org/10.1057/9780230595477_1

Iedema, R. and Scheeres, H. (2003) From doing work to talking work: Renegotiating knowing, doing, and identity. *Applied Linguistics* 24(3): 316–337. https://doi.org/10.1093/applin/24.3.316

Iedema, R. and Wodak, R. (1999) Introduction: Organizational discourses and practices. *Discourse and Society* 10(1): 5–19. https://doi.org/10.1177/0957926599010001001

Innovate UK (n.d) [Online] *Knowledge Transfer Partnerships*. Available from: http://ktp.innovateuk.org.

Irvine, J. T. and Gal, S. (2000) Language ideology and linguistic differentiation. In P. V. Kroskrity (ed.) *Regimes of Language: Ideologies, Politics, and Identities*, 35–83. Santa Fe: School of American Research Press.

Jacoby, S. and McNamara, T. (1999) Locating competence. *English for Specific Purposes* 18(3): 213–241. https://doi.org/10.1016/S0889-4906(97)00053-7

Jacquemet, M. (2005) Transidiomatic practices: Language and power in the age of globalisation. *Talk and Text* 31(4): 475–498.

Jacquemet, M. (2011) Crosstalk 2.0: Asylum and communicative breakdowns. *Text and Talk* 31(4): 475–497. https://doi.org/10.1515/text.2011.023

Jaffe, A. (2009) *Stance: Sociolinguistic Perspectives*. Oxford: Oxford University Press.

Jenkins, R. (1986) *Racism and Recruitment: Managers, Organisations and Equal Opportunity in the Labour Market*. Cambridge: Cambridge University Press.

Johnstone, B. (1990) *Stories, Community, and Place: Narratives from Middle America*. Bloomington: Indiana University Press.

Jönsson, L. and Linell, P. (1991) Story generations: From dialogical interviews to written reports in police interrogations. *Text* 11(3): 419–440. https://doi.org/10.1515/text.1.1991.11.3.419

Jupp, T., Roberts, C. and Cook-Gumperz, J. J. (1982) Language and disadvantage: The hidden process. In J. Gumperz (ed.) *Language and Social Identity*, 232–257. Cambridge: Cambridge University Press. https://doi.org/10.1017/CBO9780511620836.015

Kandola, B. (1996) Are competencies too much of a good thing? *People Management* 2(9): 21–22.

Keep, E. and James, S. (2010) Recruitment and selection: The great neglected topic. *SKOPE Research Paper No. 88*. Cardiff: Cardiff University, SKOPE.

Kelly-Holmes, H. and Mautner, G. (eds) (2010) *Language and the Market*. Basingstoke: Palgrave McMillan. https://doi.org/10.1007/978-0-230-29692-3

Kerekes, J. (2003) Distrust: A determining factor in the outcomes of gatekeeping encounters. In J. House, G. Kasper and S. Ross (eds) *Misunderstanding in Social Life*, 227–257. Harlow: Pearson Education.

Kerekes, J. (2005) Before, during, and after the event: Getting the job (or not) in an employment interview. In K. Bardovi-Harlig and B. S. Hartford (eds) *Interlanguage Pragmatics: Exploring Institutional Talk*, 99–132. New York: Routledge.

Kerekes, J. (2006) Winning an interviewer's trust in a gatekeeping encounter. *Language in Society* 35(1): 25–57. https://doi.org/10.1017/S0047404506060027

Kerekes, J. (2018) Language preparation for internationally educated professionals. In B. Vine (ed.) *The Routledge Handbook of Language in the Workplace*, 413–424. New York: Routledge. https://doi.org/10.4324/9781315690001-34

Kirilova, M. (2018) 'Oh it's a DANISH boyfriend you've got': Co-membership and cultural fluency in job interviews with minority background applicants in Denmark. In J. Angouri, M. Mara and J. Holmes (eds) *Negotiating Boundaries at Work*, 29–49. Edinburgh: Edinburgh University Press.

Kirilova, M. (2013) *All Dressed Up and Nowhere to Go: Linguistic, Cultural and Ideological Aspects of Job Interviews with Second Language Speakers of Danish.* PhD Dissertation, University of Copenhagen.

Kleifgen, J. (2013) *Communicative Practices at Work.* Bristol: Multilingual Matters. https://doi.org/10.21832/9781783090464

Komter, M. (1991) *Conflict and Co-operation in Job Interviews.* Amsterdam: John Benjamins. https://doi.org/10.1075/pbns.15

Kraft, K. (2017) *Constructing Migrant Workers: Multilingualism and Communication in the Transnational Construction Site.* PhD, University of Oslo.

Kroskrity, P. (2010) [Online] Language ideologies. *Handbook of Pragmatics Online.* Available from: https://benjamins.com/online/hop/articles/lan6.

Kulessza, M. (2002) Methods and techniques of managing de-centralising reforms in CEE countries: The Polish experience. In G. Peteri (ed.) *Mastering De-centralisation and Public Administration Reforms in Central and Eastern Europe*, 189–214. Budapest: Open Society Institute.

Kusmierczyk, E. (2014) Trust in action: Building trust through embodied negotiation of mutual understanding in job interviews. In K. Pelsmaekers, G. Jacobs and C. Rollo (eds) *Trust and Discourse: Organisational Perspectives*, 11–44. Amsterdam: John Benjamins. https://doi.org/10.1075/dapsac.56.02kus

Labov, W. (1972) *Language in the Inner City.* Philadelphia: University of Pennsylvania Press.

Labov, W. and Waletsky, J. (1967) Narrative analysis: Oral versions of personal experience. *Journal of Narrative and Life History* 7(1–4): 3–38. https://doi.org/10.1075/jnlh.7.02nar

Lamont, M., Beljean, S. and Clair, M. (2014) What is missing: Cultural processes and causal pathways to inequality. *Socio-economic Review* 12(3): 1–36. https://doi.org/10.1093/ser/mwu011

Lawson, R. and Sayers, D. (2016) Where we're going, we don't need roads. In R. Lawson and D. Sayers (eds) *Sociolinguistic Research: Application and Impact*, 7–22. London: Routledge. https://doi.org/10.4324/9781315671765-2

Lefstein, A. (2018) Moving teacher learning from the margins to the mainstream. *Practical Literacy: The Early and Primary Years* 23(1): 35–37.

Levinson, S. C. (1992) Activity types and language. In P. Drew and J. Heritage (eds) *Talk at Work: Interaction in Institutional Settings*, 66–100. Cambridge: Cambridge University Press.

Lewis, H., Dwyer, P., Hodkinson, S. and Waite, L. (2015) Hyper-precarious lives: Migrants, work and forced labour in the Global North. *Progress in Human Geography* 39(5): 580–600. https://doi.org/10.1177/0309132514548303

Linde, C. (1993) *Life Stories: The Creation of Coherence.* New York: Oxford University Press.

Linde, C. (1999) The transformation of narrative syntax into institutional memory. *Narrative Inquiry* 9(1): 139–174. https://doi.org/10.1075/ni.9.1.08lin

Linde, C. (2000) The acquisition of a speaker by a story: How history becomes memory and identity. *Ethos* 28(4): 608–632. https://doi.org/10.1525/eth.2000.28.4.608

Linell, P. (1998) Discourse across boundaries: On recontextualisations and blending of voices in professional discourse. *Text* 18(2): 143–157. https://doi.org/10.1515/text.1.1998.18.2.143

Linell, P. (2015) Mishearings are occasioned by contextual assumptions and situational affordances. *Language and Communication* 40: 24–37. https://doi.org/10.1016/j.langcom.2014.10.009

Linell, P. and Marková, I. (2013) Trust seen as embodiment, culture, language and morality: An epilogue. In I. Marková and P. Linell (eds) *Dialogical Approaches to Trust in Communication*, 255–257. Charlotte, NC: InfoAge Publishing.

Linell, P. and Sarangi, S. (eds) (1998) Discourse across the professions: Special issue on professional discourse studies. *Text* 18(2): 143–157. https://doi.org/10.1515/text.1.1998.18.2.143

Linell, P. and Thunquist, D. (2003) Moving in and out of framings: Activity contexts in talks with young unemployed people within a training project. *Journal of Pragmatics* 35(3): 409–34. https://doi.org/10.1016/S0378-2166(02)00143-1

Lipovsky, C. (2006) Candidates' negotiation of their expertise in job interviews. *Journal of Pragmatics* 38(8): 1147–1174. https://doi.org/10.1016/j.pragma.2005.05.007

Lippi-Green, R. (2012) *English with an Accent: Language Ideology and Discrimination in the United States.* (2nd ed.) New York: Routledge.

Llewellyn, N. (2010) On the reflexivity between setting and practice: The 'recruitment' interview. In N. Llewellyn and J. Hindmarsh (eds) *Organisation, Interaction and Practice: Studies in Ethnomethodology and Conversation Analysis*, 74–96. Cambridge: Cambridge University Press. https://doi.org/10.1017/CBO9780511676512.005

Lønsmann, D. and Kraft, K. (2017) Language and blue-collar workplaces. In B. Vine (ed.) *Handbook of Language in the Workplace*, 138–149. New York: Routledge. https://doi.org/10.4324/9781315690001-13

Longhi, S. and Brynin, M. (2017) *The Ethnicity Pay Gap.* Equality and Human Rights Commission: Research Report 108.

Lorente, B. P. (2010) Packaging English-speaking products: Maid agencies in Singapore. In H. Kelly-Holmes and G. Mautner (eds) *Language and the Market*, 44–55. New York: Palgrave MacMillan. https://doi.org/10.1007/978-0-230-29692-3_5

Lorente, B. P. (2012) The making of 'Workers of the World': Language and the labour brokerage state. In A. Duchêne and M. Heller (eds) *Language in Late Capitalism*, 183–206. New York: Routledge.

Lorente, B. P. (2017) *Scripts of Servitude: Language, Labour Migration and Transnational Domestic Work.* Bristol: Multilingual Matters. https://doi.org/10.21832/9781783099009

Luhmann, N. (1990) *Essays on Self-Reference.* New York: Columbia University Press.

MacLeod, N. and Haworth, K. (2016) Developing a sociolinguistically informed approach to police interviewing. In R. Lawson and D. Sayers (eds) *Sociolinguistic Research: Application and Impact*, 151–170. London: Routledge. https://doi.org/10.4324/9781315671765-9

Mäkitalo, Å and Säljö, R. (2002) Talk in institutional context and institutional context in talk: Categories and situational practices. *Text* 22(1): 57–82. https://doi.org/10.1515/text.2002.005

Makoni, S. and Pennycook, A. (2007) Disinventing and reconstituting languages. In S. Makoni and A. Pennycook (eds) *Disinventing and Reconstituting Languages*, 1–41. Clevedon: Multilingual Matters. https://doi.org/10.21832/9781853599255-003

Martin-Rojo L. (2015) The Social construction of inequality in and through interaction in multilingual classrooms. In N. Markee (ed.) *The Handbook of Classroom Discourse and Interaction*, chapter 29. n.p.: Wiley Blackwell. https://doi.org/10.1002/9781118531242.ch29

Martin-Rojo, L. (2016) Neoliberalism and linguistic governmentality. In O. Garcia, N. Flores and M. Spotti (eds) *Oxford Handbook of Language in Society*. New York: Oxford University Press.

Maryns, K. (2005) Displacement in asylum seekers' narratives. In M. Baynham and A. De Fina (eds) *Dislocations/Relocations: Narratives of Displacement*, 174–196. Manchester: St Jerome.

Maryns, K. (2006) *Asylum Speaker: Language in the Belgian Asylum Procedure*. Manchester: St Jerome.

Maryns, K. (2013) Procedures without borders: The language-ideological anchorage of legal-administrative procedures in translocal institutional settings. *Language in Society* 42(1): 71–92. https://doi.org/10.1017/S0047404512000905

Matthewman, T. (1995) Trends and development in the use of competency frameworks. *Competency* 2(4): 1–20.

Maurer, S. D., Sue-Chan, C. and Latham, G. P. (1999) The situational interview. In R. W. Eder and M. A. Harris (eds) *The Employment Interview Handbook*, 159–178. Newbury Park, CA: Sage. https://doi.org/10.4135/9781452205519.n9

Maybin, J. (2017) Textual trajectories: Theoretical roots and institutional consequences. *Text and Talk* 37(4): 415–435. https://doi.org/10.1515/text-2017-0011

McElhinny, B. (1997) Ideologies of public and private language in sociolinguistics. In R. Wodak (ed.) *Gender and Discourse*, 106–139. London: Sage. https://doi.org/10.4135/9781446250204.n6

McFarland, L. A., Ryan, A. M., Sacco, J. M. and Kriska, S. D. (2004) Examination of structured interview ratings across time: The effects of applicant race, rater race, and panel composition. *Journal of Management* 30(4): 435–452. https://doi.org/10.1016/j.jm.2003.09.004

McGregor-Smith, R. (2017) [Online] *Race in the Workplace: The McGregor-Smith Review*. Office for Business, Energy and Industrial Strategy. Available from: https://assets.publishing.service.gov.uk/government/uploads/system/uploads/attachment_data/file/594336/race-in-workplace-mcgregor-smith-review.pdf.

McIntyre, D. and Price, H. (2018) *Applying Linguistics: Language and the Impact Agenda*. London: Routledge. https://doi.org/10.4324/9781351055185-1

McNamara, T. and Shohamy, E. (2008) Language tests and human rights. *International Journal of Applied Linguistics* 18: 89–95. https://doi.org/10.1111/j.1473-4192.2008.00191.x

McNamara, T. and Roever, C. (2006) *Language Testing: The Social Dimension*. Malden, MA: Blackwell.

Mehan, H. (1993) Beneath the skin and between the ears: A case study in the politics of representation. In S. Chaiklin and J. Lave (eds) *Understanding Practice*, 241–268. Cambridge: Cambridge University Press. https://doi.org/10.1017/CBO9780511625510.010

Mey, J. (1987) Poet and peasant: A pragmatic comedy in five acts. *Journal of Pragmatics* 11(3): 281–297. https://doi.org/10.1016/0378-2166(87)90134-2

Migration Advisory Committee (2014) *Migrants in Low-Skilled Work: The Growth of EU and Non-EU Labour in Low-Skilled Jobs and its Impact on the UK.* Available from: https://assets.publishing.service.gov.uk/government/uploads/system/uploads/attachment_data/file/333084/MAC-_Migrants_in_low-skilled_work_Summary_2014.pdf.

Migration Observatory (2019) [Online] Migrants in the UK labour market: an overview. *The Migration Observatory at the University of Oxford.* Available from: https://migrationobservatory.ox.ac.uk/resources/briefings/migrants-in-the-uk-labour-market-an-overview.

Migration Observatory (2019) [Online] English language use and proficiency of migrants in the UK. *The Migration Observatory at the University of Oxford.* Available from: https://migrationobservatory.ox.ac.uk/resources/briefings/english-language-use-and-proficiency-of-migrants-in-the-uk.

Milroy, L. (2004) Language ideologies and linguistic change. In C. Fought (ed.) *Sociolinguistic Variation: Critical Reflections*, 161–177. New York: Oxford University Press.

Milroy, J. and Milroy, L. (1999) *Authority in Language: Investigating Standard English.* London: Routledge.

Miranda, A. and Zhu, Y. (2013) English deficiency and the native–immigrant wage gap. *Economics Letters* 118(1): 38–41. https://doi.org/10.1016/j.econlet.2012.09.007

Mishler, E. (1984) *The Discourse of Medicine: Dialetics of Medical Interviews.* Norwood, NJ: Ablex

Mishler, E. (2006) Narrative and identity: The double arrow of time. In A. De Fina, D. Schiffrin and M. Bamberg (eds) *Discourse and Identity*, 48–82. Cambridge: Cambridge University Press.

Modood, T., Berthoud, R., Lakey, J., Nazroo, J., Smith, P., Virdee, S. and Beishon, S. (1997) *Ethnic Minorities in Britain: Diversity and Disadvantage.* London: Policy Studies Institute.

Monbiot, G. (2016) *How Did We Get into This Mess?: Politics, Equality, Nature.* London: Verso.

Monbiot, G. (2016) [Online] Neoliberalism – the ideology at the root of all our problems. *Guardian*, 15 April 2016. Available from: https://www.theguardian.com/books/2016/apr/15/neoliberalism-ideology-problem-george-monbiot.

Morales-López, E., Prego-Vázquez, G. and Domínguez-Seco, L. (2005) Interviews between employees and customers during a company restructuring process. *Discourse and Society* 16(2): 225–268. https://doi.org/10.1177/0957926505049622

Moyer, M. (ed.) (2018) Language, mobility and work. *Journal of Language and Intercultural Development* 18(4). https://doi.org/10.1080/14708477.2018.1486271

Mumby, D. and Clair, R. (1997) Organizational discourse. In T. A. Van Dijk (ed.) *Discourse as Social Interaction: Discourse Studies. Vol. 2: A Multidisciplinary Introduction*, 181–205. Newbury Park, CA: Sage.

Noon, M. (2005) Ethnic minorities in work: Conceptual and empirical challenges. (Paper presented at the Ethnicity and Employment in the Private Sector Seminar, London, on 1 September 2005.) Available from: http://www.psi.org.uk/eeps/presentations/seminar3/noon.ppt.

Norrick, N. R. (2013) Narratives of vicarious experience in conversation. *Language in Society* 42(4): 385–406. https://doi.org/10.1017/S0047404513000444

O'Barr, W. and J. Conley (1996) Ideological dissonance in the American legal system. In C. Briggs (ed.) *Disorderly Discourse: Narrative, Conflict and Inequality*. New York: Oxford University Press.

O'Grady, C. and Millen, M. (1994) *Finding Common Ground: Cross-cultural Communication Strategies for Job Seekers*. Sydney: NCELTR, Macquarie University.

Ochs, E. and Capps, L. (1996) Narrating the self. *Annual Review of Anthropology* 25: 19–43. https://doi.org/10.1146/annurev.anthro.25.1.19

OECD (2010) *International Migration Outlook 2010*. Paris: OECD Publishing. https://doi.org/10.1787/migr_outlook-2010-en

ONS (2011) [Online] *2011 Census Data Catalogue*. Available from: http://www.ons.gov.uk/census/2011census/2011censusdata/2011censusdatacatalogue.

Pager, D. and Shepherd, H. (2008) The sociology of discrimination: Racial discrimination in employment, housing, credit, and consumer markets. *Annual Review of Sociology* 34: 181–208. https://doi.org/10.1146/annurev.soc.33.040406.131740

Palmer, D. and Campion, J. (1997) A review of structure in the selection interview. *Personnel Psychology* 50(3): 655–702. https://doi.org/10.1111/j.1744-6570.1997.tb00709.x

Park, J. S.-Y. and Bucholtz, M. (2009) Introduction. Public transcripts: Entextualization and linguistic representation in institutional contexts. *Text and Talk* 29(5): 583–500. https://doi.org/10.1515/TEXT.2009.026

Patrick, P. (2016) The impact of sociolinguistics on refugee status determination. In R. Lawson and D. Sayers (eds) *Sociolinguistic Research: Application and Impact*, 235–256. Abingdon: Routledge. https://doi.org/10.4324/9781315671765-13

Patterson, F., Tiffin, P., Lopes, S. and Zibarras, L. (2018) Unpacking the dark variance of differential attainment in exams for overseas graduates. *Medical Education* 52(7): 736–746. https://doi.org/10.1111/medu.13605

Pelsmaekers, K., Rollo, C., Van Hout, T. and Heynderickx, P. (eds) (2011) *Displaying Competence in Organizations: Discourse Perspectives*. London: Palgrave Macmillan. https://doi.org/10.1057/9780230307322

Piller, I. and Takahashi, K. (2009) [Online] Welcome to Language-on-the-Move! *Language on the Move*. Available from: http://www.languageonthemove.com/welcome-to-language-on-the-move.

Piller, I. (2016a) *Linguistic Diversity and Social Justice: An Introduction to Applied Sociolinguistics*. Oxford: Oxford University Press. https://doi.org/10.1093/acprof:oso/9780199937240.001.0001

Piller, I. (2016b) Monolingual ways of seeing multilingualism. *Journal of Multicultural Discourses* 11(1): 25–33. https://doi.org/10.1080/17447143.2015.1102921

Piller, I. and Lising, L. (2014) Language, employment, and settlement: Temporary meat workers in Australia. *Multilingua* 33(1–2): 35–59. https://doi.org/10.1515/multi-2014-0003

Plumwood, V. (1993) *Feminism and the Mastery of Nature*. London: Routledge.

Posthuma, R., Morgeson, F. and Campion, J. (2002) Beyond employment interview validity: A comprehensive narrative review of recent research and trends over time. *Personnel Psychology* 55(1): 1–81. https://doi.org/10.1111/j.1744-6570.2002.tb00103.x

Potter, J. (1996) *Representing Reality: Discourse, Rhetoric and Social Construction*. London: Sage. https://doi.org/10.4135/9781446222119

Psathas, G. (1995) *Qualitative Research Methods. Vol. 35: Conversation Analysis: The Study of Talk-in-Interaction*. Thousand Oaks, CA: Sage.

Rakić, T., Steffens, M. C. and Mummendey, A. (2011) Blinded by the accent! The minor role of looks in ethnic categorization. *Journal of Personality and Social Psychology* 100(1): 16–29. https://doi.org/10.1037/a0021522

Rampton, B. (1997) Retuning in applied linguistics. *International Journal of Applied Linguistics* 7(1): 3–25. https://doi.org/10.1111/j.1473-4192.1997.tb00101.x

Rampton, B. (2006) *Language in Late Modernity: Interaction in an Urban School*. Cambridge: Cambridge University Press. https://doi.org/10.1017/CBO9780511486722

Rampton, B. (2007) Neo-Hymesian linguistic ethnography in the United Kingdom. *Journal of Sociolinguistics* 11(5): 584–607. https://doi.org/10.1111/j.1467-9841.2007.00341.x

Rampton, B. (2009) Interaction ritual and not just artful performance in crossing and stylization. *Language in Society* 38(2): 149–176. https://doi.org/10.1017/S0047404509090319

Rampton, B. (2014) [Online] Gumperz and Governmentality in the 21st Century: Interaction, Power and Subjectivity. *Working Papers in Urban Language and Literacies, Paper 136*. Available from: https://www.kcl.ac.uk/ecs/research/research-centres/ldc/publications/workingpapers/abstracts/wp136-rampton-2014-gumperz-and-governmentality-in-the-21st-century.pdf.

Rampton, B. (2015) [Online] Post-panoptic standard language? *Working Papers in Urban Language and Literacies, Paper 162*. Available from: https://www.kcl.ac.uk/ecs/research/research-centres/ldc/publications/workingpapers/abstracts/wp162--ben-rampton-2015--post-panopticon-standard-language.

Rampton, B. (2016) Drilling down to the grain in superdiversity. In K. Arnaut, J. Blommaert, B. Rampton and M. Spotti (eds) *Language and Superdiversity*, 91–109. New York: Routledge.

Rampton, B. Maybin, J. and Roberts, C. (2015) Theory and method in linguistic ethnography. In J. Snell, S. Shaw and F. Copland (eds) *Linguistic Ethnography: Interdisciplinary Explorations*, 14–50. London: Palgrave Macmillan. https://doi.org/10.1057/9781137035035_2

Ravotas, D. and Berkenkotter, C. (1998) Voices in the text: The uses of reported speech in a psychotherapist's notes and initial assessment. *Text* 18(2): 211–239. https://doi.org/10.1515/text.1.1998.18.2.211

Reissner-Roubicek, S. (2017) Teamwork and the 'global graduate': Negotiating core skills and competencies with employers in recruitment interviews. In: J. Angouri, M. Marra, and J. Holmes (eds) *Negotiating Boundaries at Work*. Edinburgh: Edinburgh University Press.

Riddiford, N. (2017) [Online] Communicating effectively in job interviews: A resource for newcomers to New Zealand. *The Language in the Workplace Project*. Available from: www.newzealandnow.govt.nz/interviews.

Riddiford, N. and Newton, J. (2010) *Workplace Talk in Action – An ESOL Resource*. Wellington: Victoria University of Wellington.

Rienzo, C. and Vargas-Silva, C. (2016) *Migrants in the UK: An Overview*. Oxford: The Migration Observatory at the University of Oxford.

Riessman, C. K. (1993) *Narrative Analysis*. Newbury Park, CA: Sage.

Riggins, S. H. (1990) *Beyond Goffman: Studies on Communication, Institution, and Social Interaction*. Berlin: De Gruyter Mouton. https://doi.org/10.1515/9783110847291

Ritzer, G. (1999) Assessing the resistance. In B. Smart (ed.) *Resisting McDonaldization*, 234–256. London: Sage. https://doi.org/10.4135/9781446217627.n15

Rivera, L. (2012) Hiring as cultural matching. *American Sociological Review* 77(6): 999–1022. https://doi.org/10.1177/0003122412463213

Roberts, C. (2016) Translating global work experience into the institutionalised models of competency: Linguistic inequalities in the job interview. In K. Arnaut, J. Blommaert, B. Rampton and M. Spotti (eds) *Language and Superdiversity*. New York: Routledge.

Roberts, C. (2019) From the outside in: Gatekeeping the workplace. In M. Cooke and R. Peutrell (eds) *Brokering Britain, Educating Citizens: Exploring ESOL and Citizenship*, 213–226. Bristol: Multilingual Matters. https://doi.org/10.21832/9781788924634-015

Roberts, C., Atkins, S. and Hawthorne, K. (2014) *Performance Features in Clinical Skills Assessment: Linguistic and Cultural Factors in the MRCGP Exam*. London: Centre for Language, Discourse and Communication, King's College London.

Roberts, C. and Campbell, S. (2005) Fitting stories into boxes: Rhetorical and contextual constraints on candidates' performances in British job interviews. *Journal of Applied Linguistics* 2(1): 45–73. https://doi.org/10.1558/japl.v2i1.45

Roberts, C. and Campbell, S. (2006) *Talk on Trial: Job Interviews, Language and Ethnicity. DWP Research Report 344*. Sheffield: Department for Work and Pensions. Available from: library.archive@dwp.gsi.gov.uk.

Roberts, C., Campbell, S. and Brennan, F. (2006) The 'linguistic penalty' to foreign-born candidates in British interviews. *Equal Opportunities Review 157*: 22–23.

Roberts, C., Campbell, S. and Robinson, Y. (2008) *Talking Like a Manager: Promotion Interviews, Language and Ethnicity. DWP Research Report 510*. Sheffield: Department for Work and Pensions. Available from: library.archive@dwp.gsi.gov.uk.

Roberts, C. and Cooke, M. (2009) Authenticity in the adult ESOL classroom and beyond. *TESOL Quarterly* 43(3): 620–642.
https://doi.org/10.1002/j.1545-7249.2009.tb00189.x

Roberts, C., Cooke, M., Campbell, S. and Stenhouse, J. (2007) [DVD] *Frequently Asked Questions. The Great British Job Interview*. n.p.: Jobcentre Plus and King's College London.

Roberts, C., Davies, E. and Jupp, T. (1992) *Language and Discrimination: A Study of Communication in Multi-ethnic Workplaces*. London: Longman.

Roberts, C. and Moss, B. (n.d.) [DVD] *Doing the Lambeth Talk: Real Life GP-Patient Encounters in the Multi-lingual City*. London: Department of Postgraduate General Practice, NHS London Deanery.

Roberts, C., and Sarangi, S. (1999) Hybridity in gatekeeping discourse: Issues of practical relevance for the researcher. In S. Sarangi and C. Roberts (eds) *Talk, Work and Institutional Order*, 473–503. Berlin: De Gruyter Mouton.
https://doi.org/10.1515/9783110208375.4.473

Roberts, C. and Sarangi, S. (2003) Uptake of discourse research in interprofessional settings: Reporting from medical consultancy. *Applied Linguistics* 24(3): 338–359.
https://doi.org/10.1093/applin/24.3.338

Roberts, C., Sarangi, S., Southgate, L., Wakeford, R. and Wass, V. (2000) Oral examinations: Equal opportunities, ethnicity, and fairness in the MRCGP. *British Medical Journal* 320: 370–374. https://doi.org/10.1136/bmj.320.7231.370

Roberts, C. and Sayers, P. (1987) Keeping the gate: How judgments are made in interethnic interviews. In K. Knapp, W. Enninger and A. Knapp-Potthoff (eds) *Analyzing Intercultural Communication*, 111–135. Berlin: De Gruyter Mouton.

Rock, F. (2001) The genesis of a witness statement. *Forensic Linguistics* 8: 44–72.
https://doi.org/10.1558/sll.2001.8.2.44

Rock, F. (2007) *Communicating Rights: The Language of Arrest and Detention*. Basingstoke: Palgrave Macmillan.

Rolfe, A., Atkins, S., Hawthorne, K. and Roberts, C. (2015) *RCGP Insider's Guide to the CSA for the MRCGP*. London: Royal College of General Practitioners.

Rose, N. (1998) *Inventing Ourselves: Psychology, Power and Personhood*. Cambridge: Cambridge University Press. https://doi.org/10.1017/CBO9780511752179

Roy, S. (2003) Bilingualism and standardization in a Canadian call center: Challenges for a linguistic minority community. In R. Bayley and S. Schecter (eds) *Language Socialization in Multilingual Societies*, 269–287. Clevedon: Multilingual Matters.
https://doi.org/10.21832/9781853596377-019

Ryan, A. M. and Ployhart, R. E. (2000) Applicants' perceptions of selection procedures and decisions: A critical review and agenda for the future. *Journal of Management* 3(36): 565–606. https://doi.org/10.1177/014920630002600308

Sacks, H., Schegloff, E. A. and Jefferson, G. (1974) A simplest systematics for the organization of turn-taking for conversation. *Language in Society* 50(4): 696–735.
https://doi.org/10.1353/lan.1974.0010

Sandwall, K. (2010) 'I learn more at school': A critical perspective on workplace-related second language learning in and out of school. *TESOL Quarterly* 44(3): 542–574. https://doi.org/10.5054/tq.2010.229270

Sanglin-Grant, S. (2003) [Online] *Widening the Talent pool: Racial Equality in FTSE-100 Companies*. n.p.: Runnymede Trust. Available from: https://www.runnymedetrust.org/uploads/publications/pdfs/wideningTheTalentPool.pdf.

Sanglin-Grant, S. (2005) [Online] *The Space Between: From Rhetoric to Reality*. n.p.: Runnymede Trust. Available from: https://www.runnymedetrust.org/uploads/publications/pdfs.

Sarangi, S. (2015) Experts on experts: Sustaining 'communities of interest' in Professional Discourse Studies. In M. Gotti, S. Maci and M. Sala (eds) *Insights into Medical Communication*, 25–47. Bern: Peter Lang

Sarangi, S. and Roberts, C. (eds) (1999a) *Talk, Work and Institutional Order: Discourse in Medical, Mediation and Management Settings*. Berlin/New York: De Gruyter Mouton. https://doi.org/10.1515/9783110208375

Sarangi, S. and Roberts, C. (1999b) The dynamics of interactional and institutional orders in work-related settings. In S. Sarangi and C. Roberts (eds) *Talk, Work and Institutional Order: Discourse in Medical, Mediation and Management Settings*, 1–57. New York: De Gruyter Mouton. https://doi.org/10.1515/9783110208375.1.1

Sarangi, S. and Slembrouck, S. (1996) *Language, Bureaucracy and Social Control*. London: Longman. https://doi.org/10.1075/bjl.11.13sar

Sarangi, S. and Slembrouck, S. (1997) Confrontational asymmetries in institutional discourse: A socio-pragmatic view of information exchange and face management. *Belgian Journal of Linguistics* 11(1): 255–275.

Scheepers. S. (2011) Equality for those who are competent. Discourses on competencies, diversity and equality in the public sector. In K. Pelsmaekers, C. Rollo, T. Van Hout and P. Heynderickx (eds) (2011) *Displaying Competence in Organizations: Discourse Perspectives*. London: Palgrave Macmillan. https://doi.org/10.1057/9780230307322_3

Scheuer, J. (2001) Recontextualisation and communicative styles in job interviews. *Discourse Studies* 3(2): 223–248. https://doi.org/10.1177/1461445601003002004

Schiffrin, D. (1996) Narrative as self-portrait: Sociolinguistic constructions of identity. *Language in Society* 25(2): 167–203. https://doi.org/10.1017/S0047404500020601

Schiffrin, D. (2000) Mother/daughter discourse in a Holocaust oral history. *Narrative Inquiry* 10(1): 1–44. https://doi.org/10.1075/ni.10.1.01sch

Schiffrin, D. (2006) From linguistic reference to social reality. In A. De Fina, D. Schiffrin and M. G. W. Bamberg (eds) *Discourse and Identity*, 103–131. Cambridge: Cambridge University Press. https://doi.org/10.1017/CBO9780511584459.006

Scollon, R. and Scollon, S. (1995) *Intercultural Communication: A Discourse Approach*. Oxford: Blackwell.

Scollon, R. and Scollon, S. (2007) Nexus analysis: Refocussing ethnography on action. *Journal of Sociolinguistics* 11(5): 608–625. https://doi.org/10.1111/j.1467-9841.2007.00342.x

Seale, C., Butler, C., Hutchby, I., Kinnersley, P. and Rollnick, S. (2007) Negotiating frame ambiguity: A study of simulated encounters in medical education. *Communication and Medicine* 4(2): 177–188. https://doi.org/10.1515/CAM.2007.021

Sebba, M. (1993) *London Jamaican: A Case Study in Language Contact*. London: Longman.

Silverman, D. and Jones, J. (1976) *Organizational Work: The Language of Grading, the Grading of Language*. London: Collier Macmillan.

Silverstein, M. (1979) Language structure and linguistic ideology. In P. R. Clyne, W. F. Hanks and C. L. Hofbauer (eds) *The Elements: A Parasession on Linguistic Units and Levels*, 193–247. Chicago: Chicago Linguistic Society.

Silverstein, M. (2003) Indexical order and the dialectics of sociolinguistic life. *Language and Communication* 23(3–4): 193–229. https://doi.org/10.1016/S0271-5309(03)00013-2

Smith, D. (2001) Texts and the ontology of organizations and institutions. *Studies in Cultures, Organizations and Societies* 7(2): 159–198. https://doi.org/10.1080/10245280108523557

Smith, D. (2005) *Institutional Ethnography: A Sociology for People*. n.p.: Altamine Press.

Snell, J., Shaw, S. and Copland, F. (eds) (2015) *Linguistic Ethnography: Interdisciplinary Explorations*. London: Palgrave Macmillan. https://doi.org/10.1057/9781137035035

Spotti, M. (2016) Sociolinguistic shibboleths at the institutional gate. In K. Arnaut, J. Blommaert, B. Rampton and M. Spotti (eds) *Language and Superdiversity*, 261–278. New York: Routledge.

Stivers T. (2008) Stance, alignment, and affiliation during storytelling: When nodding is a token of affiliation. *Research on Language and Social Interaction* 41(1): 31–57. https://doi.org/10.1080/08351810701691123

Stivers, T., Mondada, L. and Steensig, J. (2011) Knowledge, morality and affiliation in social interaction. In T. Stivers, L. Mondada and J. Steensig (eds) *The Morality of Knowledge in Conversation*, 3–24. Cambridge: Cambridge University Press. https://doi.org/10.1017/CBO9780511921674.002

Stokoe, E. (2012) Moving forward with membership categorization analysis: Methods for systematic analysis. *Discourse Studies* 14(3): 277–303. https://doi.org/10.1177/1461445612441534

Stokoe, E. (2014) The conversation analytic role-play method (CARM): A method for training communication skills as an alternative to simulated role-play. *Research on Language and Social Interaction* 47(3): 255–265. https://doi.org/10.1080/08351813.2014.925663

Stokoe, E. and Sikveland, R. O. (2017) The conversation analytic role-play method: Simulation, endogenous impact and interactional nudges. In V. Fors, T. O'Dell and S. Pink (eds) *Theoretical Scholarship and Applied Practice*, 73–96. Oxford: Berghahn. https://doi.org/10.2307/j.ctvw04bkj.8

Stokes, R. and Hewitt, J. P. (1976) Aligning Actions. *American Sociological Review* 41(5): 838–849. https://doi.org/10.2307/2094730

Stracke, E. (2014) Applied linguistics as a meeting place: An introduction. In E. Stracke (ed.) *Intersections: Applied Linguistics as a Meeting Place*. Newcastle upon Tyne: Cambridge Scholars Publishing.

Strömmer, M. (2015) Affordances and constraints: Language learning in cleaning work. *Multilingua* 35(6): 697–711. https://doi.org/10.1515/multi-2014-0113

Stroud, C. (2004) Rinkeby Swedish and semilingualism in language ideological debates: A Bourdieuean perspective. *Journal of Sociolinguistics* 8(2): 196–214. https://doi.org/10.1111/j.1467-9841.2004.00258.x

Suchman, L. (1987) *Plans and Situated Actions*. New York: Cambridge University Press.

Svennevig, J. (2001) Institutional and conversational modes of talk in bureaucratic consultations. In A. Hvenekilde and J. Nortier (eds) *Meetings at the Crossroads*, 106–135. Oslo: Novus.

Svennevig, J. (2004) Other-repetition as display of hearing, understanding and emotional stance. *Discourse Studies* 6(4): 489–516. https://doi.org/10.1177/1461445604046591

Tannen, D. (2007) *Talking Voices: Repetition, Dialogue, and Imagery in Conversational Discourse*. (2nd ed.) New York: Cambridge University Press.

Taylor, C. (1989) *Sources of the Self: The Making of Modern Identity.* Cambridge: Cambridge University Press.

Thornborrow, J. (2002) *Power Talk: Language and Interaction in Institutional Discourse*. London: Longman.

Timmermans, S. and Epstein, S. (2010) A world of standards but not a standard world: Toward a sociology of standards and standardization. *Annual Review of Sociology* 36: 69–89. https://doi.org/10.1146/annurev.soc.012809.102629

Tracy, K. and Robles, J. (2009) Questions, questioning, and institutional practices: An introduction. *Discourse Studies* 11(2): 131–152. https://doi.org/10.1177/1461445608100941

Tranekjær, L. (2015) *Interactional Categorization and Gatekeeping: Institutional Encounters with Otherness*. Clevedon: Multilingual Matters. https://doi.org/10.21832/9781783093687

Trinch, S. L. (2003) *Latinas' Narratives of Domestic Abuse: Discrepant Versions of Violence*. Amsterdam: John Benjamins. https://doi.org/10.1075/impact.17

Trudgill, P. (ed.) (1984) *Applied Sociolinguistics*. London: Academic Press.

UK Government (2006) [Online] *The Race Relations Code of Practice Relating to Employment*. Available at: https://legislation.gov.uk/uksi/2006/630/contents/made.

Urcioli, B. (2008) Skills and selves in the new workplace. *American Ethnologist* 35(2): 211–228. https://doi.org/10.1111/j.1548-1425.2008.00031.x

van Leeuwen, T. and Wodak, R. (1999) Legitimizing immigration control: A discourse-historical Analysis. *Discourse Studies* 1(1): 83–118. https://doi.org/10.1177/1461445699001001005

Vertoveç, S. (2007) Super-diversity and its implications. *Ethnic and Racial Studies* 30(6): 1024–1054. https://doi.org/10.1080/01419870701599465

Vigouroux, C. B. (2013) Informal economy and language practice in the context of migrations. In A. Duchêne, M. Moyer and C. Roberts (eds) *Language, Migration and Social Inequalities: A Critical Sociolinguistic Perspective on Institutions and Work*, 296–328. Bristol: Multilingual Matters. https://doi.org/10.21832/9781783091010-011

Vine, B. and Marra, M. (2017) The Wellington Language in the Workplace project: Creating stability through flexibility. In M. Marra and P. Warren (eds) *Linguist at Work: Festschrift for Janet Holmes*, 181–201. Wellington: Victoria Press.

Vohra, M. (n.d.) *Impressive Interviews for All Competitions*. Delhi: New Light Publication.

Vološinov, V. N., Matejka, L. and Titunik, I. R. (1973) *Marxism and the Philosophy of Language*. New York/London: Seminar Press.

Wacquant, L. J. D. (1989) Towards a reflexive sociology: A workshop with Pierre Bourdieu. *Sociological Theory* 7: 26–63. https://doi.org/10.2307/202061

Wadsworth, J. (2017) [Online] *Immigration and the UK Economy. Paper EA039*. Centre for Economic Performance, London School of Economics. Available from: https://cep.lse.ac.uk/pubs/download/ea039.pdf.

Weber, M. and Parsons, T. (1947) *The Theory of Social and Economic Organization*. New York: Free Press.

Weinert, F. E. (2001) Concept of competence: A conceptual clarification. In D. S. Rychen and L. H. Salganik (eds) *Defining and Selecting Key Competencies*, 45–65. Ashland, OH: Hogrefe and Huber Publishers.

Werner, O. and Schoepfle, G. M. (1987) *Systematic Fieldwork*. Newbury Park, CA: Sage.

White, A. (2002) *Social Focus in Brief: Ethnicity 2002*. Norwich: Office for National Statistics.

Wodak, R. (1996) *Disorders of Discourse*. London: Longman.

Wolfram, W. (1993) Ethical considerations in language awareness programs. *Issues in Applied Linguistics* 4(2): 225–255.

Wolfram, W. (2016) Public sociolinguistic education in the United States: A proactive, comprehensive program. In R. Lawson and D. Sayers (eds) *Sociolinguistic Research: Application and Impact*, 87–108. London: Routledge. https://doi.org/10.4324/9781315671765-6

Wood, C. and Wybron, I. (2015) [Online] *Entry to, and Progression in, Work*. York: Joseph Rowntree Foundation. Available from: https://www.Jeff.org.uk/report/entry-and-progression-work.

Wood, R. and Payne, T. (1998) *Competency Based Recruitment and Selection*. Chichester: Wiley.

Woolard, K. A. (1998) Introduction: Language ideology as a field of inquiry. In B. B. Schieffelin, K. A. Woolard and P. V. Kroskrity (eds) *Language Ideologies: Practice and Theory*, 3–49. New York: Oxford University Press.

Woolf, K., McManus, I. C., Potts, H. W. W. and Dacre, J. E. (2013) The mediators of minority ethnic underperformance in final medical school examinations: A longitudinal study. *British Journal of Educational Psychology* 83(1): 135–159. https://doi.org/10.1111/j.2044-8279.2011.02060.x

Wyatt, M. and Silvester, J. (2015) Reflections on the labyrinth: Investigating Black and minority ethnic leaders' career experiences. *Human Relations* 68(1): 1–27. https://doi.org/10.1177/0018726714550890

Young, L. (1994) *Crosstalk and Culture in Sino-American Communication*. Cambridge: Cambridge University Press. https://doi.org/10.1017/CBO9780511519901

Topic Index

Author Index

CPSIA information can be obtained
at www.ICGtesting.com
Printed in the USA
JSHW052021310521
15404JS00001B/7